T0271253

The Reinterpretation of Italian Economic History
From Unification to the Great War

Post-Unification Italy was part of a wider world within which men and money circulated freely; it developed to the extent that those mobile resources chose to locate on its soil. The economy's cyclical movements reflected conditions in international financial markets, and were little affected by domestic policies. State intervention restricted the internal and international mobility of goods, and limited Italy's development: it kept the economy weak, reduced Italy's weight in the comity of nations, and paved the way for the frustrations and adventurism that would plunge the twentieth century into world war.

Stefano Fenoaltea obtained his Ph.D. in economics at Harvard University, where he studied under Alexander Gerschenkron and John R. Meyer. He has taught extensively at leading colleges and universities in the United States, and is now serving on the Faculty of Economics at the University of Rome (Tor Vergata). He has published widely in academic journals, and is best known for his work on slavery, medieval agriculture, and Italian development. He has been a member of the Institute for Advanced Study, a Guggenheim Fellow, and a consultant to the Istituto centrale di statistica and to the Bank of Italy; he is listed in *Who's Who in the World*.

The Reinterpretation of Italian Economic History

From Unification to the Great War

STEFANO FENOALTEA

Università di Roma "Tor Vergata"

CAMBRIDGE
UNIVERSITY PRESS

CAMBRIDGE
UNIVERSITY PRESS

32 Avenue of the Americas, New York NY 10013-2473, USA

Cambridge University Press is part of the University of Cambridge.

It furthers the University's mission by disseminating knowledge in the pursuit of education, learning and research at the highest international levels of excellence.

www.cambridge.org
Information on this title: www.cambridge.org/9781107658080

First published in Italian as *L'economia italiana dall'Unità alla Grande Guerra* 2006
English edition published 2011
First paperback edition 2013

A catalogue record for this publication is available from the British Library

Library of Congress Cataloguing in Publication data
Fenoaltea, Stefano.
[Economia italiana dall'Unità alla Grande Guerra. English]
The reinterpretation of Italian economic history : from unification to the great war /
Stefano Fenoaltea.
p.   cm.
Includes bibliographical references and index.
ISBN 978-0-521-19238-5 (hbk)
1. Italy – Economic conditions – 1849–1870.   2. Italy – Economic conditions –
1870–1918.   I. Title.
HC305.F39813   2010
330.945′084 – dc22   2009027793

ISBN 978-0-521-19238-5 Hardback
ISBN 978-1-107-65808-0 Paperback

For Annalina

The Reinterpretation of Italian Economic History
From Unification to the Great War

Contents

List of Tables

List of Figures

NB: *The time series are often illustrated with a logarithmic vertical axis. In such cases equal vertical displacements imply equal relative movements, and equal slopes imply equal growth rates.*

Acknowledgments

Tables 1.01, 1.03, and 1.04 and Figure 1.05 previously appeared in S. Fenoaltea, "Notes on the Rate of Industrial Growth in Italy, 1861–1913," *Journal of Economic History* 63 (2003), pp. 695–735, respectively as Table 1 (p. 698), Table 2 (pp. 710–711), Table 3 (p. 712), and Figures 2 and 3 (p. 713). Copyright © 2003 The Economic History Association. Reprinted with the permission of Cambridge University Press.

Figure 1.03 and panels (a), (d), (e), and (f) of Figure 1.06 previously appeared in S. Fenoaltea, "The Growth of the Italian Economy, 1861–1913: Preliminary Second-Generation Estimates," *European Review of Economic History* 9 (2005), pp. 273–312, respectively as Figure 4 (p. 277), Figure 5 (p. 289), Figure 18 (p. 297), Figure 19 (p. 298), and Figure 20 (p. 299). Copyright © 2005 European Historical Economics Society. Reprinted with the permission of Cambridge University Press.

Tables 2.01 and 2.03 previously appeared in S. Fenoaltea, "International Resource Flows and Construction Movements in the Atlantic Economy: The Kuznets Cycle in Italy, 1861–1913," *Journal of Economic History* 48 (1988), pp. 605–637, respectively as Table 1 (pp. 608–609) and Table 3 (p. 615). Copyright © 1988 The Economic History Association. Reprinted with the permission of Cambridge University Press.

Tables 5.01, 5.05, and 5.07 previously appeared in S. Fenoaltea, "Italy," in P. K. O'Brien, ed., *Railways and the Economic Development of Western Europe*, 1983, London, The Macmillan Press, pp. 49–120, respectively as Table 3.1 (p. 52), Table 3.9 (pp. 79–81), and Table 3.11

(p. 91). Copyright © 1983 St Antony's College, Oxford. Reproduced with the permission of Palgrave Macmillan.

Table 6.02 previously appeared in S. Fenoaltea, "Peeking Backward: Regional Aspects of Industrial Growth in Post-Unification Italy," *Journal of Economic History* 63 (2003), pp. 1059–1102, as Table 2 (p. 1069). Copyright © 2003 The Economic History Association. Reprinted with the permission of Cambridge University Press.

Preface

This book summarizes some decades of research on the economic history of Italy between Unification and the Great War. It is equally concerned with what happened then, and with how we gradually came to understand it as we now do: it is at once social science, and history of that science.

This twin concern reflects the author's sense of his discipline. Economic history invites rigorous logic, parsimonious explanations, and a confrontation with evidence that is naturally quantitative: it is, or at least can be, science in its style. Substance is another matter. Economics, history, the social "sciences" are not the cumulation of objective knowledge, but the contemporary form of the stories our distant forefathers would tell when they gathered around the campfire. Our theories, our facts – our stories, like their stories – are constructs that define and project an image of ourselves; they are shaped by fears and aspirations so deep we do not admit them to our conscious minds, by prejudices so strong we do not recognize them.

So too, specifically, economic history. The process and context that generate an interpretation, and can signal the alternatives that were never allowed a hearing, are as central to its proper evaluation as the more conventional evidence it invokes: we would have a better sense of what there is to be seen if our predecessors had told us not only what they saw, but who they were, where they stood, and how they got there.

The author's research has been constantly encouraged by the benevolent attention of his companions in the vineyard: above all Pierluigi Ciocca and Gianni Toniolo, our illustrious seniors Alberto Caracciolo and Luciano Cafagna, and then also, as they joined the profession, Vera

Zamagni, Giovanni Federico – the closest collaborator in the reconstruction of aggregate production series – and most recently Giovanni Vecchi. These close colleagues – and the giants that dominated the post-war debate on the numbers and their interpretation, Alexander Gerschenkron, Rosario Romeo – are the author's principal interlocutors.

Controversy sharpens arguments, stimulates research; it is the joyful side of scholarship. This work reviews the debates to which the author has contributed: those to which he can speak with the authority, and lack of impartiality, of a principal.

The author owes much to the exceptional assistance received from numerous libraries, in Italy and the United States. His greatest debts are to the library of the Bank of Italy, and especially to Livia Cannizzaro and Maria Teresa Pandolfi, and to the library of the Istituto centrale di statistica.

Man lives by bread as well. For financial assistance to his research on post-Unification Italy the author thanks the Ente per gli studi bancari, monetari e finanziari "Luigi Einaudi"; the National Science Foundation; the Guggenheim Foundation; the then Ministero dell'Università e della Ricerca Scientifica e Tecnologica. The investigation of the regional aspects of Italy's industrial growth has been sponsored by the Bank of Italy; the estimates and the interpretations are the author's and do not involve the responsibility of the Bank. The Associazione Guido Carli generously funded the preparation of this volume; its support is gratefully acknowledged.

The first, Italian, edition of this work went to press late in 2005.[1] The initial manuscript was much improved by the useful comments of Brian A'Hearn, Alberto Baffigi, Stefano Battilossi, Marco Belfanti, Carlo Ciccarelli, Pierluigi Ciocca, Alfredo Gigliobianco, Marco Magnani, Juan Carlos Martinez Oliva, Fabrizio Mattesini, Massimo Roccas, and Giovanni Vecchi; the author thanks them most warmly, but bears sole responsibility for the final text.

The present English edition has been partly revised in response both to the further comments received in presentations at the Ufficio Ricerche Storiche of the Bank of Italy, the Centro per la formazione in economia e politica dello sviluppo rurale (Portici), the Università Commerciale Luigi Bocconi (Milan), the Università Politecnica delle Marche (Ancona), and

---

[1] S. Fenoaltea, *L'economia italiana dall'Unità alla Grande Guerra*, Rome-Bari, 2006.

the Università di Venezia Ca' Foscari, and to the thoughtful reviews penned by Piero Bolchini, Pierluigi Ciocca, Marcello de Cecco, Giovanni Federico, Renato Giannetti, Luciano Pezzolo, Giuseppe Tattara, Gianni Toniolo, and Vera Zamagni.[2]

For their expert, selfless assistance in the search for a suitable frontispiece, special thanks are due Rod Filan, Paolo Miana, and their fellow contributors to "The Aerodrome" (www.theaerodrome.com); the photograph itself was kindly made available by the Musée de l'Air et de l'Espace at Le Bourget.

---

[2] P. Bolchini *et al.*, "A proposito di Stefano Fenoaltea, *L'economia italiana dall'Unità alla Grande Guerra*, Bari-Roma, 2006," *Rivista di storia economica* 22 (2006), pp. 331–375; R. Giannetti, "Sviluppo globale e sviluppo nazionale: riflessioni a partire da Stefano Fenoaltea, *L'economia italiana dall'Unità alla Grande Guerra*, Bari, Laterza, 2006," *Rivista di politica economica* 97 (2007), nn. 3–4, pp. 407–419; G. Toniolo, "Sviluppo nonostante lo Stato," *Il Sole-24 Ore* 142, n. 172 (June 25, 2006), p. 41; Id., "Review of Stefano Fenoaltea (2006), *L'economia italiana dall'Unità alla Grande Guerra* (Rome and Bari: Laterza)," *Journal of Modern Italian Studies* 12 (2007), pp. 130–132. L. Pezzolo's review was a private one, graciously provided at the present author's specific request.

Introduction

1. Of failure and success

Italy is again rich. It had been rich in ancient times, in the centuries of Rome's hegemony and the *pax romana*. From the collapse of the West Italy recovered sooner and better than anyone else: in the reborn medieval economy of the new millennium Europe's leading maritime, commercial, financial, finally even manufacturing powers were all Italian. For many centuries, again, Italy was rich.

That primacy was not maintained. Italy was still prosperous in the sixteenth century, the *siglo de oro* of the Iberian nations that conquered the ocean sea. But by the seventeenth century naval and commercial leadership, and financial hegemony, had passed to the Dutch; England then wrested these from the Low Countries, and in the eighteenth century it was challenged only by France, by then Europe's leading manufacturer. Italy became peripheral, underdeveloped, an importer of the manufactures and commercial services it once exported.[1]

In the nineteenth century Italy fell further behind the leaders. The Napoleonic wars had confirmed England's naval, colonial and commercial preeminence; and England pioneered the industrial revolution, the

[1] C. M. Cipolla, *Before the Industrial Revolution: European Society and Economy, 1000–1700*, New York 1980; P. Malanima, *La fine del primato. Crisi e riconversione nell'Italia del Seicento*, Milan 1998. For an introduction to the attendant debate see S. Fenoaltea, "Lo sviluppo economico dell'Italia nel lungo periodo: riflessioni su tre fallimenti," in P. Ciocca and G. Toniolo, eds., *Storia economica d'Italia. 1. Interpretazioni*, Rome-Bari 1998, pp. 15–29.

transition to the modern world of factories and machines, of sustained productivity growth, eventually of rising living standards even for the working masses. England was soon followed by her former colonies in America, and also, on the Continent, by Belgium, by Switzerland, and again by France, once more England's rival in the final triumph of European imperialism.

Post-Unification Germany too would imitate England, starting late but catching up in a few decades of rapid growth. The German challenge to the hegemony of England and France composed the quarrels between these ancient enemies, and unleashed the globe-spanning tragedies of the twentieth century.

In the half-century that followed Unification, Italy also grew and developed. It emerged from the broad ranks of the still traditional, stagnant economies: that by itself was a considerable achievement. But the young Kingdom did not match the vigor of the even younger *Reich*. It contained its lag behind the leaders, but did not reduce it; its development remained weak, partial, disappointing not only next to what was eventually achieved, but to what was expected at the time.[2] Italy would participate in the World War with lamentable economic and military weakness; the end of that bloodbath found it on the winning side, but without the weight – the political, the military, ultimately the *economic* weight – to impose its views at the Peace conference. It emerged not triumphant but frustrated, militant, *revancharde*: the shame of Fascism, the ultimate tragedy of the Carthaginian alliance were the direct consequences of united Italy's limited economic development.[3]

Italy today is rich again, but it is a *parvenue* of the last few decades. Through the middle years of the twentieth century it remained a poor cousin of the affluent West, a source of out-migration that subjected Italians abroad to the humiliations, often to the tragedies, suffered today by Italy's immigrants from Eastern Europe, Africa, and Asia. Through

---

[2] On the perceived promise of a united Italy see the fine essay by M. de Cecco, "L'Italia grande potenza: la realtà del mito," in P. Ciocca and G. Toniolo, eds., *Storia economica d'Italia. 3.2. I vincoli e le opportunità*, Rome-Bari 2003, pp. 3–36.

[3] The counterfact is of course difficult to specify. Would a stronger Italy have stayed out of the War? Would it have joined the Allies, and shortened the War perhaps by enough to avoid the Russian revolution? Or would it rather have joined Germany's challenge to the Anglo-French imperial hegemony? And if thus strengthened, would the Central Powers have reaped the quick victory they had envisaged, or would they (and Italy) have suffered ultimate defeat in a seamless combination of the two World Wars? There is little here to constrain one's hypotheses; but it seems clear enough that the history of Italy and more would have taken a very different course.

the middle years of the twentieth united Italy paid in strife and sorrow for the development failure of its first fifty years.[4]

2. The transformation of post-Unification Italy

Between Unification and the World War Italy's population grew, from 25 to 35 million within the pre-War borders, despite an outflow that increased from the 1880s to reach one million departures, counting both permanent and temporary migrants, in 1913.

The economy expanded and modernized. It was poorly documented at the time: many now standard indicators did not even exist, and have had to be reconstructed, with the difficulties and uncertainties discussed below. But progress is evident, from partial but significant data.

Living standards clearly rose, albeit from very low levels. Health and nutrition improved: infant mortality fell (from 19 percent of births in 1863 to 12 in 1913), as did mortality from contagious diseases (from eight per thousand inhabitants in 1887 to three in 1913); life expectancy at birth increased (from 31 years in 1861 to 47 in 1913), military recruits grew taller (from 163 centimeters, on average, for those born in 1861 to 166 for those born in 1913).[5] School attendance increased, at the primary level (from two fifths of the relevant population in 1861 to over nine tenths in 1913) and above (for example from 0.5 university students per thousand inhabitants in 1871 to 0.8 in 1911); illiteracy fell (from three quarters of the population over age six in 1861 to under two fifths in 1911).[6]

A modern infrastructure was put in place. The railway, born early in the century, was a revolutionary innovation: not only because of its then astonishing speed, but because for the first time in human history transportation over land became as inexpensive as transportation over

---

[4] For the contrary view that the World Wars and Fascism were mere accidents that delayed the continuation of successful development see V. Zamagni in P. Bolchini *et al.*, "A proposito di Stefano Fenoaltea, L'economia italiana dall'Unità alla Grande Guerra, Bari-Roma, 2006," *Rivista di storia economica* 22 (2006), pp. 372–373.

[5] Istat (Istituto centrale di statistica), *Sommario di statistiche storiche italiane, 1861–1955*, Rome 1958, pp. 42, 63, 69; V. Zamagni, *The Economic History of Italy, 1860–1990: Recovery after Decline*, Oxford 1993 (translation of Id., *Dalla periferia al centro: la seconda rinascita economica dell'Italia, 1861–1981*, Bologna 1990), p. 30.

[6] Istat, *Sommario*, p. 78; V. Zamagni, "Istruzione e sviluppo economico in Italia, 1861–1913," in G. Toniolo, ed., *Lo sviluppo economico italiano 1861–1940*, Bari 1973, pp. 190, 195, 202, and V. Zamagni, "Istruzione e sviluppo economico: il caso italiano, 1861–1913," in G. Toniolo, ed., *L'economia italiana 1861–1940*, Bari 1978, pp. 140, 148, 165.

water. By 1860 the railway net reached some ten to fifteen thousand kilometers in France, Germany, and Great Britain; in Italy it reached but two thousand kilometers, mostly in the north, with separate, minor networks in Tuscany, in the Papal states, and around Naples. The new Kingdom avidly pursued railway construction; by 1880 almost all the main north-south routes were in place, and myriad minor lines were added by 1895. By 1913 the Italian system reached some eighteen thousand kilometers, a respectable total even if still far below the thirty to forty thousand by then operating in Britain and France (to say nothing of the over sixty thousand in Germany, by then twice the size of Italy in population as well as in area).

Industry also grew, it is evident from the well-documented transformation of Italy's external trade.[7] From 1870 to 1913 commodity imports quadrupled (from 0.9 to 3.6 billion lire) and exports trebled (from 0.8 to 2.5 billion), at barely higher prices (plus ten percent). In 1870 the most significant imports were textile goods, of cotton (11 percent of total imports), wool (6 percent), and silk (5 percent); wheat (9 percent); sugar (8 percent) and other tropical goods (7 percent); metalware (8 percent). Imports of industrial raw materials were comparatively minor (coal, 4 percent; raw cotton, 4 percent; silk-seed and cocoons, 5 percent), imports of machinery all but trivial (under 2 percent). In 1913 the import list was headed by grain (11 percent), followed by coal and raw cotton (9–10 percent each, in quantity terms a ten-fold increase since 1870) and machinery (6 percent).

In 1870 about a third of Italy's export earnings were contributed by silk: mostly raw silk, merely reeled from the cocoons, and thus a barely processed agricultural product. Other major exports were olive oil (12 percent), wheat (6 percent), rice (5 percent), sulphur (4 percent), citrus fruit (3 percent).[8] In 1913 silk was still the leading export, but its share had dropped to a fifth; citrus fruit had kept their share (3 percent), but olive oil, rice and sulphur exports had become insignificant (1–2 percent each), and wheat exports had ended. The main exports, second only to silk, were cotton textiles, with a tenth of the total; and exports of machinery had begun (3 percent).

When it was unified, therefore, Italy was a typical underdeveloped economy that exported raw materials and imported manufactures and

---

[7] Direzione generale delle dogane e imposte indirette, *Movimento commerciale del Regno d'Italia nell'anno . . .* , annual.

[8] Wheat was thus both imported and exported; this shall be returned to below.

tropical goods; in little more than a generation, it had become an at least partly industrialized economy whose imports were mainly raw materials and whose exports included manufactures.

One notes also the "low-tech" nature of Italy's industrial development, again typical of a partly developed economy. There were some world-level advanced sectors, including in particular those supplying the Navy, a reflection of the national ambition to Great Power status; but in the main Italy seems have replicated the first industrial revolution, with textiles in the van. Germany instead spearheaded the second industrial revolution, developing "high-tech" electrical equipment and chemicals; the difference would tell in 1917.

3. The debates in the literature

There is disagreement in the literature even on the basic facts, the time path of the economy. Today's statistical bureaus provide numerous up-to-date figures, but this abundance of data is relatively recent: it dates essentially from the post-war diffusion of national income accounting, macroeconomic analysis, and anti-cyclical economic policies.

Before then (in Italy, but things were not much better abroad) economic statistics were sharply limited. The censuses, with increasing economic content, were taken every ten (or twenty) years. The high-frequency data collected at the time refer mostly to financial variables, in particular to commodity prices, interest rates, and exchange rates. Real flows were systematically observed only in the presence of some fiscal concern: thus the data on foreign trade, on the industries subject to production tax, and on mining activity. Statistics on production as such began with episodic surveys; continuous monitoring appeared slowly, beginning with agriculture in the early 1900s. For almost the entire period from Unification to the World War, for almost all the sectors of the economy, the path of production was not recorded.[9]

The first attempts to estimate production movements were by individual scholars. In the 1950s, the Istituto centrale di statistica (Istat) reconstructed Italy's national accounts from 1861 on; but that noteworthy effort was too imperfect to be considered definitive, and quantitative historians have continued their patient investigations. These are still

---

[9] A broad selection of the available data (and references to the underlying sources) appears in the successive editions of Dirstat (Direzione generale della statistica), *Annuario statistico italiano*, 1878ff.

proceeding; but the work is well along, and what can already be discerned is at times significantly different from what was, or is still, widely believed.

The interpretation of the facts is also in dispute: historians disagree on the impulses and mechanisms that shaped the growth of the economy, and on the evaluation of public policy. Here too, the new statistical reconstructions – and the rigorous application of economic analysis – call into question views that are widely shared.

The following chapters examine various related strands of the historians' debate.[10] The first considers the statistical reconstructions of industrial and aggregate development, and the broad interpretations more or less closely tied to these. The Istat series suggest a sharp increase in the growth rate near the end of the nineteenth century; the more recent estimates suggest a steadier growth rate over the long run, but with a clear cycle in industrial production. The extant interpretations (and evaluations of the role of public policy) differ widely; most tie rapid growth to the loosening of supply constraints, a quantitative analysis points rather to a garden-variety cycle in the demand for durable goods.

The second chapter examines the causes of the investment cycle, of the upswings in the 1880s and after the turn of the century. The literature tends to seek its causes within Italy itself; in fact, the Italian cycle seems part of a broad international cycle, determined in the first instance by the cycle in British exports of capital.

The third chapter considers the consumption cycle, with particular attention to the 1880s. Post-war historians consider those years a period of crisis, in agriculture and the economy at large, caused by the fall in the price of imported grain. This thesis is based on bad logic, buttressed by spurious data; the new consumption and wage series confirm that the 1880s were years of prosperity, as they were in fact remembered in the earlier literature.

The fourth chapter considers the ever-lively controversy on the impact of protection. Here too, new efforts have undermined widely held opinions. The cotton tariff was effective, despite the growth of exports; the steel tariff did not help the engineering industry, but rather tied it to the domestic market and prevented export-led growth; the grain tariff did

---

[10] These are of course the strands that have concerned the present author; comprehensive surveys have been ably provided by Zamagni, *An Economic History*, and again by J. S. Cohen and G. Federico, *The Growth of the Italian Economy, 1820–1960*, Cambridge 2001.

not limit the crisis and emigration, rather, it limited employment growth and directed Italy's peasants overseas.

The fifth chapter reexamines the impact of the railways. The new statistical reconstructions support neither the belief that the major lines built in the 1860s and '70s were essential to the subsequent development of the economy, nor the thesis that the demand for metal products generated by railway construction could have provided a significant stimulus to industrial growth; rather, they point to the growing importance of the demand for industrial goods generated by railway maintenance and repair, and to the comparative usefulness of the much-maligned minor lines built after 1880.

The sixth chapter examines the first diachronic estimates of regional industrialization. The "industrial triangle" in northwest Italy emerged in the half-century at hand: around 1870 the regions with a sub-average manufacturing sector were not so much southern as eastern, along the Adriatic and Ionian coasts from Emilia to Calabria. The North's greater progress seems tied not to an initially higher level of development, but more simply to its greater endowment of the natural resources that attracted "low-tech" industries, especially textiles. The lack of development in the South did not stimulate development in the North; rather, it was tied to the broader national failure to develop the industries at the cutting edge of technical progress.

The final chapter recapitulates the main conclusions, and ponders the novel trends in the literature.

Some of the arguments in the text relate directly to theoretical considerations, briefly recalled in the appendices.

The Time Series and the Interpretations

1. The stages of growth

In the nineteenth century England and the Western World experienced industrial development, sustained economic growth, unprecedented material progress. Progress became the new religion: in Its name, as formerly in that of the True Faith, the West justified colonial conquest and the new imperialism.

That same faith foretold the future, and interpreted the past. The future held out limitless improvement; the past was the history of progress, specifically of technical progress, of that particular progress that was the pride and miracle of the West. The triumph of that ideology has been complete: to this day we have no mental categories to describe the vast sweep of human history other than technological ones, from the "Stone Age" on.

The faith in progress would be shaken only in recent decades. Public opinion has become increasingly aware of the limits to growth, especially from the absorptive capacity of the environment. In the 1960s, too, a small number of maverick scholars – working in different disciplines, on different problems, and not, apparently, in touch with each other – produced works that shared a heterodox tendency to redeem the "primitive," and to interpret past innovations in terms of growing human effort rather than effort-saving technical progress. Together, their analyses suggested an alternative interpretation of human history as a long decadence, a progressive decline in living standards, from the late Stone Age on, due essentially to the relentless growth of the human population. Eden was not a dream, it was a distant memory.[1]

In the mid-twentieth century, when the current debate on the economic growth of post-Unification Italy began, the faith in progress was still intact. Modern economic development was identified with industrialization, and the transition from agriculture to industry was considered analogous to that from, say, the Stone Age to the Bronze Age. The key to development was the improvement in the capacity to produce: those who possessed that greater capacity moved ahead into the new age, those who lacked it remained mired in backwardness.

This tradition would culminate in Walt Rostow's famous little book appropriately titled *The Stages of Economic Growth*. Rostow proposed a universal scheme, articulated in five stages. Every society, he claimed, had been, or perhaps still was, traditional and static. In the past of the advanced societies, and in the future of those that had not yet begun to develop, he saw three transitional stages: the creation of the prerequisites for growth, the "take-off" into sustained growth, and the "drive to maturity." Every society would so reach, if it had not already reached, the final stage of "high mass consumption." Mass prosperity would thus be achieved within the capitalist system, without a marxist revolution – whence the sub-title *A Non-Communist Manifesto* selected by the author, not by chance a hawk on Vietnam.[2]

The analysis developed by Alexander Gerschenkron is less widely known, but far richer than Rostow's one-dimensional scheme. To Gerschenkron's mind the most interesting aspect of the industrialization of backward countries is that it does not await the fullness of time: the take-off (or "great spurt," as he prefers to call it) begins even before all the canonical prerequisites are in place, thanks to innovative solutions that create *substitutes* for the missing prerequisites.

For Gerschenkron the critical prerequisite is the entrepreneurial ability to accumulate and manage industrial capital: it is abundant in developed societies, but scarce in backward ones, and the more scarce, the more backward they are. In England, the most advanced economy of its day, the industrial take-off was led by the numerous individual masters of private firms. In Germany, the great spurt took place in conditions of

[1] S. Fenoaltea, "Economic Decline in Historical Perspective: Some Theoretical Considerations," *Rivista di storia economica* 22 (2006), pp. 3–39.
[2] W. W. Rostow, *The Stages of Economic Growth: A Non-Communist Manifesto*, Cambridge 1960.

relative backwardness, with meager supplies of entrepreneurial capacity; the industrial take-off was accordingly led by the entrepreneurial "mixed banks," who supported and coordinated the individual firms. In Russia, the great spurt took place in conditions of extreme backwardness, with minimal supplies of entrepreneurial capacity; the industrial take-off was accordingly fostered directly by the State, the entrepreneur of last resort.[3]

2. Gerschenkron's index and interpretation

In 1955 Gerschenkron published his study of the Italian case.[4] Building on an earlier effort by Guglielmo Tagliacarne, Gerschenkron constructed an index of Italian industrial production from 1881 to 1913 (Table 1.01 and Figure 1.01).[5] That index pointed to moderate growth (4.6 percent per year) from 1881 to 1888, stagnation (0.3 percent per year) from 1888 to 1896, rapid growth (6.7 percent per year) from 1896 to 1908, and finally reduced growth (2.4 percent per year) from 1908 to 1913. Gerschenkron saw in the years 1896–1908 Italy's "great spurt": he considered it "a period of 'long-term' growth," and not a mere cyclical upswing, because of "the ease with which [Italian industry] rode horse and foot across the intervening depression of 1900."[6]

What struck Gerschenkron, however, was that the growth rate even then fell short of the high levels (8 to 12 percent per year) that he would have expected from the experience of such similarly backward countries as Sweden, Japan, and Russia. He accordingly searched for the causes that limited the intensity of Italy's great spurt; and among these he identified labor-market strife, the lack of an "industrialization ideology," and

---

[3] A. Gerschenkron, "Economic Backwardness in Historical Perspective," in B. F. Hoselitz, ed., *The Progress of Underdeveloped Areas*, Chicago 1952, pp. 3–29, reprinted in A. Gerschenkron, *Economic Backwardness in Historical Perspective*, Cambridge MA 1962, pp. 3–30; Id., "The Approach to European Industrialization: A Post-Script," in Id, *Economic Backwardness*, pp. 355–364.

[4] A. Gerschenkron, "Notes on the Rate of Industrial Growth in Italy, 1881–1913," *Journal of Economic History* 15 (1955), pp. 360–375, reprinted in Id., *Economic Backwardness*, pp. 72–89. Subsequent page references are to the latter volume.

[5] Gerschenkron's index appears, along with partial indices for six industrial sectors (below, ch. 1A, § 3), in Gerschenkron, "Notes," p. 75; an exhaustive description of the underlying sources and methods appears in Id., "Description of an Index of Italian Industrial Development, 1881–1913," in Id., *Economic Backwardness*, pp. 367–421. For the preceding index see G. Tagliacarne, "Lo sviluppo dell'industria italiana e il commercio estero," in Ministero per la Costituente, *Rapporto della commissione economica presentato all'Assemblea costituente. II. Industria. I. Relazione*, vol. 2, Rome 1947, pp. 33–92.

[6] Gerschenkron, "Notes," p. 77.

TABLE 1.01. *Industrial production: index numbers (1900 = 100)*

	(1) Gerschenkron 1955 (EM)[a]	(2) Istat 1957 (M)[a]	(3) Vitali 1966 (EMCU)[a]	(4) Fenoaltea 1967 (MU)[a]	(5) Fenoaltea 1972 (M)[a]	(6) Carreras 1983 (EMU)[a]	(7) Maddison 1991 (EMCU)[a]	(8) Fenoaltea 2001 (EMCU)[a]
1861		57	58	37	59	49	41	52
1862		57	58	37	59	46	41	53
1863		57	58	37	60	48	42	54
1864		57	58	37	60	46	41	54
1865		62	63	36	60	46	40	56
1866		62	63	37	60	48	40	55
1867		59	60	39	61	49	41	54
1868		59	60	39	62	52	41	53
1869		65	65	40	63	55	42	54
1870		68	66	42	64	58	45	56
1871		62	62	42	64	54	46	57
1872		65	65	43	65	60	47	59
1873		70	70	45	66	62	50	61
1874		73	72	46	67	64	51	62
1875		73	72	47	67	61	51	61
1876		73	73	47	69	55	50	62
1877		73	73	48	69	60	50	63
1878		70	71	48	69	58	51	64
1879		70	71	48	69	56	51	64
1880		68	69	53	72	66	57	67
1881	54	76	77	57	74	64	61	70
1882	57	73	75	61	77	68	66	73
1883	64	76	78	65	79	69	70	76
1884	63	78	81	67	80	71	71	79
1885	65	81	84	72	83	72	77	82
1886	67	78	82	76	85	77	81	85
1887	73	84	87	88	91	84	91	87
1888	74	81	84	88	91	73	91	88
1889	72	81	83	86	91	80	89	87
1890	72	81	82	82	89	81	86	87
1891	67	76	77	73	85	79	77	86
1892	64	76	78	69	84	74	74	84
1893	70	76	78	72	85	80	76	85
1894	72	81	82	76	87	83	80	87
1895	73	84	84	78	89	85	80	88
1896	75	81	82	79	89	88	81	89
1897	78	84	84	82	91	83	84	91
1898	86	84	85	88	94	92	88	94
1899	92	89	90	97	98	96	96	98
1900	100	100	100	100	100	100	100	100
1901	104	97	99	101	101	109	102	103
1902	109	105	106	104	102	110	104	107
1903	114	108	109	113	106	117	111	111
1904	117	111	112	119	109	119	118	116
1905	126	116	118	133	116	127	131	122
1906	139	127	129	152	124	145	147	131
1907	152	141	142	172	133	157	163	140
1908	163	149	150	196	144	158	182	148
1909	168	149	150	203	148	157	190	156
1910	169	149	151	211	151	160	197	163
1911	174	151	153	218	153	168	202	165
1912	182	162	164	222	154	180	205	174
1913	184	159	161	220	153	181	202	175

[a] major sectors: extractive industries (E), manufacturing (M), construction (C), utilities (U).

Source: S. Fenoaltea, "Notes on the Rate of Industrial Growth in Italy, 1861–1913," *Journal of Economic History* 63 (2003), p. 698.

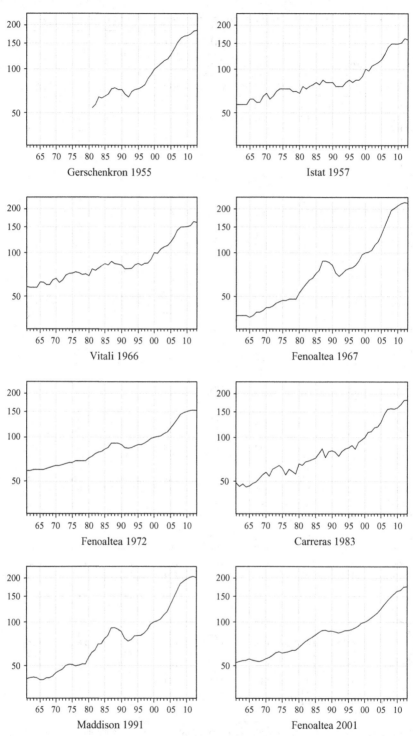

Source: Table 1.01.

FIGURE 1.01. *Industrial production: index numbers (1900 = 100)*

the weak demand for industrial products then generated by railroad construction because the railway net had in fact already been built.[7]

But to his mind the heaviest responsibilities lay with the State. The State could and should have turned the upswing of the 1880s into a great spurt; it failed to do so. Worse, the State's irrational tariff policy severely retarded industrial growth. The tariff should have protected the industries with a high growth potential, the innovative industries which did not face established competitors in the more advanced countries, engineering and chemicals above all. The tariff increases of 1878 and 1887 instead protected textiles, steel, and grain. The textile industry had pioneered the first industrial revolution, and was by then mature. A steel industry was clearly artificial in a country without coal, and the steel tariff hurt the engineering industry; the grain tariff damaged industry across the board. The protection of engineering and chemicals was opposed by the politically powerful textile and agricultural producers, who purchased machinery, dyes and fertilizer; the engineering industry obtained barely enough protection to offset the tariff on steel.[8] The State thus retarded Italy's development: "in Italian conditions a great deal of state intervention would have been in order, and in fact most desirable," but in the event "perfect inactivity of the government in economic affairs might have been more beneficial than what actually took place."[9]

If all these obstacles were nonetheless overcome, if after 1896 a great spurt of industrial growth took place all the same, it was thanks to the creation in the mid-1890s of entrepreneurial banks on the German model, with German capital and managers. These banks nurtured the new industrial firms, supplying them with capital and management; they were substitutes both for the individual capacities that were naturally scarce in

---

[7] Ibid., pp. 84–87. Labor-market conflict was exacerbated by the example provided by the unions that had meanwhile appeared in the more advanced economies; it accordingly represented (like the prior completion of the railway net) an example of the *dis*advantages of backwardness, which does not bring only the benefits of low wages, ready-made technologies, and the like (p. 86).

[8] Ibid., pp. 79–83; A. Gerschenkron, "The Industrial Development of Italy: A Debate with Rosario Romeo (with a Postscript)," in Id., *Continuity in History and Other Essays*, Cambridge MA 1968, pp. 98–127 (translation of A. Gerschenkron and R. Romeo, "Lo sviluppo industriale italiano [testo del dibattito tenuto a Roma, presso la Svimez, il 13 luglio 1960]," *Nord e Sud* 23 [1961], pp. 30–56).

[9] A. Gerschenkron, "Rosario Romeo and the Original Accumulation of Capital," in Id., *Economic Backwardness*, pp. 90–118 (translation of Id., "Rosario Romeo e l'accumulazione primitiva del capitale," *Rivista storica italiana* 71 [1959], pp. 557–586); the quotation is from p. 117. See also Id., "Notes," pp. 79–80, and Id., "The Industrial Development," p. 118.

a still backward economy, and for the leadership the inept State failed to provide. The Italian case thus presented some peculiar features, but for all that it well fit the broader pattern of prerequisite substitution in conditions of relative backwardness.[10]

3. The Istat and Vitali series

Gerschenkron's 1955 essay was soon followed by the other works that would define the post-war debate: the time series reconstructed by Istat (Italy's Bureau of statistics) and by Ornello Vitali, and the interpretation proposed by Rosario Romeo.

Between 1957 and 1959 Istat published three fundamental works. The first, the *Indagine*, reconstructed the national accounts, year by year, from 1861 on.[11] The expenditure series – consumption, investment, net imports – were presented at both current and constant (1938) prices; the production series – value added in agriculture, industry, and services – were presented only at current prices, so that their increases reflected inflation as well as real growth.

The constant-price series point to a sharp discontinuity in the half-century at hand. From 1861 to the mid-1890s aggregate output grew no faster than population: real per-capita income remained constant, real per-capita private consumption actually drifted down. After that, growth was much faster, with clear increases in production and consumption even in per-capita terms (Table 1.02 and Figure 1.02).[12]

The *Indagine* did not reconstruct the production accounts at constant prices, but it did present a 1938-price index of manufacturing output.[13] In this sector too growth appeared to have been discontinuous: the index registered relatively rapid growth from the turn of the century (5.9 percent per year from 1898 to 1908), as Gerschenkron's did, but before then it registered only very slow growth (under 1.1 percent per year,

---

[10] Gerschenkron, "Notes," pp. 87–89.

[11] Istat (Istituto centrale di statistica), *Indagine statistica sullo sviluppo del reddito nazionale dell'Italia dal 1861 al 1956*, *Annali di statistica*, serie VIII, vol. 9, Rome 1957.

[12] Table 1.02, col. 1 transcribes the estimate of the *de facto* population within the borders of 1871–1913 used to calculate the per-capita series; it interpolates decadal data or estimates, and is practically indistinguishable from a simple trend (S. Fenoaltea, "Production and Consumption in Post-Unification Italy: New Evidence, New Conjectures," *Rivista di storia economica*, 18 [2002], pp. 295, note 27). The estimates in cols. 2 and 3 are from Istat, *Indagine*, pp. 262–263, 270–271; gross national income is obtained as the sum of net national income and depreciation.

[13] Istat, *Indagine*, pp. 98–99, 218. A 1938-price series for the gross saleable product of core agriculture (cultivation and herding) was also presented (pp. 67–68, 204).

TABLE 1.02. *Total product: Istat-Vitali series (billion lire at 1938 prices)*

	(1) year-end de facto population (millions)	(2) gross national income	(3) private consump- tion	(4) agri- culture	(5) industry	(6) net services	(7) indirect business taxes	(8) gross domestic product
		Istat estimates		Vitali estimates				
				value added				
1861	25.0	49.6	46.6	22.9	9.2	17.5	2.7	52.3
1862	25.2	51.3	46.7	23.7	9.1	17.9	2.8	53.5
1863	25.4	50.1	46.3	22.8	9.1	17.8	3.0	52.8
1864	25.5	51.4	47.1	23.8	9.1	18.2	3.8	54.9
1865	25.7	53.0	48.1	25.1	9.9	18.3	4.8	58.1
1866	25.9	55.3	48.8	25.9	9.9	19.9	5.0	60.7
1867	26.1	51.4	46.5	22.8	9.5	18.6	3.1	54.0
1868	26.3	52.8	46.4	24.8	9.5	18.3	3.6	56.2
1869	26.4	54.4	47.5	25.3	10.2	18.2	3.5	57.3
1870	26.6	54.2	48.3	25.1	10.5	18.8	3.3	57.7
1871	26.8	55.0	48.1	25.5	9.8	18.6	3.5	57.4
1872	27.0	54.7	48.5	24.8	10.2	18.4	3.1	56.5
1873	27.1	57.1	49.4	26.0	11.0	18.5	2.9	58.4
1874	27.3	55.9	50.7	25.5	11.3	18.8	3.0	58.5
1875	27.5	58.1	51.7	26.6	11.4	19.1	3.8	60.9
1876	27.6	57.7	52.3	25.7	11.4	19.3	3.9	60.3
1877	27.8	58.1	52.7	25.7	11.4	19.2	3.8	60.1
1878	28.0	58.5	52.3	26.1	11.1	19.2	3.8	60.3
1879	28.1	58.7	51.9	26.6	11.2	19.2	4.0	61.1
1880	28.3	60.9	51.6	27.9	10.9	19.1	3.8	61.7
1881	28.5	57.5	52.3	23.1	12.1	19.9	4.3	59.4
1882	28.7	60.6	51.0	26.6	11.9	19.5	4.2	62.1
1883	28.9	60.0	51.7	25.3	12.3	19.9	4.5	62.0
1884	29.0	60.6	52.4	25.2	12.8	20.3	5.0	63.2
1885	29.2	60.6	54.8	25.0	13.2	20.6	4.9	63.7
1886	29.4	62.8	53.3	26.8	13.0	20.1	4.7	64.8
1887	29.7	62.5	54.4	25.6	13.7	20.8	5.4	65.5
1888	29.9	62.2	53.0	25.3	13.2	21.1	5.6	65.2
1889	30.1	59.7	53.8	22.9	13.1	21.6	5.4	63.0
1890	30.3	63.9	56.2	26.8	12.9	22.0	5.0	66.7
1891	30.5	65.7	56.4	28.3	12.2	21.9	4.7	66.9
1892	30.7	62.6	55.7	25.5	12.2	22.2	4.8	64.7
1893	30.9	64.6	55.3	27.6	12.3	21.9	4.8	66.6
1894	31.1	64.1	55.4	25.5	12.9	22.7	5.2	66.3
1895	31.3	65.2	56.4	25.8	13.3	23.4	5.2	67.6
1896	31.5	66.4	57.1	27.2	12.9	23.5	5.5	69.1
1897	31.8	63.8	56.4	23.9	13.3	23.8	5.3	66.3
1898	32.0	68.7	57.3	27.8	13.3	23.8	4.9	69.9
1899	32.2	69.5	58.4	27.2	14.2	24.4	5.1	71.0
1900	32.4	73.1	60.7	29.3	15.7	25.3	5.5	75.9
1901	32.7	77.9	61.9	33.0	15.6	25.5	5.8	79.8
1902	32.9	76.3	63.0	29.9	16.7	26.4	6.2	79.1
1903	33.1	79.9	64.7	31.9	17.2	26.3	5.9	81.3
1904	33.4	79.6	65.2	30.9	17.6	26.9	5.9	81.4
1905	33.6	83.2	66.6	31.5	18.6	27.9	6.5	84.5
1906	33.8	84.6	68.5	30.7	20.2	28.7	7.0	86.6
1907	34.1	92.9	72.5	36.0	22.4	29.3	6.4	94.0
1908	34.3	90.0	74.4	33.3	23.6	30.6	7.2	94.6
1909	34.6	95.7	76.0	36.7	23.6	32.5	7.3	100.0
1910	34.8	90.1	73.9	31.0	23.8	33.4	7.5	95.7
1911	35.0	97.1	76.8	35.5	24.1	34.1	8.1	102.0
1912	35.3	98.5	79.1	34.3	25.8	35.9	7.9	104.0
1913	35.5	101.9	79.5	38.4	25.4	36.5	8.3	109.0

Sources: cols. 1, 5–6, see text; cols. 2–3, Istat (Istituto centrale di statistica), *Indagine statistica sullo sviluppo del reddito nazionale dell'Italia dal 1861 al 1956*, Annali di statistica, serie VIII, vol. 9, Rome 1957, pp. 262–263, 270–271; cols. 4, 7–8, P. Ercolani, "Documentazione statistica di base," in G. Fuà, ed., *Lo sviluppo economico in Italia*, vol. 3, Milan 1969, pp. 401–402, 408.

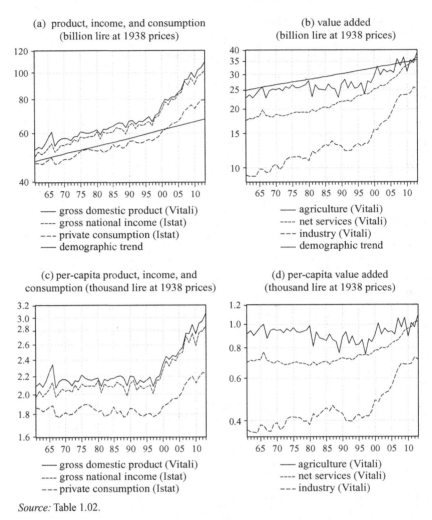

(a) product, income, and consumption
(billion lire at 1938 prices)

—— gross domestic product (Vitali)
---- gross national income (Istat)
--- private consumption (Istat)
—— demographic trend

(b) value added
(billion lire at 1938 prices)

—— agriculture (Vitali)
---- net services (Vitali)
--- industry (Vitali)
—— demographic trend

(c) per-capita product, income, and
consumption (thousand lire at 1938 prices)

—— gross domestic product (Vitali)
---- gross national income (Istat)
--- private consumption (Istat)

(d) per-capita value added
(thousand lire at 1938 prices)

—— agriculture (Vitali)
---- net services (Vitali)
--- industry (Vitali)

Source: Table 1.02.

FIGURE 1.02. *Total product: Istat-Vitali series*

barely positive in per-capita terms), with minor fluctuations around trend
(Table 1.01 and Figure 1.01). The reason for the difference between
the two indices is not clear: the *Indagine* provided only very succinct
descriptions of the underlying sources and methods, and Istat's estimates
cannot be replicated.[14]

---

[14] The difference cannot be due to the fact that Gerschenkron's index includes mining as
well as manufacturing, as the mining sector was relatively small, and in any case did not
grow from 1881 to 1888.

The *Indagine* was accompanied by the first abstract of historical statistics, the *Sommario*.[15] The *Sommario* presented time series on the weather, population, social indicators, and, in abundance, the economy: on the production of agricultural and industrial goods, transportation, foreign trade, wages and prices, even the national accounts and food consumption. The accompanying explanations are again frustratingly brief, but it is clear that the "historical statistics" in the *Sommario* are often extrapolations of limited contemporary data, or altogether new: not only in the case of the recently created national accounts, but even for example in that of agricultural production, ostensibly documented in great detail. In the case of industry, on the other hand, the *Sommario* reproduced data generated at the time, but the time series are limited in number and highly incomplete.[16] The unknown vastly exceeds the known: for those who are concerned about the reliability of the series in the *Indagine*, the *Sommario* is of no comfort at all.

Both the *Indagine* and the *Sommario* have been widely disseminated, and widely used; not so Istat's multi-volume *Le rilevazioni*, the third and perhaps most lasting of these official contributions, which reviews in superb detail the original sources of Italy's historical statistics.[17] *Le rilevazioni* reveal the lack of sources even where the *Sommario* presents complete series, and the unreliability of various historical series reproduced in the *Sommario* and presumably incorporated in the national-income aggregates of the *Indagine*. Istat's pioneering estimates cannot therefore be considered authoritative or definitive. Istat has described the sands on which it built its edifice; it is a great pity that it failed to present a detailed account of the methods and materials used to construct it.

In 1961 a further volume appeared, *I consumi*, presented as the personal effort of Benedetto Barberi, then Istat's second-in-command.[18] It contains hundreds of detailed series on consumption, in terms both of quantity and of cost, with a discussion of their long-term movements; the

---

[15] Istat (Istituto centrale di statistica), *Sommario di statistiche storiche italiane, 1861–1955*, Rome 1958.

[16] There are numerous series for the products of mining and metalmaking, and from 1893 for chemicals, derived from the reports of the Corpo delle miniere; as to the rest the only series refer to minor foodstuffs subject to production tax (sugar, beer, and a few more of even lesser significance), to tobacco (a State monopoly), to textiles (reeled silk, from 1900 cotton yarn), to engineering (ships launched, from 1905 rolling stock for the State railways), to paper (from 1907), and to power and lighting-gas.

[17] Istat (Istituto centrale di statistica), *Le rilevazioni statistiche in Italia dal 1861 al 1956*, 4 vols., *Annali di statistica*, serie VIII, vols. 5–8, Rome 1957–59.

[18] B. Barberi, *I consumi nel primo secolo dell'Unità d'Italia*, Milan 1961.

description of the sources and methods is again very succinct, and does little more than refer back to the production series in the *Sommario* and the statistics on foreign trade.

In 1963 a broad international project on the past growth of the industrial economies led in Italy to the formation of the so-called "Ancona group" headed by Giorgio Fuà. Ornello Vitali, the group's statistician, completed the *Indagine* by reconstructing the production account at constant (1938) prices. The Vitali constant-price value added series were pre-published by Fuà himself in 1966; in 1969 they appeared, again with very brief descriptions of the underlying sources and methods, along with the other studies prepared by the group.[19]

The Vitali production series identify 11 sectors (agriculture including related activities, the four major industrial groups, and six branches of the services group); they closely follow, in the large and in so far as possible in the small, the extant Istat estimates, which Vitali sought to complete rather than to amend (Table 1.02 and Figure 1.02).[20] For the manufacturing sector Vitali simply adopted the Istat index; and since manufacturing dominates total industry the Vitali index of industrial production closely follows the Istat index for manufacturing alone. Industrial growth in the 1880s is somewhat strengthened by the construction boom, but apart from that the two series are practically parallel (Table 1.01 and Figure 1.01).[21]

Considered together, the aggregate estimates for agriculture, industry, and the services tie the discontinuous path of the Istat series to essentially common movements in the first twenty years (when all three groups grow

[19] G. Fuà, *Notes on Italian Economic Growth 1861–1964*, Milan 1966; P. Ercolani, "Documentazione statistica di base," in G. Fuà, ed., *Lo sviluppo economico in Italia*, vol. 3, Milan 1969, pp. 380–460; O. Vitali, "La stima del valore aggiunto a prezzi costanti per rami di attività," in Fuà, *Lo sviluppo economico*, vol. 3, pp. 463–477.

[20] Below, ch. 1A, § 3. The series in Table 1.02, cols. 4–8 are derived from Ercolani, "Documentazione statistica," Tables XII.1.1.A and XII.1.4; cols. 5 and 6 sum the estimates for industry (extractive industries, manufacturing, construction, and utilities) and for the services (transportation and communication, commerce, banking and insurance, miscellaneous services, buildings, and public administration), deducting from these the otherwise double-counted banking and insurance business. Gross domestic product, measured by Vitali "at market prices" (col. 8), includes indirect business taxes (col. 7). Some minor statistical discrepancies apart, the differences between cols. 2 and 8 reflect the differences between national income on the Istat definition and domestic product on the international definition followed by Vitali. These differences refer to the treatment of income from foreign sources, and of business services provided by the public administration; neither item is particularly significant.

[21] The "Vitali 1966" index in Table 1.01 is simply the 1938-price series in Table 1.02, col. 5, suitably rescaled.

roughly in step with population) and again in the last fifteen years (when all three grow much faster than before), but to disparate movements in the intervening years. From 1880 almost to the end of the century the services grow continuously, at an accelerating pace; agriculture and industry experience sharp and largely opposite cycles. Up to 1887 industry grows as agriculture declines; then industry declines (and then recovers) while agriculture recovers (and then again declines). Agriculture is tied to consumption, industry to investment: it is the fall in per-capita agricultural production that accounts for the erosion of living standards after 1880 (Table 1.02 and Figure 1.02).

4. Romeo's interpretation

In the later 1950s Rosario Romeo published two major essays, the first (1956) dedicated to the recent works of marxist historians, the second (1958) to the "capitalist" – economic, industrial – growth of the Italian economy from 1861 to 1887.[22] He further refined his analysis in the following few years, in his famous debate with Gerschenkron, in his brief survey of Italian industrialization from Unification to the eve of the second World War – and then abandoned the topic to pursue other interests.[23]

Romeo's first essay contained a close criticism of the so-called "Gramsci thesis" (more appropriately attributed to Emilio Sereni, at least in its economic aspects) that the new Kingdom's failure to redistribute land delayed both Italy's political modernization, because the bourgeois State did not acquire the loyalty of the peasantry, and its economic development, because the poverty of the rural masses limited consumption and therefore industrial growth.[24] To Romeo's mind that agrarian reform was simply impossible, as the Great Powers would not have allowed it; in any

---

[22] R. Romeo, "La storiografia politica marxista," *Nord e Sud* 21 (1956), pp. 5–37, 22 (1956), pp. 16–44; Id., "Problemi dello sviluppo capitalistico in Italia dal 1861 al 1887," *Nord e Sud* 44 (1958), pp. 7–60, 45 (1958), pp. 23–57. These were then published together as Id., *Risorgimento e capitalismo*, Bari 1959. Subsequent page references are to the third edition, Rome-Bari 1998.

[23] Gerschenkron, "The Industrial Development"; R. Romeo, *Breve storia della grande industria in Italia*, Rocca San Casciano 1961. Romeo's theses would subsequently be championed by other scholars; see in particular G. Pescosolido, *Agricoltura e industria nell'Italia unita*, Rome-Bari 1994.

[24] A. Gramsci, *Il Risorgimento*, Turin 1949; E. Sereni, *Il capitalismo nelle campagne (1860–1900)*, Turin 1947. In its economic content the thesis belongs to the minority tradition that emphasizes the impulse to growth from the demand side rather than from the supply side; for a broad critique see J. Mokyr, "Demand vs. Supply in the Industrial Revolution," *Journal of Economic History* 37 (1977), pp. 981–1008.

case it would have failed, as Italy's peasants lacked capital and technical skills; and if by chance it had succeeded it would actually have delayed economic modernization, as it did in France.

Romeo's thought followed the orthodox tradition of the stages of growth: industrial growth was limited not by demand (then satisfied by imported manufactures) but by supply, by the capacity to produce, and more specifically by the accumulation of capital. The capital required for industrial production could only be generated by saving, by limiting consumption; in a backward, agricultural economy, by limiting the consumption of the peasants, of the poor.[25] An agrarian reform would have increased peasant incomes and consumption, reduced saving and the accumulation of capital; it would have retarded industrial growth. Wisely, the newborn national State refrained from agrarian reform.

Romeo's second essay and subsequent contributions developed his analysis, which he tied closely to Gerschenkron's index and to the time series just published by Istat. He confirmed there his strongly positive evaluation of the role of the State – in direct contrast to Gerschenkron, who himself produced a subtle exegesis of Romeo's work.[26]

Romeo's model is entirely classical, linear, (proto-)rostowian. The creation of the prerequisites – the "original accumulation of capital," in his marxist jargon – must precede industrial growth. In Italy, that accumulation took place in the 1860s and '70s. The growth of agricultural output (indicated by the Istat series) led to a rise not in rural wages and peasant consumption but in land rents and savings. Through the land tax and public borrowing, the State absorbed that "agrarian accumulation"; through its public-works policies, it embodied that capital in the "essential infrastructure," the major railway lines that unified the peninsula. The State thus created the prerequisites for growth: in the 1860s and '70s, it did what then had to be done.[27]

This process of accumulation was ended by the agrarian crisis of the 1880s, but by then it had played its part. With the prerequisites in place, industrial growth could begin. The 1880s saw the birth of large-scale industry, assisted by tariff protection and government contracts; to

[25] Romeo, *Risorgimento e capitalismo*, pp. 35–36.
[26] Ibid., pp. 87–184; Romeo, *Breve storia*; Gerschenkron, "The Industrial Development"; Id., "Rosario Romeo." Romeo cited Istat's *Le rilevazioni*, and questioned the reliability of the *Indagine* (Romeo, *Risorgimento e capitalismo*, pp. 103–104); but in the end he never challenged Istat's figures without the support of alternative estimates, as for example Gerschenkron's index.
[27] Romeo, *Risorgimento e capitalismo*, pp. 103–120 ("The accumulation of capital in agriculture"), 121–150 ("The creation of the infrastructure").

Romeo's mind even the creation of the steel industry was absolutely legitimate. The State, having created the prerequisites for industrialization, supported Italy's nascent industry: it could not have done more to favor the development of Italian "capitalism."[28]

Romeo's characterization of the 1880s remains somewhat ambiguous. At one point, he notes the orderly industrial development of those years, under way thanks to the efforts of the preceding decades (and confirmed by Gerschenkron's index, which he considers preferable to Istat's); elsewhere, he presents the birth of large-scale industry (perhaps displacing artisanal production, with little net growth, as suggested by the Istat index) as the institutional innovation that completed the set of prerequisites that would permit the industrial revolution from the late 1890s to the World War.[29]

Little changes if the 1880s are seen as the first stage of industrialization or as the last stage of pre-industrialization. What matters more is the fact that in the 1880s, when "agrarian accumulation" had come to an end, when large-scale industry got under way, railway construction rose to new heights. Romeo asserts that this further infrastructure was not "fundamental"; he also mentions the reduction in investment in agriculture, and points to the self-financing of the non-agrarian sectors.[30] But in so doing he is responding only to Gerschenkron's claim that the construction of the ("fundamental") railways did not have to come first; he does not come to grips with the essential difficulty, that is, the evidence that investment in infrastructure and in industry was not in fact constrained by agrarian rents and savings. This undercuts the logic of his critique of the "Gramsci thesis," the justification of the hardship imposed on the rural masses; it undercuts the logic of his sequence, which requires the *completion* of the infrastructure before the industrial take-off not because the railway from the Alps to the boot's heel is useless without the extension to its toe, but because the supply of savings is limited and can flow to industry only when it is no longer absorbed by the creation of the infrastructure.[31]

[28] Ibid., pp. 151–184 ("The birth of large-scale industry").

[29] Ibid., pp. 102, 159, 169–170; Romeo, *Breve storia*, p. 256; Gerschenkron, "The Industrial Development," pp. 111–112, 115. Romeo defends Gerschenkron's index even against Gerschenkron, who was instead ready to accept the Istat index that highlighted the discontinuity associated with the creation of the German-style banks even better than his own (ibid., p. 109).

[30] Romeo, *Risorgimento e capitalismo*, pp. 158–161.

[31] This response to Romeo's critique of the "Gramsci thesis" does not appear actually to have been formulated by the marxist historians Romeo had taken to task; if it is in the literature, the present writer missed it.

5. A new index of industrial production

The 1960s saw the birth, in the United States, of the so-called "cliometric school" that applied modern economic theory and statistical methods to the study of economic history. Its leaders included the first generation of Gerschenkron's graduate students; the present author was part of the second generation, and devoted his doctoral dissertation to post-Unification Italy.[32]

The first contribution of that work was a new index of industrial production. It was in essence a revision of Gerschenkron's index, which he had described in detail, with the aid of the new material presented by Istat: the series in the *Sommario*, and their implicit critique in *Le rilevazioni*.[33]

The revisions were of four orders. First, the index was carried back to 1861; this would permit an evaluation of the growth spurt of the 1880s, which Gerschenkron down-played on the strength of an index that began too late to reveal its beginning, duration, and overall strength. Second, the method used to aggregate the individual series was modified. Following the then standard procedure, Gerschenkron had combined the elementary series into sectoral indices, and then reweighted these to obtain the aggregate series; for the practical and theoretical reasons noted below the new index was obtained through a direct aggregation (with value added weights) of all its component series. Third, the set of component series was modified: many were added, trebling the number related to manufacturing and extending the coverage of the index to the utilities, while the extractive industries were omitted altogether. Fourth and not least, the individual series were examined, evaluated, and if necessary amended or eliminated outright.[34]

---

[32] S. Fenoaltea, "Public Policy and Italian Industrial Development, 1861–1913" (unpublished Ph.D. thesis, Harvard University, 1967), summarized in Id., "Decollo, ciclo, e intervento dello Stato," in A. Caracciolo, ed., *La formazione dell'Italia industriale*, Bari 1969, pp. 95–114. The first "cliometric italianist" was Jon Cohen, whose 1966 Berkeley dissertation extended Gerschenkron's work; see J. S. Cohen, "Financing Industrialization in Italy, 1894–1914: The Partial Transformation of a Late-Comer," *Journal of Economic History* 27 (1967), pp. 363–382. The immediately preceding work of S. B. Clough, *The Economic History of Modern Italy*, New York 1964, was instead entirely traditional.

[33] Gerschenkron, "Description"; Istat, *Sommario*; Id., *Le rilevazioni*. As noted the description of the index in Id., *Indagine*, is too brief to allow its reconstruction.

[34] Below, ch. 1A, § 4. The extractive industries were excluded because they are a primary activity, typically developed (for export) even in backward countries, and thus a poor indicator of the capacity to modernize; in the case at hand mining output (net of

The most significant of these corrections involved the grain-consumption figures, used to represent milling. The historical statistics incorporated by Gerschenkron's index and reproduced with trivial revisions by Istat (and Barberi) showed very similar levels of per-capita consumption in the late 1870s, when their overall level is confirmed by the grist tax, and in the early 1900s, when they are based on relatively sound agricultural statistics. Over the 1880s and early 1890s, when the data-gathering process was so notoriously poor that the output figures were generally disbelieved, measured per-capita grain consumption declined to roughly half its previous level; it then recovered in a sudden surge around the turn of the century, apparently as the result of interpolation. The extended decline and the subsequent rapid recovery in grain consumption, clearly improbable in their own right, thus seemed entirely bogus; the revised series eliminated these spurious fluctuations in favor of a simple trend (Figure 1.03).[35]

This critique of the historical grain production and consumption series carried over to the aggregate series that incorporate them. In 1900 milling accounts for over a quarter of Gerschenkron's index, and the spurious surge in grain consumption gives a strong boost to measured growth. At the sectoral level, only his foodstuffs index grows smartly over 1899–1902; all the other sectoral indices register a brief decline, or at least a pause (chemicals). Gerschenkron's "horse and foot" are in essence the removal of a statistical error: the years from 1896 to 1908 appear in a different light, and by his own criteria the great spurt is in doubt.[36]

The critique of the Istat (and Vitali) series was less precise, as they cannot be recalculated, but even broader. Like Gerschenkron's index, the Istat measures of industrial production increasingly underestimate

---

exports) is of little value even as an indicator of downstream industrial transformation, as metalmaking and chemical production were documented by direct evidence.

[35] Fenoaltea, "Decollo," pp. 97–98, and more extensively Id., "Public Policy," pp. 30–37. Figure 1, p. 37 (here reproduced as Figure 1.03) presents the sum of the tons of wheat and corn available for human consumption reported in Istat, *Sommario*, p. 223; the critique is based on the very rich description of the sources of the agricultural output data in Id., *Le rilevazioni*, vol. 7, pp. 3–75. On the skepticism with which the late-nineteenth century cereal production and consumption estimates were greeted see ibid., p. 73, and similarly L. Einaudi, *Cronache economiche e politiche di un trentennio*, 8 vols., Turin 1959–66, vol. 1, p. 103. As a simple trend the corrected series was obviously a first approximation: it removed the spurious movements of the existing series but did not itself incorporate any cyclical fluctuations, as the information then available did not permit. The path of such food consumption could then be considered known in the long run, but not in the short.

[36] Gerschenkron, "Notes," p. 77; Id., "Description," pp. 394, 401.

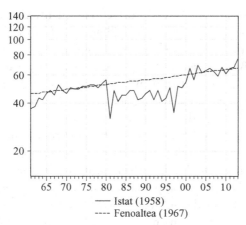

Source: S. Fenoaltea, "Public Policy and Italian Industrial Development, 1861–1913"
(unpublished Ph.D. thesis, Harvard University, 1967), Fig. 1.

FIGURE 1.03. *Wheat and corn for human consumption (million quintals)*

(foodstuffs and total) output over the 1880s and early 1890s, and overstate growth around the turn of the century. The distortions of the grain
consumption series derive from the underlying production series; given
the importance of grain-growing in its own right, and the likelihood
of analogous distortions in the other agricultural production estimates,
the Istat estimates of agricultural production would appear to be similarly distorted. The entire reconstruction of the national accounts is thus
called into question: the sudden transition in the mid-1890s from stagnation to relatively rapid growth appears vastly exaggerated if not entirely
spurious.[37]

The new index enhanced the oscillations already recorded by Gerschenkron, with sustained growth in the 1880s, decline and recovery
in the 1890s, and renewed rapid growth after 1900 (Table 1.01 and
Figure 1.01). The attendant growth rates are well above those of the
Gerschenkron index, averaging 7.9 percent per year from 1879 to 1887
and peaking at 13.3 percent per year in 1904–08. But they are not to be
taken too seriously, for the index covers no more than about half of total
production, and the residual could have moved very differently; rather,

[37] S. Fenoaltea, "Railroads and Italian Industrial Growth, 1861–1913," *Explorations in
Economic History* 9 (1972), pp. 335, 349, repeated in translation in Id., "Le ferrovie e
lo sviluppo industriale italiano, 1861–1913," in G. Toniolo, ed., *Lo sviluppo economico
italiano 1861–1940*, Bari 1973, pp. 167, 183, and again in G. Toniolo, ed., *L'economia
italiana 1861–1940*, Bari 1978, pp. 115, 131.

they reveal the sensitivity of the measured growth rate to the underlying elementary series, and to the largely arbitrary method with which they are combined.

Gerschenkron searched for the influences that retarded Italy's great spurt because he obtained an annual growth rate near 7 percent rather than over 8; given the imprecision of such estimates such differences are simply insignificant.

6. The "cyclical" interpretation

The analysis of the available production series began by identifying those that mattered most, in terms of their weight in the overall index, or of their contribution to its fluctuations. Their movements were then correlated with those of the corresponding imports and exports.[38] Three main groups of industries emerged.

The old consumer-goods industries grew relatively slowly and steadily: thus milling (in part, obviously, by assumption), and also the cotton industry. Cotton yarn and cloth production grew faster than consumption, first reducing imports (thanks also to tariff protection) and then breaking out into exports. Supply clearly grew, but relatively steadily: there was no apparent discontinuity, no particular acceleration that might point to the creation of missing prerequisites.[39]

There was instead a clear discontinuity in the growth of the new industries – fertilizer, sugar, electric power – which appeared suddenly and grew rapidly to significant levels. But not even these support the stages-of-growth interpretations, for they do not reveal a prior inability to industrialize for the lack of prerequisites already possessed by the more advanced economies. Fertilizer production grew with domestic consumption, with its market, and not by taking over a market previously supplied by more advanced producers. The rise of the sugar industry did displace imports, but it was accompanied by the diffusion of sugar-beet cultivation and growing tariff protection; again, nothing suggested a prior inability to manage the industrial transformation of the raw material.[40] In the

---

[38] Fenoaltea, "Decollo."

[39] The analysis of milling is precluded by the lack of international trade in its output; for technical reasons, it would appear, grain is traded either as the raw material (wheat) or as a finished product (pasta), but not as the intermediate good (flour).

[40] The increase in industrial production could have been due simply to an increase in agricultural supply, or to an elastic response by industrial entrepreneurs to (actual or prospective) tariff protection.

case of electric power, finally, the sudden increase in industry's ability to produce was undeniable. But the missing prerequisites were technical, world-wide; the first Italian generating plant came on stream in 1883, in Milan, just a few months after the world's first, in New York.

The third group was that of the old industries producing investment goods: engineering, and, altogether secondarily, metalmaking. Statistically it was much the most important group, as it determined the fluctuations of the aggregate: these industries, and these alone, were those that grew rapidly in the 1880s, collapsed in the crisis of the 1890s, and then boomed again after the turn of the century. In both cases production movements elastically followed the variations in domestic consumption. The metalmaking industry obtained a significant increase in its share of the domestic market, thanks to tariff protection. The market share of domestic engineering was ever very high, and practically constant from decade to decade (though it varied from year to year, in inverse proportion to consumption growth: domestic supply was less elastic than foreign supply, as if domestic industry needed some time to organize the production of goods readily available on the international market). The impulses that generated the output movements of the metal-processing industries, and the aggregate index, clearly stemmed from the demand side, and not from the supply side.

The supply-side discontinuities were thus few in number, highly specific, and tied to special circumstances. The production and consumption series provided no evidence of a take-off or great spurt tied to a broad-gauged increase in the capacity to develop industry, in the *relative* supply of Italian industrial goods thanks to the creation of prerequisites already available in the more advanced economies of the time. There was no evidence of a transition from one age or stage to another, from preindustrialization to industrialization, from traditional stagnation to modern economic growth. Gerschenkron and Romeo differed on many points, but shared the stages-of-growth approach; their interpretations were rejected together because the quantitative evidence did not support them where they were in agreement.[41]

---

[41] Their specific hypotheses of course fared no better. The econometric analysis attributed no perceptible effect, on relative supply, to the birth and growth of Gerschenkron's mixed banks. Similarly skeptical evaluations of their role were later reached by Anna Maria Biscaini Cotula and Pierluigi Ciocca, through an analysis of Italy's financial structure, and by Antonio Confalonieri, through years of research in the archives of the banks themselves: see A. M. Biscaini Cotula and P. Ciocca, "Le strutture finanziarie: aspetti quantitativi di lungo periodo (1870–1970)," in F. Vicarelli, ed., *Capitale industriale*

From 1861 to 1913 Italy's industrial growth was characterized by considerable structural continuity: the broad movements of the aggregate growth rate were tied to the instability of the demand for investment goods, which interacted with an ever-elastic supply. But in a market economy investment demand is naturally and notoriously unstable, precisely because investment is an adjustment to the desired stock of capital. The rapid growth of the 1880s, the crisis of the 1890s, and the renewed growth of later years were accordingly identified as the successive phases of an ordinary business cycle.

The work ended with a hypothesis as to the underlying causes of that cycle, and an evaluation of the role of public policy. The hypothesis tied the cycle in investment demand to the changes in the political climate, and the risk associated with industrial investment. From 1861 to 1876 Italy was governed by the Right, closely identified with its agricultural power base, and ever ready to sacrifice domestic industry to expand Italy's agricultural exports. From 1876 to 1887 the political scene was dominated by the Left's Agostino Depretis, friendly to industrial interests and to business in general; from 1887 to 1896 by Francesco Crispi, a hot-head driven by considerations of prestige and apparently unconcerned with the economic consequences of his policies. The closing years of the century were marked by a political challenge from the reactionary Right and social unrest, and in 1900 the King was murdered by an anarchist; the "return to normalcy" came with the political ascendancy of Giovanni Giolitti, and lasted right up to the War.

The hypothesis was thus simply that industrial entrepreneurs invested more under governments they trusted (Depretis, Giolitti), and less under governments they did not trust (the Right, Crispi). Economic policy apparently influenced the rate of industrial growth primarily through its impact on investment demand, as it repeatedly altered the confidence of industrial entrepreneurs.[42] Foreign entrepreneurs, interestingly, no less

---

e capitale finanziario: il caso italiano, Bologna 1979, pp. 70–71, and A. Confalonieri, *Banca e industria in Italia, 1894–1906*, 3 vols., Milan 1974–76 and Id., *Banca e industria in Italia dalla crisi del 1907 all'agosto 1914*, 2 vols., Milan 1982. The econometric identification of the railways' role was less easily established, not least because the railway net grew steadily, albeit with a reduction in the growth rate after the mid-1890s; in any case, there was no evidence of a discontinuous increase in relative supply on domestic markets that could somehow be traced to the "completion" of the infrastructure, whether "essential" (and thus associated with a sudden increase in transport services) or global (and thus associated with a sudden increase in the flow of savings into investment in industry).

[42] Fenoaltea, "Decollo," pp. 108–112; in greater detail below, ch. 2, § 1.

than domestic ones: since the currency was strong when domestic investment and net imports surged and weakened as they fell, foreign investment
must have followed a parallel cycle.[43]

But there was more. The engineering industry (which dominated the
movements of aggregate industrial output) appeared not only to have
absorbed most of the domestic market, but to have been constrained by
it, as the tariff on steel raised its costs and priced it out of world markets.
The steel tariff kept the engineering industry from continuing to grow,
expanding into export markets, when the domestic market collapsed in
the late 1880s: the domestic production cycle was the domestic investment
cycle because protection prevented export-led growth. Gerschenkron had
criticized the tariff on somewhat different grounds, but his condemnation
of Italy's trade policy was entirely justified.[44]

7. Bonelli, Cafagna, and the consensus that never was

The literature was subsequently enriched by a number of interpretive
essays, notably the 1978 essay by Franco Bonelli on "Italian capitalism,"
and two papers published by Luciano Cafagna in 1983.[45]

The subsequent reviews of the literature agree that Bonelli and
Cafagna share the "cyclical interpretation," and that the stages-of-growth
approach has been abandoned.[46] But this view is superficial: it does not

---

[43] Fenoaltea, "Decollo," p. 110; in greater detail below, ch. 2, § 5.

[44] Fenoaltea, "Decollo," pp. 112–113, and more fully Id., "Riflessioni sull'esperienza industriale italiana dal Risorgimento alla prima guerra mondiale," in Toniolo, *Lo sviluppo
economico*, pp. 121–156, and again in Toniolo, *L'economia italiana*, pp. 69–104; also
in greater detail below, ch. 4, § 4.

[45] F. Bonelli, "Italian Capitalism: General Interpretative Guidelines," in G. Federico, ed.,
The Economic Development of Italy since 1870, Aldershot 1994, pp. 99–142 (translation
of F. Bonelli, "Il capitalismo italiano. Linee generali di interpretazione," in R. Romano
and C. Vivanti, eds., *Storia d'Italia. Annali. 1. Dal feudalesimo al capitalismo*, Turin
1978, pp. 1193–1255); L. Cafagna, "Protoindustria o transizione in bilico? (A proposito della prima onda dell'industrializzazione italiana)," *Quaderni storici* 54 (1983),
pp. 971–984; Id., "La formazione del sistema industriale: ricerche empiriche e modelli
di crescita," *Quaderni della Fondazione G. G. Feltrinelli* 25 (1983), pp. 27–38. These
were reprinted in Id., *Dualismo e sviluppo nella storia d'Italia*, Venice 1989, respectively
pp. 359–372 and pp. 385–399. Page references to Cafagna's essays will be, wherever
possible, to that volume.

[46] V. Zamagni, *The Economic History of Italy, 1860–1990: Recovery after Decline*,
Oxford 1993 (translation of Id., *Dalla periferia al centro: la seconda rinascita eco-
nomica dell'Italia, 1861–1981*, Bologna 1990), pp. 79–80; G. Federico and G. Toniolo,
"Italy," in R. Sylla and G. Toniolo, eds., *Patterns of European Industrialization: The
Nineteenth Century*, London 1991, p. 149; G. Federico, "Introduction," in Id., *The
Economic Development*, p. xiii; J. S. Cohen and G. Federico, *The Growth of the Italian
Economy, 1820–1960*, Cambridge 2001, pp. 20–22. So too, regrettably, S. Fenoaltea,

look beyond the cyclical fluctuations themselves, and fails to consider the presence or absence of the deeper changes in the structure of the economy, and in its capacity to grow, that characterize the stages of growth.[47]

Cafagna himself never abandoned the stages-of-growth approach; rather, he became ever more critical of the traditional chronology. In 1961 his views were entirely rostowian: he recalled the canonical leading sectors (textiles in England, the railway on the Continent); he shared Gerschenkron's view that growth must begin with a sudden acceleration; and he described the economic growth of the early twentieth century as a true revolution.[48] In 1965 Cafagna agreed that the fundamental problem was the scarcity of capital, which limited supply; he underscored the importance both of the "agrarian accumulation" identified by Romeo, and of the financial substitutes identified by Gerschenkron. On the other hand, he suggested abandoning the notion of a great spurt; he saw in its stead a series of upswings, none of which was in fact predominant. Cafagna placed these upswings in the years 1880–87 and 1896–1908, the war years, and again 1922–29; but the key point was the denial of a massive effort concentrated in the space of a few years.[49]

"Lo sviluppo dell'industria dall'Unità alla Grande Guerra: una sintesi provvisoria," in P. Ciocca and G. Toniolo, eds., *Storia economica d'Italia. 3.1. Le strutture dell'economia*, Rome-Bari 2002, p. 151: this repetition of the general opinion was to be confirmed or amended in page proofs, but these were never received. For the subsequent reconsideration see S. Fenoaltea, "Contro tre pregiudizi," *Rivista di storia economica* 20 (2004), pp. 88–94, summarized in the following paragraphs.

[47] Zamagni, *The Economic History*, p. 80, thus attributed the "cyclical model" even to Gerschenkron, simply because his index is not, like Istat's, practically flat up to 1895; but Gerschenkron himself had carefully distinguished the "great spurt" of the following years from a mere cyclical upswing. As noted, moreover, Gerschenkron was ready to abandon his own index in favor of Istat's: Gerschenkron, "The Industrial Development," p. 109.

[48] L. Cafagna, "L'industrializzazione italiana. La formazione di una 'base industriale' in Italia fra il 1896 e il 1914," *Studi storici* 2 (1961), pp. 690–724, reprinted in Id., *Dualismo e sviluppo*, pp. 323–357; see in particular pp. 324, 329, 331–332, 334, 352. The only cycle mentioned is the very long Kondratieff cycle, whose very existence is in doubt: see for example S. Solomou, *Phases of Economic Growth: Kondratieff Waves and Kuznets Swings*, Cambridge 1987.

[49] L. Cafagna, "Intorno alle origini del dualismo economico in Italia," in A. Caracciolo, ed., *Problemi storici dell'industrializzazione e dello sviluppo*, Urbino 1965, pp. 103–150, reprinted with the addition of notes and subtitles in Cafagna, *Dualismo e sviluppo*, pp. 187–220; see in particular pp. 206, 213–214. See also Id., "The Industrial Revolution in Italy, 1830–1914," in C. M. Cipolla, ed., *The Fontana Economic History of Europe*, vol. 4, Glasgow 1972, pp. 279–328, and in particular pp. 299, 317 (where the Kondratieff cycle is again recalled), 321–323. The 1965 essay exists in English ("Discussion of the Origins of Italian Economic Dualism," in Federico, *The Economic Development*, pp. 634–653), but the translation is unreliable.

Bonelli's 1978 essay on "Italian capitalism" identified a period of "agrarian accumulation" that ended with the agrarian crisis of the 1880s, but began in the eighteenth century, long before Unification; he attributed to the State a leading role in the transition to industrial growth; and he noted the *qualitative* as well as quantitative modification of the economy, the change in the way it reacted to the opportunities of the moment. In essence, Bonelli described a lengthy progression, not without interruptions, across successive stages of growth; its long time frame apart, his interpretation closely followed that of Romeo.[50]

In 1983 Cafagna chose his definitive metaphor, proposing an analysis centered not on a great spurt but on successive "waves." He noted that these "waves" had some elements in common with a "natural" history of industry in which different sectors develop in succession, as suggested by Hoffman, and also with the "technical cycle" identified by the present author. In developing his concept he followed Hoffman, specifying the leading sectors of the successive "waves" (first textiles, then wood and engineering, and finally basic products such as chemicals, steel, and power).[51]

In the same year Cafagna published an extensive review of the extant interpretations: Sereni's, Romeo's, Gerschenkron's, and finally the "Bonelli-Cafagna view." This last was characterized by the absence of a great spurt; rather, it emphasized gradual change, Italy's slow and difficult progress as growth alternately quickened and slackened. But it was otherwise close to Romeo's: it too saw a critical period of "agrarian accumulation" – a point on which "Romeo was perfectly right, save only that *it was a century-long phenomenon*" – followed by "preindustrialization," then in the 1880s by the beginning of industrial growth, and finally by the decisive upswing of the pre-war years.[52]

The "Bonelli-Cafagna view" is essentially Romeo's in slow motion, and clearly a stages-of-growth interpretation. In that context the image of the wave is misleading. A wave passes, like the present author's demand cycles, without changing the sea; Cafagna's "waves" are in fact the successive hops of a lengthy and difficult take-off, different in this but only

---

[50] Bonelli, "Italian Capitalism," pp. 100, 103, 107, 110–113, 117, 131.

[51] Cafagna, "Protoindustria," pp. 361, 370–371.

[52] Cafagna, "La formazione," especially pp. 396–398 (author's translation; italics in the original). The "Bonelli-Cafagna view" also emphasizes the openness of the Italian economy: the North's long "agrarian accumulation" is tied to its exports to the more advanced areas of Europe, and each stage of development is characterized by a specific solution to the balance-of-payments problem. Both these issues will be returned to below.

in this from the take-off contemplated by Rostow, by Gerschenkron, and by Romeo. Equally clearly, and despite the widespread claims to the contrary, the stages-of-growth approach is far from dead, and the properly (or merely) cyclical interpretation is anything but agreed-upon.

At a deeper level, the literature offers two opposing conceptions of the economy of post-Unification Italy, two different models of the economy in general. The one sees the national economy as limited to and by its internal endowment of financial, institutional, and technological resources. These must therefore be patiently accumulated (or substituted by gerschenkronian innovations); when they reach sufficiency the economy acquires a greater set of capacities, and passes from a given stage to the next. This may happen quickly or slowly, with monotonic or cyclical movements; the story changes, but the underlying model is one and the same.

The other model sees in the growth of the capacity to produce, in the accumulation of capital, in technical progress, the key to economic growth in the (western) world at large. But these are the background to *national* development: Italy was but a region of a wider world, and it developed to the extent that firms, capital, and technical experts chose to locate within its territory rather than elsewhere. These resources were internationally mobile, and could readily relocate if it was convenient to do so: history registers a sequence of equilibria that are quickly reached, not the slow movement from one equilibrium to another. The supply of resources is elastic, the past matters little.

In the first ("stages-of-growth") model Italy produces what it can produce; in the second ("cyclical") model Italy produces what is advantageously produced within its borders. In the event, the policies of its governments did not make Italy a region in which it was convenient to produce for the rest of the world: output was limited to what was advantageously produced for the domestic market, and accordingly followed the cycle in domestic demand. But it could have been otherwise: the same model generates the hypothesis of sustained industrial growth, led by engineering exports, with a different tariff policy.[53]

Even the second model is thus consistent with a sudden acceleration in the rate of growth as well as with cyclical fluctuations: what characterizes it is the elasticity of supply, the ever-present readiness to take advantage of the opportunities offered by the market, and not the actual time path of such opportunities. The heart of the "cyclical" model is not the cycle but the economy's always adequate capacity to produce; in the alternative

---

[53] Above, § 6, note 44.

"stages-of-growth" model that capacity is taken to develop slowly over time, with the creation of the necessary prerequisites.

There are often discussions in which the parties involved fail to understand each other because they express similar concepts with different words; Italy's economic historians have failed to understand each other because different concepts have been expressed with similar words, and a consensus has been perceived where none existed.[54]

8. The evolution of the time series: industry

The present author's first index was, as noted, a simple weighted sum of the available time series: it thus recorded the movements of documented production, and served to identify its most significant components. The underlying sample was not representative: it seemed to contain the entire cyclical group and most of the new industries, but a much smaller share of the traditional industries that presumably grew slowly or even declined. In 1972 the author proposed a second index, for manufacturing alone, that sought to represent that sector as a whole. That new index attributed to the non-documented industries a constant growth rate equal to that of Italy's population: the modification obviously conserved the cyclical path of the first index, but much reduced its variability and trend growth rate (Table 1.01 and Figure 1.01).[55] The curious result was that this new index closely matched the corresponding Istat series – save of course over the 1880s and 1890s, when Istat underestimated foodstuffs production – as if the latter actually incorporated a similar correction.

In 1983 Albert Carreras completed his doctoral dissertation comparing the industrial development of Italy and Spain.[56] He produced an

---

[54] The confusion of these different models seems due to the image of the "wave," and perhaps also to Cafagna's own suggestion, recalled above, that his "waves" are kin to the "technical cycle" of the present author (Cafagna, "Protoindustria," p. 361). Moreover, Cafagna's review of the extant interpretations did not separately consider the present author's, strengthening the suggestion that it could be assimilated to the Bonelli-Cafagna view.

[55] This index was published as five-year averages in Fenoaltea, "Railroads," pp. 333, 349. The subsequent literature seems not to have noted this correction to the 1967 index, and the "Fenoaltea index" has remained the first (subsequently published, with a clearly inadequate commentary, in Id., "Italy," in P. K. O'Brien, ed., *Railways and the Economic Development of Western Europe*, London 1983, pp. 54–56): see for example Cohen and Federico, *The Growth*, p. 47, Zamagni, *The Economic History*, p. 79, and especially the works of Carreras and Maddison, returned to below.

[56] A. Carreras, "La producció industrial espanyola i italiana des de mitjan segle XIX fins a l'actualitat" (unpublished Ph.D. thesis, Universitat Autònoma de Barcelona, 1983); Id., "La producción industrial en el muy largo plazo: una comparación entre España e Italia de 1861 a 1980," in L. Prados and V. Zamagni, eds., *El desarrollo económico en la*

entirely new index of Italian industrial production from 1861 to 1980; with respect to the earlier indices of the present author, the number of elementary series was practically doubled.[57] Many of these were altogether new, or significant corrections of existing series; oddly, however, Carreras retained the Istat cereal-consumption series, even though he noted its defects.[58] Over the post-Unification period the Carreras index lies between the two indices of the present author, but with the upswing of the 1880s flattened by the underestimation of flour production: the overall pattern is one of relatively steady growth, with neither the sudden acceleration of the Istat-Vitali series nor the strong cycle picked up by Gerschenkron and by the present author (Table 1.01 and Figure 1.01).[59]

Yet another index appeared in 1991: it was obtained by Angus Maddison, who recalculated the growth of the Italian economy as part of his vast project on world development.[60] For the decades at hand Maddison borrowed the present author's first (1967) index, extending it with a few additional series also compiled by the present author. He made no use of the second (1972) index, which attributed a slow growth rate to the industries missed by the first; not surprisingly, Maddison's index strongly resembles the 1967 series, and reproduces its strong cycle and rapid growth (Table 1.01 and Figure 1.01).

The most recent index of Italian industrial production is the author's own, at 1911 prices, computed in 2001 (Table 1.01 and Figure 1.01).[61] It covers all industry, grouped in 15 sectors (Table 1.03 and Figure 1.04);

Europa del Sur: España e Italia en perspectiva histórica, Madrid 1992, pp. 173–210. A broad synthesis of his results for Italy appeared later in A. Carreras, "Un ritratto quantitativo dell'industria italiana," in F. Amatori, D. Bigazzi, R. Giannetti and L. Segreto, eds., *Storia d'Italia. Annali. 15. L'industria*, Turin 1999, pp. 179–272.

[57] Below, ch. 1A, § 4. The series are summed directly, with 1970 value added weights, without calculating intermediate, sectoral indices; all the major groups are represented, save construction.

[58] Carreras, "Un ritratto quantitativo," pp. 239–240. His decision to do so may have reflected his interest in very long-term growth, and a reduced concern for medium-term cyclical movements.

[59] Ibid., p. 195. For Carreras, too, the "Fenoaltea index" is the first, of 1967.

[60] A. Maddison, "A Revised Estimate of Italian Economic Growth, 1861–1989," *BNL Quarterly Review* 177 (1991), pp. 225–241; Id., *Monitoring the World Economy, 1820–1992*, Paris 1995; Id., *The World Economy: A Millennial Perspective*, Paris 2001; below, ch. 1A, § 4.

[61] Used in S. Fenoaltea, "La crescita industriale delle regioni d'Italia dall'Unità alla Grande Guerra: una prima stima per gli anni censuari," Banca d'Italia, *Quaderni dell'Ufficio Ricerche Storiche*, n. 1, Rome 2001, it was then presented in Id., "Lo sviluppo dell'industria," pp. 141–152, and in greater detail in Id., "Notes on the Rate of Industrial Growth in Italy, 1861–1913," *Journal of Economic History* 63 (2003), pp. 708–714 and 720–731. It is undergoing revision, but the recent emendations are minor, and not considered here.

TABLE 1.03. *Industrial production: value added, by sector*
(million lire at 1911 prices)

	(1) extrac-tive indus-tries	(2) food-stuffs	(3) tobacco	(4) tex-tiles	(5) cloth-ing	(6) leather	(7) wood	(8) metal-making	(9) engi-neering
					manufacturing				
1861	35	434	20	122	88	110	155	7	188
1862	37	433	20	118	87	113	132	7	190
1863	40	435	20	121	87	116	127	6	195
1864	41	437	20	119	89	119	127	6	197
1865	41	438	20	114	92	122	156	6	199
1866	41	439	20	117	90	125	169	6	202
1867	43	441	20	117	91	129	160	6	206
1868	47	443	20	118	91	132	131	6	211
1869	49	446	19	125	93	136	136	6	219
1870	49	450	20	128	93	139	146	6	226
1871	49	455	21	140	94	143	136	7	231
1872	54	459	23	140	97	147	141	7	234
1873	59	463	23	147	101	151	142	7	240
1874	58	467	24	149	103	155	137	8	245
1875	52	468	22	149	104	159	141	9	255
1876	57	469	24	137	106	163	156	9	260
1877	58	470	25	135	106	167	156	9	267
1878	61	474	22	143	106	172	156	10	274
1879	67	474	21	140	104	176	141	10	278
1880	70	481	22	150	110	181	136	12	292
1881	71	491	21	166	120	186	151	15	317
1882	80	494	20	166	122	190	156	15	329
1883	82	500	21	175	124	194	156	18	350
1884	82	506	24	177	131	199	171	20	364
1885	84	513	24	185	137	203	190	22	380
1886	82	520	24	192	143	208	219	25	401
1887	80	526	23	203	145	212	228	30	442
1888	81	533	23	220	142	217	204	35	447
1889	83	535	22	221	140	222	176	37	434
1890	85	542	22	229	143	227	176	32	412
1891	85	545	21	228	141	232	176	28	383
1892	86	547	22	224	140	237	171	25	363
1893	85	554	22	228	144	243	171	27	374
1894	83	565	22	252	148	248	175	27	380
1895	78	577	22	267	157	254	180	29	396
1896	80	584	21	273	162	259	194	29	395
1897	87	591	21	279	162	265	204	32	403
1898	90	601	21	293	164	271	223	35	418
1899	98	616	21	310	170	277	242	39	447
1900	98	631	22	308	170	284	233	40	464
1901	102	644	22	324	173	290	247	39	453
1902	106	661	22	339	181	291	257	39	456
1903	111	680	23	343	187	292	272	44	484
1904	113	684	23	358	189	293	277	49	514
1905	118	706	24	371	194	294	301	58	557
1906	121	739	24	402	214	295	311	69	627
1907	122	776	25	442	241	296	331	73	675
1908	123	799	26	450	248	297	360	85	762
1909	127	799	27	450	250	298	389	97	796
1910	136	823	28	433	243	299	410	104	821
1911	142	827	28	428	243	300	386	105	828
1912	148	872	29	475	255	301	367	119	880
1913	149	909	26	475	253	302	362	115	856

TABLE 1.03 *(continued)*

	(10)	(11)	(12)	(13)	(14)	(15)	(16)	(17)
		manufacturing *(cont.)*						
	nonmet. mineral prod.	chemicals, rubber	paper, printing	sundry manuf.	total	construction	utilities	total
1861	46	15	25	8	1,218	285	8	1,547
1862	53	15	26	8	1,202	324	8	1,572
1863	54	15	26	8	1,211	336	9	1,596
1864	56	17	27	8	1,222	331	9	1,603
1865	57	16	29	8	1,257	334	9	1,641
1866	48	17	30	8	1,272	287	10	1,609
1867	47	17	31	8	1,273	262	10	1,588
1868	46	17	33	8	1,257	259	11	1,573
1869	47	18	34	8	1,288	253	11	1,601
1870	49	18	36	8	1,320	266	12	1,646
1871	51	19	37	9	1,343	274	13	1,678
1872	55	21	39	9	1,372	294	13	1,733
1873	64	21	39	9	1,407	325	13	1,805
1874	68	22	42	9	1,428	336	14	1,836
1875	59	22	44	9	1,442	293	14	1,802
1876	57	24	46	10	1,460	284	15	1,816
1877	61	25	47	10	1,476	292	16	1,842
1878	61	25	49	10	1,503	297	16	1,876
1879	63	27	51	10	1,495	305	17	1,883
1880	68	28	53	10	1,545	329	18	1,961
1881	71	31	56	11	1,636	340	19	2,066
1882	80	32	59	11	1,674	387	20	2,161
1883	85	33	62	11	1,730	412	21	2,245
1884	89	34	65	11	1,790	423	22	2,317
1885	93	35	69	11	1,860	434	24	2,402
1886	95	36	73	11	1,947	444	27	2,500
1887	93	38	76	12	2,030	437	29	2,575
1888	94	39	80	12	2,045	439	31	2,596
1889	94	40	83	12	2,016	423	32	2,555
1890	97	42	87	12	2,022	418	34	2,559
1891	96	45	91	13	1,997	410	36	2,529
1892	92	47	96	13	1,975	389	38	2,489
1893	94	49	99	13	2,018	375	41	2,519
1894	95	52	103	13	2,079	374	41	2,578
1895	89	54	108	14	2,145	321	44	2,587
1896	89	56	111	14	2,188	307	47	2,621
1897	91	61	114	14	2,239	311	49	2,686
1898	93	64	116	14	2,314	308	55	2,767
1899	97	69	119	15	2,423	312	59	2,892
1900	102	75	121	15	2,464	322	62	2,947
1901	109	78	123	16	2,519	339	66	3,026
1902	121	83	128	17	2,595	368	72	3,141
1903	131	90	130	18	2,693	386	80	3,270
1904	141	99	150	19	2,796	405	90	3,404
1905	153	104	177	20	2,959	433	98	3,608
1906	163	113	206	21	3,185	460	107	3,874
1907	174	122	211	22	3,388	483	122	4,115
1908	186	136	224	23	3,597	513	138	4,371
1909	213	145	237	24	3,726	586	154	4,592
1910	242	159	248	25	3,826	661	169	4,793
1911	260	168	242	27	3,843	697	190	4,872
1912	273	184	270	28	4,052	713	211	5,124
1913	276	192	273	29	4,067	707	233	5,155

Source: S. Fenoaltea, "Notes on the Rate of Industrial Growth in Italy, 1861–1913," *Journal of Economic History* 63 (2003), pp. 710–711.

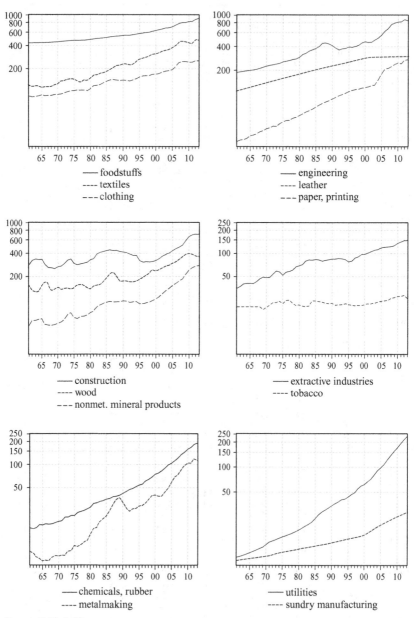

Source: Table 1.03.

FIGURE 1.04. *Industrial production: value added, by sector*
(million lire at 1911 prices)

but it is still provisional, as the set of sector-specific estimates carefully built up over many years is completed by rough estimates for the remaining sectors.[62]

Over the long run the new index largely confirms the Carreras index. From 1861 to 1913, according to the new estimates, aggregate industrial output (and aggregate manufacturing output, which dominates the total) increased by a factor of 3.3, for an average annual growth rate of 2.3 percent. Comparable growth rates were manifested by the extractive industries, which increased by a factor of 4.3, and by construction, which despite the pre-war boom increased by a factor of only 2.5. The utilities, which benefited far more from technical and social progress, increased in contrast by a factor of almost 30.

Within manufacturing, too, the spectrum of sectoral growth rates was relatively broad. The most dynamic sectors were metalmaking and chemicals, which thanks to technical progress (and growing protection, in the case of metalmaking) grew by a factor near 15; paper and printing grew by a factor near 10, thanks presumably to growing literacy. Lower but still above-average growth rates were displayed by non-metallic mineral products, engineering, and textiles, which grew by factors near 6, 5, and 4, respectively.[63] Below-average growth rates were displayed instead by clothing and leather, which did not so much as triple; by foodstuffs and woodworking, which more nearly doubled; and by tobacco, which barely grew at all. The relative weight of the different groups and sectors – measured, like the series themselves, at constant prices – accordingly varied significantly over time (Table 1.04).[64]

The elementary series reveal widely differing growth rates even within the individual groups and sectors. Their component industries are at times simply independent (like mining on the one hand and quarrying on the other), at times direct rivals (like the various textile industries).[65] "New"

---

[62] The former include the estimates for the three non-manufacturing groups (the extractive industries, construction, and the utilities) and seven of the twelve manufacturing sectors. The preliminary estimates are the series for the tobacco, engineering, and sundry manufacturing industries, specific to each sector but highly aggregated; for the leather-working industries, constructed as a simple interpolation of a handful of census benchmarks; and for the foodstuffs industry, constructed on the assumption that food consumption followed, with a reduced elasticity, the movements of non-food consumption (below, ch. 1A, § 5).

[63] Sundry manufacturing also grew by a factor of 4, but this is largely assumed.

[64] Current-price measures would clearly be preferable, but they are not yet available (below, ch. 1A, § 1).

[65] S. Fenoaltea, "The Extractive Industries in Italy, 1861–1913: General Methods and Specific Estimates," *Journal of European Economic History* 17 (1988), pp. 117–125,

TABLE 1.04. *Industrial production: sector shares (percent)*

	(1) 1861	(2) 1871	(3) 1881	(4) 1891	(5) 1901	(6) 1911
extractive industries	2.3	2.9	3.5	3.3	3.4	2.9
foodstuffs	28.0	27.1	23.8	21.6	21.3	17.0
tobacco	1.3	1.3	1.0	.8	.7	.6
textiles	7.9	8.3	8.1	9.0	10.7	8.8
clothing	5.7	5.6	5.8	5.6	5.7	5.0
leather	7.1	8.5	9.0	9.2	9.6	6.2
wood	10.0	8.1	7.3	6.9	8.2	7.9
metalmaking	.5	.4	.7	1.1	1.3	2.2
engineering	12.1	13.7	15.4	15.1	15.0	17.0
nonmet. mineral products	3.0	3.1	3.5	3.8	3.6	5.3
chemicals, rubber	1.0	1.1	1.5	1.8	2.6	3.5
paper, printing	1.6	2.2	2.7	3.6	4.1	5.0
sundry manufacturing	.5	.5	.5	.5	.5	.5
manufacturing	78.8	80.0	79.2	79.0	83.2	78.9
construction	18.4	16.3	16.5	16.2	11.2	14.3
utilities	.5	.8	.9	1.4	2.2	3.9
TOTAL	100.0	100.0	100.0	100.0	100.0	100.0

Source: S. Fenoaltea, "Notes on the Rate of Industrial Growth in Italy, 1861–1913," *Journal of Economic History* 63 (2003), p. 712.

industries contained traditional components (like soap and candle-making within chemicals), and vice versa (like the sugar or combed wool industries); and even some old industries, with traditional technologies, grew with youthful vigor (thus the distribution of water, which increased approximately ten-fold).[66]

At this level of disaggregation the most meaningful distinction appears to be once again that between the production of durables (and their inputs), tied to investment, and that of (other) non-durables, tied to consumption: on the one hand the extractive, woodworking, metalmaking, engineering, non-metallic mineral processing, and construction industries, on the other the foodstuffs, tobacco, textiles, clothing, leather, paper and sundry manufacturing industries, plus the utilities. The first group alternated periods of growth and periods of decline, with cyclical peaks in 1865, 1874, 1887 and 1912 (Figure 1.05): all four peaks appear in the construction-related industries, at least the last two in the

---

and Id., "Textile Production in Italy, 1861–1913," *Rivista di storia economica* 18 (2002), pp. 3–40.

[66] Fenoaltea, "Notes"; Id., "The Growth of Italy's Wool Industry, 1861–1913: A Statistical Reconstruction," *Rivista di storia economica* 16 (2000), pp. 119–145; Id., "The Growth of the Utilities Industries in Italy, 1861–1913," *Journal of Economic History* 42 (1982), pp. 601–627.

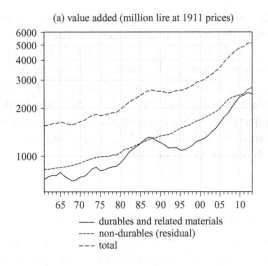

(a) value added (million lire at 1911 prices)

—— durables and related materials
---- non-durables (residual)
--- total

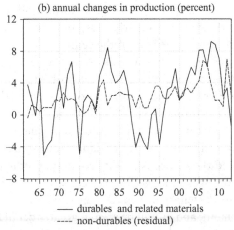

(b) annual changes in production (percent)

—— durables and related materials
---- non-durables (residual)

Sources: Table 1.03 and text.

FIGURE 1.05. *Industrial production: major aggregates*

metal-processing industries as well (Figure 1.04).[67] The second group grew altogether more regularly; the aggregate thus followed, in dampened form, the cycle in the production of durables (and related inputs: Figure 1.05). Once again, therefore, aggregate output seems to vary with the production of durable goods, that is, with investment.

---

[67] The estimates of metal processing in the 1860s and '70s are very rough, and may miss the output cycle.

In the production of non-durable goods (in essence, consumption), the cycle reappears in the annual growth rate: the latter was almost always positive, but typically above average when the production of durables also expanded (Figure 1.05). The point is *sub judice*, however, to the extent that the underlying data reveal this pattern only for the non-food group, and its extension to food production and consumption is only a reasonable conjecture.[68] In the Italian context, moreover, that conjecture goes to the heart of the debate on the "agrarian crisis" of the 1880s, and, correspondingly, on the merits of Italy's protectionist response; but these are the subjects of later chapters.[69]

9. The evolution of the time series: total product

As noted above, the Istat-Vitali reconstruction of the national accounts had soon been criticized: the sudden increase in the growth rate seemed due to the growing underestimation of agricultural (and related industrial) production over the 1880s and early '90s, and the reabsorption of that error in the years around the turn of the century.[70]

The literature's reaction to this criticism has been curiously schizophrenic. On the one hand, Italy's historians came to disbelieve the Istat-Vitali series, and the discontinuity in industrial and aggregate growth. The Bonelli-Cafagna view that development occurred in successive "waves," rather than with a sudden acceleration, was widely accepted; the authoritative surveys by Gianni Toniolo and Vera Zamagni explicitly criticized the extant Istat-Vitali series; and the overhaul of the historical accounts was among the projects sponsored by the Bank of Italy in view of its centenary in 1993.[71]

On the other hand, and as will be seen in greater detail below, the profession at large came to believe that the 1880s were a decade of crisis and hardship, with an agricultural collapse that offset the industrial boom,

---

[68] The author's first indices represented milling as a simple trend, as the likely cyclical deviations were then unknown; some thirty years on, those deviations can be hypothesized with reasonable confidence.

[69] Below, chs. 3 and 4.

[70] Above, § 5.

[71] Above, § 7; G. Toniolo, *An Economic History of Liberal Italy, 1850–1918*, London 1990 (translation of Id., *Storia economica dell'Italia liberale 1850–1918*, Bologna 1988), pp. 148–149; Zamagni, *The Economic History*, pp. 79–80; G. M. Rey, "Introduzione," in Id., ed., *I conti economici dell'Italia. 2. Una stima del valore aggiunto per il 1911*, Collana storica della Banca d'Italia, serie "statistiche storiche," vol. I.II, Bari 1992, p. vii.

and a reduction of consumption that offset the growth of investment – even though the only statistics that can be cited to support this view are the very Istat-Vitali series that are generally considered unreliable, and that are in fact distorted precisely because over those years they increasingly underestimate agricultural production, foodstuffs manufacturing, and consumption.

Giovanni Federico noted this contradiction. In 1982 one of his earliest articles developed the critique of the extant agricultural statistics; and he then took on the thankless task of reestimating the time series for agricultural production.[72]

From about 1990 a number of authors proposed modifications of the Istat-Vitali series. The first effort – and much the most important, not least because it would become the international standard – was Angus Maddison's reconstruction of the production account.[73] For industry, as seen above, Maddison essentially replaced the Vitali series with the present author's first index, which grew much more rapidly; for agriculture and the services he lacked alternatives to the Vitali series, but he nonetheless increased the aggregate's growth rate by reweighting them. That reweighting is illogical but not unmotivated: by raising the end-to-end growth rate, given the series' terminal value, Maddison reduced its initial level to a figure that was altogether more reasonable, in international perspective, than that calculated by Istat and Vitali.[74] Maddison's series imply that per-capita output grew from Unification on, but they retain the sharp acceleration around the turn of the century that characterized the original estimates (Table 1.05 and Figure 1.06). The subsequent efforts did no more than reweight Maddison's series, or even the original Istat-Vitali series, with predictably limited results.[75]

---

[72] G. Federico, "Per una valutazione critica delle statistiche della produzione agricola italiana dopo l'Unità (1860–1913)," *Società e storia* 15 (1982), pp. 87–130.

[73] Maddison, "A Revised Estimate," and above, § 8, note 60; below, ch. 1A, § 4. Maddison estimated total product "at factor cost," equal to total value added, with no adjustment for indirect business taxes.

[74] For a more detailed discussion see below, ch. 1A, § 4.

[75] The best known of these efforts is N. Rossi, A. Sorgato and G. Toniolo, "I conti economici italiani: una ricostruzione statistica, 1890–1990," *Rivista di storia economica* 10 (1993), pp. 1–47. For a review of these revisions see C. Bardini, A. Carreras and P. Lains, "The National Accounts for Italy, Spain and Portugal," *Scandinavian Economic History Review* 43 (1995), pp. 116–124, and, in brief, Cohen and Federico, *The Growth*, pp. 9–11. For the reasons noted below Figure 1.06 illustrates the Maddison series multiplied by a constant.

TABLE 1.05. *Total product: Maddison series (million lire at 1870 prices)*

	(1) agriculture	(2) industry	(3) services	(4) G.D.P.[a]	(5) per-capita G.D.P.[a] (lire)
1861	4,471	1,535	2,191	8,197	328
1862	4,628	1,564	2,254	8,446	335
1863	4,452	1,574	2,253	8,280	326
1864	4,647	1,559	2,320	8,525	334
1865	4,901	1,509	2,348	8,758	341
1866	5,057	1,510	2,596	9,163	354
1867	4,452	1,555	2,392	8,399	322
1868	4,842	1,558	2,378	8,778	334
1869	4,940	1,602	2,328	8,870	336
1870	4,901	1,690	2,425	9,016	339
1871	4,979	1,736	2,400	9,115	340
1872	4,842	1,786	2,352	8,980	333
1873	5,077	1,886	2,368	9,331	344
1874	4,979	1,928	2,393	9,300	341
1875	5,194	1,920	2,453	9,566	348
1876	5,018	1,878	2,468	9,364	339
1877	5,018	1,901	2,441	9,360	337
1878	5,096	1,936	2,467	9,498	340
1879	5,194	1,935	2,480	9,608	342
1880	5,448	2,143	2,477	10,067	356
1881	4,510	2,318	2,560	9,388	330
1882	5,194	2,484	2,533	10,210	356
1883	4,940	2,647	2,593	10,181	353
1884	4,921	2,668	2,665	10,254	353
1885	4,881	2,895	2,690	10,467	358
1886	5,233	3,047	2,651	10,931	371
1887	5,038	3,432	2,762	11,232	379
1888	4,940	3,444	2,810	11,195	375
1889	4,471	3,367	2,875	10,713	356
1890	5,233	3,238	2,927	11,398	377
1891	5,526	2,915	2,912	11,352	373
1892	4,979	2,778	2,957	10,714	349
1893	5,389	2,856	2,961	11,205	363
1894	4,979	3,023	3,046	11,047	355
1895	5,038	3,035	3,146	11,218	358
1896	5,311	3,055	3,159	11,526	365
1897	4,667	3,157	3,191	11,016	347
1898	5,428	3,333	3,236	11,998	375
1899	5,311	3,633	3,334	12,278	381
1900	5,721	3,774	3,467	12,962	400
1901	6,444	3,839	3,522	13,803	423
1902	5,838	3,937	3,643	13,418	408
1903	6,229	4,200	3,631	14,058	424
1904	6,034	4,437	3,720	14,189	425
1905	6,151	4,933	3,898	14,981	446
1906	5,994	5,532	4,017	15,543	459
1907	7,029	6,143	4,123	17,296	508
1908	6,502	6,883	4,327	17,713	516
1909	7,166	7,179	4,735	19,081	552
1910	6,053	7,442	4,892	18,389	528
1911	6,932	7,640	5,015	19,586	559
1912	6,697	7,752	5,296	19,745	559
1913	7,498	7,627	5,463	20,589	579

[a] at factor cost.

Source: A. Maddison, "A Revised Estimate of Italian Economic Growth, 1861–1989," *BNL Quarterly Review* 177 (1991), pp. 236–237.

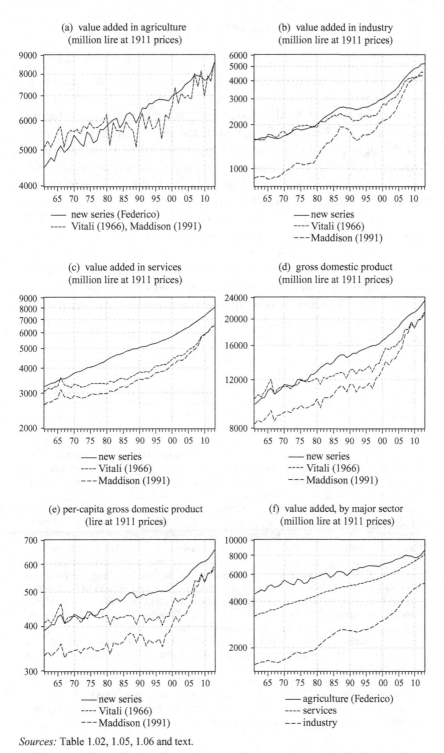

(a) value added in agriculture
(million lire at 1911 prices)

—— new series (Federico)
- - - - Vitali (1966), Maddison (1991)

(b) value added in industry
(million lire at 1911 prices)

—— new series
- - - - Vitali (1966)
- - - Maddison (1991)

(c) value added in services
(million lire at 1911 prices)

—— new series
- - - - Vitali (1966)
- - - Maddison (1991)

(d) gross domestic product
(million lire at 1911 prices)

—— new series
- - - - Vitali (1966)
- - - Maddison (1991)

(e) per-capita gross domestic product
(lire at 1911 prices)

—— new series
- - - - Vitali (1966)
- - - Maddison (1991)

(f) value added, by major sector
(million lire at 1911 prices)

—— agriculture (Federico)
- - - - services
- - - industry

Sources: Table 1.02, 1.05, 1.06 and text.

FIGURE I.06. *Total product: old and new series*

Deeper revisions would require basic research. The Bank of Italy's project on the revision of the historical accounts, entrusted to Guido Rey, led initially to the reestimation of aggregate product at current prices in 1911; the detailed recalculation of the sectoral value added figures was assigned to Federico (agriculture), the present author (industry), and Zamagni (services). These estimates appeared in 1992; they were retouched almost a decade later, when parallel current-price estimates were compiled for 1891, 1938, and 1951.[76] Of the Istat current-price estimates for 1911, only those for agriculture were essentially confirmed (−2 percent); those for industry and especially the services were revised upward (+15 percent and +22 percent, respectively).[77]

Very recently, the individual efforts to reconstruct the entire time series have yielded their first fruits, and an independent recalculation of the national accounts has at last become possible (Table 1.06 and Figure 1.06).[78] The first series to appear were those for industry, at 1911 prices, discussed above (Table 1.03); to calculate gross domestic product in the conventional manner the corresponding total is here slightly increased.[79]

---

[76] G. Federico, "Il valore aggiunto dell'agricoltura," S. Fenoaltea, "Il valore aggiunto dell'industria italiana nel 1911," and V. Zamagni, "Il valore aggiunto del settore terziario italiano nel 1911," all in Rey, *I conti economici dell'Italia. 2*, respectively pp. 3–103, 105–190, and 191–239; G. Federico, "Una stima del valore aggiunto dell'agricoltura italiana," S. Fenoaltea and C. Bardini, "Il valore aggiunto dell'industria," and V. Zamagni and P. Battilani, "Stima del valore aggiunto dei servizi," all in G. M. Rey, ed., *I conti economici dell'Italia. 3°. Il valore aggiunto per gli anni 1891, 1938, 1951*, Collana storica della Banca d'Italia, serie "statistiche storiche," vol. I.III.2, Rome-Bari 2000, respectively pp. 3–112, 113–238, and 239–371.

[77] Federico, "Una stima del valore aggiunto," p. 19; Fenoaltea and Bardini, "Il valore aggiunto," p. 119; Zamagni and Battilani, "Stima del valore aggiunto," p. 245.

[78] The new series reconstruct the production accounts at 1911 prices. To illustrate the joint effect of the new time paths and the new current-price estimates for 1911, in Figure 1.06 the new series are compared with the 1911-price series obtained by scaling the Vitali and Maddison series (Tables 1.02 and 1.05) to interpolate the Istat estimates of value added in 1911 (7,912 million lire in agriculture, 4,288 in industry, and 6,020 in the services), and the corresponding gross domestic product (19,788 million lire): Istat, *Indagine*, pp. 234, 238, 244, and G. M. Rey, "Nuove stime di contabilità nazionale (1891–1911): primi risultati," *Rivista di storia economica* 19 (2003), p. 319. As can be seen, Maddison's reweighting of the six Vitali series for the services slightly increases the growth rate of the entire group.

[79] S. Fenoaltea, "The Growth of the Italian Economy, 1861–1913: Preliminary Second-Generation Estimates," *European Review of Economic History* 9 (2005), pp. 273–312, and below, ch. 1A, § 5. The increase corresponds to the value of the principal raw materials consumed by the extractive industries.

TABLE 1.06. *Total product: new series (million lire at 1911 prices)*

	(1) agriculture (Federico)	(2) industry	(3) net services	(4) indirect business taxes	(5) G.D.P.	(6) per-capita G.D.P. (lire)
1861	4,488	1,568	3,231	478	9,765	390
1862	4,620	1,593	3,287	501	10,001	397
1863	4,768	1,619	3,355	534	10,277	405
1864	4,659	1,627	3,370	667	10,323	404
1865	4,978	1,665	3,454	847	10,945	426
1866	5,126	1,633	3,518	885	11,162	431
1867	4,924	1,614	3,530	550	10,617	407
1868	5,009	1,601	3,590	630	10,831	413
1869	5,157	1,631	3,667	623	11,077	419
1870	5,476	1,676	3,769	587	11,508	432
1871	5,328	1,707	3,815	616	11,466	428
1872	5,188	1,765	3,865	550	11,369	422
1873	5,110	1,840	3,931	508	11,389	420
1874	5,585	1,871	4,012	531	11,999	440
1875	5,483	1,833	4,046	679	12,042	439
1876	5,219	1,851	4,081	693	11,845	429
1877	5,297	1,877	4,144	665	11,983	431
1878	5,670	1,913	4,230	679	12,493	447
1879	5,663	1,924	4,280	715	12,581	447
1880	5,795	2,004	4,389	670	12,857	454
1881	5,912	2,110	4,485	762	13,269	466
1882	6,020	2,209	4,569	745	13,544	473
1883	6,075	2,295	4,657	791	13,817	479
1884	5,725	2,366	4,689	883	13,662	470
1885	5,896	2,453	4,753	865	13,967	478
1886	6,215	2,549	4,860	833	14,458	491
1887	6,293	2,622	4,911	948	14,774	498
1888	6,184	2,645	4,984	998	14,810	496
1889	5,904	2,604	4,995	946	14,449	481
1890	6,153	2,610	5,062	876	14,700	486
1891	6,479	2,580	5,113	823	14,995	492
1892	6,456	2,541	5,134	849	14,980	488
1893	6,658	2,571	5,218	851	15,299	495
1894	6,658	2,628	5,264	911	15,462	497
1895	6,775	2,634	5,311	916	15,637	499
1896	6,837	2,670	5,381	969	15,857	503
1897	6,822	2,740	5,472	936	15,969	503
1898	6,806	2,823	5,545	874	16,048	502
1899	6,775	2,952	5,635	908	16,270	505
1900	6,962	3,007	5,749	980	16,698	515
1901	7,063	3,089	5,859	1,021	17,032	521
1902	7,148	3,206	6,000	1,102	17,456	531
1903	7,273	3,337	6,140	1,046	17,795	537
1904	7,483	3,472	6,286	1,046	18,286	548
1905	7,592	3,678	6,372	1,146	18,789	559
1906	7,716	3,946	6,578	1,240	19,481	576
1907	7,973	4,188	6,731	1,127	20,019	588
1908	7,918	4,444	6,919	1,251	20,533	598
1909	7,887	4,667	7,115	1,283	20,952	606
1910	7,685	4,872	7,292	1,341	21,190	609
1911	7,778	4,954	7,520	1,440	21,693	619
1912	8,051	5,209	7,758	1,405	22,422	635
1913	8,587	5,241	8,042	1,461	23,332	656

Source: S. Fenoaltea, "The Growth of the Italian Economy, 1861–1913: Preliminary Second-Generation Estimates," *European Review of Economic History* 9 (2005), pp. 286–288.

In 2003 Federico published his similarly preliminary estimates of agricultural production, also at 1911 prices. This series considers the ten most important products; it interpolates or extrapolates the few reliable historical statistics assuming reasonable reactions by producers and consumers to changes in relative prices (and in real incomes, provisionally estimated from limited evidence).[80] It widely replaces the historical statistics incorporated by the Istat-Vitali series with new estimates constructed, as the original figures could not be, with the benefit of hindsight: in full knowledge, that is, of the outputs recorded, at the end of the period at hand, by the new statistical service. The new series tends to confirm the old claim that that the Istat-Vitali figures increasingly underestimate output in the 1880s and early 1890s; it further suggests that those figures somewhat overestimate production in the preceding decades.

The production account is completed by the brand-new (and again preliminary) series for the services estimated by the present author. These extrapolate the new Zamagni estimates of value added in 1911 with a variety of sector-specific indicators. Some of these, as for example the movement of railway vehicles or the stock of buildings, had already been computed to estimate the corresponding industrial value added in maintenance; others are derived from total commodity production, or constructed even more simply by interpolating census-year labor-force benchmarks.[81] The new aggregate series for the services also differs strongly from the preceding Istat-Vitali series: the latter displays accelerating growth (from initial rates inferior even to the rate of population growth), the new series remains close to a steady growth path.

The new, preliminary estimates of gross domestic product (at 1911 prices) are obtained by summing these new series for agriculture, industry, and the services.[82] From 1861 to 1913 estimated growth is closer to

---

[80] G. Federico, "Le nuove stime della produzione agricola italiana, 1860–1910: primi risultati e implicazioni," *Rivista di storia economica* 19 (2003), pp. 357–381, and below, ch. 1A, § 6. The series appears also in Id., "Heights, Calories and Welfare: A New Perspective on Italian Industrialization, 1854–1913," *Economics and Human Biology* 1 (2003), pp. 289–308, and, in graph form, in Id., "L'agricoltura italiana: successo o fallimento?" in Ciocca and Toniolo, *Storia economica d'Italia*. 3.1, p. 113.

[81] Fenoaltea, "The Growth of the Italian Economy," and below, ch. 1A, § 6. The series in Table 1.06 are net of otherwise double-counted credit and insurance business services.

[82] Gross domestic product "at market prices" equals total value added (gross domestic product "at factor cost") plus indirect business taxes. The estimate of these last at 1911 prices (Table 1.06) simply extrapolates the recent Vitali estimate for 1911 with the aid of Vitali's 1938-price series; see O. Vitali, "Gli impieghi del reddito nell'anno 1911," in Rey, *I conti economici dell'Italia*. 2, pp. 302, 304, and above, Table 1.02. The

Maddison's results than to Istat's: total product increases by a factor of 2.4 (against Maddison's 2.5 and Istat's 2.1), corresponding to a per-capita improvement of 68 percent (against Maddison's 77 percent, and Istat's 44 percent). At the same time, the terminal value of the new series reflects the new, higher estimates for 1911 obtained for the Bank of Italy. As one moves back in time the higher growth rate and the higher terminal level tend to offset each other: the new 1861 output estimate practically coincides with the Istat-Vitali estimate, and exceeds Maddison's figure by almost one fifth.[83]

The time path of the new aggregate series is very different from that of all the earlier estimates. The turn-of-the-century acceleration that characterized the Istat-Vitali series (and their subsequent reweightings) – in the dock for over thirty years – has all but disappeared: the new series grows, from Unification to the World War, without that sharp discontinuity.

The growth rate varied of course over time, following a long cycle that includes the familiar expansions of the 1880s and the early 1900s, and the slower growth of the early decades and of the 1890s. If the three major sectors are considered together it is apparent that the cycle of the aggregate was the cycle of industrial production, the smallest but also, over the medium term, the most volatile of the three (Figure 1.06). Agricultural production remained close to a steady trend, with only short and presumably natural cycles; the services also followed the long cycle of the aggregate, but with only minimal deviations from trend.

As seen above, within industry the cycle was in the sectors producing durable goods (Figure 1.05). Aggregate output thus appears to have followed the investment cycle: an utterly commonplace story, new in this specific context only because it was masked by the distortions of the early estimates.

---

new GDP (and sector-specific) estimates are preliminary not only because they include elementary time series that are themselves preliminary, but because the elementary series are combined, very simply, with 1911-price value added weights; proper measures reflect changes in relative prices (below, ch. 1A, § 1), but require information that has not yet been assembled. The new aggregate series were partly anticipated in G. Toniolo, "La storia economica dell'Italia liberale: una rivoluzione in atto," *Rivista di storia economica* 19 (2003), p. 254, where the new series for industry and agriculture are combined with the Vitali series for the services.

[83] The problem identified by Maddison, that in international perspective the early Italian figure seems too high, is thus recreated. The error may well be in the estimates for the other European countries, as those indices were obtained with the traditional methodology that tends to overestimate growth and underestimate the magnitudes calculated by backward extrapolation; see below, ch. 1A, § 2.

10. The evolution of the literature

This utterly commonplace story has not yet proved utterly convincing. A number of the author's closest colleagues continue to see more than a cyclical acceleration in the final upswing before the War. This strand of the literature is considered below, following the investigation of the investment cycle itself.[84]

But at least the competing interpretations are no longer seen as one. The deeper issue has at last been joined: the "cyclical interpretation" is heir to distinguished dissent, and the view that domestic capital must be patiently accumulated has found new champions.

The most thoroughgoing rejection of the "cyclical" model is that of Piero Bolchini.[85] To his mind the model gratuitously assumes that mobile resources flowed readily into and out of Italy; he overlooks its inductive basis, its derivation from the empirical evidence.[86] That evidence is in fact overwhelming, as the international mobility of (Italian) labor is beyond serious question; the mobility of capital is established by the appreciation of the exchange rate when domestic investment and net imports increased; and the mobility of skilled personnel is documented by the very names of Italy's firms of the day, of its still-extant soccer clubs that trace their beginnings to that time.[87]

Be all that as it may, Bolchini sees in domestic saving the driving force behind Italy's progress; and in this he is echoed by Pierluigi Ciocca and Marcello de Cecco.[88] The revival of the older literature is only partial,

---

[84] Below, ch. 2, § 10. The first econometric investigation of the new series' trends and cycles is briefly reviewed in the Appendix (ch. 1A, § 7).

[85] P. Bolchini in P. Bolchini et al., "A proposito di Stefano Fenoaltea, *L'economia italiana dall'Unità alla Grande Guerra*, Bari-Roma, 2006," *Rivista di storia economica* 22 (2006), pp. 331–338.

[86] Bolchini (ibid., p. 331) cites a long "deductive" passage that appears in fact in chapter 6, where the focus is on the implications for regional development of the "stages of growth" model on the one hand and the "cyclical" model on the other. Marcello de Cecco (ibid., p. 345) similarly suggests that the "cyclical" model sees the past through the prism of "the events of the last twenty years"; but the "cyclical" model was evolved long before that, in the 1960s. It is applied in S. Fenoaltea, "Railroads and Italian Industrial Growth, 1861-1913," *Explorations in Economic History* 9 (1972), pp. 325–351, which abandons the then conventional "social saving" measures based on the outward movement of a given production-possibilities curve precisely because Italy is modeled as "a small open economy with international factor mobility" (p. 325).

[87] Thus the "Milan Foot-Ball and Cricket Club," born in 1899 and now the "Associazione Calcio Milan" (sic), and the "Genoa Foot-Ball and Cricket Club," born in 1893 and still so called, both of course founded by expatriate Britons.

[88] Bolchini in Bolchini et al., "A proposito," pp. 333–338; P. Ciocca, ibid., pp. 341–342; de Cecco, ibid., pp. 344–346. Bolchini's contribution alone has a separate subtitle: "In lode del risparmio" ("In praise of saving").

as the accumulation of capital is taken to determine not the (slow or sudden) acceleration of the growth rate, but the trend on which the cycle was superimposed; but the essential point is that development depends on the accumulation of internal resources, and the "cyclical" model's emphasis on resource mobility is considered seriously misleading.

What is prudence in the conduct of every private family can scarce be folly in that of a great kingdom: surely, our intuition tells us, Italy's progress was tied to Italian saving. Resource mobility seems empirically established, and to imply the opposite; but the contradiction can be resolved in a variety of ways.

Bolchini's way – to affirm the first proposition and deny the second, if only because foreign loans must ultimately be repaid – is only one; another, clearly, is to affirm the second and deny the first. This is what the "cyclical" interpretation suggests, and Giuseppe Tattara, for one, seems comfortable with that.[89] In favor of this second way one might add that probably no one would be uncomfortable if the proposition that local development does not depend on local saving were applied to a town, a province, a region – to anything, in fact, short of a nation. Nations resonate differently with us, perhaps for no better reason than that we have yet to reject our fathers' nationalism as we have rejected their equally noxious racism.

But there is a third and more ecumenical way. Mobile resources render domestic savings irrelevant to domestic development for some purposes but not for others: it all depends on the observer's specific concern, on what is in fact meant by "domestic." International mobility does imply that if a city is ripe for gas lighting a gas company will be set up in short order, whatever the domestic supply of capital or technical experts; and once in place, even if foreign-owned and foreign-staffed, it produces locally and enters "gross domestic product." The company may remain forever foreign-owned, for foreign *direct* investment need never be repaid: capital mobility breaks the bond between domestic saving and investment in the long run as well as the short, and the explanation of the path of production in Italy – production by anyone at all, Italy a mere geographic expression – legitimately ignores domestic capital.

Gross *national* product is something else again, it is what is produced by a country's residents rather than simply within its borders. From this different and no less legitimate perspective, if a company in Italy remains forever owned and staffed by Englishmen that corner of a foreign field is indeed forever England. The emphasis on internal saving and on the

[89] Bolchini, ibid., p. 338; G. Tattara, ibid., pp. 353–355.

accumulation of "domestic" capital – human, no less than financial –
thus seems entirely appropriate if one is concerned with the economic
progress of Italians, rather than with the economic progress of Italy; but
these do not coincide, and what is central to the one need not be, and
in fact is not, central to the other.[90] De Gaulle loved France; Pétain, it is
said, loved the French.

---

[90] de Cecco (ibid., p. 345) rejects the notion that resource mobility can render domestic
development painless; the suggestion here is that if it is, for the domestic population,
entirely painless, it is also essentially fruitless. Not for that place, but for those people,
there is no substitute for the accumulation of wealth and skills.

1A

The Measurement of Production Movements

1. Methodology: the measurement of "real" product

The product of an industry can be measured in physical units ("tons of sugar"); but to compare or sum different industries measurement must be in a meaningful common unit, a unit of value. Industry does not create, it transforms; its product in value terms is identified with its value added, measured by the difference between the value of its output and the cost of the corresponding raw material.[1]

Value measures suffer however from the inconstancy of the value of the monetary unit; to obtain "real" measures the measures at current prices must somehow be deflated.[2]

The traditional method calculates the "real" product series through the so-called "double deflation" of value added, that is, by valuing both the output and the raw material at constant prices. This is equivalent to the deflation of value added by a price index – an index of output and raw material prices – that not only depends on the "base year" that supplies the prices that are held constant, but is also specific to the industry in question.[3]

---

[1] $VA_{it} = p_{it}Q_{it} - z_{it}R_{it}$, where VA is value added, Q is output in physical units, p is the price of the product (its value per physical unit), R is the consumption of the raw material also in physical units, and z is the unit price of the raw material; i and t identify the industry and the time period to which the measure refers.

[2] S. Fenoaltea, "Real Value Added and the Measurement of Industrial Production," *Annals of Economic and Social Measurement* 5 (1976), pp. 113–139, here partly summarized; similarly G. Fuà, *Crescita economica. Le insidie delle cifre*, Bologna 1993.

[3] $v_{ito} = p_{io}Q_{it} - z_{io}R_{it}$, where v is "real value added"; p_{io} and z_{io} are the prices of the product and the raw material in the "base year" o. Equivalently, $v_{ito} = VA_{it}/d_{ito} =$

The indices used to deflate the value added of different industries are accordingly different. As relative prices change, their paths will differ; the ratios among different industries' "real" value added will accordingly differ from those calculated at current prices, except of course in the base year itself. Any year can be selected as the base year: the traditional procedure generates multiple alternative measures, as many as the possible base years, of the relative "real" size of different industries.[4]

In a complete and logically coherent accounting system the value of the services of the primary factors of production (labor and equipment) are valued at their current (shadow) price, and value added is indifferently measured by deducting the value of the raw material from that of output, or by summing the values of the services of those primary factors of production.[5] The measure of "real" value added obtained as the latter sum at constant prices is equivalent to the deflation of value added by an index of the rental prices of the corresponding labor and equipment; that index is again specific to the individual industry, and different from the index for the same industry obtained from the prices of its output and its raw material. The traditional approach thus generates a double multiplicity of alternative measures, all of them "real," of the relative size of different industries.[6]

$(p_{it}Q_{it} - z_{it}R_{it})/d_{ito}$, where the deflator $d_{ito} = (p_{it}Q_{it} - z_{it}R_{it})/(p_{io}Q_{it} - z_{io}R_{it})$; d_{ito} is an index of the prices p_i and z_i with base o. The negative component of v_{ito} can exceed the positive one, whence the problem of "negative real value added."

[4] Consider two industries j and k in two years m and n. Given different variations in p_{jt}, z_{jt}, p_{kt}, and z_{kt}, the indices d_{jtm}, d_{jtn}, d_{ktm}, and d_{ktn} will differ. Two different values of v_{jt}/v_{kt} are therefore obtained, the one as v_{jtm}/v_{ktm}, the other as v_{jtn}/v_{ktn}; and $v_{jto}/v_{kto} = VA_{jt}/VA_{kt}$ only if $t = o$, so that $d_{jto} = d_{kto} = 1$.

[5] $VA_{it} = p_{it}Q_{it} - z_{it}R_{it} = r_{it}K_{it} + w_{it}L_{it}$, where K represents equipment in physical units, r is its rental value per unit, L is the labor consumed (also in physical units), and w is its unit price. If industry is limited to the process of transformation, it excludes the activity (and industrial value added excludes the earnings) of any speculators and monopolizers (even if internal to the firm, in which case the relevant unit value of output p_{it} is also a shadow price).

[6] The alternative measure of "real value added" is $v_{2ito} = r_{io}K_{it} + w_{io}L_{it}$, where r_{io} and w_{io} are the unit remunerations of the primary factors of production in the "base year" o. Equivalently, $v_{2ito} = VA_{it}/d_{2ito} = (r_{it}K_{it} + z_{it}R_{it})/d_{2ito}$, where the deflator $d_{2ito} = (r_{it}K_{it} + w_{it}L_{it})/(r_{io}K_{it} + w_{io}L_{it})$: d_{2ito} is an index of the unit prices r_i and w_i with base o. Consider two industries, j and k, and two years m and n. With changing ratios among p_{jt}, z_{jt}, p_{kt}, z_{kt}, r_{jt}, w_{jt}, r_{kt}, and w_{kt}, the deflators d_{jtm}, d_{2jtm}, d_{jtn}, d_{2jtn}, d_{ktm}, d_{2ktm}, d_{ktn} and d_{2ktn} differ. Four alternative measures of the same "real" ratio are thus obtained, respectively as v_{jtm}/v_{ktm}, v_{jtn}/v_{ktn}, v_{2jtm}/v_{2ktm}, and v_{2jtn}/v_{2ktn}. With one hundred possible "base years," there are two hundred possible measures of the two industries' "real" relative size in a given year, and so on.

This statistical confusion vanishes once it is understood that what is to be measured is not "real" (constant-price) value added, but "real value" (value in a unit of unchanging worth) added. This measure is obtained by deflating the current-price value added of each and every industry, however equivalently calculated, by *one and the same deflator*, which itself corresponds to the value at current prices of the unit of unchanging worth (which is also arbitrary, though an hour of common labor is a widely accepted standard). With a single, common deflator all the alternative intratemporal "real" measures of relative industry size coincide; only the alternative intertemporal measures differ, and that is inevitable because they depend on the chosen deflator.[7]

Historical reconstructions are typically constrained by a lack of continuous data on value added and on the consumption of raw materials; the "real product" series are often simple sums of physical output series, combined with the value added weights obtained for some "base year."[8] For the traditional methodology such measures are imperfect approximations to the desired "double-deflated" measures; considered as approximations to the measures obtained with a common deflator they are again imperfect, but they are typically *less* distorted than the "double-deflated" measures themselves.[9]

2. Methodology: estimating "unknown" series

Historical reconstructions are typically constrained by a lack of continuous data on physical production as well.

These gaps can to an extent be filled by using the typically abundant figures relating to foreign trade. The sum of the output and net imports of an intermediate good yields the total supply of the raw material available for

[7] Deflating VA_{it} with the same deflator d_t^*, that does not depend on i, the intratemporal real value added relatives $v_{jt}^*/v_{kt}^* = (VA_{jt}/d_t^*)/(VA_{kt}/d_t^*)$ will be identical, and correspond to VA_{jt}/VA_{kt}, whether industrial value added is computed (with the correct unit values) as $p_{it}Q_{it} - z_{it}R_{it}$ or as $r_{it}K_{it} + w_{it}L_{it}$; the problem of "negative real value added" simply disappears. The choice of d^* remains arbitrary, and intertemporal measures remain ambiguous, precisely because we lack an agreed-upon standard unit of constant worth. If that unit is identified with an hour of common labor, all production is measured in such hours; if with a basket of goods, all production is measured in such baskets. Over time productivity grows, and production grows less if measured in hours of labor than in baskets of goods; but given the decreasing marginal utility of goods the hours-of-labor measure may be the more accurate measure of the "real" growth of welfare.

[8] The "real" estimate of value added is simply $vs_{it} = Q_{it}(VA_{io}/Q_{io})$, that is, it extrapolates VA_{io} using the ("real") index of physical production, Q_{it}/Q_{io}.

[9] Fenoaltea, "Real Value Added," pp. 131–136.

the subsequent transformation, and thus an estimate of the corresponding output. With this method a single production or final consumption series can be made to yield estimates for each stage of the corresponding production sequence.[10] Even so, however, it is typically impossible to obtain direct estimates of output for each and every industry.

The common procedure measures the movements of total product from those of the available series; "unobserved production" is thus assumed to have moved exactly as "observed production" did, and that assumption is considered not only legitimate but inevitable.[11] In practice, however, the better-documented industries are those that were more visible, more interesting, more modern, in a word the new and growing factory industries; the declining artisanal sectors received much less attention, and are typically underrepresented in the data. The traditional method attributes the growth of the documented industries to industry as a whole, and tends therefore to overestimate aggregate growth.

The common procedure also reconstructs the aggregate series in two steps: the elementary series are first combined (with value added weights) into sector-specific indices, and the latter are then combined (with weights that correspond to the value added of the entire sector) into the desired aggregate index. Within each sector total "unobserved production" is assumed to move with total "observed production"; if entire sectors are unobserved, their total is similarly taken to have moved with the total product of the (at least partially) observed sectors. In the aggregate series, therefore, each elementary component receives a triple weight. The value added (in the base year) in that specific production is only the first: its weight is then inflated, in the calculation of the sectoral series, in inverse proportion to the series' coverage of the entire sector, and again, in the calculation of the aggregate, in inverse proportion to the coverage of the total by the available sector-specific series. A small industry belonging to a large and poorly documented sector receives a total weight greater than that of much larger industries in better-documented sectors.

---

[10] Consider two industries j and k, assuming that the second transforms the output of the first. One can estimate Q_k from Q_j (or vice versa) through the equations $Q_k = a_k R_k$ and $R_k = Q_j + M_j$, where a_i is the technical coefficient Q_i/R_i, and M_i measures net imports. If the a_i coefficients are constant, if only by assumption, R_i and Q_i follow identical paths, and "double deflation" reduces to the weighting of the product (or the raw material) by the corresponding value added in the base year: $v_{ito} = p_{io}Q_{it} - z_{io}R_{it} = p_{io}Q_{it} - z_{io}(Q_{it}/a_i) = (p_{io} - (z_{io}/a_i))Q_{it} = (VA_{io}/Q_{io})Q_{it}$.

[11] Thus, explicitly, C. H. Feinstein, *National Income, Expenditure and Output of the United Kingdom, 1855–1965*, Studies in the National Income and Expenditure of the United Kingdom, vol. 6, Cambridge 1972, p. 207.

The defects of this procedure are easy to see. On the one hand, the overall weighting of the elementary series is determined, artificially and arbitrarily, by the selected accounting system that defines the different sectors: the same data, combined with the same method, yield different results if the industries are differently grouped.[12] On the other hand, and with equal nonchalance, individual undocumented industries are assumed to be adequately represented by others ("of the same sector") that may have operated in very different markets, or produced goods that were substitutes rather than complements; and in such cases their output movements were more plausibly independent, or even inversely related, than parallel to each other.

The direct aggregation of all the available series (with their individual value added weights) renders the resulting total independent of the accounting system; but if the resulting aggregate is taken to measure total production the path of the documented industries (together) is again attributed to the undocumented industries (again together).

In fact, if some industries or entire sectors are not documented in the conventional manner, the only reasonable procedure is to construct the corresponding estimates in a reasoned manner. Any amount of reflection will produce explicit hypotheses more plausible than the implicit ones of the common procedure; and further research typically reveals some access to the undocumented sequences, using if nothing else the plausible regularities of supply and demand functions, and the relatively abundant data on relative prices.

3. The production series: Gerschenkron, Istat, and Vitali

The indices of industrial production recalled above are characterized by their different statistical procedures, and by certain idiosyncratic elements. Not every researcher wishes to reconstruct the path of industry as a whole: those interested specifically in the process of modernization might ignore the sectors it least touched, as for example construction. Not every researcher begins with a critical examination of the primary sources, and the reconstruction, if necessary, of the basic series themselves: some

---

[12] Imagine that the only documented chemical industry is the production of sulphuric acid, and that the rubber industry is not documented. One researcher uses an accounting system that includes rubber-processing among the chemical industries, and assumes that it grew in step with sulphuric acid production; another uses a system that considers it a separate sector, and accordingly assumes that it grew in step with the weighted sum of all the available elementary series.

use the time series already available in the historical sources, others limit themselves to recombining the sectoral estimates already present in the secondary literature.

The indices produced by Gerschenkron (1955), Istat (1957), and Vitali (1966) are traditional indices, constructed in two steps and making use, where possible, of "double deflation." They also share an imprudent readiness to rely uncritically on the series present in the sources: not even Istat seems to have been concerned about their reliability, for all the precious evidence on that very issue that it itself presented under separate cover.[13]

Gerschenkron's index incorporates 19 elementary series, for individual industries. From these, weighted at 1898 prices, he obtained six sectoral indices, which he then combined with weights proportional to the entire sectors' value added in 1903. The sectors refer to the extractive industries (represented by the production of iron, zinc, lead, and copper ores, of solid mineral fuel, sulphur, and pyrites), metalmaking (the production of iron and steel, copper, and lead, and also of refined petroleum), textiles (raw cotton imports, and the output of reeled silk), engineering (iron and steel production plus net imports, net of rails), foodstuffs (beer and sugar production, and also milling, indexed by the supply of wheat available for human consumption), chemicals (the production of sulphuric acid). The series he used are typically taken from the historical sources, but a few were borrowed directly from Tagliacarne. Gerschenkron estimated that his index covered, in 1903, some 65 percent of the corresponding total; but that is the share of the six sectors represented in his aggregate, gross of whatever component industries his elementary series missed altogether.[14]

The Istat manufacturing index is described only in very summary terms. The elementary series, weighted by value added at 1938 prices, appear to have been combined into six sectoral indices, for foodstuffs, textiles, metalmaking, engineering, non-metallic mineral products, and chemicals; the aggregate index appears to have been obtained by summing these with (over the period at hand) value added weights calculated for 1906–10. The foodstuffs and textile indices apparently combine 20 elementary series, obtained from the sources or calculated from the availabilities of

---

[13] Istat (Istituto centrale di statistica), *Le rilevazioni statistiche in Italia dal 1861 al 1956*, 4 vols., *Annali di statistica*, serie VIII, vols. 5–8, Rome 1957–59.

[14] A. Gerschenkron, "Description of an Index of Italian Industrial Development, 1881–1913," in Id., *Economic Backwardness in Historical Perspective*, Cambridge MA 1962, pp. 367–421. His aggregate index would have been different if he had included refined petroleum in the chemical industries rather than, arbitrarily, in metalmaking.

the underlying agricultural products: this is probably where the aggregate picks up the artisanal sectors, reducing the long-term growth rate. The metalmaking and chemical indices seem to chain heterogeneous series, obtained from unspecified elements; the index for non-metallic mineral products seems to be the 1938-price value of production, itself largely inferred from the path of related sectors. The engineering industry was apparently indexed by metal consumption, as in Gerschenkron's measure; but of the sharp cycle in that consumption the Istat index shows no sign.[15]

Vitali separately estimated value added at 1938 prices in the extractive industries, manufacturing, construction, and the utilities. The index for the extractive industries is a sum of the product series in the *Sommario*, which refer essentially to mining; the same path is implicitly attributed to quarrying. His manufacturing index is simply the Istat index. The index for construction is the Istat 1938-price series for investment in housing and in public works, plus a share of the corresponding series for investment in plant and equipment. The index for the utilities has as its only real components the production of power and, from 1908, the production of gas, reported in the *Sommario*; these are extended to the rest of the sector (gas to 1907, water) with the aid of the current-price estimates in the *Indagine*.[16]

Vitali reconstructed the rest of the production account in similar fashion. For agriculture he used the 1938-price production series for cultivation and herding supplied by the *Indagine*, adding the forestry and fishing series supplied by the *Sommario* with 1938-price weights; his series is

---

[15] Istat (Istituto centrale di statistica), *Indagine statistica sullo sviluppo del reddito nazionale dell'Italia dal 1861 al 1956, Annali di statistica*, serie VIII, vol. 9, Rome 1957, pp. 98–99, and, for additional details on the individual sectors, pp. 80–94, *passim*. The current-price estimate for engineering considers blacksmiths as well; the constant-price series may too, even though it is not mentioned in the corresponding text. According to A. Carreras, "La producción industrial en el muy largo plazo: una comparación entre España e Italia de 1861 a 1980," in L. Prados and V. Zamagni, eds., *El desarrollo económico en la Europa del Sur: España e Italia en perspectiva histórica*, Madrid 1992, pp. 180–185, and again A. Carreras, "Un ritratto quantitativo dell'industria italiana," in F. Amatori, D. Bigazzi, R. Giannetti and L. Segreto, eds., *Storia d'Italia. Annali. 15. L'industria*, Turin 1999, pp. 200, 205, the Istat index underestimates growth over the early decades because it includes the hemp industry, then in decline, with an excessive weight that reflects the autarky prices of 1938. That may be; but in Istat (Istituto centrale di statistica), *Sommario di statistiche storiche italiane, 1861–1955*, Rome 1958, the only hemp series begins in 1909 (p. 109), and autarky should have increased the prices of the raw material (and the final products) rather than processing costs and value added per unit.

[16] O. Vitali, "La stima del valore aggiunto a prezzi costanti per rami di attività," in G. Fuà, ed., *Lo sviluppo economico in Italia*, vol. 3, Milan 1969, pp. 468–470.

"double deflated," as he deducted the current-price input costs (reported in the *Indagine*) deflated by the wholesale price index (in the *Sommario*). His six series for the services sector (transportation and communication, commerce, credit and insurance, sundry services, buildings, government) were obtained by deflating the corresponding current-price series in the *Indagine*; in the spirit of "double deflation" he used different deflators for the different sectors.[17]

4. The production series: the author, Carreras, and Maddison

The author's first index (1967) was derived from Gerschenkron's.[18] Even though the mining sector was excluded, the use of Istat's recent *Sommario* allowed a doubling of the number of elementary series, which became 37: nine refer to foodstuffs and tobacco, two to textiles (cotton yarn and cotton cloth), six to metalmaking, one to engineering (represented, as in Gerschenkron's index, by the consumption of iron and steel), 14 to chemicals, and five to the utilities (gas and power).

The series were subjected to a first critical evaluation. The series for reeled silk was thus eliminated, as measured output too often fell short of net exports; other series were corrected, including those for the milling industry (discussed in the text), for sulphuric acid, and for engineering.[19]

The elementary output series were weighted by estimates of unit value added at 1911 prices, and directly summed, without computing intermediate sectoral indices; the aggregate index measured the path of documented production, and served to identify the most significant industries within the documented subset.[20]

The author's second index (1972) aimed instead at representing the entire manufacturing sector, documented only in part. Departing from conventional practice, it did not simply assume that undocumented production moved as the documented part; rather, the first index (amended to exclude the utilities) was complemented by a direct estimate of the time

---

[17] Ibid., pp. 467–468, 470–473.

[18] S. Fenoaltea, "Public Policy and Italian Industrial Development, 1861–1913" (unpublished Ph.D. thesis, Harvard University, 1967).

[19] Sulphuric acid output data are available from 1893; the series was brought back to 1861 on the basis of pyrite production, correcting the figures Gerschenkron had taken from Tagliacarne. Gerschenkron's engineering figures for 1881–1905 were retouched, as through an oversight his estimates of raw material consumption failed to exclude imported rails.

[20] With the two-step procedure an undocumented industry can turn out to be highly significant, merely because it is part of a large sector "represented" by a small component.

path of the undocumented residual. The estimate is extremely crude – the undocumented sectors, which account for roughly half of total value added in 1903, are simply attributed a constant product per capita – but it is reasoned, and justified by the prevalently artisanal nature of those sectors.[21]

The Carreras index (1983) is exhaustively documented in the author's doctoral dissertation.[22] The index covers every industrial sector, save only construction, from 1861 to 1980. It avoids double deflation, and the calculation of intermediate, sectoral indices; it directly aggregates, with 1970 value added weights, no fewer than 86 series, but even so it covers, in its base year, no more than about 60 percent of total output. The elementary series refer to energy production (8 series, including the utilities), the extractive industries (14 series), metalmaking (10 series), non-metallic mineral processing (one series, for cement), chemicals (16 series), engineering (15 series), foodstuffs and tobacco (8 series), textiles (10 series), paper and related industries (3 series), rubber (one series).[23] These are reconstructed from the sources, borrowed from Istat's compilations, or estimated from raw material consumption; many are entirely or partly new. As noted, the Istat grain-consumption series is criticized, but finally accepted without modification.

Maddison's series (1991) revise the entire production account estimated by Vitali.[24] He found the estimates for the 1860s, obtained by backward extrapolation, excessively high next to the figures calculated for other European countries. To reduce them to reasonable levels, he sought to increase the subsequent rate of growth; he obtained the desired result, simply recombining existing series, through two main devices.

First, he modified the path of industry, replacing the four Vitali series by equivalent ones derived by the present author. For the minor sectors (the extractive industries, construction, and the utilities) he used the new 1911-price series; for the manufacturing group he used the author's first index (revised only to exclude the utilities, and to include the new series

[21] S. Fenoaltea, "Railroads and Italian Industrial Growth, 1861–1913," *Explorations in Economic History* 9 (1972), pp. 333, 349.

[22] A. Carreras, "La producció industrial espanyola i italiana des de mitjan segle XIX fins a l'actualitat" (unpublished Ph.D. thesis, Universitat Autònoma de Barcelona, 1983). Carreras also produced an analogous index for Spain.

[23] Some of these refer to goods that appeared after the period at hand; in 1911 his index actually contains 68 series (Carreras, "Un ritratto quantitativo," p. 207).

[24] A. Maddison, "A Revised Estimate of Italian Economic Growth, 1861–1989," *BNL Quarterly Review* 177 (1991), pp. 225–241.

for the silk industry).[25] He ignored the 1972 index for manufacturing as a whole, which (like the Istat index used by Vitali) barely trebled from 1861 to 1913; Maddison attributed to the industries omitted by the first index the rapid growth (and strong cycle) of those it included, and obtained a five-fold increase in production from 1861 to 1913.

For agriculture and the services Maddison lacked alternatives to the seven Vitali series, which roughly double, together, from 1861 to 1913. He further increased the overall growth rate by changing the weights attached to the eleven series in his sample. He used as weights the current-price estimates of value added in 1870 that Istat had obtained *by backward extrapolation*: he thus attributed to manufacturing, which grew rapidly, the relatively high early weight it would have had, had it in fact grown slowly.

Rapid growth with a high initial weight generates an even higher terminal weight, and according to Maddison's series Italy was already by 1911 more industrial than agricultural. Maddison's revision thus removed one incongruity only by creating another, no less significant than the first.[26]

5. The new production series: industry

The latest industrial index by the present author aims at complete coverage, in the specific sense that every industry is explicitly represented by a series estimated directly and with due care; the elementary series can thus be subaggregated at will, without affecting the aggregate.[27] The elementary series in the index number in the hundreds.[28] Those contained in the historical sources are often reconstructed and revised on the basis of the

---

[25] The series used by Maddison are drawn from Fenoaltea, "Public Policy," Id., "The Growth of the Utilities Industries in Italy, 1861–1913," *Journal of Economic History* 42 (1982), pp. 601–627, Id., "Construction in Italy, 1861–1913," *Rivista di storia economica* 4 (1987), International Issue, pp. 21–54, Id., "The Extractive Industries in Italy, 1861–1913: General Methods and Specific Estimates," *Journal of European Economic History* 17 (1988), pp. 117–125, and Id., "The Growth of Italy's Silk Industry, 1861–1913: A Statistical Reconstruction," *Rivista di storia economica* 5 (1988), pp. 275–318.

[26] Maddison, "A Revised Estimate"; C. Bardini, A. Carreras and P. Lains, "The National Accounts for Italy, Spain and Portugal," *Scandinavian Economic History Review* 43 (1995), p. 120; above, Table 2.05.

[27] The aggregate also varies, obviously, if total industry is also defined in different ways, for example if the maintenance of durable goods is attributed to the services sector rather than to industry itself.

[28] For an exhaustive list of the products represented by the elementary series see S. Fenoaltea, "Il valore aggiunto dell'industria italiana nel 1911," in G. M. Rey, ed., *I conti*

underlying local data; many are entirely new, and are either derived from previously unused sources, or estimated, in the absence of direct evidence, on the basis of reasonable hypotheses.

The elementary series have been subaggregated to represent fifteen sectors. Twelve belong to the manufacturing group; the other three represent the other, minor groups (the extractive industries, construction, and the utilities), and are essentially those already used by Maddison.

The series for the utilities incorporates eight elementary series; these cover not only gas and power but also, for the first time, direct estimates for the distribution of water.[29] The construction series incorporates 30 elementary series: 13 refer to the new construction and maintenance of rail- and tramways (indexed by the growth, or the extent and use, of the corresponding nets), another 13 refer to other infrastructure (obtained in part by deflating expenditure for non-railway public works, in part by evaluating at constant prices the investments of the utilities), and four refer to the new construction and maintenance of private buildings (subject to tax, and exempt). The aggregate estimates much exceed the Istat-Vitali figures, perhaps because these neglect the public-works expenditure hidden in other budgets (education, health, etc.).[30] The series for the extractive industries in turn includes 32 elementary series, which incorporate the familiar data on mining output, suitably reexamined and revised, and new estimates of quarrying output, not documented in the sources. The aggregate is very different from the earlier Gerschenkron and Istat-Vitali series, constructed with the standard methodology: the new series assume that quarrying followed construction (which consumed its output) rather than the documented part of the same sector (mining, whose products were consumed by the metalmaking and chemical industries, or simply exported).[31]

Within the manufacturing group seven sectors have been researched with similar care. The textile sector is represented by eight series for the silk industry, estimated back from textile production (documented

economici dell'Italia. 2. Una stima del valore aggiunto per il 1911, Collana storica della Banca d'Italia, serie "statistiche storiche," vol. I.II, Bari 1992, pp. 105–190.

[29] Fenoaltea, "The Growth of the Utilities." The water supply industry grew rapidly, but less rapidly than gas and power together; the overall rate of growth is accordingly revised downward.

[30] S. Fenoaltea, "Railway Construction in Italy, 1861–1913," *Rivista di storia economica* 1 (1984), International Issue, pp. 27–54; Id., "Public Works Construction in Italy, 1861–1913," *Rivista di storia economica* 3 (1986), International Issue, pp. 1–33; Id., "Construction."

[31] Fenoaltea, "The Extractive Industries."

by loom counts) and therefore consistent by construction with the corresponding export figures; ten for the wool industry, built up from a new estimate of the clip; two for the cotton industry, but so calculated as to pick up quality change (and the effect of protection, about which more anon); and another 14 for the linen, hemp, jute, and artificial silk industries.[32] The clothing sector is represented by 13 series, of which seven refer to different textiles and six to hats and their intermediate inputs (felts and straw braid). The wood industry, poorly documented by the sources, is represented by two series only, for the initial, and subsequent, processing of the material; these are derived by averaging over separate estimates of wood production and consumption. Metalmaking is represented by 15 series, that incorporate the historical data; the processing of non-metallic minerals, by 11 series that use construction movements to extrapolate the limited available data. Chemicals are represented by series for over 80 products, typically of the well-documented modern component of the industry; the path of its traditional component (soap, fats, etc.) is instead estimated from a few census-based benchmarks. The paper and printing industry, finally, is represented by three series, for the successive stages of production; these are built up from data on the industry's stock of machines.[33]

These estimates, carefully constructed over the years, are complemented by preliminary series for the remaining sectors: foodstuffs and tobacco, leather, engineering, and sundry manufacturing. This last industry is practically insignificant; the corresponding series sums over an estimate for photographic materials, and a simple trend. The tobacco series extrapolates value added in 1911 on the basis of the total weight of processed goods reported in the *Sommario*; and the leather-goods series merely interpolates a few census-based benchmarks, leaving to future research the identification of its cyclical movements and the explanation (or correction) of its surprising deceleration after 1900.

The engineering industry, which dominated the author's first index, has been reestimated as the sum of four series. Two of these, for

---

[32] Fenoaltea, "The Growth of Italy's Silk Industry"; Id., "The Growth of Italy's Wool Industry, 1861–1913: A Statistical Reconstruction," *Rivista di storia economica* 16 (2000), pp. 119–145; Id., "The Growth of Italy's Cotton Industry, 1861–1913: A Statistical Reconstruction," *Rivista di storia economica* 17 (2001), pp. 139–171; Id., "Textile Production in Italy, 1861–1913," *Rivista di storia economica* 18 (2002), pp. 3–40; below, ch. 4, § 3.

[33] The underlying sources and methods are described in S. Fenoaltea, *Italian Industrial Production, 1861–1913: A Statistical Reconstruction* (in progress).

blacksmithing and goldsmithing, are again simple interpolations of census-year benchmarks. A third, for the maintenance of machinery, follows energy consumption (net of firewood), considered an index of the work performed by the machines themselves; and the fourth is again the iron-and-steel consumption series (net of rails), but it represents only the manufacture of new products, and not, as in the first index, the industry as a whole.[34]

The time path of foodstuffs production, finally, has been provisionally estimated from that calculated for the entire residual group of non-durable goods, which serves here as an index of non-food consumption, assuming an elasticity of 40 percent (as implied by the recent estimates for 1911 and, at 1911 prices, 1891); the final estimate incorporates minor corrections to reflect changes in the structure of international trade (the growth of pasta and canned-tomato exports, and the decline of sugar imports).[35]

Gross domestic product (Table 1.06) is here calculated in the conventional manner, and the value added of the extractive industries accordingly includes the value of the consumed reserves that are in fact their raw material. The total obtained by summing the sector-specific estimates (Table 1.03) is accordingly increased by adding two series, which extrapolate the value of the reserves consumed in 1911 by mining and by quarrying, respectively, in proportion to the corresponding 1911-price value added in mining and in quarrying.[36]

6. The new production series: agriculture, services, and GDP

Giovanni Federico's reconstruction of the agricultural production series has also been proceeding for very many years; a first preliminary aggregate series has recently been published. It incorporates seven new series for the

---

[34] The series for the engineering industry thus maintains the cyclical path of the 1967 estimate, but both the amplitude of the cycle and the long-term growth rate are much reduced.

[35] Fenoaltea, "Il valore aggiunto," and S. Fenoaltea and C. Bardini, "Il valore aggiunto dell'industria," in G. M. Rey, ed., *I conti economici dell'Italia. 3°°. Il valore aggiunto per gli anni 1891, 1938, 1951*, Collana storica della Banca d'Italia, serie "statistiche storiche," vol. I.III.2, Rome-Bari 2000, pp. 113–238.

[36] S. Fenoaltea, "The Growth of the Italian Economy, 1861–1913: Preliminary Second-Generation Estimates," *European Review of Economic History* 9 (2005), pp. 273–312. The estimated values of the reserves consumed appear in Id., "Il valore aggiunto," pp. 113–114; the 1911-price value added series for mining and for quarrying appear in Id., "The Extractive Industries," pp. 122–123.

main food products (grain, wine, oil, beef, lamb, pork, and milk) and three textile-fiber series derived from the corresponding industrial estimates.[37]

The new series are typically averages of demand-side and supply-side estimates. The former deduct net imports from estimated consumption, which is presumed to vary, with reasonable elasticities, with real incomes and relative prices; the latter assume slow exogenous productivity growth, and a response to changes in relative prices that reflects the constraints imposed by the given land. The results are partial and preliminary, but it is already clear that the discontinuities of the earlier series are not confirmed by the movements of prices and incomes.

The complementary series for the services, also preliminary, have been very recently calculated by the present author.[38] They extrapolate the estimates of value added in 1911 recently compiled by Vera Zamagni with appropriate indices of the corresponding "real" product.

Within the transportation and communication sector those indices are, for rail transportation, the axle-kilometers of railway vehicles, the total rolling stock of machine tramways, and the track length of horse tramways; for other inland transportation, total commodity production (measured by agricultural and industrial value added at constant prices); for maritime transportation, the registered tonnage of Italy's commercial (sail- and steam-powered) fleets; for communication, total mailings, private telegrams, and telephone subscribers.

Value added in commerce is indexed by a weighted sum of 1911-price value added in commodity production and in transportation, with weights selected to reproduce the aggregate change suggested by the new estimates for 1891 and 1911. The credit and insurance sector, net of otherwise double-counted business services, is very small; it is indexed by census employment benchmarks, linked together by a weighted average of various cyclical series. The series for sundry services and for public administration directly interpolate census benchmarks, weighted to reflect the relative earnings of different sub-groups. The services of buildings are indexed directly by the real housing stock.

The new GDP series simply sums the new, preliminary 1911-price value added estimates for agriculture, industry, and the services (and Vitali's 1938-price estimates of net indirect taxes, suitably rescaled, to

---

[37] G. Federico, "Le nuove stime della produzione agricola italiana, 1860–1910: primi risultati e implicazioni," *Rivista di storia economica* 19 (2003), pp. 357–381, here partly summarized.

[38] Fenoaltea, "The Growth of the Italian Economy."

obtain a measure "at market prices").[39] In point of method this series, and its components, are only first approximations, as the desired measures are not in fact aggregates at constant prices, but deflations of current-price value added series with a common price index (above, § 1). The necessary current-price series are not yet available, and only constant-price estimates can be constructed with the limited information at hand.[40]

7. The new production series: trends and cycles

The new series for GDP and the three major branches of production have been subjected to formal analysis that extracts the "trend" and the "cycle."[41] The series are decomposed with two alternative methods: one uses a standard band-pass filter, the other relies on a general structural time series model with uncorrelated components.[42] These alternative methods reflect very different statistical approaches, but both identify a high-frequency "business cycle" and a flexible "trend" that incorporates low-frequency fluctuations (the "long cycles" of the traditional literature); in the case at hand they yield very similar results.[43]

To an extent, these results confirm the conclusions suggested by a visual examination of the new series (Figures 1.05, panel *a*, 1.06, panels *d* and *f*): to a first approximation the (short) cycle of the new GDP series is that of its agricultural component, while the trend fluctuation (the long cycle) is that of industrial production (and specifically of durable-goods production). The (short) cycle in agriculture and GDP, roughly four

---

[39] Above, ch. 1, § 9, note 82.

[40] Annual current-price estimates remain beyond the horizon, but a significant improvement could be obtained in the relatively near term even with a small number of widely spaced benchmarks; see S. Fenoaltea, "The Reconstruction of Historical National Accounts: The Case of Italy," presented at the International Economic History Congress, Helsinki, 2006, session 103. Absent current-price estimates, the actual weight of the services sector in the early post-Unification years is simply unknown; compare V. Zamagni in P. Bolchini *et al.*, "A proposito di Stefano Fenoaltea, *L'economia italiana dall'Unità alla Grande Guerra*, Bari-Roma, 2006," *Rivista di storia economica* 22 (2006), p. 374.

[41] C. Ciccarelli and S. Fenoaltea, "Business Fluctuations in Italy, 1861–1913: The New Evidence," *Explorations in Economic History* 44 (2007), pp. 432–451, here partly summarized.

[42] M. Baxter and R. G. King, "Measuring Business Cycles: Approximate Band-Pass Filters for Economic Time Series," *Review of Economics and Statistics* 81 (1999), pp. 575–593; A. C. Harvey and A. Jaeger, "Detrending, Stylized Facts and the Business Cycle," *Journal of Applied Econometrics* 8 (1993), pp. 231–247.

[43] The calculated Baxter-King "trend" is in fact a simple seven-year moving average with given triangular weights, and the "trend" of the aggregate is the simple sum of the "trends" of its components.

years long, is quite sharp until about 1890; subsequently, those cyclical variations are much reduced.[44] This "passing of the agricultural cycle" seems without equivalents in other countries, and is not easily confirmed by the available independent evidence; it may be a figment of the data.

The decomposition also reveals an unexpected fluctuation in the "trend" of agricultural production, with peaks (or troughs) some twelve to fifteen years apart. Interestingly, these fluctuations change shape over time: the "trend" growth rate was above its long-term average in most years before 1870 and again after 1900, but only comparatively rarely between those dates. The even longer cycle that thus emerges parallels the Kondratieff cycle in commodity prices, which is essentially a cycle in the relative price of agricultural goods.[45] In the early 1900s, it would seem, agriculture too benefited from improved opportunities.

The analysis of "trend" GDP points in turn to a "trend break" or "structural break" in 1900: after that date mean growth rates were higher than before, and the difference is statistically significant. The break is in the statistical structure that generates the series; a break in the structure of the economy – the behavioral parameters that capture the reaction to given opportunities – is something else again, and the one does not imply the other. Faster growth may reflect a change in those parameters, as the "stages-of-growth" interpretations would have it, or merely the improved opportunities of the "cyclical" interpretation; as argued above both models are comfortable with sudden accelerations as with cyclical swings, and the evidence of a statistical break does not discriminate between them.

---

[44] The relative variability of the economy can be measured only across periods spanned by homogeneous series; meaningful comparisons across longer-term time spans are precluded because the available estimates for pre-war, inter-war, and post-war Italy, constructed with different methodologies, are not equally sensitive to actual production movements.

[45] W. A. Lewis, *Growth and Fluctuations, 1870–1913*, London 1978.

2

The Investment Cycle

1. The "political cycle": birth, death, and life after death

The first index constructed by the present author was dominated by the cycle of the metalmaking and engineering industries, which followed the parallel cycle in the consumption of their products.[1]

Since those products were then almost exclusively "producer durables" (investment goods), that consumption cycle was interpreted as an investment demand cycle.[2] Investment demand is naturally unstable, precisely because it is a demand for durable goods. Investment renews, and "net" investment increases, the stock of physical capital; and the durability of that stock has two immediate consequences. First, the desired stock of capital depends on the *expectations* of the businessmen who plan production; those expectations are surrounded by uncertainty, and, like those that determine the movements of financial markets, subject to sudden change. Second, a *permanent* increase in the desired stock of capital generates only a *transitory* demand for the net investment that increases that

---

[1] S. Fenoaltea, "Decollo, ciclo, e intervento dello Stato," in A. Caracciolo, ed., *La formazione dell'Italia industriale*, Bari 1969, p. 108 and above, ch. 1, § 6. The engineering industry appears as noted to have been limited to the domestic market, and prevented from developing significant exports, by the tariff on steel, discussed in greater detail below.
[2] The alternative of a supply cycle was not considered. The relative paths of production and consumption and the inverse relation between their ratio and consumption growth exclude an autonomous cycle in domestic supply; and a cycle in world supply due to variations in raw material prices can also be excluded, as the relative price of metal rose in the 1880s and 1890s, and fell in the early 1900s, following a cycle very different from that of the consumption of finished metalware. Istat (Istituto centrale di statistica), *Sommario di statistiche storiche italiane, 1861–1955*, Rome 1958, pp. 172, 187.

stock.[3] Investment will be high when business wants to increase its stock of productive capital, and low when it wishes only to maintain it or even to reduce it.

The desired stock of capital increases as expected production does: as the latter grows so does the former, raising investment demand. In the case at hand, however, the investment cycle did not seem to have been set in motion by a cycle in the growth of the other sectors, which grew quite steadily; rather, the investment cycle seemed due to changes in the desired stock of capital for given levels of production.

The hypothesis of a "political cycle" tied the cycle in investment demand to changes in the confidence of industrial entrepreneurs in the governments of the day, that is, to changes in the perceived probability of policies favorable or unfavorable to industry.[4]

The specific hypothesis was that the desired capital stock depends directly on expected production, and also, inversely, on the risk attached to the corresponding commitment. With constant risk levels, the slow and steady growth of expected output would generate a similarly slow and steady growth in the desired stock of capital, and therefore in investment (to maintain that growing capital, and steadily to increase it). But the equilibrium path of the capital stock depends parametrically on the level of risk: with a constant level of risk output and capital grow together, but the capital–output ratio that is thus maintained will be lower if the perceived risk level is higher, and so on.

Simplifying, one can imagine two regimes, corresponding respectively to "low" perceived risk (if industry trusts the government) and "high" perceived risk (in the opposite case); in the first regime industry desires a "high" capital–output ratio, in the second a "low" one. The cyclical impulse stems from the shift from one regime to another: a change for the better induces industry to bring the capital–output ratio up from the "low" level to the "high" one, and over the transition investment will be exceptionally high; a change for the worse has opposite effects,

---

[3] If the stock of capital passes from a constant level of 100 to an again constant level of 110, for example, there will be a net investment of 10 only in the transition period. In theory, admittedly, the increase in investment may so increase production as to feed back on the desired stock of capital and generate a further increase in investment, and so on, in a sequence that tends to explode; but this requires unrealistically rigid behavior, and seems in any case irrelevant to the case at hand.

[4] When it was formulated this hypothesis was in the air. Investment had grown rapidly in the early 1960s, the years of the "Italian miracle," and had then suddenly declined; it was said that the industrial entrepreneurs had been frightened by the "opening to the Left" that brought the Socialists into the government.

and over the transition investment will be exceptionally low, even below mere replacement. Always *over the transition*: that is the characteristic of stock-adjusting flows, which are naturally cyclical.

In the specific case at hand the slow and steady growth of the consumption of engineering goods from 1861 to the late 1870s seemed to approximate a constant-risk equilibrium path – in a high-risk regime, as the Right then in power was clearly tied to agriculture and little interested in industry. With the fall of the Right in 1876, and the return to protection in 1878, the regime changed for the better: industry could trust Depretis, and investment shot up to augment the capital stock.

That investment boom was inherently transitory; but the sharp reduction in investment after the death of Depretis in 1887 seemed due to another regime change, this time for the worse. Crispi, who succeeded Depretis, immediately dragged Italy into a disastrous tariff war with France, whose much richer and stronger economy then represented Italy's principal export market: industry distrusted his adventurism, and sought a reduction in the capital stock commensurate with the increase in risk.[5]

The fall in investment was also inherently transitory: in the 1890s the stock of capital apparently reached its new desired level, and, from very low levels, investment began again to grow. It would probably have continued to grow, even with an unchanged regime, as the equipment put in place in the 1880s came up for replacement; but recovery gave way to a second boom as the troubles that marked the end of the century came to an end, Giolitti restored confidence, and the risk regime changed once more, for the better. The desired capital–output ratio rose again: from the turn of the century investment surged, generating a new cyclical upswing entirely analogous to that of the 1880s.

In sum, therefore, industry was taken to have invested little under the governments the entrepreneurs considered deaf to their interests, and much under the "trustworthy" governments of Depretis and Giolitti. The

[5] Industrial duties, increased in 1878, were increased again by the new tariff of 1887 (and by the punitive duties on French goods; the countervailing French duties were aimed at the exports generated by Italy's agriculture, and those most heavily hit were the producers of wine and of silk). Investment rose sharply after 1878, and fell sharply after 1887; it did not seem to respond directly to changes in the industrial duties (and the related changes in expected production), whence the hypothesis that the critical variations were rather in the perceived risk of harmful policies. Today, with a heightened awareness of the industrial costs of the grain tariff introduced in 1887, it might be tempting to argue that industry clearly benefited from net protection after 1878, but not necessarily after 1887; but this line of inquiry has been overtaken by the reinterpretation of the investment cycle, discussed below.

hypothesis that the investment cycle in post-Unification Italy was thus a "political cycle" has been well received.[6] It would not long survive, however, as the investment cycle turned out not to be limited, as the author thought, to industrial investment in Italy. The cycle in Italy was in investment of all types; it could not have been due to the expectations and confidence specific to the industrial interests. The cycle in Italy followed the broad world-wide "Kuznets" cycle; it could not have been due to events specific to Italy.[7] The early hypothesis that identified a "political cycle" has thus been decapitated; but like Saint Denis, patron of Paris, it has miraculously remained alive.[8]

2. The Kuznets cycle in the world and in Italy

The international economy of the later nineteenth century was characterized by long swings in transoceanic resource flows. The transoceanic movement of European migrants and capital peaked in the early 1870s, the late 1880s, and again on the eve of the First World War, and reached intervening minima in the late 1870s and near the turn of the century. In the receiving countries, which include Canada, Argentina, and Australia as well as the United States, construction displayed this very same long swing; in Britain, the dominant exporter of capital as well as a major source of migrants, construction displayed its mirror image, peaking when transoceanic resource flows and New World construction were weakest, and vice versa.

This complex of long swings was discovered in the post-war years by Simon Kuznets and his school, as they documented the quantitative aspects of modern economic growth in America and elsewhere. In their interpretation the swings in construction and in resource flows are related: migration shifted the demand for infrastructure investment from the Old-World countries of origin to the New-World destination countries; construction thus fell in the former and rose in the latter, and this reallocation of investment set in motion the parallel flow of capital. The analysis was

---

[6] L. Cafagna, "La politica economica e lo sviluppo industriale," in *Stato e società dal 1876 al 1882: atti del XLIX Congresso di storia del Risorgimento italiano (Viterbo, 30 settembre – 5 ottobre 1978)*, Rome 1980, pp. 141–157, reprinted in Id., *Dualismo e sviluppo nella storia d'Italia*, Venice 1989, pp. 261–278.

[7] S. Fenoaltea, "International Resource Flows and Construction Movements in the Atlantic Economy: The Kuznets Cycle in Italy, 1861–1913," *Journal of Economic History* 48 (1988), pp. 605–637, summarized in what follows.

[8] J. S. Cohen and G. Federico, *The Growth of the Italian Economy, 1820–1960*, Cambridge 2001, p. 20.

captured in the description of construction as "population-sensitive capital formation."[9]

The present author became aware of these works only after a culpable delay.[10] Their pertinence to the Italian case would be confirmed by the new construction series: the 1911-price value added series in the recent index discussed above, a 1911-price series for investment in new structures, and an index of urban construction (Table 2.01 and Figure 2.01).[11] The aggregate new-construction series displays an early

[9] M. Abramowitz, "The Nature and Significance of Kuznets Cycles," *Economic Development and Cultural Change* 9 (1961), pp. 225–248, and Id., "The Passing of the Kuznets Cycle," *Economica* 140 (1968), pp. 349–367; A. Cairncross, *Home and Foreign Investment, 1870–1913: Studies in Capital Accumulation*, Cambridge 1953, and Id., "Economic Growth and Stagnation in the United Kingdom before the First World War," in M. Gersovitz, C. F. Diaz Alejandro, G. Ranis and M. R. Rosenzweig, eds., *The Theory and Experience of Economic Development: Essays in Honor of Sir W. Arthur Lewis*, London 1982, pp. 287–299; A. C. Kelley, "Demographic Change and Economic Growth: Australia, 1861–1911," *Explorations in Entrepreneurial History* 5 (1968), pp. 207–277; S. S. Kuznets, *Capital in the American Economy: Its Formation and Financing*, Princeton 1961; B. Thomas, *Migration and Economic Growth: A Study of Great Britain and the Atlantic Economy*, Cambridge 1954, and Id., *Migration and Urban Development: A Reappraisal of British and American Long Cycles*, London 1972; J. G. Williamson, *American Growth and the Balance of Payments, 1820–1913: A Study of the Long Swing*, Chapel Hill 1964. Other scholars were skeptical of any causal relation among the observed long swings, but theirs was a minority view. See H. J. Habakkuk, "Fluctuations in House-Building in Britain and the United States in the Nineteenth Century," *Journal of Economic History* 22 (1962), pp. 198–230; P. J. O'Leary and W. A. Lewis, "Secular Swings in Production and Trade, 1870–1913," *The Manchester School of Economic and Social Studies*, 23 (1955), pp. 113–152; S. B. Saul, "House Building in England, 1890–1914," *Economic History Review* 15 (1962), pp. 119–137. The "Kuznets cycle" at issue here is at times called the "international Kuznets cycle," to distinguish it from another long cycle – in the distribution of income – also discovered by Kuznets; see S. S. Kuznets, "Economic Growth and Income Inequality," *American Economic Review* 45 (1955), pp. 1–28.

[10] In the late 1970s the author stumbled on the unexpected concordance between the industrial investment cycle in Italy and the construction cycle in Australia (Kelley, "Demographic Change," p. 243). The Kuznets swing in the new Italian series had in fact been immediately noted, ten years earlier, by Arthur Bloomfield; but the present author did not then grasp its significance. See A. I. Bloomfield, *Patterns of International Investment Before 1914* (Princeton Studies in International Finance No. 21), Princeton 1968, p. 32.

[11] The value of new construction is construction value added, less its maintenance component, plus the value of the materials consumed; the index of urban construction is obtained by chaining an average of the growth rates of binder consumption in a sample of (mostly northern) cities, documented by the local tax on construction materials. For a more complete description see S. Fenoaltea, "Railway Construction in Italy, 1861–1913," *Rivista di storia economica* 1 (1984), International Issue, pp. 27–54; Id., "Public Works Construction in Italy, 1861–1913," *Rivista di storia economica* 3 (1986), International Issue, pp. 1–33; Id., "Construction in Italy, 1861–1913," *Rivista di storia economica* 4 (1987), International Issue, pp. 21–54.

TABLE 2.01. *Construction*

	(1)	(2)	(3)	(4)	(5)
	new construction (million lire at 1911 prices)				index of urban construction (1911 = 100)
	social overhead capital		private buildings	total	
	railways	other			
1861	188	109	100	396	30.6
1862	210	114	158	482	40.3
1863	214	143	134	492	35.9
1864	191	145	153	490	38.5
1865	182	179	128	490	37.9
1866	157	132	98	387	31.8
1867	113	114	110	337	33.3
1868	111	127	89	327	30.4
1869	96	116	107	320	32.4
1870	106	140	95	341	32.4
1871	114	128	122	364	34.2
1872	122	153	126	401	36.4
1873	136	167	174	476	38.3
1874	141	149	212	502	38.1
1875	111	140	152	404	36.4
1876	97	140	139	376	35.6
1877	83	166	137	387	34.2
1878	89	172	127	388	34.2
1879	123	156	120	399	34.2
1880	147	167	126	440	36.8
1881	168	154	147	469	37.5
1882	211	171	178	559	39.0
1883	236	196	175	607	42.3
1884	231	219	183	632	46.6
1885	234	218	207	659	48.9
1886	223	238	209	671	55.4
1887	198	277	160	635	56.4
1888	205	298	116	619	56.7
1889	176	286	124	585	52.0
1890	175	247	164	586	45.9
1891	181	210	181	572	42.7
1892	179	182	163	524	38.6
1893	151	166	186	503	38.9
1894	165	151	183	498	36.1
1895	73	143	177	393	35.7
1896	43	142	177	361	36.4
1897	46	141	176	363	36.0
1898	36	143	176	356	40.9
1899	34	154	177	365	44.1
1900	43	165	183	391	42.3
1901	51	173	204	428	44.3
1902	60	191	239	490	47.6
1903	58	202	274	533	49.9
1904	70	198	306	573	54.7
1905	73	226	335	635	56.9
1906	83	278	329	690	70.8
1907	91	302	349	742	72.1
1908	95	337	373	805	78.6
1909	116	413	444	973	84.6
1910	141	477	519	1,137	89.3
1911	150	495	555	1,201	100.0
1912	155	506	564	1,225	100.9
1913	151	501	547	1,199	91.6

Source: S. Fenoaltea, "International Resource Flows and Construction Movements in the Atlantic Economy: The Kuznets Cycle in Italy, 1861–1913," *Journal of Economic History* 48 (1988), pp. 608–609.

(a) aggregate value of new construction
(million lire at 1911 prices)

(b) value of new construction: railways
(million lire at 1911 prices)

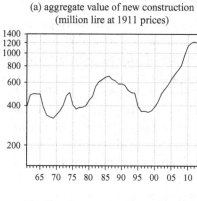
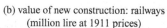
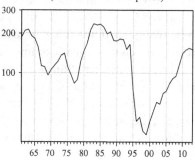

(c) value of new construction: other public
works (million lire at 1911 prices)

(d) value of new construction: private
buildings (million lire at 1911 prices)

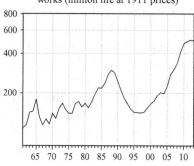

(e) index of urban construction
(1911 = 100)

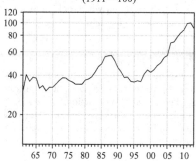

Source: Table 2.01.

FIGURE 2.01. *Construction*

post-Unification cycle, with a collapse following the defeats and budget crisis of 1866, and then the classic Kuznets cycle, with sharp peaks in 1874, 1886, and 1912, and equally clear minima in 1876 and 1898.[12] The cycle reappears in the index of urban construction, and, with some variation, in each of the main components of aggregate construction.[13]

The collapse after 1866 and the subsequent rapid growth into the early 1870s are evident in urban construction, railway construction, and non-railway public works.[14] Over the mid-1870s three of four series decline sharply; the only exception is non-railway public works construction (and within that, too, the private component tied to utility-industry investment markedly contracts).[15] All four series then grow rapidly, through the better part of the 1880s. The subsequent crisis also involves all the sectors of the industry, even if with differences in detail.[16] The crisis does not last beyond the turn of the century: in the subsequent years all four series again grow rapidly, right up to 1912.

After the early 1860s, clearly, construction in Italy too followed the Kuznets cycle. The upswings of industrial investment in the 1880s and again in the early 1900s are therefore part of a general cycle in capital formation: they cannot be due (other than secondarily) to changes in the confidence of Italy's *industrial* entrepreneurs in the government of the day, to changes in the sensitivity of public policy to their specific interests. In fact, there is reason to believe that industrial investment followed the Kuznets cycle even in the early decades. From 1870–71 to 1872–74, net

---

[12] The new series differs from the corresponding Istat-Vitali series, which fails to pick up the cycle in the 1860s and 1870s, and registers the boom, bust, and recovery between 1880 and ca. 1905, but not the subsequent growth beyond the previous peak. See S. Fenoaltea, "The Growth of the Italian Economy, 1861–1913: Preliminary Second-Generation Estimates," *European Review of Economic History* 9 (2005), Figure 8.

[13] Econometrically, the cycle in urban construction seems tied to non-railway public works and (with a reduced weight) to the construction of private buildings, but not to railway construction, which was primarily extra-urban (Fenoaltea, "Construction," note 14).

[14] The cycle appears in the construction of private buildings, too, but over the 1860s it is estimated through urban construction; it is independently estimated from the data on the buildings-tax base only from 1872 (ibid., Table 2).

[15] Fenoaltea, "Public Works," Table 3.

[16] Railway construction declines slowly from 1885 to 1894, and then drops suddenly to very low levels; other public works construction (and urban construction) grow until 1888, and then decline, returning by the mid-'90s to the levels of the mid-'70s; the construction of private buildings collapses in 1887, when the speculative bubble bursts, but recovers by the early 1890s. The speed of this recovery is surprising, and one wonders whether it may not result from some accounting change in the data (like that which in the Istat-Vitali series produced the spurious collapse in public works in 1870: ibid., pp. 339–340); but no evidence to that effect could be found.

imports of machinery double, only to return to their initial levels by the end of the decade; and the early 1870s are remembered as a period of feverish speculation, which saw the creation of many new industrial and financial concerns.[17]

Investment in both industry and infrastructure thus seems to have followed the Kuznets cycle from the 1860s on. Save for a very few years in the immediate aftermath of Unification, the Italian cycle seems part of a world-wide phenomenon; and it is in that context that it must be understood.

3. The Italian cycle: demographic flows

For Kuznets and his school, as noted, the mirror-image construction cycles in Britain and overseas were due to the migration cycle, which shifted the demand for infrastructure (and generated a parallel cycle in capital flows). Italy too was actively involved in the international (and intercontinental) flows of labor and capital, and in Italy too construction followed the long swing of the Kuznets cycle; but Italy was a country of *emigration*, and construction in Italy followed the cycle of the countries of *immigration*. The Italian case would fit the kuznetsian norm, with inverse cycles in construction and emigration, if Italian migration followed a cycle that was itself opposite to that of total migration out of Europe (and into the receiving countries); it would be an exception to that norm if (as one would in fact expect) Italian migration followed the cycle in aggregate transoceanic migration.

The Italian migration statistics are unfortunately very imprecise. The *Sommario* reports the Istat series for total emigration (Table 2.02 and Figure 2.02).[18] As Arthur Bloomfield had noted, this series follows around its own trend a Kuznets cycle that is *positively* correlated with construction in Italy and overseas.[19] The data are unreliable, however, as they

---

[17] S. Battilossi, *Annali*, P. Ciocca and G. Toniolo, eds., *Storia economica d'Italia. 2*, Rome-Bari 1999, pp. 116–121. The estimates of engineering output do not grow in the early 1870s, but they are then very rough. Until 1881 the consumption of iron and steel that represents the industry is estimated not from metal production data, but from metal production estimates derived from the production of pig iron and net imports of pig and scrap iron; there is no evidence on domestic scrap iron supply.

[18] Istat, *Sommario*, p. 65.

[19] Bloomfield, *Patterns of International Investment*, pp. 32, 49, affirms that Italian emigration displays a clear long swing that is correlated with internal fluctuations (extensions to the railway net, industrial production as measured by the present author), but even more strongly tied to, and influenced by, the Kuznets cycle in the United States. Similarly,

TABLE 2.02. *Migration and demographic growth (thousand individuals)*

	(1) Istat series (1913 borders) gross emigration	(2) Giusti series (current borders) net emigration	(3) Giusti series (current borders) de facto pop.[a]
1861			21,777
1862		22	21,899
1863		18	22,049
1864		14	22,215
1865		10	22,392
1866		6	25,207
1867		1	25,264
1868		1	25,383
1869	135	2	25,616
1870	107	2	25,789
1871	122	2	26,801
1872	146	33	26,963
1873	152	35	27,101
1874	108	30	27,197
1875	103	32	27,358
1876	109	35	27,613
1877	99	32	27,823
1878	96	34	27,989
1879	120	45	28,173
1880	120	49	28,214
1881	136	53	28,460
1882	162	55	28,679
1883	169	60	28,896
1884	147	66	29,181
1885	157	71	29,449
1886	168	76	29,615
1887	216	82	29,857
1888	291	111	30,045
1889	218	96	30,330
1890	216	104	30,514
1891	294	124	30,728
1892	224	118	30,918
1893	247	127	31,141
1894	225	119	31,349
1895	293	144	31,514
1896	307	148	31,704
1897	300	163	31,948
1898	284	173	32,114
1899	308	184	32,317
1900	353	179	32,437
1901	533	113	32,663
1902	532	114	32,911
1903	508	115	33,097
1904	471	102	33,377
1905	726	126	33,600
1906	788	133	33,836
1907	705	125	34,068
1908	487	105	34,328
1909	626	119	34,582
1910	651	119	34,919
1911	534	119	35,146
1912	711	309	35,346
1913	873	466	35,355

[a] at year end.

Sources: col. 1, Istat (Istituto centrale di statistica). *Sommario di statistiche storiche italiane, 1861–1955*, Rome 1958, p. 65; cols. 2–3, F. Giusti, "Bilanci demografici della popolazione italiana dal 1861 al 1961," in Istat (Istituto centrale di statistica), *Sviluppo della popolazione italiana dal 1861 al 1961*, *Annali di statistica*, serie VIII, vol. 17, Rome 1965, p. 116.

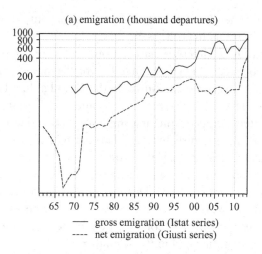

(a) emigration (thousand departures)

—— gross emigration (Istat series)
---- net emigration (Giusti series)

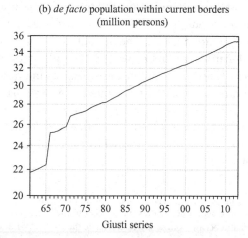

(b) *de facto* population within current borders
(million persons)

Giusti series

Sources: Table 2.02.

FIGURE 2.02. *Migration and demographic growth*

actually registered the number of passports (authorized or issued) rather than actual departures; and the return flow was high (and highly variable).

F. Lauricella, "Emigrazione italiana di massa in Argentina e in Brasile e ciclo agricolo (1876–1896)," in F. Assante, ed., *Il movimento migratorio italiano dall'Unità nazionale ai giorni nostri*, vol. 2, Geneva 1978, pp. 372, 382–383, computes an eleven-year moving average of the changes in Italy's transoceanic migration. This series follows a long cycle with high levels in the 1880s and from 1896 to 1909, and minima in the early 1890s (and again after 1910, when the moving average includes the war years); the author attributes the first upswing to the fall in grain prices in Italy, and the second to the improvement in overseas labor-market conditions.

The data do not therefore register the net, "permanent," migration considered by the Kuznets hypothesis.[20]

Net emigration is directly measured only over longer periods, from the difference between the natural increase (births minus deaths) and the actual increase between two censuses. In the period at hand five censuses were taken, in 1861, 1871, 1881, 1901, and 1911 (that due in 1891 was unfortunately skipped); the first three were taken December 31, the fourth February 10, the fifth June 10. The census data yield rates of net migration that increase constantly, from 0.1 per thousand in 1862–71 to 1.3 per thousand in 1872–81, 3.8 per thousand in 1882–1901, and 4.7 per thousand in 1901–11.[21] This last rate seems to be something of an overestimate, however, as the June census date captures a larger share of the census-year departures, concentrated in the first semester, than of the return flow, concentrated in the second.[22]

Annual estimates of net migration and (given the natural increase) the year-end *de facto* population have been constructed by Franco Giusti (Table 2.02 and Figure 2.02).[23] The annual net migration figures were obtained by allocating the intercensal totals (adjusted as necessary to reflect a number of full years) on the basis of gross migration; they imply average annual rates equal to 1.3 per thousand in 1872–81 (as above), 2.8 in 1882–91, 4.6 in 1892–1901, and 3.6 in 1902–11. According to these estimates, therefore, at least over the last three decades net migration and construction varied inversely, as posited by the traditional analysis of the Kuznets school.

---

[20] Istat, *Sommario*, pp. 5, 65, 67. The passports authorized, and even more those issued, surely underestimate actual departures, both because the same passport could be used more than once, and because one could in fact leave the country without a passport. The ratio of passports to departures changes in 1901, when passports became mandatory for transoceanic travel. Before that date the New-World countries' data on immigration from Italy exceed the Italian data on departures for those countries by about a quarter; that discrepancy then diminishes or even changes sign. Repatriation data are available only from 1902, and only for the transoceanic flow, as they are taken from ships' passenger lists. See F. Coletti, "Dell'emigrazione italiana," in R. Accademia dei Lincei, *Cinquanta anni di storia italiana*, vol. 3, Milan 1911, pp. 10–11, 14–15, 38, 74; J. D. Gould, "European Inter-Continental Emigration. The Road Home: Return Migration from the USA," *Journal of European Economic History* 9 (1980), pp. 79, 84–85, 88–90; E. Sori, *L'emigrazione italiana dall'Unità alla seconda guerra mondiale*, Bologna 1979, p. 55.

[21] M. Livi Bacci, "I fattori demografici dello sviluppo economico," in G. Fuà, ed., *Lo sviluppo economico in Italia*, vol. 2, Milan 1969, p. 21.

[22] Gould, "European Inter-Continental Emigration," p. 82.

[23] F. Giusti, "Bilanci demografici della popolazione italiana dal 1861 al 1961," in Istat (Istituto centrale di statistica), *Sviluppo della popolazione italiana dal 1861 al 1961*, *Annali di statistica*, serie VIII, vol. 17, Rome 1965, p. 116.

TABLE 2.03. *Construction and demographic change*

	(1) 1862– 1871	(2) 1872– 1881	(3) 1882– 1891	(4) 1892– 1901	(5) 1902– 1911
1. total construction (billion lire at 1911 prices)	4.030	4.242	6.125	4.182	7.779
2. rate of net emigration (percent per year)	.01	.13	.37	.38	.39
3. population growth rate (percent per year)	.69	.60	.69	.70	.71
4. population increment (millions)	1.784	1.659	2.011	2.192	2.383
5. marriages (millions)	2.031	2.147	2.316	2.293	2.578
6. ratio of row 1 to row 4	2.3	2.6	3.0	1.9	3.3
7. ratio of row 1 to row 5	2.0	2.0	2.6	1.8	3.0

Source: S. Fenoaltea, "International Resource Flows and Construction Movements in the Atlantic Economy: The Kuznets Cycle in Italy, 1861–1913," *Journal of Economic History* 48 (1988), p. 615.

These estimates of net migration can however be questioned on a number of grounds. A first problem concerns the discontinuities that appear in the census years 1901 and 1911 (Figure 2.02): these find no counterpart in the gross-migration data, and are not very plausible in and of themselves. A second problem concerns temporary migration, which is the difference between gross and net migration. Giusti's estimates of net migration imply that the share of temporary migrants in the total flow was relatively low in the 1870s and 1890s, and relatively high in the 1880s and especially the early 1900s. This cycle is also implausible, as the share of net migration presumably grew steadily, from decade to decade, as transport technology improved (and especially as steamships replaced sailing ships).[24]

The share of temporary emigrants in the transoceanic total was negligible in the 1870s, and near 60 percent in the first decade of the 1900s; if one assumes that it equaled 20 percent in the 1880s and 40 percent in the 1890s one obtains a net migration rate, from 1881 on, that is practically constant from decade to decade (Table 2.03).[25] But gross migration grew rapidly in the 1880s and early 1900s, and net migration presumably

[24] A third problem that is noted to complete the list refers to short-run movements, and disappears over the longer time-spans relevant to the Kuznets cycle. From year to year, according to Giusti, net migration varied less than gross migration (Figure 2.02); it presumably varied more, as the conditions which encouraged departures discouraged returns, and vice versa.

[25] Fenoaltea, "International Resource Flows," pp. 615 and 635–637. The estimate of the population at the end of 1911 is also slightly reduced.

did too (Figure 2.02). Net migration was thus apparently high around 1891 and low around 1901: if the series does not present discontinuities, between these two dates net migration must have been declining. The annual series has not yet been reconstructed, but the available evidence suggests that net migration from Italy followed the Kuznets cycle of total European migration to the New World.[26]

The path of migration is in any case only the first problem that the Italian case creates for the Kuznets school's interpretation. Italy's population growth was determined essentially by the natural increase, far greater (and steadier) than the net flow of migrants; border changes apart, even Giusti's estimated population series barely differs from a simple trend (Figure 2.02).

From decade to decade population growth was practically constant: whether one considers the increase in total numbers, or the number of new families created by marriage, the construction cycle is clearly a cycle in construction *per demographic unit* (Table 2.03), and cannot be traced back to an underlying demographic cycle.[27] In Italy, infrastructure investment cannot be described as "population-sensitive capital formation": the Italian case does not fit the kuznetsian paradigm.

4. The Italian cycle: financial flows

Italy's construction cycle (unlike its demographic cycle) was parallel to that of the overseas lands; and so was the cycle in its financial flows. In Italy, too, capital imports were typically high when British capital exports were high, and low when these were low.

Italy's capital imports were also poorly documented. The least uncertain components of the balance of payments refer to the movement of goods, registered in quantity terms by the customs officials and then converted into values by a committee of experts.[28] The Istat series for net

---

[26] One thus returns in essence to Bloomfield's observation, recalled above: after 1881 net migration follows a flat trend, and its cycle was presumably that of gross migration around its own (rising) trend.

[27] On marriages see S. Somogyi, "Nuzialità," in Istat, *Sviluppo della popolazione*, p. 375. Table 2.03 uses the demographic estimates presented in Fenoaltea, "International Resource Flows," but the critical cycle, in row 6, is obtained even with Giusti's figures (Table 2.02).

[28] The "balance of payments" is a cash account. The positive items are those that generate an inflow of foreign currency: exports of goods, exports of services (the earnings from Italian workers abroad, or foreign tourists in Italy), and capital imports. The negative

trade in goods (the "trade deficit") shows that Italy was normally a net importer of goods; and those net imports also followed a cycle, with clear peaks in 1864–65, 1874, 1887, and 1912, very close to the Kuznets cycle followed by construction (Table 2.04 and Figure 2.03).[29]

Net imports of goods are not due, as is often claimed, to an inadequate domestic output: when in the 1840s the Irish potato crop miserably failed, and the need for imported food was very great, Ireland lacked the means to pay for imports, and the Irish by the million left the country or starved. The international market is heartless, and allows a negative balance in one part of the foreign account only if it is covered by a positive balance elsewhere: Italy's recurrent trade deficit was financed, permitted, in fact *created* by the net income from abroad under other headings of the balance of payments.[30]

These net earnings, not well documented at the time, include those from the export of services – including, importantly, the repatriated earnings of Italy's migrants – and capital imports.[31] The Istat estimates of net capital inflows vary over a range in excess of one billion lire, almost as much as the net disbursements due to the trade deficit, and the estimates of migrants' earnings over a range of 800 million (Table 2.04 and

---

items are, obviously, their opposites: imports of goods, and so on. The overall accounting balance is zero; with fixed exchange rates, the "surplus" or "deficit" refers to a specific item, which depends on the specific nature of the currency and of the exchange-rate regime. Under a "gold standard," the currency is gold, or paper freely convertible into gold at its nominal value; the exchange rate is fixed beause it is defined by the gold content of the different monetary units, and the "surplus" in the balance of payments is identified with the net inflow of gold. Under the "gold-exchange" standard of the 1950s and 1960s the exchange rate was fixed by the central bank, that bought or sold foreign currency, on demand, at a given price (625 lire to the dollar); the "surplus" was then identified with the net purchases of foreign currency by the central bank. With flexible exchange rates, as prevail today, the net "balance of payments" is zero in every sense: national currencies lack intrinsic value (a gold content), the central banks do not fix the exchange rate, and day by day the exchange rate is whatever clears the market, equalizing the demand for foreign currency (from the negative items of the account) and the corresponding supply (from the positive items).

[29] Istat (Istituto centrale di statistica), *Indagine statistica sullo sviluppo del reddito nazionale dell'Italia dal 1861 al 1956*, *Annali di statistica*, serie VIII, vol. 9, Rome 1957, pp. 253–254.

[30] Below, ch. 4, § 2.

[31] The national accounts count as "exports of services" the repatriated earnings of temporary migrants, and as "unilateral transfers" the remittances of permanent migrants. This distinction is here immaterial, and remittances will also be considered earnings by labor abroad.

TABLE 2.04. *International financial flows*

	(1)	(2)	(3)	(4)	(5)
	\multicolumn{4}{c}{Istat balance-of-payments series (million lire)}	British
	net imports of goods	net imports of capital	labor income	residual	capital exports[a]
1861	313	325	10	−22	12
1862	223	244	9	−30	14
1863	231	255	13	−37	31
1864	367	410	20	−63	28
1865	367	392	25	−50	41
1866	219	262	23	−66	46
1867	109	158	33	−82	52
1868	71	116	39	−84	42
1869	101	113	44	−56	51
1870	101	95	45	−39	55
1871	−152	−144	35	−43	76
1872	−35	−44	46	−37	97
1873	96	37	57	2	86
1874	264	182	66	16	78
1875	132	20	75	37	57
1876	62	−58	87	33	31
1877	171	72	89	10	10
1878	−6	−101	92	3	23
1879	121	31	87	3	31
1880	35	−88	98	25	33
1881	27	−88	101	14	60
1882	36	−68	107	−3	61
1883	51	−72	112	11	49
1884	204	77	114	13	70
1885	452	358	108	−14	62
1886	373	293	110	−30	78
1887	524	452	121	−49	88
1888	220	132	128	−40	91
1889	363	195	143	25	83
1890	362	203	166	−7	107
1891	194	−26	241	−21	72
1892	161	−58	242	−23	63
1893	172	−39	209	2	57
1894	9	−202	184	27	50
1895	84	−168	200	52	55
1896	68	−209	232	45	50
1897	18	−292	254	56	41
1898	101	−259	294	66	29
1899	−29	−429	354	46	47
1900	244	−192	390	46	34
1901	246	−393	572	67	19
1902	166	−467	549	84	24
1903	240	−414	527	127	43
1904	214	−442	492	164	52
1905	234	−742	781	195	88
1906	494	−550	844	200	121
1907	813	−129	729	213	162
1908	1,059	103	642	314	150
1909	1,098	217	603	278	142
1910	1,028	−31	739	320	174
1911	1,035	−22	778	279	204
1912	1,155	106	835	214	203
1913	991	−95	834	252	234

[a] million pounds.

Sources: cols. 1–4, Istat (Istituto centrale di statistica), *Indagine statistica sullo sviluppo del reddito nazionale dell'Italia dal 1861 al 1956*, Annali di statistica, serie VIII, vol. 9, Rome 1957, pp. 255, 258–259, 264–265; col. 5, M. Edelstein, *Overseas Investment in the Age of High Imperialism: The United Kingdom, 1850–1914*, New York 1982, pp. 313–314.

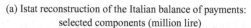

(a) Istat reconstruction of the Italian balance of payments:
selected components (million lire)

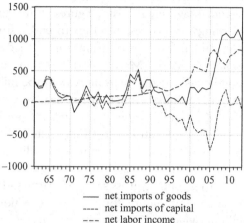

——— net imports of goods
---- net imports of capital
– – – net labor income

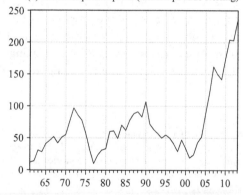

(b) British capital exports (million pounds sterling)

Source: Table 2.04.

FIGURE 2.03. *International financial flows*

Figure 2.03).[32] Subtracting these inflows from that outflow one obtains
a residual that corresponds closely to the net income from other exports
of services (in essence, net income from tourism less net expenditure for
transportation and for the repatriated earnings of foreign capital). That
residual is long very small, and then grows, in the early 1900s, to some
300 million lire.[33]

---

[32] Istat, *Indagine*, pp. 255, 258–259, 264–265.
[33] Ibid., pp. 256–257.

Istat seems to have estimated directly the flows due to labor and other services, and to have obtained capital flows as a residual.[34] Near the end of the period at hand, however, the Istat figures seem significantly to overestimate the earnings of services, and thus to underestimate capital imports. The recent estimates of those earnings in 1911 carefully compiled (and documented) by Mauro Marolla and Massimo Roccas already reduce the corresponding Istat estimate by more than 100 million lire; but even their estimate of the earnings from tourism, near 500 million, seems too high next to Vera Zamagni's contemporaneous and much more solid estimate of value added in the entire sector that includes hotels, restaurants, and the like. The latter estimate comes to 408 million lire, of which only 82 for hotels and rooming houses.[35] Attributing to foreigners a reasonable share of the corresponding gross sales, net earnings from tourism seem limited to some 200 million lire, for a global correction to the Istat figure near 400 million (which are to be deducted from the income from services, and added to capital imports).[36]

Over time, too, the Istat labor-income figures seem excessively variable. Those estimates appear to be based on the gross *flow* of migrants, which similarly jumps up in 1901 and in 1905 (Table 2.02 and Figure 2.02); but remittances seem more reasonably tied to the savings by the *stock* of Italians abroad, which grew according to the figures of the time from

---

[34] Ibid., pp. 160–177.

[35] M. Marolla and M. Roccas, "La ricostruzione della bilancia internazionale dei servizi e trasferimenti unilaterali dell'anno 1911," in G. M. Rey, ed., *I conti economici dell'Italia. 2. Una stima del valore aggiunto per il 1911*, Collana storica della Banca d'Italia, serie "statistiche storiche," vol. I.II, Bari 1992, pp. 241–282; one notes the hypothesis that foreigners remained in Italy, on average, almost four weeks (p. 259), which seems much too high (not least in view of the incidence of business travel). Zamagni's estimates are based relatively directly on the census data for the sector's labor force; see V. Zamagni, "Il valore aggiunto del settore terziario italiano nel 1911," in Rey, *I conti economici dell'Italia. 2*, pp. 193–195.

[36] The value added of hotels and the like near 82 million lire may correspond to sales near 130 million, of which perhaps 40 percent (some 50 million lire) may be attributed to foreigners. Quadrupling that to allow for meals and other expenses one obtains a total of some 200 million lire, which (neglecting on the one hand the earnings from foreign tourists that rented villas, and on the other all the spending by Italian tourists abroad) seems a reasonable upper limit to net earnings from tourism. This reduction (by some 300 million lire) of the estimate by Marolla and Roccas is in addition to their own 100-million-lire reduction of the Istat estimate of net income from exported services, whence a total reduction of 400 million lire. The critique of the Istat figures in Fenoaltea, "International Resource Flows," p. 622, suggested a similar correction, but attributed it entirely to labor income; it is here corrected in light of the cited, more recent research results.

under one million in 1871 to some six million in 1911.[37] The probable path of this item is accordingly one of relatively steady growth; and this means that the capital-import cycle presumably followed the trade-deficit cycle relatively closely, albeit around a trend that grew more slowly, with a final maximum close to 300–400 million lire rather than one billion.

As far as capital flows are concerned, then, Italy seems altogether analogous to the overseas lands. Like these, Italy was part of the financial periphery, normally an importer of capital; and like theirs, Italy's capital imports followed the Kuznets cycle, rising and then falling over the 1870s, rising again in the 1880s, falling again in the 1890s, and then rising once more after 1900, with or at least like the outflow of capital from Great Britain (Table 2.04 and Figure 2.03).[38] The only exception to these generally parallel movements, the only peculiarly Italian episode once again concerns the early 1860s, when Italian capital imports were high but transoceanic flows were minimal.

5. The Italian cycle: the causes of the trade deficits

The trade deficit and capital inflows tend to move together, as noted, because of the reduced importance, and reduced variability, of the other components of the balance of payments. In general, either may cause the other; in specific cases, causal priority is revealed by the movement of the exchange rate.

The balance of payments tends to reach equilibrium through movements in the relative value of the goods of the trading countries, that is, in the so-called "real exchange rate" (or "terms of trade"). The real exchange rate varies both with the nominal exchange rate, and with relative domestic price levels: our goods will thus be worth 10 percent more,

---

[37] The larger part of the income from Italian labor abroad consisted of remittances, and not of the savings of temporary migrants: Marolla and Roccas, "La ricostruzione," p. 254. F. Balletta, "Emigrazione italiana, cicli economici e rimesse (1876–1976)," in G. Rosoli, ed., *Un secolo di emigrazione italiana 1876–1976*, Rome 1978, p. 81, illustrates the Istat migration and labor-income series ("remittances," but the figures include income from temporary migration). The latter follows the movements of the former only so long as it was estimated, that is, up to the Second World War; it subsequently grows very steadily (until it suddenly collapses, when Italians abroad understood that Italy was no longer poor, and that their sacrifices were no longer justified).

[38] The British capital export series is taken from M. Edelstein, *Overseas Investment in the Age of High Imperialism: The United Kingdom, 1850–1914*, New York 1982, pp. 313–314.

in terms of foreign goods, if with unchanged domestic prices our currency is worth 10 percent more (so that the foreign currency that used to cost 100 lire now costs only 91), and also if with an unchanged nominal exchange rate our domestic price level increases, relative to the foreign level, by 10 percent. The higher our real exchange rate, the cheaper foreign goods will appear to us, and the dearer our goods will appear to foreigners; the higher also, therefore, our trade deficit.

The equilibrium real exchange rate is that which maintains equilibrium in the balance of payments, that is, that which generates a trade deficit that offsets capital imports (and other net inflows, if any). With flexible exchange rates, as today between the euro and the dollar, equilibrium in the balance of payments is maintained by movements in the nominal exchange rate. With fixed exchange rates, as under the gold standard, the balance of payments tends to equilibrium through the changes in relative domestic price levels induced by the changes in the money stock created by the foreign imbalance itself: under the gold standard, the country with a foreign deficit loses gold, and the country with a foreign surplus acquires it.

An international equilibrium can be disturbed by impulses that arise in the market for goods, or in the market for capital. Imagine, to illustrate the first case, that for some reason (an increase in internal demand, or some foreign innovation) we tend to import more goods than before at the current real exchange rate (which was up to then the equilibrium rate). The trade deficit increases, an overall deficit appears; and this deficit will tend to reduce our real exchange rate (either through a devaluation of the currency, with flexible exchange rates, or through a reduction of our internal price level, relative to the foreign one). The growing trade deficit may be covered at least in part by induced capital movements: with flexible exchange rates the devaluation of our currency may be seen as temporary, causing speculative purchases of our currency in view of its subsequent recovery; with fixed exchange rates the loss of currency causes a net demand for liquidity that attracts foreign loans. In the event, the trade deficit and capital imports increase together, accompanied by a decline in the real exchange rate. If the initial equilibrium is disturbed in the opposite sense, by an increase in our exports, the trade deficit and capital imports decline together, while the real exchange rate increases.

Imagine, to illustrate the alternative scenario, that a disequilibrium in the balance of payments appears because for some reason (for example, a wave of infrastructure investment) we import more capital than before.

At the prevailing real exchange rate (which was up to then the equilibrium rate) an overall surplus appears, and our real exchange rate accordingly rises (as our currency appreciates, or our domestic price level increases relative to the foreign one). This rise in the real exchange rate in turn increases the trade deficit: the trade deficit and capital imports again rise together, and the real exchange rate rises too. If the initial equilibrium is disturbed in the opposite sense, by a reduction in our capital imports, the trade deficit and capital imports decline together, and the real exchange rate also declines.

The trade deficit and capital imports move together in any case: but with parallel movements in the real exchange rate if the initial impulse is in financial markets and the capital flows cause the trade deficits, and with opposite movements in the real exchange rate if the initial impulse is in the goods market and the trade deficits cause the flows of capital.

In the period at hand the Italian lira was defined by its metal content (equal to that of the French franc), but the convertibility of the paper lira was suspended during the crisis of 1866, reestablished in 1883, and then again abandoned a few years later.[39] The nominal exchange rate of the lira was therefore semi-flexible, in the sense that it could fall below the metal parity of the currency unit but not rise above it (save by the very small margin allowed by the cost of transporting the metal coins themselves).

The nominal exchange rate (the value in paper lire of a metal lira) is well documented (Table 2.05 and Figure 2.04).[40] Apart from a brief episode in the very early 1870s the lira was strong when the trade deficits and capital flows were high, and weak when they were low. The simple correlation of the trade deficit and the nominal exchange rate equals 0.517; and it would surely have been higher had the nominal exchange rate been fully flexible, and not limited, upward, by the lira's metal parity.

The real exchange rate seems to have moved with the trade deficit and capital imports even after parity was reached in the early 1880s and again in the early 1900s. With the nominal exchange rate at par, the real exchange rate rises with an increase in the domestic price level, relative to that abroad (world-wide, commodity prices fell from the early 1870s to the mid-1890s, and then rose steadily). But the domestic prices of

[39] Non-convertibility reappeared officially in 1894, *de facto* by 1888: Battilossi, *Annali*, pp. 107, 135, 139–140, 153, 163.
[40] Istat, *Sommario*, p. 166.

TABLE 2.05. *Interest and exchange rates*

	(1) exchange rate (gold lire/ paper lira)	(2) rent indices (1911 = 1,000) nominal	(3) real	(4) annual consol yield (percent) Italian	(5) British	(6) Italian yield premium[a]
1861	1.000			7.17	3.32	53.7
1862	1.000			7.39	3.27	55.8
1863	1.000			7.22	3.28	54.6
1864	1.000			7.08	3.37	52.4
1865	1.000			8.00	3.39	57.6
1866	.943			8.91	3.45	61.3
1867	.932			9.90	3.27	67.0
1868	.913			9.54	3.24	66.0
1869	.964			8.32	3.27	60.7
1870	.958			8.35	3.28	60.7
1871	.953			7.34	3.27	55.4
1872	.923	492	410	6.07	3.28	46.0
1873	.867	502	399	6.35	3.28	48.3
1874	.902	513	438	6.35	3.28	48.3
1875	.934	524	469	5.96	3.24	45.6
1876	.933	535	503	5.93	3.16	46.7
1877	.919	546	486	5.97	3.14	47.4
1878	.918	557	480	5.68	3.15	44.5
1879	.907	571	493	5.22	3.08	41.0
1880	.929	586	524	4.92	3.05	38.0
1881	.990	600	545	4.97	2.90	41.6
1882	.984	615	585	5.03	2.94	41.6
1883	1.003	631	627	5.05	2.83	44.0
1884	1.007	646	688	4.67	2.72	41.8
1885	1.001	663	737	4.61	2.85	38.2
1886	1.007	679	772	4.46	2.81	37.0
1887	.994	696	788	4.51	2.72	39.7
1888	.996	684	761	4.57	2.62	42.7
1889	.999	673	725	4.64	2.63	43.3
1890	.990	661	694	4.65	2.67	42.6
1891	.988	655	687	4.77	2.68	43.8
1892	.977	648	698	4.71	2.65	43.7
1893	.931	642	734	4.69	2.60	44.6
1894	.915	635	738	5.05	2.55	49.5
1895	.960	629	727	4.39	2.29	47.8
1896	.940	635	710	4.39	2.06	53.1
1897	.960	641	719	4.21	1.96	53.4
1898	.931	648	730	4.11	2.00	51.3
1899	.938	654	738	4.06	2.18	46.3
1900	.946	661	748	4.09	2.53	38.1
1901	.968	667	753	4.03	2.67	33.7
1902	.997	674	754	3.94	2.66	32.5
1903	1.009	681	771	3.97	2.75	30.7
1904	1.009	698	775	3.96	2.84	28.3
1905	1.013	733	819	3.88	2.78	28.4
1906	1.003	784	870	3.80	2.83	25.5
1907	1.001	839	927	3.73	2.97	20.4
1908	1.013	898	957	3.69	2.91	21.1
1909	1.009	943	975	3.66	2.98	18.6
1910	1.001	971	993	3.66	3.09	15.6
1911	.999	1,000	1,000	3.71	3.15	15.1
1912	.994	1,030	1,018	3.64	3.28	9.9
1913	.986	1,061	1,045	3.62	3.40	6.1

[a] 100 ((col. 4–col. 5)/col. 4).

Sources: cols. 1, 4–6, S. Fenoaltea, "International Resource Flows and Construction Movements in the Atlantic Economy: The Kuznets Cycle in Italy, 1861–1913," *Journal of Economic History* 48 (1988), pp. 620–621; col. 2, S. Fenoaltea, "Construction in Italy, 1861–1913," *Rivista di storia economica* 4 (1987), International Issue, pp. 30–31; col. 3, see text.

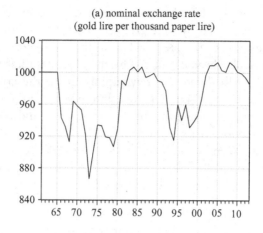

(a) nominal exchange rate
(gold lire per thousand paper lire)

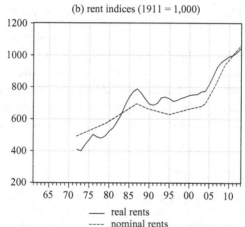

(b) rent indices (1911 = 1,000)

—— real rents
---- nominal rents

Source: Table 2.05.

FIGURE 2.04. *Indicators of the real exchange rate*

imported goods remain tied to their foreign prices, converted into lire at a constant exchange rate; the relative increase in the domestic price level is due entirely to the increase in the price of the goods least subject to import competition, real estate and services first and foremost.[41] The main component of the cost of services is the cost of labor; and as shall

---

[41] This change in domestic relative prices occurs even with changes in the nominal exchange rate. If the lira appreciates, for example, import prices fall, in lire, and the price level remains unchanged, on average, because of the absolute and relative rise in the prices of the goods least subject to import competition.

be seen in greater detail in the next chapter the two periods in which real wages rose most sharply were precisely the 1880s (up to the crisis of 1887), and the years of the pre-war boom. Indices of nominal and real rental rates have also been calculated by the present author (Table 2.05 and Figure 2.04). Real rentals grew rapidly up to the crisis of 1887 (accompanied by the well-known real-estate boom), and then declined; their growth resumed around the turn of the century, and was especially rapid during the boom years from 1904 to 1908.[42]

With the brief exception of the early 1870s, in sum, the cycle in the real exchange rate is parallel to that in the trade deficit and capital imports: the trade-deficit cycle was clearly generated by the capital-import cycle, and not vice versa.[43]

6. The Italian cycle: the causes of capital flows

In the analysis of the Kuznets school, too, the swings in the American trade deficit were caused by those in capital imports (as in the experience of the Reagan years, which seemed novel only because the historical precedents had been forgotten); but the capital flows were themselves induced by the opposite construction cycles caused by the cycle in transoceanic migration.[44] In the Italian case, as noted, the construction cycle does

[42] The nominal rent series is from Fenoaltea, "Construction" (Table 2, col. 3). The real series is that same series deflated by the cost of living index in Id., "Production and Consumption in Post-Unification Italy: New Evidence, New Conjectures," *Rivista di storia economica* 18 (2002), pp. 282–283 (Table A.1, col. 9; below, Table 3.03, col. 6), and rescaled to set its level in 1911 equal to 1.00. P. Ciocca and A. Ulizzi, "I tassi di cambio nominali e 'reali' dell'Italia dall'Unità nazionale al Sistema Monetario Europeo (1861–1979)," in S. Cardarelli *et al.*, *Ricerche per la storia della Banca d'Italia. Volume I*, Collana storica della Banca d'Italia, serie "contributi," vol. I, Bari 1990, pp. 341–368, reconstruct the movements of the real exchange rate not from the relative prices of traded and non-traded goods, but directly from the nominal rates and the indices of wholesale prices in Italy and abroad. Their series is characterized by substantial stability until the mid-1870s, and again, after a decade-long appreciation, from the mid-1880s on (pp. 353, 366–367). The wholesale price indices are built up from the prices of goods, traded goods, and as the authors note the tendency to "real exchange rate stability" may be simply due to relatively unified commodity markets (pp. 344–345); from this perspective the only puzzle is the apparent transition from one equilibrium to another, perhaps in response to changing tariffs and transport costs.

[43] The trade-deficit cycle is attributed to the capital-import cycle already in B. Stringher, "Il commercio con l'estero e il corso dei cambi," *Nuova Antologia di Scienze, Lettere ed Arti*, serie III, 54 (1894), in particular pp. 21–22, 25–26, 29–31, 41–42.

[44] The pioneering work on the American balance of payments was Williamson, *American Growth*.

not seem traceable to demographic causes; and the evidence suggests that it was itself the effect, rather than the cause, of the cycle in capital imports.

The link between the construction cycle and the capital-import cycle is clarified by the behavior of financial markets. An increase in construction can cause a parallel increase in capital imports, as in the kuznetsian interpretation: investment demand exceeds domestic saving, and the resulting tension in financial markets attracts foreign capital. Alternatively, an autonomous increase in capital imports can cause a parallel increase in construction: the foreign capital increases the supply of finance, and stimulates investment.

The behavior of financial markets is illustrated in part by the path of interest rates. The reference rate is the yield of Italian consols (Table 2.05 and Figure 2.05).[45] The simple correlation between that yield and construction is negative (−0.534); as construction and capital imports rose the interest rate clearly fell, as construction and capital imports declined the interest rate tended instead to rise or to remain constant.

The consol yield was near 7 percent in the early 1860s, with high construction and capital imports, and then rose to some 10 percent as construction and capital imports fell. From the late 1860s to the early 1870s the yield fell by almost two fifths, to some 6 percent, while construction and capital imports recovered (with the exception once again of the anomalous flows in 1871, due presumably to the Franco-Prussian war). The yield then remained practically constant almost to the end of the 1870s, while construction and capital imports declined; it then fell again, by almost a quarter, in the decade to 1887, as construction and capital imports surged. The crisis of the 1890s was marked by declining construction and capital imports, while yields rose, at least slightly (by half a percentage point, to some 5 percent); and the strong recovery of construction and capital imports over the pre-war boom was again accompanied by a decline in the consol yield, which had fallen, by 1913, to just 3.6 percent.

[45] Consols are government bonds with no maturity date; their income stream is perpetual, and the corresponding interest rate is simply the ratio between the constant value of the coupon and the variable value of the bond itself. The yield series is taken from B. Bianchi, "Appendice statistica: il rendimento del consolidato dal 1862 al 1946," in F. Vicarelli, ed., *Capitale industriale e capitale finanziario: il caso italiano*, Bologna 1979, pp. 156–158; it is extrapolated to 1861 through the analogous series in M. Da Pozzo and G. Felloni, *La borsa valori di Genova nel secolo XIX*, Turin 1964, p. 469.

(a) consol yield (percent per year)

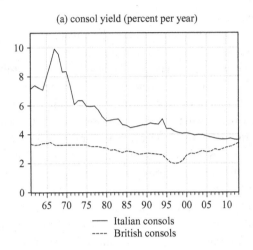

— Italian consols
---- British consols

(b) Italian yield premium

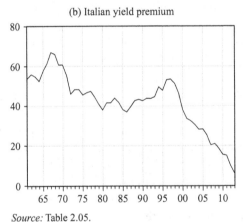

Source: Table 2.05.

FIGURE 2.05. *Italian and British interest rates*

The path of the consol yield thus suggests that the waves of foreign investment in Italy were due to an abundance of foreign supply, and not to the pressure of domestic demand: that they were the cause, and not the effect, of the construction cycle.[46]

---

[46] The model of investment behavior remains that described above (ch. 2, § 1), with two modifications. First, it is applied to all capital, including infrastructure, and not to industrial capital alone; second, the changes in the desired stock of capital are tied to changes in the interest rate rather than to changes in risk. A one-shot decline in the interest rate generates a one-shot increase in the desired stock of capital; investment is high until that desired level is reached, and only until then.

Consol yields are not however a comprehensive indicator of the state of financial markets, for at least three reasons. First, the measured yield is the nominal yield, and it is an uncertain measure of the relevant interest rate, which is in fact the real rate; the difference between the two is the expected rate of inflation, which is simply unknown.[47] About real interest rates, more will be said below; for the moment, it is enough to recall that prices drifted down into the mid-1890s and then drifted up, and that it is reasonable to assume that changing expectations (from deflation to inflation) made for a decline in real interest rates, in the early 1900s, even greater than that in nominal rates.[48] Second, the yield of government bonds is an imperfect index of the interest rate in private transactions, as it could include a premium for the risk that the sovereign State might simply repudiate its debt: a risk that was not negligible especially after 1866, when Italy's public finances were in desperate straits.[49] Third, the market for credit is notoriously different from the market for goods, in which the buyer purchases all he wants at the given price. At any interest rate, bank loans are rationed, granted or denied to those who seek them;

[47] The "real" interest rate calculated from contemporaneous interest and inflation rates corresponds to the expected real rate only if the inflation rate is not expected to change: a 10 percent yield with 2 percent inflation thus implies an 8 percent real rate if the expected rate of inflation is also 2 percent, and a 3 percent real rate if the expected rate of inflation is 7 percent. Analogously, the "real" rates actually earned over a period of time can be interpreted either as *ex ante* rates, assuming that expectations were error-free (so that expected inflation and measured inflation coincide), or, conversely, as measures of the expected inflation rate (and of its error), assuming given (*ex ante*) real interest rates. A realized real return of 10 percent thus reveals an expected return of 10 percent, assuming that expected and realized inflation coincide, or (for example) a realized inflation rate 7 percentage points below the expected rate, assuming an *ex ante* real return of 3 percent.

[48] The change in the expected rate of inflation may have been gradual ("adaptive"), as it came to be recognized that prices were indeed drifting up, or sudden ("rational"), if tied to the discovery of significant new supplies of gold, near the end of the century, in Alaska and in South Africa.

[49] The State had retained the option to repurchase its bonds at par, and eventually exercised it with the conversion of the public debt in 1906 (Battilossi, *Annali*, p. 191): the State in fact repurchased the old 5-percent bonds, and issued new, 3-percent bonds. The State's option capped the bonds' market value (and sustained their current yield) when market yields fell below their nominal yield: with a market rate of 4 percent, for example, a 5-percent perpetuity would be worth 125 lire, but investors fearful of repurchase at par would not offer more than the 100 lire they would receive from the State. The conversion of the debt was experienced, and described, as a triumph: it certainly confirmed the flattering fact that the State could borrow at low rates (which could equally have been confirmed by the sale of 5-percent bonds at prices above their par value, had the State abandoned its option), but beyond that there is no clear justification for self-congratulation.

at any interest rate the banks will be more willing to lend if their reserves are ample, and less willing if these are scarce.

Beyond the interest rate, therefore, it is worth considering more general indicators of the state of financial markets, and the presence or absence of crowding-out. For example, a wave of railway investment (for political reasons) could create tension in the financial market and induce an inflow of foreign capital; but in that case the increase in railway investment would reduce the finance available for residential, industrial and other investment, which would accordingly be crowded out.

In the period at hand there is no trace of crowding out. As seen above, the various components of construction generally move together; and high construction (and capital imports) coincided with high investment of every sort. The same cycle appears in construction and, as also seen above, industrial investment. A very similar cycle appears in public spending (especially on defence) and public borrowing, with peaks in the early 1860s, the 1880s, and at the end of the period at hand, and again in the stock markets of Milan and Genoa.[50]

The absence of crowding-out tells the same story as the movements of the interest rate: construction and industrial investment in post-Unification Italy were clearly high in periods of financial abundance, and low in periods of financial stringency. This financial cycle follows the cycle in capital imports; it cannot have been due to an autonomous cycle in domestic saving, which would have generated an *opposite* cycle in capital imports.

The macroeconomic variables thus rule out the hypothesis that the cycle in industrial and infrastructure investment had internal causes. Investment of all types followed the cycle in the supply of finance, and that cycle was due to the cycle in the supply of foreign capital.

The pioneering hypotheses of Gerschenkron and Romeo had been cast in terms of stages of growth, and focused on the domestic developments

---

[50] A. Pedone, "Il bilancio dello Stato e lo sviluppo economico italiano: 1861–1963," *Rassegna economica* 31 (1967), pp. 285–341. Da Pozzo and Felloni, *La borsa valori*, pp. 499–508, indicate for the Genoa exchange peaks in 1864 (46), 1873 (93), and 1887 (98), and troughs in 1867 (33), 1877 (72), and 1896 (44), when the series ends. The weighted stock-price index in S. Baia Curioni, *Modernizzazione e mercato. La borsa di Milano nella "nuova economia" dell'età giolittiana (1888–1914)*, Milan 2000, pp. 39–44, 205–210, starts in January 1888 (100); it hits a minimum in July 1894 (74), and then recovers. A speculative peak was reached in 1905 (174, in September), but the index then settles down to levels that remained high by historical standards (130–140; at then end of 1913 the index equals 134).

that satisfied the prerequisites for industrialization; a cycle imported from abroad might seem entirely at odds with their views. In Gerschenkron's scheme, however, the German-style "mixed banks" represented an improvement in financial intermediation (as well as in managerial skills); in Romeo's, capital flowed into industry once it was no longer absorbed by public works. Both Gerschenkron and Romeo thus tied the changes in the rate of industrial growth to changes in the supply of capital; and that central point sensed by those eminent scholars reappears fully, if in different terms and by different means, in the interpretation of Italy's industrial progress suggested by further research.

7. The Italian cycle: the supply of foreign capital

Construction in Italy largely paralleled that in the overseas lands, but it apparently responded to shifts in capital supply rather than to demographic change; it behaved as "finance-sensitive," rather than "population-sensitive," capital formation. The Italian case thus does not fit the kuznetsian paradigm: it must be explained either as an exception to that paradigm, or by so changing the paradigm itself that Italy, Britain, and the overseas lands are all comfortably accommodated in a single general scheme.

An alternative account of the Kuznets cycle is naturally suggested by the observation that construction is everywhere notoriously "finance-sensitive," simply because its products are extraordinarily durable; that construction follows a similar cycle in Italy (the early 1860s apart) and in the overseas lands, and an inverse cycle in Britain; and that as far as capital flows are concerned Italy and the overseas lands were all in the same group, of capital importers, whereas in the present sample of countries only Britain was a capital-exporter. The obvious hypothesis is that the cycle in capital exports from the British core generated a cycle in the supply of capital in the entire periphery, in southern Europe as well as across the oceans.

The cycle in the supply of foreign capital that apparently generated the Italian construction cycle would thus be attributed (after the early 1860s) to the cycle in British capital exports. It matters little that Britain was not the only exporter of capital, and that first France and then Germany invested more in Italy than Britain did. British capital exports were then the dominant component of international financial flows, especially with respect to their variation, and they alone clearly follow the long swing now known as the Kuznets cycle.[51] British, French, and German capital competed the world over. When and where British capital exports increased, French and German capital was crowded out; it was pushed into opportunities that offered a lower return, in Italy and elsewhere.

The more serious problem for this alternative hypothesis is rather the inverse cycle in construction, and therefore (on this logic) in the supply of capital, in Britain and the periphery. Capital was mobile, financial markets closely tied; the natural presumption is that there was a single "world" interest rate, and therefore that the supply of capital moved as one in the core and in the periphery. This is in fact presumed by the paradigm of the Kuznets school: if the supply of capital is common to all, the inverse cycle in investment can only stem from an inverse cycle in the *demand* for capital, attributed in the case at hand to the geographic shift in the demand for infrastructure induced by migration.

The analysis of the Italian case illustrates the limits to financial globalization. The path of Italian consol yields differs markedly from that of British consol yields (Table 2.05 and Figure 2.05): the simple correlation between these series is practically nil (.039). Italian construction, correlated negatively with the Italian yield (−0.534), displays a slight positive correlation with the British yield (.158), thanks to their broadly parallel movements over the last two pre-war decades (with a sharp fall and then recovery in the 1890s, and then sustained growth).[52]

There is a good deal of variation in the relative difference between those yields, calculated as a percentage of the Italian figure (Table 2.05 and Figure 2.05); and this series seems particularly significant. First of all, since investors could readily switch between Italian and British bonds, the "Italian premium" was presumably an equilibrium amount, that equalized the *ex ante* yields allowing for risk.[53] An equilibrium yield premium

[51] Bloomfield, *Patterns of Internatinal Investment*, pp. 8, 47; A. Fishlow, "Lessons from the Past: Capital Markets during the 19th Century and the Interwar Period," *International Organization* 39 (1985), pp. 388–389, 393–395.

[52] The British consol yield is taken from C. K. Harley, "The Interest Rate and Prices in Britain, 1873–1913: A Study of the Gibson Paradox," *Explorations in Economic History* 14 (1977), p. 87, over 1873–1913, and extrapolated back to 1861 using the corresponding series in S. Homer, *A History of Interest Rates*, New Brunswick 1963, p. 196.

[53] If the British yield is risk-free, and the only risk attached to the Italian yield is a probability p of permanent default, then the British yield will equal $(1 - p)$ times the Italian yield, and the relative yield premium calculated here is exactly the perceived probability of default p. Capital mobility means in fact not that differences in yields are necessarily zero, but that such differences are necessarily contained within the limits allowed by

is of course at one and the same time a measure of the inducement to hold the higher-yielding bond, and of investors' reluctance to hold it. The simple correlation between the Italian trade deficit, which remains as noted the best cyclical indicator of capital imports, and the "Italian premium" is strongly negative (−0.769): the cycle in Italian capital imports was governed by changes in foreign investors' reluctance to hold Italian bonds at given levels of inducement more than by changes in the inducement at given levels of reluctance.[54]

The simple correlation of Italian construction with that premium is also strongly negative (−0.854), and stronger than its negative correlation with the Italian yield alone (−0.534). This can be explained by recalling the quantitative restrictions on credit, which were presumably loosened when foreign investors were more willing to hold Italian bonds; a fall in the risk premium would thus be an index of an increase in the supply of capital in Italy. But that is not all: since real interest rates in individual countries presumably varied more than their average, the changes in the premium may well capture the movements in the real interest rate that actually determined the construction cycle, but are not otherwise observed.[55]

In general, therefore, in the Italian case the construction cycle seems due to changes in the supply of foreign capital due not to parallel changes in the supply of capital in the country of origin, but to changes in the premium required to attract that capital into Italy. Construction may have been everywhere "finance-sensitive," and capital markets may have been unified up to the limit set by that premium; but as that premium

---

substitution – exactly as the "law of one price" for traded goods, properly understood, means not that interlocal price differences are necessarily zero, but that they are necessarily limited to the cost of the goods' movement (transport costs, and applicable tariffs).

[54] In light of this, Michele Fratianni and Franco Spinelli's claim that "net capital inflows... were responding to a high interest-rate differential" and their contempt for contemporary economists' stress on investors' attitudes both seem unwarranted: M. Fratianni and F. Spinelli, "Currency Competition, Fiscal Policy and the Money Supply Process in Italy from Unification to World War I," *Journal of European Economic History* 14 (1985), p. 483.

[55] The negative association between construction and the "Italian premium" seems lacking only at the end of the 1870s, when construction is at a cyclical trough but the premium is not at a cyclical peak. This may be due to the improvement in those years of Italy's public finances (Pedone, "Il bilancio dello Stato," p. 333), and to the decrease in the risk attached specifically to government bonds, even as the risk attached to private bonds increased: in those years, the sectors of construction that decline are the essentially private ones (railways and residential buildings).

varied the local supply of capital, and with it construction, would follow an inverse cycle in the capital-exporting country on the one hand and the capital-importing country on the other.

8. The world cycle: the relative supply of British capital

The cycle in construction (and other capital formation) in Italy would therefore stem from the cycle in the premium required by investors to compensate for the greater risk attached to Italian bonds, that is, in those investors' *confidence*. In the 1860s, when construction in Italy did not follow the Kuznets cycle, that premium seems to vary with specifically Italian events: it shoots up in conjunction with military defeat and the near-bankruptcy of the State. Over the following decades Italian construction follows the Kuznets cycle common to the capital-importing countries; the variations in the "Italian premium" seem then to represent changes in investors' confidence not specific to Italy but common to the entire financial periphery.

The variations in the "periphery premium" had soon been noted by the minority that did not accept the kuznetsian interpretation (which instead neglected those variations, presuming instead as was noted above that the supply of capital was common to Britain and the overseas lands): Hrothgar Habakkuk and then Arthur Lewis had specifically emphasized that in Britain in the 1890s foreign bonds had fallen out of favor, and dragged each other down through bandwagon effects.[56] The data on the nominal yields of various categories of British and foreign bonds subsequently collected by Michael Edelstein confirm their observation, and illustrate the phenomenon over a longer time span.[57]

Table 2.06 is constructed from Edelstein's annual figures, with observations at roughly decennial intervals and near the Kuznets-cycle turning points. Line 1 transcribes directly from the source the reported yield of

---

[56] See in particular Habakkuk, "Fluctuations in House-Building," p. 226, and W. A. Lewis, *Growth and Fluctuations, 1870–1913*, London 1978, p. 180. According to Lewis the reluctance to lend to foreign countries went "beyond any point that objective economic analysis of their own economic solutions could justify"; but that sentence must be understood as excluding by hypothesis the predicted effect of the general disfavor even on "innocent" countries. The consequences of the panic are "objectively" predictable even if the panic is not "objectively" justified.

[57] Edelstein, *Overseas Investment* (unpublished Appendix 7, kindly transmitted by the author).

TABLE 2.06. *Percentage premia for groups of British and foreign bonds*

	(1) 1876	(2) 1886	(3) 1896	(4) 1906	(5) 1913
A. *reference yield (percent per year)*					
1. British consols	3.19	3.00	2.29	2.91	3.38
B. *percentage premia: other British bonds*					
2. corporations	17.8	15.5	16.7	19.6	18.7
3. railways	18.2	13.3	13.6	15.4	15.7
4. industrial and commercial firms	–	–	34.0	31.2	26.6
5. social overhead	–	18.3	20.2	16.9	14.5
C. *percentage premia: colonial and related bonds*					
6. colonial and provincial governments	26.7	24.2	30.8	23.4	23.2
7. Australasian governments	26.2	23.3	29.8	23.0	20.0
8. colonial corporations	38.1	29.6	39.4	28.9	27.3
9. Canadian railways	51.1	29.1	40.5	22.4	20.4
10. United States railways	48.1	34.3	46.9	22.4	18.1
11. Latin American railways	43.8	33.2	41.4	26.3	22.1
12. social overhead	45.2	35.9	44.8	35.9	26.7
D. *percentage premia: European governments*					
13. French consols	24.6	18.3	22.1	7.9	0.9
14. Italian consols	46.2	32.7	47.8	23.4	3.9
E. *percentage premia: simple averages, by group*					
15. group B (British)	24.6	19.7	21.1	20.8	18.9
16. group C (colonial and related), public	26.5	24.3	30.3	23.2	21.6
17. group C (colonial and related), private	45.3	32.4	42.6	27.2	22.9

Sources: see text.

British consols (which differs slightly from that in the preceding table). Lines 2–14 in turn present the premia relative to that yield, analogous to the Italian premium discussed above (Table 2.05), calculated for various groups of bonds, British and foreign, public and private.[58] Lines 15–17 present the simple averages calculated, for different sets of groups, from the figures in the preceding lines.[59]

Between 1886 and 1906 the yield on British consols collapses and then recovers (line 1). A similar cycle appears in the yield of British private bonds: the average premium for this set remains practically constant, near 20 or 21 percent (line 15). The decline and recovery in the yields of British bonds, public and private, do *not* appear in the yields of "colonial and

[58] Each of these premia is calculated directly from the corresponding series in the source, which reports the average yield for that group of bonds. The labels in the source are very terse, as they perforce are here; the components of each group are not described, and a weighted average across groups cannot be calculated. The source does not report the yield of Italian consols; line 14 presents the premium calculated from the Italian yields in Table 2.05 and the British consol yield in line 1.

[59] The average for the British set is obtained by chaining successive indices, to allow for the variation of the underlying sample.

related" bonds, public and private: the corresponding premia increase by a quarter or more from 1886 to 1896, and then decline, reaching new minima, to 1906 (lines 16–17).

The financial troubles of the early 1890s clearly induced, among investors in the British market, a specific distrust of foreign bonds. Had investors distrusted all bonds which were not, like British consols, absolutely safe, the premium earned by British private bonds (line 15) would have displayed a cycle similar to that of the premium on non-British bonds (lines 16–17); had investors distrusted private bonds, the cycle in the premium would have appeared in these and only these (that is, in lines 15 and 17, and not in line 16). Investors distrusted *foreign* bonds, the bonds of the capital-importers, exactly as Habakkuk and Lewis had said.

The long cycle in the "periphery premium" is apparent in the earlier decades as well: the premia on "colonial and related" bonds were high in 1876 as in 1896, low in 1886 as in 1906.[60] The decades of growth in the outflow of British capital, and rising construction in the overseas lands, were characterized by a declining reluctance to invest in those countries; the intervening decade is their mirror image.

Over these decades Italy seems to participate fully in the financial relations between the core and the periphery; in fact, the yield premia suggest that between 1876 and 1906 the Italian State was considered equivalent to a North or South American railway (lines 9–11, 14). It would differ from these in the following years: between 1906 and 1913 the premia on "colonial and related" bonds continue to fall, reaching new lows (and British capital exports climb to new highs, Figure 2.03), but the Italian yield premium drops much more. This relative improvement may reflect a "European" phenomenon (the French premium practically disappears, line 13); it may be also be specific to Italy (and reflect perhaps a "reputation effect" of the victorious war against Turkey, opposite to that of the defeats of 1866). In any case it appears only at the very end

---

[60] The only, limited exception concerns "colonial and related" *government* bonds: their premium was not very high in 1876, and declined relatively little over the ensuing decade. The difference between rows 16 and 15 is only some 10 percent of the difference between rows 17 and 15 in 1876, against some 40 percent in 1886, 1896, and 1906, and some 70 percent in 1913: perhaps because of the colonies' growing autonomy, "colonial and related" government bonds increasingly resembled "colonial and related" private bonds rather than (non-government) British bonds.

of the period at hand, too late (as Gerschenkron would have put it) to change its general character.[61]

Over the central decades of the half-century at hand the Italian experience seems to be that of the entire periphery. The world cycle stems from the long swing in the confidence of market participants, and in particular of British savers, in investment in the periphery (a long swing analogous to that which over the past century generated major stock-market peaks around 1930, 1970, and 2000).[62] As that confidence increased the equilibrium difference between interest rates in the core and in the periphery declined, and capital flows increased; in the periphery the supply of finance increased, real interest rates fell, and construction rose, while in the core the supply of finance fell, real interest rates rose, and construction fell.[63] The long cycle in investors' confidence appears to have generated the long cycle in capital flows, and the opposite construction cycles in the core and the periphery; Italy was like the overseas lands part of the periphery, and the Italian cycle in capital formation was naturally parallel to theirs.

In this perspective the migration cycle is itself explained by the construction cycle. The prospective migrant, who has decided to leave, must still decide when to do so; he will pick a time when he expects little difficulty in obtaining work on arrival, and construction is the employer of first resort for the unskilled workers who leave the farm. Departures from the British country-side appear to have been relatively steady, but with a cycle in the destination – domestic or foreign – that reflected the inverse cycle in British and overseas construction.[64] The Italian construction cycle was parallel to that overseas: internal and external migration moved together, generating a strong cycle in total departures from the

---

[61] A. Gerschenkron, "Notes on the Rate of Industrial Growth in Italy, 1881–1913," *Journal of Economic History* 15 (1955), pp. 360–375, reprinted in Id., *Economic Backwardness in Historical Perspective*, Cambridge MA 1962, pp. 72–89 (and in particular p. 84).

[62] The length of the cycle seems due on the one hand to the cumulative processes induced by largely self-fulfilling expectations, and on the other to the loss of historical memory with demographic renewal: each generation experiences its bubble, and then becomes disenchanted.

[63] And vice versa, obviously, in the opposite case. In Britain too the strong variations in capital formation near the end of the century are far more plausibly related to the similarly strong variations in interest rates than to the necessarily muted demographic cycle, confirming that construction was and is, first and foremost, finance-sensitive. The data appear in C. H. Feinstein, *National Income, Expenditure and Output of the United Kingdom, 1855–1965*, Studies in the National Income and Expenditure of the United Kingdom, vol. 6, Cambridge 1972, pp. 192, T88–89.

[64] Thomas, *Migration and Urban Development*, pp. 20–58.

country-side. Overseas, external migration was of course an inflow rather than an outflow; but there too internal migration (from the areas of the initial colonies to those of more recent settlement) moved with external migration.[65]

In summary, the Kuznets cycle is reinterpreted by distinguishing the capital-exporting core and the capital-importing periphery. When non-British investment was out of favor, capital was relatively abundant in Britain and relatively scarce abroad, construction boomed in England and collapsed abroad, Britons migrated within Britain and non-Britons postponed migration to better days; when investors favored non-British investment, capital was relatively scarce in Britain and relatively abundant abroad, construction collapsed in Britain and boomed abroad, Britons migrated abroad and non-Britons migrated – within the old lands, within the new, and of course within the broader non-British world from the old to the new.

9. The Italian cycle: the reinterpretation

On the evidence now available, it seems clear that the Italian investment cycle was a general cycle in capital formation – in industry, in infrastructure, in residential housing – induced by shifts in the supply of foreign capital. In the 1860s the Italian cycle was idiosyncratic: the rapture induced by Unification was modified by the military defeats and budget crisis of 1866, and the willingness of non-Italians to invest in Italian assets fell sharply. A similar mechanism may have come into play, at the very end of the period at hand, with Italy's victory in the Turkish war. Over the intervening decades, however, the Italian cycle seems to have been no more than the Italian component of a world-wide cycle: the willingness of non-Italians to invest in Italy rose and fell with their willingness to invest in foreign assets in general, without significant peculiarities tied to developments in Italy itself.

The world-wide cycle is itself reinterpreted in light of the Italian evidence. In the new *Genesis* the cycle in the confidence with which British savers viewed foreign investment begat the cycle in capital flows, which begat the inverse construction cycles, which begat the cycle in migration. The basic vision remains that of the Kuznets school, which saw a causal link between the construction cycles and the resource flows; but the

---

[65] R. A. Easterlin, *Population, Labor Force, and Long Swings in Economic Growth: The American Experience*, New York 1968, p. 31.

direction of causality is inverted, as the critics of that school suggested, and this explains why construction moved inversely in the capital-importing and capital-exporting countries rather than in the labor-importing and labor-exporting countries.

The initial hypothesis of a "political cycle" attributed Italy's investment cycle to domestic political changes, including changes in political style, that impinged on the confidence of industrial entrepreneurs; the more recent Kuznets-cycle hypothesis removes from center stage the politics, and economic policies, of the governments of the time. This does not mean that those governments could not have done much worse, or much better, with even major effects on the economy's average growth rate; this was noted above, and will be returned to in greater detail below. Rather, it means that the Italian *cycle* in capital formation (and, derivatively, in industrial and total production) was set in motion, to a first approximation, not by internal political changes but by external, globe-spanning events over which Italy's governments had no control.

The prosperity of the Depretis years was sustained (indirectly but fundamentally) by the abundance of British capital exports. The ensuing crisis of the 1890s marked what Luzzatto called "the darkest years" of the new Kingdom's economy.[66] But that crisis was due only secondarily to Crispi's adventurism: the Italian economy was pushed into deflation and depression by the withdrawal of foreign capital (which lowered the equilibrium real exchange rate), but so was the entire periphery. The entire periphery similarly benefited from the subsequent recovery of British capital exports: Italy shared the prosperity of the *belle époque*, but not because of any particular merit of Giolitti's policies, not because the Italian economy was then better managed than before. The prosperity of the Giolitti years replicated almost exactly that of the 1880s, with rising investment and (as shall be seen in the next chapter) consumption, growing emigration, and the appearance of "twin deficits" (in the State budget, and the external current account); it may seem different in retrospect, but only because the World War suspended the mechanism of the Kuznets cycle before the next crisis developed, and the period ends on a cyclical high note.[67]

---

[66] G. Luzzatto, *L'economia italiana dal 1861 al 1894*, Turin 1968 (Milan 1963), p. 177.

[67] The fluctuations in Italy's commercial deficit, and capital imports, seem more violent than those in British capital exports. In speculative bubbles, the last instruments to rise and the first to collapse are typically the worst; the experience of those decades seems thus to confirm the observation in L. Cafagna, "Contro tre pregiudizi sulla storia dello sviluppo economico italiano," in P. Ciocca and G. Toniolo, eds., *Storia economica d'Italia. 1. Interpretazioni*, Rome-Bari 1998, p. 299, to the effect that from the Risorgimento to the

This interpretation dovetails nicely with the widely accepted Bonelli-Cafagna view, and would in fact explain the chronology of the "waves" in the international context the "political cycle" neglects.[68] It is also kin to that proposed at the time by Luigi Einaudi. The global (Kuznets) cycle in capital flows had not yet been documented, and Einaudi did not of course anticipate it; but he noted the abundance of capital imports in the (prosperous) 1880s and again after the crisis of the 1890s, and tied the decline of the interest rate in Italy to "the internationalization of the money market." Einaudi also traced the giolittian upswing to external rather than domestic causes: the (Kondratieff) cycle in commodity prices was already well known, and Einaudi claimed that after two decades of falling prices rising gold production and inflation had generated a world-wide boom. This last argument is weak, and sits poorly with Einaudi's well-known monetary conservatism; from his own point of view, the Kuznets-cycle story is a better one.[69]

Despite this illustrious ancestry, despite those potential suitors, the present interpretation has not been welcomed by the literature. Until it turned eighteen, and even as its decapitated elder sibling continued to dance at Court, this one had no social life to speak of; and now that it has come out properly, between hard covers, it is received more often than not with manifest disapproval.

10. The evolution of the literature

The Kuznets-cycle explanation of production movements in post-Unification Italy has yet to receive close criticism. It has not been found wanting in its logic or its supporting evidence: the long refusal to come to

---

present day Italy has always suffered from a poor financial reputation. *Always*: over the period at hand, not less with Giolitti than with Depretis (Figure 2.03).

[68] Above, ch. 1, § 7. F. Bonelli, "Italian Capitalism: General Interpretative Guidelines," in G. Federico, ed., *The Economic Development of Italy since 1870*, Aldershot 1994 (translation of F. Bonelli, "Il capitalismo italiano. Linee generali di interpretazione," in R. Romano and C. Vivanti, eds., *Storia d'Italia. Annali. 1. Dal feudalesimo al capitalismo*, Turin 1978, pp. 1193–1255), pp. 110–111, assigned to foreign capital "a decisive role in the various stages of the cycle [of the 1880s]"; but he sees capital imports as an endogenous variable that merely amplified the cycle, and "it was state expenditure which provided the impetus for the business boom."

[69] L. Einaudi, *Cronache economiche e politiche di un trentennio*, 8 vols., Turin 1959–66, vol. 1, pp. 64, 86 (for the quoted phrase), 169–170, 370–371, 450, vol. 2, pp. xx, 454, vol. 3, p. 51, 458, 475; also P. Ciocca, "Einaudi e le turbolenze economiche fra le due guerre," *Rivista di storia economica* 20 (2004), pp. 279–283 (where Einaudi's notorious dislike of Giolitti is also recalled), and S. Fenoaltea, "Einaudi commentatore e protagonista della politica economica: aspetti dell'età giolittiana," *Rivista di storia economica* 20 (2004), pp. 271–278.

grips with it, the heterogeneity of the current complaints suggest a lack of sympathy that is not so much reasoned as visceral.

One source of such antipathy may have to do with the difference in the mind set of economists on the one hand and historians on the other (and with very few exceptions Italy's economic historians are by training historians rather than economists). The Italian experience does not fit the classic interpretation of the Kuznets school: one must either explain why the Italian case was exceptional, or change the model to encompass the Italian case as well. Economists seek general models, and prefer, if it can be found, the second solution; historians pursue the particular, the specific, and may well prefer the first.[70]

A further and more general source cuts across disciplinary lines. Historians and economists alike tend to give importance to the object of their study, to consider it autonomous and active rather than merely passive; Italianists are naturally loath to accept that the major fluctuations of Italy's growth rate were determined by the changing moods of Britain's widows and orphans rather than within Italy itself.[71] So far, in fact, only Marcello de Cecco and Vera Zamagni have declared themselves satisfied that Italy was a small country that "took" a world cycle as it "took" world prices.[72] The more common reaction is to find the Kuznets-cycle story misleading or seriously incomplete; and some can so little stand the sight of it that they fail to see it at all, and fire round after round at non-existent targets.[73]

---

[70] The preference for models that are simple and general ("elegant," "powerful") is said to characterize the scientist; the classic example comes from astronomy, and the success of the copernican model that explained the apparent motion of the planets without the complex "epicycles" required by the ptolemaic model. In fact, that preference seems to characterize the human mind in general: a husband becomes convinced that his wife is having an affair when he realizes that a multitude of curious episodes, each of which has been given its own particular explanation, can be explained together with one simple, powerful hypothesis – that he is, in fact, a cuckold.

[71] Within the Kuznets school the "americanists" typically trace the cycle ultimately to American developments, the "anglicists" ultimately to British ones; the attribution of the Third World's underdevelopment to its commercial ties to Europe, once popular among left-wing intellectuals, is now seen as the expression of a reactionary white paternalism that would deny the autonomy of other races; and further examples abound.

[72] M. de Cecco and V. Zamagni, both in P. Bolchini *et al.*, "A proposito di Stefano Fenoaltea, *L'economia italiana dall'Unità alla Grande Guerra*, Bari-Roma, 2006," *Rivista di storia economica* 22 (2006), pp. 346, 372.

[73] Thus the complaints that the above interpretation denies that domestic policies *could have* influenced the path of capital imports and total product; that it applies to Italy the original interpretation of the Kuznets school; that it overlooks the preponderance of French and German investment in Italy; and so on. All rather humbling, for one writing in his mother tongue.

The dissenting comments vary widely, but have a common thread that suggests a common source: the ambition to recover a proper story with proper Italian heroes. Giovanni Federico simply suggests another waltz with the headless hypothesis.[74] Giuseppe Tattara's thoughtful and sympathetic piece explores the merits of an exchange rate policy that "shadowed gold."[75] The suggestion is perplexing, as such a policy would seem to reap neither the credibility benefits of convertibility nor the flexibility benefits of a floating rate; but there may be more to it than meets the eye.

Piero Bolchini and Gianni Toniolo both make much of institutional improvements. Toniolo's heroes are again Italy's ruling elite, as the courageous end-of-the-century reforms of the financial system and more allowed Italy to participate in the ensuing international upswing.[76] Bolchini's heroes are instead Italy's anonymous savers: the accumulation of capital progressively strengthened Italy's financial intermediaries, and the almost painless solution to the bank crisis of 1907 stands in sharp contrast to the catastrophic failures of the 1890s.[77] Reforms there certainly were, and courageous they may have been, but as seen above over that period Italy's credit-worthiness relative to that of its capital-importing peers changed not a whit; and all else aside in 1907 the financial system was clearly buttressed by the rising tide of British capital exports exactly as in the 1890s it had been sapped by the withdrawal of British capital from world markets.[78]

---

[74] G. Federico in Bolchini *et al.*, "A proposito," p. 348.

[75] G. Tattara in Bolchini *et al.*, "A proposito," pp. 355–359; also G. Tattara, "Paper Money but a Gold Debt: Italy on the Gold Standard," *Explorations in Economic History* 40 (2003), pp. 122–142.

[76] G. Toniolo in Bolchini *et al.*, "A proposito," pp. 369–370, and G. Toniolo, "Review of Stefano Fenoaltea (2006), *L'economia italiana dall'Unità alla Grande Guerra* (Rome and Bari: Laterza)," *Journal of Modern Italian Studies* 12 (2007), p. 132. In this last, echoing Tattara, Toniolo also praises the policy of "shadowing gold."

[77] P. Bolchini in Bolchini *et al.*, "A proposito," pp. 335–337. As noted above (ch. 1, § 10), Bolchini altogether rejects the "cyclical" interpretation, and returns to the stages-of-growth tradition.

[78] Toniolo, "Review," p. 132, asserts that "in order to profit from the international boom, Italy had to abandon expensive colonial adventures and put order to its public finances" (as well as rebuild, as noted, its banking system). The argument is reasonable, but Clio is not a tidy housewife: Italy's credit rating improved relative to the rest of the periphery not while it avoided those adventures and maintained a quasi-balanced budget, but only in the final run-up to the World War, when it (successfully) resumed colonial expansion and, with the Turkish war, the deficit again ballooned. See G. Tattara and M. Volpe, "Italy, the Fiscal Dominance Model, and the Gold-Standard Age," in M. C. Marcuzzo, L. H. Officer and A. Rosselli, eds., *Monetary Standards and Exchange Rates*, London 1997, p. 234.

Toniolo also suggests that the boom of the Giolitti years was more than a mere cyclical upswing. He points to the unprecedented magnitude of that boom; but the statistical point carries little weight, for British capital exports also rose, and Italian interest rates fell, far beyond their previous ranges. Without strong restrictions on the relevant elasticities the possible residual cannot be identified at all.[79]

A more promising road to a similar conclusion is that taken by Pierluigi Ciocca. With his peerless grasp of the actual workings of the Italian economy from the past right up to the present day, of its institutions and decision-making processes, he traces the chronic weakness of the Italian economy to the lack of competition, to the State's protection of monopoly rents, which stifles the incentive to invest and expand. Twice, in its post-Unification history, the Italian economy grew exceptionally fast because it was, by its own standards and all too briefly, exceptionally competitive: in the post-war years that culminated in the "economic miracle" of the early 1960s; and in the Giolitti years, when competitive pressures were increased by the rise in the exchange rate, the reduction of tariff protection, the State's neutrality in labor disputes, the containment of public deficits and subsidies, the opening of markets to potential entrants.[80]

All this under Giolitti and thanks to Giolitti: Ciocca unabashedly admires the man, whom he sees as very different from a Depretis (or a Crispi). The present author does not, has not studied him at all closely, and (as can be said of Einaudi) perhaps strains his own logic to deny Giolitti his due; but it would seem that the stronger lira, the lower average tariff, and the healthier State budget were all more closely tied to (Kuznets- and Kondratieff-cycle) changes in the world at large than to policy innovations in Giolitti's Italy.[81]

---

[79] Toniolo in Bolchini *et al.*, "A proposito," p. 369, Toniolo, "Review," p. 132; above, ch. 1A, § 7. A perhaps more subtle attempt to undercut the notion that the giolittian boom was a mere cyclical upswing may be seen in Toniolo's repeated affirmations that the present author set out decades ago to prove exactly that ("A proposito," pp. 367, 368, 369, "Review," pp. 130, 131). The author has a very different recollection, which need not of course be free of distortion; those who knew him as a graduate student may speak to the issue, but Toniolo is not among them.

[80] P. Ciocca in Bolchini *et al.*, "A proposito," p. 342, and earlier P. Ciocca, "Einaudi e le turbolenze economiche," pp. 279–282; also Id., *Ricchi per sempre? Una storia economica d'Italia (1796–2005)*, Turin 2007, and Id., "Interpreting the Italian Economy in the Long Run," *Rivista di storia economica* 24 (2008), pp. 241–246. On the "economic miracle" see also G. Nardozzi, "The Italian 'Economic Miracle'," *Rivista di storia economica* 19 (2003), pp. 139–180.

[81] The tariff is discussed below, ch. 4; see, on Giolitti, § 1, note 4.

The empirical questions may be clarified by further research, and the clutter of false issues will surely be cleaned up in God's own good time; but the deeper debate is unlikely to reach closure. The search for national heroes is strongly motivated, and cannot ultimately be thwarted: one can exult that things were not worse as lief as lament they were not better, and since events have complex antecedents one can assign merit, or blame, with infinite variety.

3

The Consumption Cycle and the "Crisis" of the 1880s

1. Conditions in the 1880s

The fluctuations in industrial production, and in investment, have been interpreted in different ways; but on the "stylized" facts themselves, on the time paths of the corresponding variables, there has long been relatively general agreement. There has been no agreement, however, even on the time paths of agricultural production and of consumption, and, with these, of the aggregate economy.

The controversy specifically concerns the 1880s, and stems from the weakness of the agricultural statistics of the time.[1] The quantitative evidence improved only slowly, but the later years are in any case clearly characterized by the crisis of the early 1890s, and then by the growing prosperity of the Giolitti years; both were clearly general, and involved consumption as well as investment, agriculture as well as industry. The 1860s and '70s are less transparent; for the old believers the rapid growth of agricultural production allowed Romeo's "original accumulation," but the orthodox opinion has long been that over those decades the changes in the real economy, for good or ill, were relatively mild.[2] The 1880s appear marked instead by strong but heterogeneous movements, with progress in industry but a crisis in at least a good part of agriculture. The

---

[1] Above, ch. 1, § 5, § 9.
[2] G. Pescosolido, *Unità nazionale e sviluppo economico*, Rome-Bari 1998, pp. 118–119, 186–197. Over the 1870s the data generated by the grist tax indicate no more than a slow growth in the consumption of grain, and in the corresponding production; and the new estimates of agricultural production have removed the contrast between the growth of the initial decades and the ensuing stagnation (above, ch. 1, § 5, § 9).

path of the aggregate economy depends on these sectors' relative weight; it is not self-evident, and has been evaluated in very different ways.

Over the 1880s, two major external developments impinged on the Italian economy. One was obviously the rising tide of British foreign investment, which lifted the Italian boat as it did others. As seen in the previous chapter, the increase in the supply of foreign capital loosened financial constraints, stimulated investment, raised the equilibrium real exchange rate; it generated a current-account deficit and a net inflow of resources, and tended to raise wages and consumption.

The second development stemmed from the progress of transportation and colonization, the invasion of European markets by the cheap grain of overseas grasslands. In the early 1880s, in Italy, the price of imported grain fell by a third. Italy's grain was not protected, the market price was the import price; the duty on grain would be raised only near the end of the decade, with the tariff of 1887. The reduction of the import price and the tariff increase obviously had opposite effects, and the interpretation of the one carries with it the interpretation of the other; the controversy over the 1880s is tied to that over tariff protection, considered in the next chapter below.

The historiography of the last few decades pays little attention to the impact of capital flows. The fall in the price of grain is considered much the most significant economic event of the period; and it is considered a negative event, that caused an economic crisis, an impoverishment of the working masses, and an upsurge in emigration. No one denies the growth of industry, and of investment, until late in the decade; the general crisis is said to have begun some five years earlier, with the "agrarian crisis" generated by the fall in the price of grain.

The standard analysis of foreign trade – the traditional model of "comparative advantage" – suggests a very different evaluation. The fall in the price of imported grain should have generated an increase in welfare, in real wages, in consumption; it should have been generally beneficial, and its favorable effects would have reinforced those of the Kuznets-cycle upswing.

The "comparative advantage" model of trade was developed in post-Napoleonic England, by the brilliant mind of David Ricardo.[3] It was understood that foreign trade was beneficial if the countries involved possessed complementary "absolute advantages," so that each could specialize in what it produced easily and obtain in exchange what it could

---

[3] D. Ricardo, *On the Principles of Political Economy and Taxation*, London 1817.

produce only with difficulty. With a simple numerical example Ricardo proved that trade was mutually beneficial even if one country possessed an absolute advantage in every sector, for each possessed a "comparative advantage" where its absolute advantage was relatively high or its absolute disadvantage relatively low; trade increased consumption in both countries because each specialized in what it produced at least cost *in terms of other goods.*[4]

In its modern version the model assumes an economy with given resources (and a given technology). These generate the basic constraint on its "production possibilities": once the available resources are fully (and efficiently) employed, the production of one good can be expanded only by reducing that of another. Economic analysis shows that a competitive economy tends to reach that constraint, and to choose, among the possible combinations of outputs, the one that has the highest value at the prevailing market prices. Absent trade, those prices are obviously domestic prices, and consumption is constrained directly by production.

If, absent trade, domestic relative prices differ from those prevailing on world markets (because relative costs differ; absolute costs are irrelevant, as Ricardo had grasped), trade increases consumption possibilities: the banana that we produce ourselves at the cost of three apples costs us, if we import it, only two apples, and if it costs only one so much the better. The point seems trivial, but it is fundamental: the fall in the price of grain *increased* the difference between relative prices in trade-less Italy and relative prices on world markets, and therefore *increased* Italy's gains from trade; if the fall in the price of grain had been harmful in and of itself, trade in general would have been harmful, and autarky would have been preferable.[5]

---

[4] Imagine for example a country A with one thousand workers, each of whom can produce in a given period one barrel of wine or three yards of cloth; and assume that, absent trade, they produce and consume 500 barrels of wine and 1,500 yards of cloth. Imagine another country, B, also with one thousand workers, each of whom can produce only half a barrel of wine, or one yard of cloth; and assume that, absent trade, they produce and consume 250 barrels of wine and 500 yards of cloth. Imagine now that B specializes in wine, where its disadvantage is lower, and produces for example 400 barrels of wine and 200 yards of cloth; that A specializes in cloth, where its advantage is higher, and produces for example 380 barrels of wine and 1,860 yards of cloth; and that they then exchange (at a relative price between those of the two countries) 130 barrels of wine from B against 320 yards of cloth from A. With trade, consumption rises to 510 barrels of wine and 1,540 yards of cloth in A, and to 270 barrels of wine and 520 yards of cloth in B.

[5] Below, Appendix 2, § 1. Vera Zamagni at least appears to have grasped this logic: to her mind the fall in the price of grain was harmful, and international trade in general is best discouraged (below, ch. 4, § 2, note 11).

In an open economy the relative prices of traded goods are those prevailing in world markets, modified by the relevant tariffs. As relative prices change, so does the output mix: some sectors suffer and shrink, releasing resources to the sectors that instead prosper and expand. In the wake of the decline in the price of grain one sees euphoric growth in industry and in specialized agriculture – the extension of the Apulian vineyards is particularly noteworthy – while grain production suffers a crisis and contracts. These have been described as "the contradictions of the 1880s"; they are in fact the logical reaction of the economy to the change in relative prices.[6]

As the output mix changes, there is an increase in the demand for the resources used intensively in the sectors that expand, and a decline in the demand for the resources used intensively in those that contract. Because the resources are given, in fixed supply, changes in demand change their market price; the change in the output mix changes the relative remuneration of the different factors of production. In the case at hand grain is land-intensive: that is why it is cheap where land is abundant, and dear in the densely settled countries, which correspondingly possess a comparative advantage in such labor-intensive sectors as industry and specialized agriculture. As these expand at the expense of grain-growing the demand for labor increases, raising real wages, and the demand for land falls, reducing rents. The fall in the price of imported grain reduces in Italy the abundance of labor and the scarcity of land: every agricultural pursuit becomes less intensive, saves labor, and reduces yields per unit of land.[7]

The fall in the price of imported grain should therefore have increased total consumption; it should have specifically benefited the working poor, who earned wages and consumed land-intensive subsistence goods, and hurt the landowners, who earned rents and consumed labor-intensive luxury goods and services.[8] These presumptive benefits for the economy in general and the working classes in particular are to be added to those that stemmed from the rise in the inflow of foreign capital. There are

---

[6] G. Toniolo, *An Economic History of Liberal Italy, 1850–1918*, London 1990 (translation of Id., *Storia economica dell'Italia liberale 1850–1918*, Bologna 1988), p. 73; compare S. Fenoaltea, "Politica doganale, sviluppo industriale, emigrazione: verso una riconsiderazione del dazio sul grano," *Rivista di storia economica* 10 (1993), p. 68.

[7] Below, Appendix 2, § 2, § 3.

[8] Various complications can be added, but they change little. Renters, for example, absorb the fall in the rental value of the land for the duration of the contract; a landowning peasant is also a worker, and a poor consumer, and thus both gains and loses; and so on.

no visible contrary, harmful developments: the general crisis and the hardships of the poor which the literature read into the 1880s would need to be explained.

2. The construction of the "crisis"

In fact, nothing suggests that the general crisis of the 1880s actually occurred.

In the press of the time economists like Vilfredo Pareto and Luigi Einaudi remember the 1880s as a period of prosperity; their tone is not polemical, their readers share their memories. In their analyses, in the splendid empirical survey produced in the early 1900s by Guido Sensini, the fall in the price of imported grain hurt grain-growing, but benefited consumers and workers, industry and specialized agriculture, on balance the economy as a whole; the downturn that will lead to the general crisis of the early 1890s dates from 1887, and it is attributable at least in part to the increase in Italy's tariffs.[9]

Between the wars the "general prosperity" of the Depretis years was still remembered, it was beyond question.[10] But this optimistic view of that period disappeared from the later literature, to be replaced by the pessimistic view that saw a crisis in all agriculture, in the entire economy. In this new interpretation the crisis that would reach its nadir in the early 1890s began a decade earlier: investment and industrial production grew until 1887, but in an economy that was already sliding towards the abyss, and that agricultural protection would at least partly restore.

This shift in the literature seems to date from the post-war years: one sees it in the writings of Gino Luzzatto and Rosario Romeo. Luzzatto too recalls the "general prosperity" of the Depretis years, but polemically dismisses it as not real, merely "apparent." Rather, those years were

---

[9] These authors also note the variations in capital imports, and their effect on aggregate resource supply, but do not appear to consider them of major importance (and they of course ignore the international Kuznets cycle, identified only by more recent statistical reconstructions, above, ch. 2, § 2): V. Pareto, *Lettres d'Italie. A cura di Gabriele De Rosa*, Rome 1973, pp. 35, 52; L. Einaudi, *Cronache economiche e politiche di un trentennio*, 8 vols., Turin 1959–66, vol. 1, pp. 64, 86, 102, 135, 169–170; G. Sensini, *Le variazioni dello stato economico dell'Italia nell'ultimo trentennio del secolo XIX*, Rome 1904, pp. 23, 89–90, 145, 161, 320. For Bonaldo Stringher, too, the downturn was in the late 1880s, but it was not due to the tariff increase, of which he approved; see B. Stringher, "Il commercio con l'estero e il corso dei cambi," *Nuova Antologia di Scienze, Lettere ed Arti*, serie III, 54 (1894), pp. 23–25.

[10] B. Croce, *Storia d'Italia dal 1871 al 1915*, 9th ed., Bari 1967 (1927), pp. 46, 173.

characterized by the "agrarian crisis" which was "determined... by the fall in world prices" and "aggravated... by the competition of American grain": "agriculture remained the foundation of the economy," and "the ever worse condition of the rural classes" could only cause "an economic malaise... that worsened from year to year."[11]

Romeo took a different path: he came to the general crisis not with logic but against logic, in conflict not with the earlier literature but with himself. In the 1880s Romeo sees, obviously, the progress of industry; but he also sees the progress of specialized agriculture, and considers the "agrarian crisis," of the entire sector, an invention of the protectionist lobby. But he is faced with the Istat series, newly published and apparently authoritative, that register in the 1880s levels of per-capita food and total consumption lower than at any other time. In fact, as noted, Istat itself recognized the utter unreliability of the agricultural-output data that underlie their consumption figures, but in a separate and less accessible source, which Romeo cites but seems not to have examined in any depth. Romeo accepts the decline in per-capita consumption he sees in the data with obvious reluctance, he even imagines a demographic spurt to minimize its implications for aggregate growth; but in the end he accepts it, and also describes the 1880s as a decade of overall crisis.[12]

The ascendancy of the Istat series lasted perhaps a decade. Around 1970, scholars were warned that in the 1880s and 1890s those series badly underestimated cereal production and consumption, and with these all higher-level aggregates; around 1980, Giovanni Federico devoted one of his earliest contributions to the weaknesses of the underlying output data, and began the long march that would lead to their revision; by 1990, and in view of its coming centenary, the Bank of Italy sponsored the revision of the historical national accounts.[13]

The literature would nonetheless adhere to the pessimistic interpretation, without Romeo's doubts and qualms. For Valerio Castronovo, for example, in those years "the hardships of agricultural day-laborers increased, swarms of the unemployed invaded the cities looking for

---

[11] G. Luzzatto, *L'economia italiana dal 1861 al 1894*, Turin 1968 (Milan 1963), pp. 168–173 (translations by the present author): "the agrarian crisis" is the subtitle (p. 168), the other quoted phrases are taken, not in order, from p. 169. Luzzatto's volume was published after Romeo's, but it had a long gestation (pp. 3–5), and the very sources it is based on confirm that it was in fact written earlier.

[12] R. Romeo, *Risorgimento e capitalismo*, 3[d] ed., Rome-Bari 1998 (Bari 1959), pp. 103, 154–156, and above, ch. 1, § 3.

[13] Above, ch. 1, § 5, § 9.

work"; for Guido Pescosolido, "the crisis of the grain-producing sector...generated a serious decline in per-capita consumption"; for Vera Zamagni, "the persistence of the agricultural crisis eventually led to a general economic crisis, as agriculture was still the basis of the economy, and this led to both social unrest and emigration" (and to "the introduction of protectionist measures" in 1887).[14] Gianni Toniolo differed only in part: he noted that the fall in grain prices should have pushed Italy further into more labor-intensive crops (entirely to the benefit of its working masses), but this long-run tendency would not have prevented "negative effects...in the medium term," and specifically the tragedy of "an overall fall in per capita food consumption...in an economy already close to subsistence level."[15]

Historians knew that the early production data are few and unreliable, that the Istat series are not to be trusted; they knew their interpretation of the period could not rely simply on the extant figures, that these were themselves in need of revision on the basis of reasonable hypotheses. In the recent literature it is the pessimistic interpretation of the 1880s which itself supports the Istat series: if these do not prove at least they illustrate, they capture the essential features of a general crisis, and of a reduction in living standards, already established by a process of deduction.[16] Romeo yielded to the "data," the historians of the succeeding generation support them with syllogisms.

Toniolo's syllogism is not explicit; his would seem to be a macroeconomic argument, tied to balance-of-payments equilibrium, about which more below. The canonical syllogism of the "pessimists" is instead entirely clear: the fall in grain prices surely hurt cereal cultivation, *ergo* surely all agriculture, *ergo* surely the entire economy, then predominantly agricultural; emigration increased, *ergo* the working masses had surely

---

[14] V. Castronovo, *Storia economica d'Italia*, Turin 1995, p. 52, and Pescosolido, *Unità nazionale*, p. 201 (translations by the present author); V. Zamagni, *The Economic History of Italy, 1860–1990: Recovery after Decline*, Oxford 1993 (translation of Id., *Dalla periferia al centro: la seconda rinascita economica dell'Italia, 1861–1981*, Bologna 1990), pp. 62, 116.

[15] Toniolo, *An Economic History*, p. 74.

[16] Toniolo, for example, questions the time profile of the Istat series, and does not believe that per-capita output stagnated almost to the end of the century (ibid., p. 149); he fails to add that the very same distortion is present in the agricultural-output and food-consumption estimates cited to document the presumed decline in living standards in the 1880s (pp. 74, 161). Zamagni notes the "insecure foundations" of the Istat series, but considers them "broadly indicative" of actual developments (*The Economic History*, pp. 59–60).

been impoverished. Their logic is simple and seductive; it is Luzzatto's logic.

3. The inferences of the "pessimists"

In the "pessimistic" interpretation that dominates the post-war literature the Istat series and deductive logic support each other. The weakness of first was pointed out decades ago; the equal weakness of the second was pointed out altogether more recently, and that interpretation has finally been taken to task.[17]

The inferences of the "pessimists" do not survive analysis, they contradict common experience. The surge in emigration, in particular, does not prove that the workers' living standards declined. Emigration can increase for a host of other reasons, a rise in wages and employment abroad, a decline in the cost of movement; and in the 1880s this last can confidently be presumed, as the fall in grain prices in Europe's markets was due precisely to the fall in the cost of transportation from (and within) the overseas lands.[18] Italy's economic historians are also well aware that the second surge in emigration came precisely in the Giolitti years, when the economy's prosperity is neither disputable nor disputed; but this is not considered relevant, perhaps because of the *forma mentis* of the historian, who seeks individual, particular explanations for every single event.

Nor do the "pessimists" consider the incongruity of what they see in the 1880s. The opposite paths of consumption and investment, for example, are consistent with the neoclassical model, but only because in that utopia general crises are ruled out and full employment is always maintained. The Great Depression convinced even mainstream economists that real-world economies are not so stable: the intuition at the root of the keynesian

---

[17] S. Fenoaltea, "Production and Consumption in Post-Unification Italy: New Evidence, New Conjectures," *Rivista di storia economica* 18 (2002), pp. 251–298, summarized in what follows; it adds little to what was already in Sensini, *Le variazioni*. That article does not consider the hypothesis of a macroeconomic crisis, but as will be seen below it provides all the evidence needed to discard it.

[18] The available data suggest that the increase in migration was entirely in its transoceanic component, and point to the increasing attractiveness of New-World destinations; Istat (Istituto centrale di statistica), *Sommario di statistiche storiche italiane, 1861–1955*, Rome 1958, p. 65. Their increasing attractiveness may have been absolute (because of falling transport costs, the Kuznets upswing), or even merely relative, should the "agrarian crisis" have affected the Old World in its entirety; by themselves, these data prove nothing.

revolution is precisely that consumption tends to vary not in opposition to investment, stabilizing aggregate output and employment, but in parallel, driven by the income generated by investment itself. A fall in consumption as investment rose would be an exception to macroeconomic norms, it cannot be taken for granted.

The instability of market economies stems from self-reinforcing cyclical movements: prosperity improves expectations, further boosting investment and incomes, depression leads to pessimism that further reduces investment and sends the economy spiraling downward. If it is hardly plausible that consumption fell as investment increased, it is equally unlikely that investment increased as consumption fell and the economy slid into a crisis: nothing would explain the optimism of (domestic and foreign) entrepreneurs, the euphoria that generated the real-estate bubble.

There is a further incongruity within the Istat series, which register a decline in total consumption only as a balance between a decline in food consumption and a smaller *increase* in non-food consumption. The Istat series are neither transparent nor authoritative, but of the two the weaker is without a doubt the food-consumption series: it is based directly on the very poor agricultural production estimates of the day, while non-food consumption is based at least in part on more reliable evidence, on industrial production and foreign trade.[19]

The actual path of some consumption series will be investigated below; for the moment the point is simply that food is a primary good, and as income falls the consumption of relative luxuries is sacrificed before that of necessities. The decline of food consumption accompanied not by an even larger decline, but by an actual increase, in non-food consumption would be an exception to microeconomic norms, it too cannot be taken for granted.[20]

The "pessimists" also forget our own experience with the OPEC-imposed rise in the price of crude oil. That too marked a sudden change in the relative price of a basic good, an imported good. It had widespread, differentiated effects on our economies: all sorts of markets reached new equilibria, and resources shifted from the sectors that suffered to those that gained. Overall, however, for us importers the rise in the price of

---

[19] Istat (Istituto centrale di statistica), *Indagine statistica sullo sviluppo del reddito nazionale dell'Italia dal 1861 al 1956*, Annali di statistica, serie VIII, vol. 9, Rome 1957, pp. 80–82, 183–184.

[20] It is not impossible, of course, and might be explained by a massive redistribution of income in favor of the better off; but this too is returned to below.

oil marked a serious deterioration of our terms of trade, a reduction in our capacity to consume, a clear loss of welfare. The "pessimists" attribute all these negative effects to the contrary impulse, to the *reduction* in the price of a basic import; this too can hardly be taken for granted.

This is in fact the central flaw in the logic of the "pessimists." Had Italy been an *exporter* of grain, it would surely have suffered from a decline in its price, from the rise of new competitors: as it was surely hurt in early modern times when the development of manufacturing in northern Europe deprived it of its industrial leadership, or early in the last century when the extraction of sulphur in Louisiana deprived it of a centuries-old monopoly. Italy was largely agricultural, but its exports were the labor-intensive products of its specialized agriculture; grain is a typical land-intensive product, Italy logically imported it.[21]

The fall in the price of grain and of its substitutes surely hurt the producers of *those* goods: in the 1880s the crisis of the grain-growing sector can indeed be taken for granted. But – as recognized by Italy's economists of the day, and more recently by Toniolo – its *predictable* effects on other sectors and on the entire economy were surely positive; and to these benefits were added those of rising capital imports, of the resulting trade deficit which further increased the supply of resources and loosened the constraint on consumption.

The general crisis of Italy's agriculture and of its entire economy, the hardships of the working classes, the reduction in consumption cannot be established by deduction. The "pessimistic" interpretation can neither rest on the Istat series, nor validate them with its own logic: those series and that interpretation stand together like a house of cards, the entire structure collapses at the first breath of reason.

4. The path of consumption

The general crisis of the 1880s suggested by the Istat series and described by the recent literature seems entirely invented. Reliable data are scarce, if they were not the path of the economy over that decade would not be disputed; but such as they are they clearly support the opinion of the day, the assertion of the older literature, that the 1880s were a decade of prosperity.

---

[21] Below, Appendix 2, § 2.

A first indication to this effect comes from those few elements of food consumption for which documentation is actually available, because the goods were themselves taxed, or obtained from raw materials that were entirely imported: beer, coffee, and sugar. Table 3.01 reports their average per-capita consumption, by decade; for coffee and sugar it also reports consumer prices in both nominal and real terms (that is, deflated by a cost of living index about which more below), and the real expenditure calculated as physical consumption times the corresponding real price.[22]

In the 1880s per-capita physical consumption, real prices, and real expenditure all reach new *highs*: the increase in demand is undeniable, and points to an increase in consumers' real incomes. Similar gains appear, as expected, from the 1880s to the early 1900s (and also from the 1860s to the 1870s). The crisis is clearly in the 1890s alone, when per-capita consumption falls: the consumption of these goods is notoriously price-inelastic, and the decline in demand is revealed by the relative stability of real expenditure as real prices rose.[23]

At the time, to be sure, the per-capita consumption of beer, coffee, and sugar was extremely limited, and these changes in demand may well refer to consumers who were relatively well off. The reliable food-consumption series prove very little, but what little they prove certainly sits poorly with the "pessimistic" interpretation.

The more significant series, from this point of view, are the relatively new series that track the per-capita consumption of (non-luxury) textile fibers, of cotton and of wool. Table 3.01 reports these as well, by decade and by year; it also reports the (nominal and real) wholesale prices of the raw fibers, and the corresponding real expenditure. The reported prices are treated as indices of the (unavailable) retail prices of the finished goods; the real expenditure series are therefore also mere indices, that can be compared over time but not across fibers.[24]

---

[22] The consumption and nominal price series are as reported by Istat; for further details, and the annual series, see Fenoaltea, "Production and Consumption," pp. 258–263. Beer prices are unknown. The annual series are not reported here, as they need in any case to be smoothed to eliminate what appear to be wild swings in inventories induced by announced changes in tariffs.

[23] With a given price-inelastic demand curve (and given consumer incomes), expenditure increases as the price rises; if the price rises, expenditure fails to increase only if the demand curve has itself shifted, and lower quantities than before are demanded at every price.

[24] For further details on the sources and methods see Fenoaltea, "Production and Consumption," pp. 263–268.

Per-capita fiber consumption increased from decade to decade. The annual series show that consumption growth was slow and relatively regular, but exceptionally rapid in two sub-periods: between 1905 and 1908, when the growth of the Giolitti years was most intense, and again in the 1880s (Figure 3.01). Nominal and real prices varied significantly; real expenditure followed a sharp cycle, reaching levels in the 1880s and again in the early 1900s well above those of the 1870s and 1890s.[25] In the 1880s, as in the Giolitti years, the consumption of ordinary consumer goods increased; nothing suggests a decline in the consumption of basic necessities, in aggregate consumption.

In the 1880s (and 1890s) the consumption of basic necessities is not documented. That consumption could have fallen, even as that of other goods increased, in the presence of a massive redistribution of income that further impoverished the already poor. But not even this possibility

TABLE 3.01. *Per-capita consumption of selected foods and textiles*

A. food consumption: beer, coffee, and sugar (annual averages, by decade)

	(1)	(2)	(3)	(4)	(5)	(6)	(7)	(8)	(9)
		per-capita consumption (kgs)			retail prices (lire/kg)			real per-capita spending (lire)	
				(nominal)		(deflated)			
	beer[a]	coffee	sugar	coffee	sugar	coffee	sugar	coffee	sugar
1861–70	.24	.44	2.31	2.17	1.33	2.37	1.46	1.04	3.35
1871–80	.46	.47	2.73	3.50	1.43	3.09	1.26	1.44	3.43
1881–90	.75	.51	2.80	3.42	1.51	3.67	1.61	1.85	4.49
1891–00	.56	.42	2.48	4.19	1.55	4.76	1.76	1.99	4.36
1901–10	1.30	.59	3.42	3.35	1.47	3.72	1.64	2.19	5.58

B. textile consumption: cotton and wool[b] (annual averages, by decade)

	(1)	(2)	(3)	(4)	(5)	(6)	(7)	(8)
	per-capita fiber consumption (kgs)			wholesale fiber prices (lire/kg)			real per-capita spending (lire)	
			(nominal)		(deflated)			
	cotton	wool	cotton	wool	cotton	wool	cotton	wool
1861–70	1.37	1.63	3.13	2.50	3.47	2.71	4.54	4.42
1871–80	1.67	1.70	2.02	2.93	1.78	2.59	2.96	4.40
1881–90	2.51	2.13	1.53	2.31	1.62	2.46	4.07	5.23
1891–00	3.01	2.24	1.02	1.77	1.16	2.01	3.46	4.51
1901–10	3.81	2.66	1.27	1.71	1.41	1.90	5.40	5.05

[25] The method by which these estimates are obtained clearly overstates real expenditure on cotton in the 1860s. The "cotton famine" due to the American Civil War raised the price of the raw fiber and reduced value added in its processing; the ratio of the price of the finished good to that of the raw fiber, which the calculations consider constant, was in fact exceptionally low.

TABLE 3.01 *(continued)*

C. textile consumption: cotton and wool[b]

	(1)	(2)	(3)	(4)	(5)	(6)	(7)	(8)
	per-capita fiber consumption (kgs)		wholesale fiber prices (lire/kg)				real per-capita spending (lire)	
			(nominal)		(deflated)			
	cotton	wool	cotton	wool	cotton	wool	cotton	wool
1861	1.65	1.53	1.69	2.71	1.82	2.92	3.01	4.48
1862	1.18	1.53	3.41	2.44	3.78	2.70	4.46	4.14
1863	1.07	1.53	4.59	2.26	5.21	2.57	5.57	3.94
1864	1.10	1.62	5.43	2.20	6.48	2.62	7.16	4.24
1865	1.42	1.67	3.75	2.05	4.38	2.40	6.20	4.01
1866	1.39	1.64	3.25	2.33	3.55	2.54	4.94	4.18
1867	1.44	1.76	2.31	2.65	2.35	2.70	3.38	4.74
1868	1.46	1.62	2.27	2.75	2.37	2.86	3.45	4.63
1869	1.62	1.73	2.49	2.70	2.66	2.89	4.30	5.00
1870	1.43	1.63	2.05	2.89	2.09	2.95	2.99	4.81
1871	1.44	1.57	2.18	2.97	1.96	2.67	2.82	4.20
1872	1.39	1.63	2.22	2.97	1.88	2.51	2.62	4.09
1873	1.72	1.69	2.33	2.86	1.88	2.30	3.23	3.88
1874	1.86	1.66	2.42	3.11	2.10	2.70	3.91	4.48
1875	1.86	1.74	1.95	2.80	1.77	2.54	3.29	4.43
1876	1.79	1.80	1.81	2.69	1.73	2.56	3.09	4.61
1877	1.78	1.80	1.84	2.83	1.66	2.56	2.96	4.60
1878	1.66	1.71	1.73	2.85	1.51	2.49	2.51	4.25
1879	1.55	1.68	1.80	3.07	1.57	2.69	2.45	4.54
1880	1.63	1.73	1.87	3.15	1.70	2.86	2.77	4.95
1881	2.12	1.92	1.68	2.81	1.55	2.59	3.28	4.97
1882	2.25	1.84	1.80	2.70	1.74	2.61	3.91	4.79
1883	2.50	1.91	1.46	2.26	1.47	2.28	3.66	4.36
1884	2.40	2.11	1.57	2.19	1.69	2.37	4.07	5.01
1885	2.61	2.23	1.49	2.23	1.68	2.52	4.38	5.62
1886	2.57	2.22	1.31	2.23	1.51	2.58	3.89	5.73
1887	2.55	2.37	1.38	2.23	1.59	2.57	4.06	6.09
1888	2.54	2.21	1.45	2.10	1.64	2.37	4.15	5.24
1889	2.64	2.21	1.54	2.19	1.68	2.39	4.45	5.29
1890	2.89	2.25	1.59	2.20	1.69	2.34	4.90	5.26
1891	2.84	2.22	1.34	2.14	1.42	2.28	4.04	5.07
1892	2.64	2.18	1.09	1.90	1.19	2.07	3.15	4.52
1893	2.66	2.19	1.05	1.79	1.21	2.08	3.22	4.56
1894	2.90	2.16	.97	1.75	1.14	2.06	3.30	4.45
1895	3.20	2.33	.93	1.65	1.09	1.94	3.49	4.52
1896	3.11	2.30	.99	1.80	1.12	2.05	3.48	4.71
1897	3.21	2.33	.87	1.62	.99	1.84	3.18	4.29
1898	3.17	2.18	.83	1.55	.95	1.77	3.02	3.87
1899	3.22	2.29	.95	1.77	1.08	2.03	3.49	4.65
1900	3.11	2.24	1.18	1.75	1.36	2.01	4.21	4.50
1901	2.96	2.41	1.14	1.46	1.31	1.67	3.87	4.03
1902	3.35	2.54	1.09	1.44	1.24	1.63	4.15	4.16
1903	3.45	2.46	1.25	1.57	1.43	1.81	4.94	4.45
1904	3.35	2.47	1.36	1.48	1.54	1.66	5.15	4.11
1905	3.43	2.39	1.14	1.83	1.30	2.07	4.44	4.96
1906	3.72	2.54	1.34	2.04	1.51	2.29	5.62	5.83
1907	4.60	2.73	1.35	2.00	1.52	2.24	6.98	6.12
1908	5.05	3.01	1.30	1.95	1.41	2.11	7.10	6.36
1909	4.43	3.05	1.33	1.88	1.39	1.97	6.17	6.01
1910	3.77	3.00	1.41	1.45	1.47	1.51	5.53	4.51
1911	3.36	2.94	1.46	1.87	1.48	1.90	4.99	5.59
1912	4.26	3.10	1.51	2.12	1.51	2.12	6.46	6.58
1913	3.76	3.00	1.56	2.25	1.56	2.25	5.89	6.74

[a] liters.

[b] greasy wool.

Source: S. Fenoaltea, "Production and Consumption in Post-Unification Italy: New Evidence, New Conjectures," *Rivista di storia economica* 18 (2002), pp. 261, 264–265, 267.

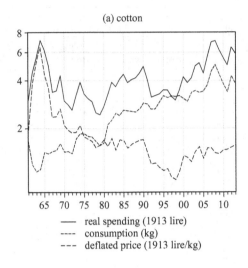

(a) cotton

— real spending (1913 lire)
---- consumption (kg)
--- deflated price (1913 lire/kg)

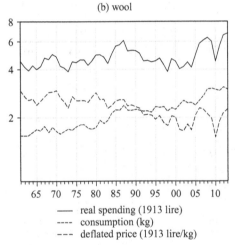

(b) wool

— real spending (1913 lire)
---- consumption (kg)
--- deflated price (1913 lire/kg)

Source: Table 3.01.

FIGURE 3.01. *Per-capita consumption of cotton and wool*

can rescue the "pessimists," for there is no evidence that inequality and poverty increased. The Istat data on the heights of army recruits show a long-term increase presumably tied to nutritional and epidemiological improvements; they show no increase in the *dispersion* of heights for the recruits born in the twenty years from 1875 to 1895, the coefficient of variation is in fact marginally reduced.[26] Giovanni Vecchi has in turn reconstructed a broad sample of family budgets from Unification on; this independent evidence points in the 1880s not to an increase but to a *reduction* in inequality.[27]

If inequality did not increase, if the distribution of income remained stable or improved, the increase in the consumption of ordinary goods rules out a decline in the consumption of basic necessities. In the 1880s Italians spent more to clothe themselves; they may have spent less to feed themselves, thanks to the fall in the price of grain, but they cannot have reduced their levels of nutrition, there cannot have been "an overall fall in per capita food consumption... in an economy already close to subsistence level."

5. The path of nominal wages

The "pessimistic" position is in any case annihilated by the evidence on wages.

The wage series from 1862 to 1903 published at the time by Dirstat shows continuous growth in their nominal level (and, in the early 1880s, a sixty-percent increase in their purchasing power measured in wheat). The "pessimists" could ignore it: the underlying sample was of workers in the textile industries that had received tariff protection, the rise may have been in the return to their "human capital," to their specialized skills, rather than to their "labor."[28]

---

[26] The *mean* can vary in the short to medium run because of an epidemiological onslaught that affects all social classes, but the well off are immune to the cyclical declines in consumption that affect the poor; the dispersion of the data is accordingly the better measure of cyclical movements. A reduction in the avoidance of military service in the regions with lower average heights would lower the heights' average, but increase their dispersion; it is not implausible over the early decades, and especially in war-time (as suggested by the figures for those born between 1897 and 1900). See Fenoaltea, "Production and Consumption," pp. 277–278; also G. Federico, "Heights, Calories and Welfare: A New Perspective on Italian Industrialization, 1854–1913," *Economics and Human Biology* 1 (2003), pp. 289–308.

[27] G. Vecchi, "I bilanci familiari in Italia: 1860–1960," *Rivista di storia economica* 11 (1994), pp. 9–95; N. Rossi, G. Toniolo and G. Vecchi, "Is the Kuznets Curve Still Alive? Evidence from Italian Household Budgets, 1881–1961," *Journal of Economic History* 61 (2001), p. 918.

[28] Dirstat (Direzione generale della statistica), *Annuario statistico italiano 1887–1888*, p. 436, *1904*, p. 360. The more recent construction-wage series in S. Fenoaltea, "Public Works Construction in Italy, 1861–1913," *Rivista di storia economica* 3 (1986), International Issue, pp. 18–19, may similarly reflect only the high earnings of specialized

They cannot however ignore the path of the wages of *unskilled* workers, now also available.[29] The new series for nominal wages in industry (Table 3.02) is obtained from data on the remuneration of manual laborers in a variety of industries and locations, chained and weighted to eliminate composition effects. These wages too increase over the early decades, with a peak growth rate between 1884 and 1888; they slip back in the 1890s only to recover and reach new highs after the turn of the century (Figure 3.02).

Since manual labor in industry was the practical alternative to agricultural labor, this first series should approximate the movements of agricultural wages as well; in fact, in Italy's then predominantly agricultural economy, it was presumably the going rate for agricultural day laborers that determined the earnings of unskilled workers in industry.

Direct evidence on the wages of agricultural day laborers is very scanty. The present series (Table 3.02) incorporates data for all Italy only from 1905; in 1881–1904 it tracks wages only in Lombardy; and before then it is estimated from the industrial series, and contains no additional evidence whatsoever. Such as they are, these data suggest that the wages of unskilled workers in agriculture and in industry moved very similarly (Figure 3.02). Between 1881 and 1913 the simple correlation between the two series exceeds 0.99; the only divergence of any note appears right in the early 1880s, when only (Lombard) farm wages dipped slightly (1882–84), but then these too rose smartly and reached new highs right up to 1888.

The general crisis of the 1880s never happened. It might have happened, as Toniolo suggested, for macroeconomic reasons. The fall in grain prices tended to raise real wages, but with the lira then convertible it might have required a decline in Italy's price level obtainable only with a (smaller) decline in nominal wages; with imperfectly flexible wages their reduction might have necessitated unemployment, a decline in production that might in turn adversely affect expectations and investment, and thus push the economy into depression. There are many "might haves" here – it is particularly hard to believe that wages were inflexible, since those of

---

workers during the building boom. The silk-spinning wage series constructed by Giovanni Federico may similarly be unrepresentative, and in any case it follows a trend he imposed on the data; see G. Federico, *Il filo d'oro. L'industria mondiale della seta dalla restaurazione alla grande crisi*, Venice 1994, pp. 375–377, 524–525, and, for further discussion, Fenoaltea, "Production and Consumption," pp. 268–272, 288.

[29] For a description of its derivation see Fenoaltea, "Production and Consumption," pp. 272–276, 286–293.

TABLE 3.02. *Wages of unskilled workers (lire/day)*

	(1) industrial wages	(2)	(3) agricultural wages[a]	(4)
	nominal	real[b]	nominal	real[b]
1861	1.377	1.486	1.194	1.288
1862	1.385	1.536	1.198	1.328
1863	1.399	1.588	1.207	1.370
1864	1.411	1.682	1.214	1.448
1865	1.427	1.666	1.226	1.430
1866	1.447	1.583	1.240	1.356
1867	1.469	1.495	1.255	1.277
1868	1.484	1.544	1.265	1.316
1869	1.502	1.607	1.277	1.366
1870	1.520	1.552	1.290	1.316
1871	1.544	1.389	1.306	1.176
1872	1.565	1.323	1.321	1.117
1873	1.567	1.264	1.319	1.064
1874	1.568	1.358	1.317	1.140
1875	1.571	1.426	1.316	1.195
1876	1.593	1.520	1.332	1.270
1877	1.612	1.457	1.344	1.215
1878	1.625	1.420	1.351	1.181
1879	1.638	1.436	1.359	1.191
1880	1.649	1.497	1.365	1.239
1881	1.662	1.532	1.372	1.264
1882	1.675	1.618	1.379	1.332
1883	1.689	1.703	1.356	1.367
1884	1.715	1.854	1.349	1.458
1885	1.749	1.974	1.366	1.542
1886	1.814	2.094	1.393	1.607
1887	1.863	2.142	1.418	1.631
1888	1.899	2.144	1.440	1.626
1889	1.909	2.087	1.442	1.577
1890	1.888	2.011	1.441	1.535
1891	1.879	2.000	1.421	1.512
1892	1.866	2.039	1.420	1.551
1893	1.869	2.168	1.415	1.640
1894	1.860	2.193	1.416	1.670
1895	1.843	2.162	1.418	1.664
1896	1.846	2.095	1.435	1.630
1897	1.879	2.138	1.466	1.668
1898	1.946	2.225	1.478	1.690
1899	2.026	2.321	1.502	1.721
1900	2.090	2.400	1.537	1.765
1901	2.126	2.436	1.619	1.855
1902	2.161	2.455	1.653	1.878
1903	2.227	2.561	1.682	1.934
1904	2.302	2.593	1.667	1.878
1905	2.387	2.707	1.730	1.962
1906	2.468	2.780	1.800	2.028
1907	2.561	2.870	1.900	2.130
1908	2.667	2.885	2.000	2.163
1909	2.751	2.888	2.033	2.134
1910	2.838	2.944	2.100	2.179
1911	2.923	2.966	2.200	2.233
1912	3.006	3.016	2.267	2.274
1913	3.074	3.074	2.333	2.333

[a] hourly wages, multiplied by 10.

[b] at 1913 prices.

Source: S. Fenoaltea, "Production and Consumption in Post-Unification Italy: New Evidence, New Conjectures," *Rivista di storia economica* 18 (2002), pp. 273–274.

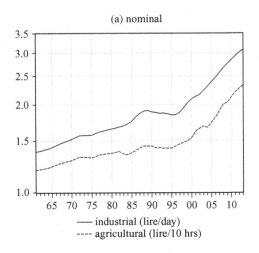

(a) nominal

—— industrial (lire/day)
---- agricultural (lire/10 hrs)

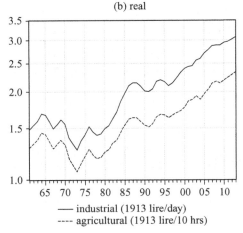

(b) real

—— industrial (1913 lire/day)
---- agricultural (1913 lire/10 hrs)

Source: Table 3.02.

FIGURE 3.02. *Wages of unskilled workers*

farm laborers varied from day to day – but one need not go beyond the first: the decline in the price level was small enough to be absorbed by the rise in real wages, and far from falling nominal wages actually rose faster than before.[30]

---

[30] Both the fall in grain prices and the rise in capital imports tended to raise real wages; but where the former tended to reduce nominal wages and prices, the latter had the opposite effect. The Istat wholesale price index (*Sommario*, p. 172) falls sharply in the 1880s, but it is dominated by traded goods, and largely ignores the goods the relative price of which tended to increase (above, ch. 2, § 5).

Prices fell, but wages rose, even for unskilled laborers. This is enough to prove that swarms of the unemployed never invaded the cities looking for work, that the "agrarian crisis" was indeed an invention of the protectionist lobby, that there was no general crisis in the 1880s.[31] There is no evidence, in the 1880s, of a depression; everything points to a rise in the living standards of the masses, to an increase in consumption as well as investment, to an improvement in the economy as a whole.

6. The path of real wages, consumption, and income

The estimates of real wages (and of the real prices and expenditure discussed above) are obtained through deflation by a cost of living index.

The deflator is not the Istat cost of living index, but a new index obtained by combining that index with a separate index, also constructed from Istat data, of the cost of bread, of wheat flour, and of corn flour (Table 3.03 and Figure 3.03).[32] The Istat index apparently includes the price of bread, but not of flour, and thus neglects inferior grains.[33] Moreover, the weight of these basic foods in the Istat index is so slight that the cost of living in 1874 was supposedly only 6.5 percentage points higher than in 1913, while bread then cost over 30 percent more, and bread and flour together over 50 percent more: the Istat index may be representative for the better off, certainly not for the masses that could meet little more than their basic food needs.[34] The new index thus includes the Istat index, but increases the weight of bread, and adds wheat and corn flour. It should better capture the cost of living of the laboring poor;

[31] The wage increases in northern agriculture are in fact noted by Pescosolido, *Unità nazionale*, p. 199. He sees them as an increase in costs for the farms already hurt by the decline in product prices; he does not realize that wages would rise only if the demand for labor actually increased, in agriculture (contrary to the thesis of the "agrarian crisis"), or at least in the economy at large (contrary to the thesis of the *general* crisis).

[32] The component series are from Istat, *Sommario*, pp. 172 (cost of living), 182 (wholesale prices of flour), and 196 (retail price of bread). The cost-of-bread-and-flour index is a simple average of the indices of the prices of wheat flour, corn flour (with a double weight), and bread. The new cost of living index is itself a three-year moving average of that index (with a double weight) and the Istat index, with the final series rescaled to one in 1913. For further details see Fenoaltea, "Production and Consumption," pp. 281–286.

[33] If the Istat index is imagined to be an average of a "cereal" index and an index for everything else, this second index can be obtained as a residual; it displays an absurd time path if the "cereal" index includes flour, but not if it includes bread alone.

[34] Food's share of consumption notoriously declines, over time and across social groups, with rising incomes; Italy was a poor country, and food represented more than half of total consumption even in the mid-twentieth century (Istat, *Sommario*, p. 220).

TABLE 3.03. *Cost of living indices (1913 = 1.000)*

	(1)	(2)	(3)	(4)	(5)	(6)
		Istat indices			bread	new
	cost		prices		and flour	cost of
	of	wheat	corn		price	living
	living	flour	flour	bread	index	index
1861	.820	.999	.989	.976	.988	.927
1862	.825	1.078	1.046	.927	1.024	.902
1863	.801	.891	.882	.878	.883	.881
1864	.779	.924	.926	.878	.913	.839
1865	.766	.830	.902	.805	.860	.857
1866	.774	.878	1.071	.902	.981	.914
1867	.793	1.237	1.206	1.024	1.168	.983
1868	.825	1.167	1.140	1.122	1.142	.961
1869	.830	.869	.787	.976	.855	.935
1870	.842	1.064	1.016	1.000	1.024	.980
1871	.868	1.190	1.508	1.098	1.326	1.111
1872	.981	1.284	1.508	1.220	1.380	1.183
1873	1.040	1.400	1.174	1.268	1.254	1.240
1874	1.065	1.349	1.639	1.317	1.486	1.155
1875	.912	.952	1.061	1.024	1.025	1.102
1876	.965	1.018	1.032	1.122	1.051	1.049
1877	1.004	1.145	1.387	1.171	1.272	1.106
1878	.967	1.125	1.384	1.146	1.260	1.144
1879	.955	1.128	1.335	1.122	1.230	1.140
1880	.990	1.110	1.384	1.171	1.262	1.102
1881	.926	.992	1.186	1.049	1.103	1.085
1882	.904	.948	1.384	1.000	1.179	1.035
1883	.875	.846	1.285	.951	1.092	.992
1884	.858	.824	1.038	.854	.939	.925
1885	.877	.821	.939	.854	.888	.886
1886	.876	.823	.989	.854	.913	.867
1887	.874	.812	.840	.878	.843	.870
1888	.885	.838	.939	.878	.899	.885
1889	.900	.888	1.038	.927	.973	.914
1890	.932	.880	.989	.927	.946	.939
1891	.929	.962	1.030	.927	.987	.940
1892	.921	.869	1.010	.976	.966	.915
1893	.901	.756	.872	.902	.850	.862
1894	.897	.689	.765	.829	.762	.848
1895	.892	.788	1.009	.854	.915	.852
1896	.888	.856	.910	.829	.876	.881
1897	.886	.951	.893	.854	.898	.879
1898	.892	1.025	.835	.927	.905	.875
1899	.878	.918	.804	.927	.863	.873
1900	.882	.931	.855	.927	.892	.871
1901	.883	.949	.875	.902	.900	.873
1902	.877	.911	.851	.878	.873	.880
1903	.903	.876	.954	.878	.916	.870
1904	.914	.858	.830	.829	.837	.888
1905	.915	.905	1.004	.829	.936	.882
1906	.932	.898	.884	.829	.874	.888
1907	.976	.868	.804	.854	.832	.892
1908	.966	.955	.957	.854	.931	.925
1909	.939	1.071	1.062	.878	1.018	.953
1910	.965	.895	1.009	.951	.966	.964
1911	.989	.970	.969	.976	.971	.985
1912	.998	1.071	1.163	.951	1.087	.997
1913	1.000	1.000	1.000	1.000	1.000	1.000
1914	1.000	1.007	.970	.976	.981	

Source: S. Fenoaltea, "Production and Consumption in Post-Unification Italy: New Evidence, New Conjectures," *Rivista di storia economica* 18 (2002), pp. 282–283.

(a) bread and flour price index and Istat cost
of living index (1913 = 1)

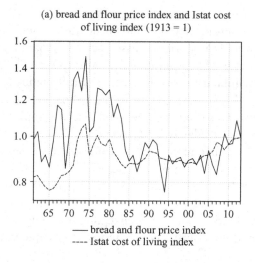

—— bread and flour price index
---- Istat cost of living index

(b) alternative cost of living indices (1913 = 1)

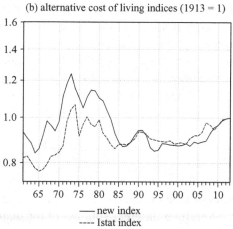

—— new index
---- Istat index

Source: Table 3.03.

FIGURE 3.03. *Cost of living indices*

next to the Istat index, in the 1880s it registers a greater decline in living
costs.

The nominal wages of unskilled workers increased in the 1880s, and
even more in the Giolitti years; but the cost of living rose in that later
period, whereas it fell sharply in the earlier. The deflated series point to the
1880s, and to the Giolitti years, as the two periods of significant real wage
growth (plus 40 percent or so, in the first as in the second); they dovetail
perfectly with the observed simultaneous increases in consumption, with
the cycle in investment and capital inflows.

The 1880s appear to have been prosperous: the paths of real and nominal wages confirm that unemployment was not increasing, that the purchasing power of the working classes increased, that the only plausible hypothesis is that food consumption then also rose.

The new preliminary series for the foodstuffs industry is based on the hypothesis of sustained growth in the 1880s, like that of the other consumer-goods industries; the new (and also preliminary) agricultural production series calculated by Giovanni Federico is similarly based on the hypothesis that in the 1880s consumption rose as real wages did.[35] These series do not prove the actual paths, as the preceding Istat series could not; but the new series illustrate paths that are plausible in light of the evidence and analysis now available, whereas the Istat series have per-capita food consumption changing in an implausible direction in the 1880s, and by absurd amounts in the 1880s and even more in the 1890s.[36]

These two criticisms must be distinguished, they differ in their origin and implications. The first specifically concerns the 1880s, the crisis or prosperity of those years; the second concerns the path of the economy over the longer run, the relative continuity or discontinuity of Italy's economic growth from Unification to the Great War. As seen above, indeed, the new series tend to eliminate the turn-of-the-century discontinuity evident in the Istat aggregates; but the latter correction does not depend on the "optimistic" interpretation of the 1880s.

This is apparent from the works and days. Scholars have known for forty years that the Istat series underestimate growth in the 1880s and '90s, that they overestimate subsequent growth: that much was evident from the absurdities of their grain-consumption series, and confirmed by Istat's own description (in a different volume) of the quality of the agricultural production data they relied on. The simple trend then imposed on grain consumption eliminated Istat's patently spurious variations, but did not impose an alternative cycle, as its path could not then be imagined (Figure 1.03). Today we can comfortably hypothesize a specific cycle, based on the revived "optimistic" interpretation of the 1880s; that much is permitted and justified by the time series reconstructed over the intervening decades.

---

[35] Above, ch. 1, § 8, § 9, ch. 1A, § 5, § 6; G. Federico, "Le nuove stime della produzione agricola italiana, 1860–1910: primi risultati e implicazioni," *Rivista di storia economica* 19 (2003), pp. 357–381.

[36] Above, ch. 1, § 5; S. Fenoaltea, "Decollo, ciclo, e intervento dello Stato," in A. Caracciolo, ed., *La formazione dell'Italia industriale*, Bari 1969, pp. 97–98; Federico, "Heights," pp. 294–296.

It is apparent, too, from the new time series themselves. The new production series for the foodstuffs industry incorporates "optimistic" cyclical consumption movements, but these are minimal; the series barely differs from a simple trend, it would change little even if one were to invert the cycle (Figure 1.04). The new agricultural production series compiled by Giovanni Federico also deviates from its trend, but those deviations are minor and short-lived (Figure 1.06); this series too would change little if one were to assume cyclical consumption movements opposite in sign but equally reasonable in magnitude. In both cases the significant correction to the Istat series reflects the elimination of the absurdly large fluctuations in the consumption of basic goods, its long decline in the 1880s and 1890s, its rapid recovery around the turn of the century; and this correction would remain even if the "pessimistic" interpretation of the 1880s should prove after all to have been right.

The major revision to the Istat series – the elimination of the sharp discontinuity in the aggregate growth rate – is correspondingly robust; it does not depend on an "optimistic" view of the 1880s. What does depend on that view is the comparatively minor further revision that captures the consumption cycle: the latter is as it is because it reflects that view, because the series were reconstructed by "optimists." But not even that is happenstance: if one digs into the evidence as one has to to reconstruct the time series, one becomes an "optimist."[37]

7. The evolution of the literature

The "pessimistic" interpretation of the 1880s dominates the literature of the last half-century; it displaced the earlier "optimistic" view that has now been revived. The controversy, long latent, is finally out in the open; and at this point the "optimists" can claim a resounding tactical success.[38] Their interpretation seems to have become the new orthodoxy, and even such leading "pessimists" as Gianni Toniolo and Vera Zamagni now declare themselves "optimists."[39]

---

[37] Not even economists are born "optimists," even if the crisis of the 1880s is not explained by our standard models: the problem can be resolved either by reconsidering the sources and showing that the facts have been misrepresented, or by reconsidering the models and enriching them to make sense of those puzzling facts.

[38] Strategic success is altogether less clear; see below, ch. 4, § 10.

[39] Both apostasies have their curious aspects. Toniolo, here the mirror image of Romeo, changed his mind when he saw the new estimates of agricultural output (the Federico series discussed above, ch. 1, § 9, ch. 1A, § 6). He describes his conversion as a reasonable response to the changing state of the evidence; what is odd is the suggestion that in the late 1980s the evidence consisted in substance of the Istat-Vitali series, to the exclusion of the

But there remain pockets of resistance. Elio Cerrito has sprung to the defense of the "pessimistic" interpretation in a long and complex work that defends "the data," cites the protectionist writings of the day, repeats that the prosperity of the 1880s was merely apparent.[40]

Cerrito maintains that the agricultural statistics of the day are internally consistent and, from a variety of points of view, quite reasonable; but he does not mention the resulting path of per-capita consumption, he does not meet the point that it is simply absurd. He asserts that the historical "data" are simply as such authoritative, surely more solid than recent "estimates"; but the "data" were only the first estimates produced at the time, and they can surely be improved with the aid of further information that was then not available or not considered.[41] The historical statistics are weak, the "pessimistic" interpretation can draw no strength from them.

Cerrito cites at length the 1886 report of Vittorio Ellena, a leading protectionist, praising his "extraordinary perspicacity," his "synthesis of the contradictory phenomena of those years." "Depression there is," concludes Ellena (with a polemical vigor that reflects the need to counter prevailing opinion); contradiction too, as Ellena himself recognizes that "consumption has grown much more rapidly than in the past thanks to the rise in wages and the fall in prices."[42] For an "optimist" that would be enough, any "depression" accompanied by so much progress can readily be granted.

Nothing daunted, Cerrito recasts Ellena's analysis: the increase in nominal and real wages did not make workers better off, the rise in consumption noted by the "optimists" results from redistribution.[43] In his own analysis nominal wages increase but the wage bill falls because employment is reduced by the widespread reduction in the intensity of cultivation;

---

long-available evidence that they underestimated output and consumption in the 1880s and 1890s. See G. Toniolo, "La storia economica dell'Italia liberale: una rivoluzione in atto," *Rivista di storia economica* 19 (2003), p. 253, and Id. in P. Bolchini *et al.*, "A proposito di Stefano Fenoaltea, *L'economia italiana dall'Unità alla Grande Guerra*, Bari-Roma, 2006," *Rivista di storia economica* 22 (2006), p. 368; also above, ch. 1, § 5, note 37. V. Zamagni in Bolchini *et al.*, "A proposito," p. 374, seems instead to deny that there was ever a "pessimistic" belief in a general crisis.

[40] E. Cerrito, "Depressioni. Caratteri e genesi della depressione di fine XIX secolo, più altre tre (e un'altra ancora)," *Studi storici* 44 (2003), pp. 927–1005.

[41] Ibid., pp. 934, 937–940; one recalls for example the silk-production "data," which imply long periods of negative consumption (above, ch. 1A, § 4).

[42] Ibid., pp. 963–964 (all translations by the present author).

[43] Ibid., p. 933. The evidence does not support the latter claim (above, § 4), but Cerrito does not confront it.

the growth of real wages is, as in the 1930s, a product and symptom of the depression.[44]

Cerrito appeals to Keynes, without noticing that in the keynesian analysis it is precisely this perverse increase in real wages as nominal wages fall less rapidly than prices that warrants monetary expansion to end their downward spiral; if nominal wages are being bid *upward* even as prices fall there is no depression, the rise in real wages is not a perverse result of unemployment.

Cerrito does not explain why nominal wages should rise despite a reduction in the demand for labor (and a fall in the price level); he simply notes that they rose even in the 1890s, when the economy was undeniably depressed. His source is the historical "data," the Dirstat wage series recalled above; he seems unaware that it refers primarily to skilled workers in the textile industries that had obtained tariff protection and were then rapidly expanding.[45]

Capitalist firms are not charities, they can hardly have increased wages to offset a reduction in their demand for labor. Logically, farmers reduced the intensity of *every* cultivation, the labor they used to grow any specific crop, because of the rise in wages induced by the aggregate *increase* in the demand for labor: this is the predictable effect if the economy reacts to the fall in the relative price of grain by shifting further into labor-intensive specialized agriculture.[46] The reduction in yields actually shows that the demand for labor was high, not that it was low: depression there wasn't.

Cerrito's long "depression" seems ultimately based, like Luzzatto's, on no more than the general fall in the price level, the downward phase of the Kondratieff cycle.[47] But falling prices do not imply crises, for over time productivity and real wages grow. As no harm is done by increases

---

[44] Ibid., pp. 974–976. Cerrito elsewhere ties the rise in real wages to emigration (p. 957): emigration then rapidly increased, but next to the size of the labor force its levels remained absolutely trivial. Still elsewhere Cerrito decries the elasticity of grain supply, which he is in fact concerned to document, as if the reduction in production were a pure loss rather than evidence that resources were being shifted to more rewarding pursuits in specialized agriculture, and industry, which were then rapidly expanding (pp. 942–943, 948).

[45] Ibid., p. 957, and above, § 5.

[46] Below, Appendix 2, § 3. The reduction in the intensity of cultivation and of average yields is the natural result of the reduction in the relative scarcity of land: the intensive and the extensive margins move together, and the abandonment of marginal lands is naturally accompanied by a decline, rather than a rise, in average yields. There is no reason to be surprised by the fall in wheat yields, and even less to invent a transfer out of wheat of the "best land" (Toniolo, *An Economic History*, p. 74); the assumption that agricultural land varies in quality and overall quantity is simply *praeter necessitatem*.

[47] Cerrito, "Depressioni," p. 969; above, § 2.

in nominal wages if prices do not rise, no harm is done by reductions in prices if nominal wages do not fall: one can call it deflation, but it is not depression, it does not imply unemployment and welfare losses. The real crisis, real in both the technical and the colloquial sense, came in the 1890s, not in the 1880s.

On the evidence, "optimism" is fully justified. Less so without the quotation marks, for the controversy is not over yet: the leading "pessimists" now declare themselves "optimists," but as will be seen forthwith the depth of their conversion is very much in doubt.

4

Protection and Migration

1. The evolution of trade policy and protection

Protection has a long history: the medieval city-states, the first nation-states protected their industry and trade with every means, including violence. In the nineteenth century England, the first industrial nation, became the first to embrace free trade. The Continent followed England and also liberalized trade both with unilateral tariff cuts and with treaties that guaranteed the contracting parties the lowest duties, those granted "the most favored nation" by other, even later, treaties.

This liberalization had its intellectual support in the new "political economy" that proclaimed the advantages of untrammeled exchange in external trade as in domestic markets. It had its practical, political support in the natural complementarity between England, the "workshop of the world," and the still traditional, agricultural Continent.

That political support would disappear, on the Continent, after just a few decades. Continental industry grew, despite its increased exposure to English competition; it was always protectionist, and that lobby became progressively stronger. In the 1880s, with the growing competition of overseas agriculture and the collapse of grain prices in European markets, significant agricultural interests also became protectionist. England would not abandon free trade; on the Continent industry and cereal-growing joined forces to push through a wave of tariff increases, and by the end of the century protection was again the rule.

Italy followed these Continent-wide shifts. Cavour's Piedmont had taken part in the first liberalization of trade. The new Kingdom inherited its policy: the mild Piedmontese tariff was extended to the entire country (subjecting the long-protected manufactures of the South to the competition of foreign industry, even before that of the North), and duties were further reduced through a series of international treaties. Then came the return to protection: it was bitterly condemned by the academic economists of the day, whose political influence was negligible, and supported by interventionist "economists" who lacked analytical arguments and rejected academic abstractions in favor of a "pragmatic" approach.[1]

Italy reversed its course as early as 1878 with a tariff that protected industry, and in particular cotton goods and steel. Within a few years the protectionist lobby was joined by the grain-growers: the 1887 tariff sharply raised the industrial duties, and protected wheat as well. That protectionist alliance was not inspired by any particular ideology, rhetoric aside it simply pursued its private interests: grain-growers and cotton-manufacturers purchased machinery, fertilizer, and dyes, the protection granted the chemical and engineering industries remained negligible.

Similarly private interests inspired the formal or informal associations that opposed those tariffs; these represented not Italy's consumers or unskilled workers – the unorganized and politically voiceless masses – but other entrepreneurs in industry or agriculture. These typically lobbied for higher duties on what they sold, and lower duties on what they bought: a foregone reaction that nonetheless points to the redistributive, zero-sum aspects of the tariff game. Most telling is the opposition to protection voiced by Italy's exporters, and in particular by the silk interests, the producers of cocoons and thread, who accounted by themselves for a third and more of Italy's exports: not because of any academic abstraction, but because they knew that limitations on imports limited exports, *their* exports.[2]

The 1887 tariff defined an epoch. In the next few years only a few rates were retouched, albeit strongly. The duty on grain in particular was

---

[1] V. Zamagni, *The Economic History of Italy, 1860–1990: Recovery after Decline*, Oxford 1993 (translation of Id., *Dalla periferia al centro: la seconda rinascita economica dell'Italia, 1861–1981*, Bologna 1990), pp. 111–112. According to the Italian text (p. 148) this "pragmatic" school merely *expressed* the official view, and it did not in fact "inspire" public policy.

[2] Thus in more recent times Boeing Aircraft has opposed the protection of the American automobile industry. Even the ideological liberalism of the Manchester interests that spearheaded the repeal of the Corn Laws served the private interests of the cotton industry, and hurt those of other producers: see S. Fenoaltea, "Manchester, manchesteriano … dekwakoncoz?" in L. Cafagna and N. Crepax, eds., *Atti di intelligenza e sviluppo economico. Saggi per il bicentenario della nascita di Carlo Cattaneo*, Bologna 2001, pp. 500–511, and below, § 5.

raised further in 1888, in 1894, again in 1895. The tariff on sugar was also raised in steps to 1895, while further protection derived from the production tax that was levied at the legal rate on foreign sugar and at *de facto* lower rates on domestic sugar. The extraction of sugar from the domestic beet at last became profitable: over a handful of years around the turn of the century domestic beet cultivation and sugar-extraction boomed, imports fell to nothing, and – at the cost of a sugar price among the highest in the world – Italy became self-sufficient.[3]

In the Giolitti years tariffs remained practically unchanged. There were a few cuts, but they seem to be so much window-dressing: at least in the case of the duties on cotton goods the only reductions were to those that had no impact on market prices, because the good was not imported.[4] Protection nonetheless fell sharply, with unchanged tariff rates, for two reasons.

Italy's tariffs were then normally not *ad valorem*, but specific: the duty was defined not as a percentage of the good's value, but as so many lire per quintal or other physical unit.[5] A duty's effect depends however on the resulting percentage increase in the good's price, that is, on its *ad valorem* equivalent; the weight of a specific rate increases if the good's price falls, and vice versa. World prices rose until 1873, then fell into the mid-1890s, and then rose again: in the Giolitti years wholesale prices rose by a third, the price of wheat by half.[6]

A weak exchange rate also protects domestic production, as, like a duty, it raises the domestic price of foreign goods; toward the end of its

[3] Istat (Istituto centrale di statistica), *Sommario di statistiche storiche italiane, 1861–1955*, Rome 1958, pp. 108, 126; G. Federico and A. Tena, "Was Italy a Protectionist Country?", *European Review of Economic History*, 2 (1998), p. 81.

[4] S. Fenoaltea, "Product Heterogeneity, Trade and Protection: The Cotton Industry in Post-Unification Italy," in A. M. Falchero, A. Giuntini, G. Nigro and L. Segreto, eds., *La storia e l'economia. Miscellanea di studi in onore di Giorgio Mori*, vol. 1, Varese 2003, pp. 280–281. Giolitti himself opposed any reduction in the tariffs that mattered, including those on steel and on grain: see G. Carocci, *Giolitti e l'età giolittiana*, Turin 1961, pp. 19, 44–45, 52–54.

[5] The practice was aimed at facilitating collection, by avoiding controversies over the good's value; to tie the actual tariff to the good's value all the same, tariff rates took quality into account, using criteria that lent themselves to objective measurement but were at times highly complex. Cotton textiles, for example, were subject to duties per quintal that varied both with the cloth's weight, and with the number of threads it contained, per unit area; the tariff seems nonetheless irrational, in the sense that with the same information one could have applied duties that were tied more closely to the cloth's actual quality and thus technically superior (Fenoaltea, "Product Heterogeneity," pp. 277, 280).

[6] W. A. Lewis, *Growth and Fluctuations, 1870–1913*, London 1978, p. 25; Istat, *Sommario*, pp. 172, 173, 192ff.

sorry history the lira was repeatedly devalued to recover the competitiveness lost through relatively high domestic inflation. Between 1861 and 1913 the lira was strong in the early 1860s, in the 1880s, in the 1900s, and weak in the intervening periods.[7]

After 1887 tariffs were not raised (wheat and sugar apart); but into the early 1890s prices fell, the lira depreciated, and protection increased. These tendencies then reversed themselves, and in the Giolitti years protection fell: not because of what Italy's government did, but rather, if one will, because it failed to do anything at all.

2. The issues: protection in general

The Italian tariff debate has moved from the political arena to the historical literature without losing vigor. It is a broad-gauged debate that concerns protection in general, individual duties, and with reference to the 1880s, as noted, even the path of the economy.

Protection as such has been seen in different ways at different times and by different groups. The economists of the day (and of later days) did not consider protection useful to development, which they associated rather with free trade, the widening of markets, specialization, the exploitation of comparative advantages.[8] To their mind protection did not generate net benefits for the national economy, rather, it reduced national wealth; it was a tax that some had the political power to impose on the rest of the nation to their own private benefit, it subsidized the strong at the expense of the weak, it was a "bourgeois socialism" that paved the way for the real thing.[9]

The ancient notion that protection could favor development would be revived by experience, by the interpretation of history. By the early twentieth century the protected industry of the United States and Germany had grown to match England's; free trade seemed to be the winning strategy for the leader, not for those trying to catch up. The ideology of progress

[7] Above, Figure 2.04. Duties were then set (and collected) in gold; had they not been devaluation would have reduced the percentage weight of the duties too, but it would have increased protection all the same.

[8] Below, Appendix 2, § 1. A neo-mercantilist school has recently arisen in the United States, prompted it would seem by the Japanese challenge, that appeals to models with multiple equilibria to justify the protection of new industries with increasing returns; but it does not question that free trade is "subsequently" beneficial.

[9] For example, L. Einaudi, *Cronache economiche e politiche di un trentennio*, 8 vols., Turin 1959–66, vol. 1, pp. 80–84, vol. 3, pp. xix–xxiii, xxviii, pp. 600–609; V. Pareto, *Lettres d'Italie. A cura di Gabriele De Rosa*, Rome 1973, pp. 15, 27–28, 116–117, 219–222, 289–290, 575–578.

also saw the industrial stage as the most advanced, so whatever favored industry was considered good, whatever its immediate costs. Romeo thus justified the limits placed on the consumption of Italy's poorest in the post-Unification years, and, without asking himself too many questions, the subsequent shift to protection. Gerschenkron generally favored industrial protection, and condemned the Italian tariff only because it protected the wrong industries, and worse yet agriculture, reducing industrial growth.[10] In the succeeding literature the usefulness of protection is taken for granted; even technical criticism of the tariff's structure is relatively rare, and the typical complaint is that certain duties were not high enough.[11]

In that literature protection can also favor economic development by avoiding balance-of-payments disequilibrium, by loosening the external constraint. Luciano Cafagna and Franco Bonelli both dedicated to the problem of the external balance entire sections of their syntheses; Giovanni Federico defined "the equilibrium of the balance of payments in the long run" as "a necessary condition for Italy's economic development," and defended the grain tariff that avoided "serious problems for the balance of trade"; Vera Zamagni repeated the latter argument, quoting Federico with approval.[12]

That the need to balance foreign transactions creates an external constraint is taken for granted; but that constraint exists only in highly specific

[10] Above, ch. 1, § 2.

[11] For example, G. Pescosolido, *Unità nazionale e sviluppo economico*, Rome-Bari 1998, p. 108; G. Toniolo, *An Economic History of Liberal Italy, 1850–1918*, London 1990 (translation of Id., *Storia economica dell'Italia liberale 1850–1918*, Bologna 1988), pp. 82–84; Zamagni, *The Economic History*, pp. 110–117. The most thoroughgoing protectionist is Vera Zamagni: to her mind any reduction in external trade is beneficial, and the "fundamental problems" of the early tariffs were resolved in 1921, "when all sectors . . . were given protection" (p. 115). Zamagni also emphasizes that protection is, in fact, the historical norm (ibid.); the same case can be made for wife-beating.

[12] F. Bonelli, "Italian Capitalism: General Interpretative Guidelines," in G. Federico, ed., *The Economic Development of Italy since 1870*, Aldershot 1994 (translation of F. Bonelli, "Il capitalismo italiano. Linee generali di interpretazione," in R. Romano and C. Vivanti, eds., *Storia d'Italia. Annali. 1. Dal feudalesimo al capitalismo*, Turin 1978, pp. 1193–1255), pp. 117–123; L. Cafagna, "The Industrial Revolution in Italy, 1830–1914," in C. M. Cipolla, ed., *The Fontana Economic History of Europe*, vol. 4, Glasgow 1972, pp. 300–303, and L. Cafagna, "La formazione del sistema industriale: ricerche empiriche e modelli di crescita," *Quaderni della Fondazione G. G. Feltrinelli* 25 (1983), pp. 27–38, reprinted in Id., *Dualismo e sviluppo nella storia d'Italia*, Venice 1989, p. 397; G. Federico, "Per una analisi del ruolo dell'agricoltura nello sviluppo economico italiano: note sull'esportazione di prodotti primari (1863–1913)," *Società e storia* 5 (1979), p. 379, and Id., "Commercio dei cereali e dazio sul grano in Italia (1863–1913). Una analisi quantitativa," *Nuova rivista storica* 68 (1984), p. 85 (translations by the present author); Zamagni, *The Economic History*, p. 116.

circumstances. With a flexible exchange rate, it cannot exist at all: the equilibrium rate is determined day by day in the market for foreign currencies, and that market is constantly and automatically cleared.[13] But as David Hume pointed out long ago the key to foreign equilibrium is the flexibility of the *real* exchange rate (the relative value of domestic and foreign *goods*, or "terms of trade"), which varies both with the nominal exchange rate (given domestic prices) and with domestic prices (given the nominal exchange rate and foreign prices); with a gold standard nominal exchange rates are fixed, and external equilibrium is automatically maintained by movements in relative price levels.[14] The analysis does not rule out changes in the level of activity, which push prices and wages to their new equilibrium levels; but the more prices and wages are flexible the more the real exchange rate is also flexible, and the more the gold standard is equivalent to a regime with flexible nominal exchange rates. Under both regimes, short-run transitions aside, external equilibrium is guaranteed and maintained by the flexibility of the real exchange rate, and the only effect of protection is to raise the real rate consistent with equilibrium; if tariffs reduce imports the real exchange rate appreciates, our goods become relatively more expensive, and because we import less we also export less.[15]

The macroeconomic models constructed in the post-war years reflect a different logic. They ignore the real exchange rate altogether; exports are taken as given, because they depend on demand generated by the rest of the world, while imports vary with domestic income, investment, and consumption. The external balance is obviously not guaranteed, the growth of income boosts imports and can generate a balance-of-payments

---

[13] Above, ch. 2, § 4, note 28.

[14] The gold flows that cover the external imbalance push relative price levels in an equilibrating direction. On Hume's "specie flow" theory see for example R. Backhouse, *A History of Modern Economic Analysis*, Oxford 1985, p. 45. Hume's analysis implies, among other things, that a rapidly growing economy on the gold standard will tend to a chronic balance of payments *surplus*, as the growing demand for means of payment attracts specie; also, obviously, that with a given demand for means of payment an increase in specie-substitutes (convertible paper money, checking accounts) leads to specie *exports*, and thus a balance-of-payments deficit.

[15] A. de Viti de Marco, *Un trentennio di lotte politiche*, Rome c.1930, p. 135; Einaudi, *Cronache*, vol. 3, p. 422; Pareto, *Lettres*, p. 44. Bonaldo Stringher ties the trade deficit to capital inflows (above, ch. 2, § 5, note 43), but would have the tariff increases of 1887 reduce the deficit and actually stimulate exports; see B. Stringher, "Il commercio con l'estero e il corso dei cambi," *Nuova Antologia di Scienze, Lettere ed Arti*, serie III, 54 (1894), p. 25.

crisis; the external constraint is very much there, and protection can loosen it by limiting import growth as the economy grows.[16]

Those models reflect the institutional innovations of the post-war days, the policy commitment to stabilize the economy in general and the price level in particular, to maintain fixed nominal exchange rates (with the "gold-exchange standard," created by international agreement, which left only the American dollar tied directly to gold).[17] With the price level and the nominal exchange rate thus fixed the real exchange rate was also fixed, and could no longer play its equilibrating role. Other international agreements limited the recourse to tariff protection, so when all was said and done income growth was limited by export growth. The booming countries of those years were those that boasted rapid export growth, the former Axis powers, and also France (who cynically devalued the franc to boost its exports); England slept, because its exports languished, and any attempt to revive the economy had quickly to be abandoned because imports soared and the pound sterling, held in large quantities by the other Commonwealth countries, could not be allowed to risk devaluation.

In post-Unification Italy prices were flexible, and so were wages: the economy was dominated by agriculture, and day-laborers' wages varied day by day following the seasonal cycle in the demand for labor. The nominal exchange rate was also flexible, if not upward once it had reached parity and the balance-of-payments surplus boosted domestic prices and wages, certainly downward: Italy's governments had always shown themselves willing to protect the circulation of bank notes rather than convertibility, to let the lira float below par. The real exchange rate was flexible, doubly flexible: "the equilibrium of the balance of payments in the long run" was automatic, it did not constrain Italy's economic development.

The historians recalled above came of age in the post-war period, nourished by the texts and models of those years; they simply *knew* that growth is subject to a balance-of-payments constraint, that tariffs

---

[16] The external constraint is obviously loosened as well by capital imports, and by the remittances of emigrants; Cafagna ("La formazione," pp. 398–399) sees the great contribution of the South to the industrial development of the North precisely in the remittances of its migrants.

[17] The nominal exchange rates of the other currencies are kept at their par values by the central banks' willingness to buy or sell any amount of foreign currency at the specified rates (above, ch. 2, § 4, note 28). In practice, if the external balance is negative the central bank can maintain the exchange rate only so long as it has reserves of foreign currency to sell – whence the system's periodic crises, accompanied by changes in parities.

can boost the one by loosening the other. They failed to notice that the external constraint derived from historically specific institutions: precisely because they were by training historians and not economists, they simply applied a preconceived theoretical model to the past, to a context in which the model's assumptions are contradicted by the facts.[18]

3. The tariff on textiles and "manchesterian" growth

The industrial revolution began in late eighteenth-century England with the mechanization of cotton spinning. The miraculous increase in productivity much reduced the cost and price of cotton goods: production, consumption, and exports grew explosively, cotton mills proliferated, and Manchester became the first modern "industrial district." Mechanization would subsequently be extended to the further processing of cotton, in particular to weaving; the golden age of the hand-loom weaver lasted only a few decades, the technical progress that created it soon destroyed it. Mechanization spread in time to other textile fibers, that bear the strains of machine processing less well than cotton, with varying lags that altered their relative prices and consumption.

The textile industry in post-Unification Italy reflected these developments. The recent estimates of value added at constant prices point to very different time paths from fiber to fiber: between 1861 and 1913 the initially small cotton industry multiplied itself thirteen-fold, and became much the largest; the wool industry grew five-fold, also increasing its relative weight; the glorious silk industry failed even to double, and slipped from a third of the total to a quarter; linen and hemp proved instead difficult to mechanize, and their processing industries declined even in absolute terms, falling from a third of the total to a bare twentieth.[19]

Italy's silk industry was an export industry (and in favor of free trade), and thanks to the high unit value of its products by far Italy's largest export earner; Italy also exported hemp products, and imported wool and linen goods, but these were minor items. Silk aside, the *grand commerce*

---

[18] Federico, who has admirably continued to improve his technical skills, has recently and not by chance recognized his youthful error, granting that "most economists today (sic) would argue that this preoccupation with the trade balance is misplaced in a world of reasonably flexible prices and wages, and for the most part, flexible exchange rates" (J. S. Cohen and G. Federico, *The Growth of the Italian Economy, 1820–1960*, Cambridge 2001, p. 22).

[19] S. Fenoaltea, "Textile Production in Italy, 1861–1913," *Rivista di storia economica* 18 (2002), pp. 36–37.

in textiles was in cotton goods; and over time that commerce changed radically. In the early decades after Unification cotton yarn and cloth were among Italy's major imports. These then dwindled; in the 1890s the net flows reversed themselves, and by the eve of the World War Italy's exports of cotton goods were second only to its exports of silk.

The tariffs of 1878 and 1887 raised duties on all imported textiles, but the literature has concerned itself primarily with those on cottons. Gerschenkron and Toniolo censure them not so much in themselves as because tariff policy should have favored the industries of the future, and not catered to the special interests of those that were already mature: a complaint that is logically impeccable, but perhaps underestimates the difficulty of predicting the course of technology and identifying *ex ante* the winners of the future.[20]

The reversal of trade flows in the 1890s suggests in any case that the cotton duties soon became ineffective. A tariff increases the market price only if it limits the flow of *imports*; if the industry is competitive and *exporting*, the domestic market price does not exceed the world price, and the tariff is simply irrelevant.[21]

This point has been made by Luciano Cafagna. Cafagna does not see the South as the victim of Unification: he does not believe that Italy's regional imbalances were created by the national State, and exacerbated by the protection of northern industry. Cafagna emphasizes rather the competitive, "manchesterian" nature of the North's progress: the textile tariff, at least, "did not after all support artificial positions, as is proved

---

[20] A. Gerschenkron, "Notes on the Rate of Industrial Growth in Italy, 1881–1913," *Journal of Economic History* 15 (1955), pp. 360–375, reprinted in Id., *Economic Backwardness in Historical Perspective*, Cambridge MA 1962, pp. 72–89 (and in particular p. 81); Toniolo, *An Economic History*, pp. 82–84. The errors in the predictions even of the most expert is illustrated for example by the Boeing 747 "Jumbo Jet," designed with its characteristic hump to serve as a front-loading freighter; it was then foregone that long-haul passenger traffic would soon move on to supersonic aircraft. Toniolo also sees in the cotton tariff a technical error, a lack of net protection for textiles; but the evidence does not confirm it (Fenoaltea, "Product Heterogeneity," p. 281, and below).

[21] The domestic price increases by the full amount of the duty only if the latter is not prohibitive, and imports continue; a prohibitive tariff increases the domestic price by less than the duty itself (below, Appendix 1, § 1). The fact that the duty is only the upper limit to the induced price increase means that the rates of "effective protection" cannot be calculated, as they have been, by considering only the duties on the product and its raw materials; see for example G. Federico and A. Tena, "Did Trade Policy Foster Italian Industrialization? Evidence from Effective Protection Rates, 1870–1930," *Research in Economic History* 19 (1999), p. 126, and Fenoaltea, "Product Heterogeneity," pp. 278–280.

by the rapid growth of exports in the following years."[22] The Southern question will be returned to in due course; the present concern is with the effect of the cotton tariff, unexpectedly illuminated by the reconstruction of the production series.[23]

The series incorporated in the early indices of industrial production measured the production of cotton yarn and cloth by its weight (calculated from the apparent consumption of the raw materials, allowing for weight losses). Pound for pound, however, a product of higher quality – a finer yarn, a cloth woven with more and finer threads – is worth more, and incorporates a greater value added; in fact, value added is close to directly proportional in spinning not to the weight but to the length of the yarn produced, and in weaving not to the weight of the cloth produced but to the length of the yarn it incorporates. The new series accordingly measure cotton yarn and cloth by the length of the yarn spun and woven; they thus capture the quality improvements the earlier series neglected and implicitly assumed away.[24]

The length series move much like the weight series, save in the 1880s, when – especially after 1887 – the length series surge ahead; this documents the increase in production tied to tariff-induced quality improvements, which the traditional weight series simply missed (Table 4.01 and Figure 4.01).

The detailed trade statistics further reveal that in the last years of the period at hand Italy was an exporter not of cotton goods in

---

[22] L. Cafagna, "Contro tre pregiudizi sulla storia dello sviluppo economico italiano," in P. Ciocca and G. Toniolo, eds., *Storia economica d'Italia. 1. Interpretazioni*, Rome-Bari 1998, pp. 307–308 (translation by the present author). In a much earlier piece, Cafagna had instead attributed the strong growth of the cotton industry through (and despite) the crisis of the 1890s precisely to tariff protection ("The Industrial Revolution," p. 294).

[23] S. Fenoaltea, "The Growth of Italy's Cotton Industry, 1861–1913: A Statistical Reconstruction," *Rivista di storia economica* 17 (2001), pp. 139–171.

[24] The ratio of length to weight is known as the yarn's "count," which in the French system used in Italy corresponds to the yarn's length in kilometers per half-kilogram of weight. Italy's trade statistics measure yarn and cloth by weight, but the tariff categories were finely subdivided by quality (and applicable duty); the average count and aggregate length of the imported yarn, and of the yarn in the imported cloth, can thus be estimated year by year directly from the data. For national production, the average count is known only in 1910; allowing for the known weights produced and imported, and the known lengths imported, one can calculate the average count of the yarn consumed as cloth. The production series in length are calculated on the assumption that the average count *consumed* remained constant, and working back through the same system of equations. The average counts spun and woven emerge from the comparison of the weight and length series; their variation over time derives from that of the quantities imported and exported.

TABLE 4.01. *Estimated output of cotton goods*

	(1)	(2) yarn	(3)	(4)	(5) cloth	(6)
		production			production	
	weight (thousand tons)	length (trillion meters)	average count (Nf)	weight (thousand tons)	length (trillion meters)[a]	average count (Nf)[a]
1861	16.8	.29	8.63	28.6	.65	11.40
1862	13.9	.24	8.67	20.2	.46	11.45
1863	14.2	.25	8.72	18.7	.43	11.50
1864	17.0	.30	8.76	20.7	.48	11.55
1865	19.1	.34	8.80	26.3	.61	11.60
1866	19.0	.34	8.85	26.8	.62	11.65
1867	19.6	.35	8.89	27.7	.65	11.70
1868	19.6	.35	8.94	28.3	.67	11.75
1869	20.6	.37	8.98	30.3	.72	11.80
1870	20.7	.37	9.02	28.2	.67	11.85
1871	19.5	.35	9.07	28.1	.67	11.90
1872	19.7	.36	9.11	27.5	.66	11.95
1873	24.6	.45	9.15	35.5	.85	12.00
1874	29.3	.54	9.20	40.2	.97	12.05
1875	26.0	.48	9.24	37.9	.92	12.10
1876	23.4	.43	9.29	36.8	.89	12.15
1877	25.5	.48	9.33	38.2	.93	12.20
1878	25.8	.48	9.37	34.4	.84	12.25
1879	26.3	.50	9.42	32.8	.81	12.30
1880	29.4	.56	9.46	35.1	.87	12.35
1881	32.5	.62	9.50	44.4	1.10	12.40
1882	41.5	.85	10.24	50.6	1.26	12.45
1883	47.8	.99	10.36	56.8	1.42	12.50
1884	46.4	.97	10.48	54.3	1.36	12.55
1885	53.1	1.16	10.94	60.8	1.53	12.60
1886	55.3	1.26	11.42	61.4	1.55	12.65
1887	56.9	1.34	11.75	61.3	1.56	12.70
1888	62.1	1.78	14.30	65.1	1.95	15.00
1889	67.3	1.93	14.34	70.6	2.14	15.21
1890	77.7	2.30	14.80	80.3	2.47	15.42
1891	77.8	2.31	14.85	79.6	2.45	15.50
1892	75.4	2.28	15.12	76.5	2.38	15.67
1893	78.5	2.40	15.29	79.0	2.49	15.85
1894	90.5	2.88	15.91	90.4	2.93	16.30
1895	100.9	3.22	15.96	101.2	3.29	16.34
1896	102.4	3.36	16.41	101.8	3.40	16.73
1897	108.5	3.57	16.45	105.7	3.55	16.82
1898	117.8	3.93	16.68	110.6	3.76	17.03
1899	122.4	4.10	16.75	115.0	3.94	17.16
1900	117.3	3.98	16.97	112.1	3.84	17.16
1901	119.4	4.08	17.09	110.5	3.83	17.36
1902	130.9	4.48	17.11	122.8	4.24	17.29
1903	139.0	4.81	17.30	130.6	4.56	17.48
1904	142.0	4.91	17.29	133.4	4.65	17.45
1905	146.6	5.06	17.26	137.1	4.76	17.38
1906	159.7	5.61	17.56	150.2	5.27	17.60
1907	185.8	6.59	17.73	179.1	6.36	17.79
1908	198.0	6.72	16.97	192.2	6.57	17.13
1909	188.5	6.39	16.95	179.8	6.17	17.19
1910	173.9	5.83	16.76	162.1	5.55	17.16
1911	171.8	5.82	16.94	157.6	5.44	17.30
1912	197.4	6.74	17.07	184.9	6.39	17.31
1913	195.2	6.87	17.60	181.5	6.43	17.75

[a] of the yarn incorporated in the cloth.

Source: S. Fenoaltea, "The Growth of Italy's Cotton Industry. 1861–1913: A Statistical Reconstruction," *Rivista di storia economica* 17 (2001), pp. 152–155.

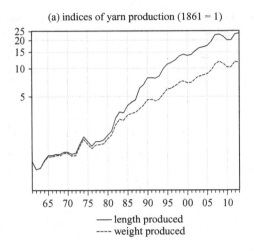

(a) indices of yarn production (1861 = 1)

—— length produced
---- weight produced

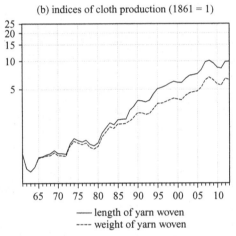

(b) indices of cloth production (1861 = 1)

—— length of yarn woven
---- weight of yarn woven

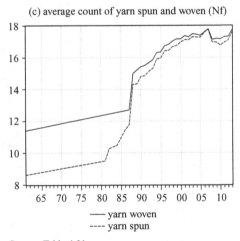

(c) average count of yarn spun and woven (Nf)

—— yarn woven
---- yarn spun

Source: Table 4.01.

FIGURE 4.01. *Estimated output of cotton goods*

TABLE 4.02. *The composition of trade in cotton textiles*[a]

(1) sub-cate-gory	(2) cloth weight (Kg/100 sq m)[b]	(3) number of threads in a 5 mm) square[c]	(4) implied range of the count (Nf)	(5) export value[d]	(6) export ratio[e]	(7) estimated average count (Nf)
a	13 plus	up to 27	up to 23	260	84	15
d	11 to 13	up to 27	up to 27	265	77	16
b	13 plus	27 to 38	up to 32	270	35	21
g	7 to 11	up to 27	up to 41	275	12	29
e	11 to 13	27 to 38	23 to 38	325	7.9	32
h	7 to 11	27 to 38	27 to 60	345	6.5	34
c	13 plus	over 38	uncertain	400	5.9	35
l	3 to 7	up to 27	up to 99	345	2.3	45
f	11 to 13	over 38	over 32	415	.90	56
i	7 to 11	over 38	over 38	445	.29	70
m	3 to 7	27 to 38	42 to 139	365	.16	80
n	3 to 7	over 38	over 60	525	.04	105

[a] categories 359, 362–364, 367–370, and 372 in 1913.
[b] the ranges include the lower bound and exclude the upper bound.
[c] the ranges exclude the lower bound and include the upper bound.
[d] lire per quintal of plain grey cloth, from the 1908 *Movimento commerciale*.
[e] ratio of total tonnage exported to total tonnage imported, 1905–13.
Source: S. Fenoaltea, "The Growth of Italy's Cotton Industry, 1861–1913: A Statistical Reconstruction," *Rivista di storia economica* 17 (2001), p. 157.

general, but only and specifically of low-quality cotton goods; higher-quality cottons continued to be imported (Table 4.02). Cafagna's unprotected, exporting, "manchesterian" industry was only part of the cotton industry; another good part produced behind tariff walls that continued to keep out imports. According to a first rough estimate, in 1913 the tariff increased the total output of cotton goods by at least forty percent.[25]

4. The tariff on steel and the engineering industry

The industrial revolution was born in England's cotton mills, but it soon involved heavy industry, the production of iron, of coal, of machinery; the railway conjoined them, and became the symbol of the new age. As and even more than the textile industry, iron-making was transformed by

[25] Below, Appendix 1, § 2, and Fenoaltea, "Manchester," pp. 499–500. The estimate is obtained by comparing actual production in 1913 to what it would have been had the average count been near 11 in spinning and 14 in weaving, as suggested by extrapolating the pre-tariff trends (Figure 4.01). Value added is reduced in proportion to the count (implicitly assuming that weaving and finishing were tied to the quality of the cloth itself), but the tariff is allowed no effect on the total weight of output. That the tariff effectively protected higher-quality cottons had been noted at the time by Italy's economists; see Einaudi, *Cronache*, vol. 1, p. 103.

technical progress: the reduction of unit costs, the spectacular increases in production and consumption were due not only to mechanization but to the development of a new production process based on coal, in England abundant, instead of charcoal, ever more expensive because of progressive deforestation.

The reduction of the ores, the subsequent refining of the iron all take place at high temperatures, using considerable quantities of fuel. This energy consumption declined over time, with the progress of technology; but in the nineteenth century iron-making used far more coal than ore or scrap, and it was cheaper to bring the iron to the coal rather than vice versa. The iron industry thus grew spontaneously near the coal mines, in the *pays noirs* of northwest Europe; far from the coal mines the iron industry was a greenhouse plant.

In Italy, the modern iron and steel industry would live behind the protection of high tariff walls, nourished by public orders at favorable prices. From its birth in the early 1880s it grew rapidly until the cyclical contraction of the early 1890s, and then surged again over the *belle époque* to reach the unprecedented output of one million tons per year. It was not for all that much to be proud of – it represented but the fiftieth part both of Italy's industry, and of Europe's iron industry – but it was clearly the product of State support, in this case (and within those limits) certainly effective.[26]

On that much contemporary observers, and later economic historians, agree. The dispute that has remained alive for a century and more concerns the cost of the national steel industry, the harm the steel tariff may have wrought to Italy's industrial development by increasing the cost of the engineering industry's raw materials. That harm was decried at the time not only by Italy's economists, who were in any case free-traders, but also by its engineering-industry entrepreneurs; and it was decried in the historical literature by Alexander Gerschenkron, who was not a free-trader at all.[27]

For Gerschenkron, as noted, the tariff should have protected the new industries, less subject to established hegemonies, and in the specific case

---

[26] S. Fenoaltea, "Il valore aggiunto dell'industria italiana nel 1911," in G. M. Rey, ed., *I conti economici dell'Italia. 2. Una stima del valore aggiunto per il 1911*, Collana storica della Banca d'Italia, serie "statistiche storiche," vol. I.II, Bari 1992, pp. 107, 145–148; B. R. Mitchell, *European Historical Statistics*, London 1975, pp. 399–401.

[27] Even Stringher, not averse to the tariff protection of industry, asked himself whether the steel tariff may not have reached harmful levels ("Il commercio con l'estero," pp. 24–25).

of Italy those characterized by high value added and low energy consumption, less handicapped by the high cost of imported coal. The tariff should have protected engineering and chemicals, certainly not "ferrous metalmaking[,] . . . a coal-consuming industry *par excellence.*" In fact the engineering industry also received protection, but the duties on its products barely offset the steel tariff; it received no *net* protection at all. The "natural" industry, with great potential, was thus sacrificed to the artificial industry, with no future; the steel tariff retarded Italy's industrial growth.[28]

Rosario Romeo was totally untouched by these arguments: without even giving them a hearing he simply repeated that he found it "difficult to doubt the legitimacy of Italy's iron and steel industry."[29]

The present author's early efforts reached a conclusion similar to Gerschenkron's, but by a different route. If, as it seemed, in the underdeveloped Italy of the time production was constrained not by supply (which was elastic because resources were mobile, across countries as within them) but by demand, precisely because the country was poor and consumed little, protection could do little good: the royal road to industrial growth was not the substitution of limited imports, but the development of potentially "infinite" exports for the world market.

From this perspective the serious harm done to the engineering industry by the steel tariff was not that it reduced its share of the domestic market (with respect to what it would have captured with the net protection Gerschenkron would have preferred); it was that it raised its costs above international levels, and cut it off from export markets. The cycle in industrial production was the cycle in engineering production, in domestic investment; with free trade (at least in steel), without the tariff that limited it to domestic customers, after the domestic boom of the 1880s the engineering industry could have continued to grow, increasing aggregate industrial output too, by breaking out of the domestic market and producing to export order.[30]

---

[28] Gerschenkron, "Notes," pp. 81–82.

[29] A. Gerschenkron, "The Industrial Development of Italy: A Debate with Rosario Romeo (with a Postscript)," in Id., *Continuity in History and Other Essays*, Cambridge MA 1968 (translation of A. Gerschenkron and R. Romeo, "Lo sviluppo industriale italiano [testo del dibattito tenuto a Roma, presso la Svimez, il 13 luglio 1960]," *Nord e Sud* 23 [1961], pp. 30–56), p. 122.

[30] S. Fenoaltea, "Decollo, ciclo, e intervento dello Stato," in A. Caracciolo, ed., *La formazione dell'Italia industriale*, Bari 1969, pp. 95–114, and more extensively Id., "Riflessioni sull'esperienza industriale italiana dal Risorgimento alla prima guerra mondiale," in G. Toniolo, ed., *Lo sviluppo economico italiano 1861–1940*, Bari 1973, pp. 136–145,

Shortly thereafter Gianni Toniolo also addressed these issues. He recognized that the engineering industry had been harmed by the steel tariff, but he did not consider the damage significant. To counter Gerschenkron's claims he calculated that with prohibitive protection for engineering and no steel tariff at all, around 1907 the engineering industry would have been half again as large as it actually was; but this would have represented only a limited increase in aggregate industrial production (7.3 percent) and *a fortiori* in gross national product (1.4 percent).[31]

These estimates would confirm that the conquest of the domestic market was not the royal road to economic development. According to Toniolo, however, that was the Italian engineering industry's only option: even without the steel tariff, it could not have exported because it had not yet reached the technical, *qualitative*, level necessary to succeed in world markets. This objection proved to be an ace: it has been repeated with approval for example by Luciano Cafagna, then by Vera Zamagni, then again by Jon Cohen and Giovanni Federico. But there are at least three good reasons not to join that chorus. First, underdeveloped countries always begin by exporting technologically unsophisticated goods, and then climb the quality gradient as they catch up to the leaders: Japan, for example, exported textiles, then ships and cars, and finally computers. Second, Italy's engineering industry does not seem to have been particularly backward: it proved capable before the end of the century of exporting major naval vessels, then the very pinnacle of technological sophistication. Third and most of all, the historical record speaks directly to the issue. Over the final decades of the nineteenth century Italian engineering firms made continuous efforts to obtain the right to process duty-free foreign steel to export order, and their understanding of their actual possibilities surely trumps ours.[32]

and again in G. Toniolo, ed., *L'economia italiana 1861–1940*, Bari 1978, pp. 84–93. The hypothesis of engineering-export-led growth was also natural, given the then recent Italian experience; but it was suggested by the sources, about which more below.

[31] G. Toniolo, "Effective Protection and Industrial Growth: The Case of Italian Engineering," *Journal of European Economic History* 6 (1977), pp. 665, 672; see also Id., *An Economic History*, p. 145.

[32] To prove that the obstacle to engineering exports was not the duty on steel Toniolo cites the very limited use of the duty-free imports, for processing and re-export, allowed in general from 1903 and for specific goods even before that. The official sources document not only, from the 1870s, the requests for duty-free imports but also, later, the complaints that the law was frustrated by administrative procedures that in fact rendered duty-free imports impossible; after 1903 this evidence of frustration disappears, both because the law and the administrative procedures were themselves revised, and because with domestic consumption growing by leaps and bounds the firms were already taxed by

Vera Zamagni goes so far as to claim that the steel industry was "highly strategic ... above all, for the support it provided to the engineering and military sectors," so much so that "the engineering industry in fact developed hand in hand with the metallurgy industry."[33] Were it true one would wonder why it was not understood at the time by the engineering interests; but it is not true, the argument has the cart pulling the horse. The only industries that need domestic sources of supply are those that process perishable goods, like sugar-beet; in the case of non-perishable goods, like steel or raw cotton, the parallel movements of the production and subsequent transformation of the raw material result from the tariff itself. Imagine that the cultivation of cotton in Italy had been considered "strategic" for the textile industry, and protected by a prohibitive duty. Clearly, the output of Italy's cotton industry too would have grown hand in hand with that of its domestic raw material; and equally clearly, with the attendant increase in its costs, that industry would never have exported so much as a bobbin of yarn or a bolt of cloth. Without a duty

their domestic orders. In a minor key Toniolo denies that the elasticity of foreign demand was high, even though for a single small producer (as for a single firm in a competitive industry) it is conventionally considered infinite; he denies that the other industrial nations would have allowed themselves to be invaded by Italian goods, forgetting both the ample market represented by the rest of the world and, by the standards of the leaders, the small scale of Italian production; he denies that the domestic elasticity of supply was high, apparently not satisfied that when the domestic market surged output (net of maintenance) maintained growth rates of 20 percent per year (enough to increase production 240 times over, in thirty years), with prices capped by import competition. See on the one hand Toniolo, "Effective Protection," pp. 662, 665, 672, Id., *An Economic History*, p. 145, L. Cafagna, "La politica economica e lo sviluppo industriale," in *Stato e società dal 1876 al 1882: atti del XLIX Congresso di storia del Risorgimento italiano (Viterbo, 30 settembre – 5 ottobre 1978)*, Rome 1980, pp. 141–157, reprinted in Id., *Dualismo e sviluppo*, pp. 261–278 (and in particular pp. 276–277), Zamagni, *The Economic History*, pp. 115–116, and Cohen and Federico, *The Growth*, p. 65; on the other Fenoaltea, "Riflessioni," 1973, pp. 136–139, 1978, pp. 84–87, and for example Einaudi, *Cronache*, vol. 1, p. 104, Pareto, *Lettres*, pp. 100–102, and A. Cottrau, *Le industrie meccaniche e il regime doganale*, Rome 1891. Cottrau produced truss bridges and roofing, and apparently had no difficulty (the steel tariff apart) in exporting such relatively unsophisticated products.

[33] Zamagni, *The Economic History*, p. 116 (with the substitution of "hand in hand with" for "at about the same pace as" to render the much stronger "di pari passo" of the original, Id., *Dalla periferia al centro*, p. 152); also pp. 94–95. There is no doubt that the Terni works were established (in 1884) with an eye to their contribution to naval armaments (ibid.), and they seem in fact to have been placed well inland to keep them out of range of enemy cannon-fire; but their potential usefulness in war-time was clearly nil. If Italy's allies controlled the seas, steel too could be imported; if they did not, as in the second war, steel could not be produced in Italy in any case because coal could not be imported either.

on the raw material Italy imported foreign cotton to work it up and sell the finished product abroad; steel was like raw cotton, that is why the engineering interests denounced the steel tariff.

5. The tariff on grain and the paradox of ricardian trade

In the 1860s and 1870s in Italy imported grain cost some 30 lire per quintal; the corresponding duty was then just 1.40 lire, a bare five percent *ad valorem*, and essentially fiscal rather than protective. The price of imported grain fell in the early 1880s, to 20 lire per quintal; it fell further in the early 1890s, to just 14–15 lire per quintal in the middle of that decade. The Italian State reacted by raising the duty to 3 lire per quintal in 1887, then to 5 lire, then to 7, and finally, in 1895, to 7.50 lire: at that point the duty raised the price of imported wheat, the price of wheat in the domestic market, by no less than 50 percent.

After 1895 the price of wheat drifted upward; in 1898, with the Spanish-American war, it reached 23 lire per quintal. In 1899 it was back to 18 lire; it remained approximately that for a decade, then rose again to settle around 21–22 lire after 1908. The tariff remained at 7.50 lire per quintal, still a third of the import price at the end of the period at hand; but precisely in 1898, from February to August, it was temporarily reduced to 5 lire, from early May – when the army fired on the demonstrators in Milan – through June it was lifted altogether.[34]

The duty on grain was harshly censured by the economists of the day. They censured it as they did other tariffs, because protection in any form impoverishes the country; they censured it more than other tariffs, for its specific, harmful redistributive effects. The tariff on grain was a "tax on hunger," no less than the hated grist tax of the 1870s; but where with the grist tax the increase in the cost of bread went entirely to the fisc, with the tariff that increase went mostly to the landowners, who were subsidized in direct proportion to their wealth.[35] The certainty that the grain tariff

---

[34] Istat, *Sommario*, p. 192; B. Stringher, "Gli scambi con l'estero e la politica commerciale," in R. Accademia dei Lincei, *Cinquanta anni di storia italiana*, vol. 3, Milan 1911, p. 180.

[35] For example Einaudi, *Cronache*, vol. 1, pp. 81–84, 204–210, vol. 3, p. 606; Pareto, *Lettres*, pp. 14–15; A. de Viti de Marco, "Finanze e politica doganale," *Giornale degli economisti* ser. 2, 2-I (1891), pp. 41–47, and U. Mazzola, "L'aumento del dazio sul grano," *Giornale degli economisti* ser. 2, 2-I (1891), pp. 193–197, reprinted in A. De Bernardi, ed., *Questione agraria e protezionismo nella crisi economica di fine secolo*, Milan 1977, pp. 179–190. Even Stringher, who favored industrial protection, considered the duties on the basic foods of the working people "an odious head-tax levied on the property-less in favor of landed property": B. Stringher, "La Gran Bretagna e le

harmed the poor was shared by the government, by the mob: that is why the duty was suspended in 1898, in the months of popular unrest.

In more recent times the duty on grain has been censured by other Italian economists, not uninterested in economic history; and in Gerschenkron's judgment Italy "never should have dared subject the tender plant of its industrial growth to the rigors of a protectionist climate in agriculture."[36] The subsequent literature has paid enormous attention to Gerschenkron's views, but not to this one. Of the duty on wheat it sees as noted not the harm done to industry but the benefits for the balance of payments, for the entire economy: the crisis of the 1880s had been caused by the fall in the price of grain, the duty was a contrary impulse as beneficial as the other had been harmful.[37]

In fact, as also noted, the fall in the price of grain seems to have been followed by all the beneficent effects predicted by the standard "comparative advantage" model of trade. Whether one evaluates the fall in the price of grain with that model, as Italy's economists did at the time, or by considering the subsequent path of the economy, as the historians have done, the conclusion one reaches is one and the same: the fall in the price of grain benefited Italy's workers, its industry, its specialized agriculture, its economy as a whole. The duty on wheat was a contrary impulse, it had the opposite effects: the economists of the day were right to oppose it, Gerschenkron was right to condemn it.

The "comparative advantage" model was developed by David Ricardo, and is still taught, to demonstrate that free trade benefits all parties. To be exact, it shows that free trade benefits every *country*, not everybody within each country. The abolition of tariffs alters the relative prices of goods, and the relative incomes of the factors of production, in each domestic market; the factor of production that trade renders locally less scarce obviously comes out the loser. Every change in prices and the production mix alters market equilibria and redistributes incomes – whence of course the clashes over tariff policy, the contrasting pressures brought to bear by different interest groups. The model considers these but downplays them, it emphasizes not these sectoral gains and losses but the overall national gain.[38]

concorrenze mondiali," *Nuova Antologia di Scienze, Lettere ed Arti*, serie III, 3 (1886), pp. 713–714 (translation by the present author).

[36] P. Sylos Labini, *Problemi dello sviluppo economico*, Bari 1970, pp. 138–141; Gerschenkron, "Notes," p. 81.

[37] Above, ch. 3, § 2, § 5.

[38] Below, Appendix 2, § 1–§ 3.

As the model is applied to the empirical evidence, however, it yields a paradoxical result: the general gain the model focuses on turns out to be trivial, the model that would emphasize it illustrates rather the clash of opposing interests. The empirical analysis yields significant sectoral gains and losses, significant changes in the real return to the different factors of production; but because the model assumes given resources and a given set of production possibilities these large effects are inevitably of opposite sign and mutually offsetting up to a trivial residual. What the "comparative advantage" model actually shows is that the tariff game is practically zero-sum.

This is apparent in Jeffrey Williamson's estimates of the effects of the Corn Laws in mid-nineteenth-century England. Using a sophisticated 19-equation general equilibrium model that assumes given resources, he calculated that the abolition of the grain duty raised real wages and manufacturing production by perhaps a fifth – at the expense of everybody else, as total product was barely affected (plus 1.5 percent). In the Italian case the present author used a sophisticated supply-and-demand diagram to reach very similar conclusions. Assuming a unit-elastic grain supply curve, the removal of the tariff would in 1911 have saved resources worth some 335 million lire in import-competing grain production. These resources, which would have moved to the export sectors, were enough almost to double, for example, the textile industry; but the grain that would have been imported because it was no longer produced would have cost 285 million lire, for a net gain that was, next to a gross product near 20,000 million lire, obviously insignificant.[39]

The traditional model of trade thus actually leaves room for opposite evaluations of the grain tariff. If one believes, as Gerschenkron did, in the stages of growth, if one sees in industry a level above that of the traditional economy, the tariff is clearly to be condemned because of its effects on the most modern sector, regardless of its overall effects: by repealing grain duties England chose industry and embraced the future, by instituting them Italy sacrificed industry and remained tied to the past.

If one does not share that interpretation of history, if one does not see a hierarchy among the economy's sectors, one's view of the tariff can be

---

[39] J. G. Williamson, "The Impact of the Corn Laws Just Prior to Repeal," *Explorations in Economic History* 27 (1990), pp. 123–156; S. Fenoaltea, "Politica doganale, sviluppo industriale, emigrazione: verso una riconsiderazione del dazio sul grano," *Rivista di storia economica* 10 (1993), pp. 67–68.

altogether milder, even favorable: the reallocation of resources and the redistribution of incomes have their economic and human costs that the trade model neglects, and one can certainly conclude that the small overall gain obtainable with free trade was not worth the candle. Indeed, if one's first priority is to ensure that the better off have the capacity to save and accumulate, the grain tariff is certainly to be praised precisely for its redistributive effects: the consumption of the masses had been increased by the fall in the price of grain as it would have been by a "gramscian" land reform, the State certainly did well to roll it back.[40]

6. The tariff on grain and real wages

Giovanni Federico has recently reconsidered, with different coauthors, various aspects of Italian protection. The effects of the tariff have been calculated using a general equilibrium model, that assumes given resources, similar to that constructed by Jeffrey Williamson to measure the effects of the Corn Laws.[41] The results are in the main what one would expect: protection had major effects on the output of individual sectors and the remuneration of individual factors of production, but a very small net effect on the economy as a whole.[42]

The grain tariff itself supposedly had a negligible effect not only on aggregate output, but also on the real wages of unskilled labor, cutting

[40] This particular defense of the grain tariff seems to be missing from the literature: for Romeo, Bonelli and Cafagna the period of "agrarian accumulation" *precedes* industrial development, which is then financed by other means (above, ch. 1, § 4, § 7); for Zamagni the savings of the well-to-do are always important, but the grain tariff was generally beneficial because it limited the general crisis caused by the fall in the price of grain (Zamagni, *The Economic History*, pp. 62, 116, 245–246). By supporting land rents the State actually supported the yield of the land tax; the attribution to the State only of the duties it collected underestimates the contribution of the tariff to the public budget, and correspondingly overestimates the net gain of the landowners.

[41] G. Federico, "Protezione e sviluppo economico italiano: molto rumore per nulla?," in Cafagna and Crepax, *Atti di intelligenza*, pp. 451–489, which draws on Federico and Tena, "Was Italy?" and "Did Trade Policy?" and G. Federico and K. O'Rourke, "Much Ado About Nothing? Italian Trade Policy in the 19th Century," in S. Pamuk and J. G. Williamson, eds., *The Mediterranean Response to Globalisation before 1950*, London 2000, pp. 269–296; Williamson, "The Impact."

[42] Federico, "Protezione," p. 467. Protection is said for example to have doubled grain production, reduced textile production by a fifth (presumably because of the duty on grain), and much altered the real wages of various categories of workers with specific skills.

these in 1911 by a bare two percent.[43] This is an unexpected result, in more than one way a surprising one.

The first surprise is that it should be proposed by Federico. It sits comfortably with his youthful assertions – he once defended the grain tariff, it's a short step from that to seeing no reason to condemn it – but not with his more mature efforts, his ongoing work. His new estimates of agricultural production and food consumption presume that these increased in the 1880s, as real wages rose; and the statistical increase in real wages stems more from the fall in the price of wheat, in the cost of living, than from the inflation of nominal wages (above, Figure 3.02).

If real wages were not sharply cut by the duty on wheat, they cannot earlier have been sharply increased by the contrary impulse, the fall in the price of wheat. With the lira then convertible the fall in the world price of wheat sharply cut the cost of living; if it left real wages substantially unchanged, it must have caused a substantial reduction in *nominal* wages; and if these were not perfectly flexible this in turn implies the unemployment needed to drive them down, it implies the macroeconomic "crisis of the 1880s" adumbrated by Toniolo.[44]

The rise in nominal wages even as the cost of living rapidly declined can be understood, it seems, if the rise in capital imports and the fall in the price of wheat both raised real wages; the Kuznets-cycle upswing in capital imports does not seem large enough, by itself, to counteract the strong deflationary pressure on nominal wages (and other prices) which Federico's result ties to the fall in the price of wheat. The claim that the duty on wheat did not materially reduce real wages pulls the rug out from under the "optimistic" interpretation of the 1880s, to which Federico himself subscribes.

Federico's result is also surprising on technical grounds, as it differs from those normally obtained with the tools he uses: Williamson's prototype recalled above ties to a duty no more than twice as high an effect on wages more than ten times greater. These models are so complex the sorcerers themselves are mere apprentices, and the exact source of a particular result can only be guessed; but one notes that in the model

---

[43] Federico (ibid., p. 479) concludes that this was surely too little to have had a significant impact on migration; the latter issue is returned to below.

[44] Above, ch. 3, § 5. Conversely, since the grain tariff appears to have raised the workers' cost of living by 10 to 20 percent (Fenoaltea, "Politica doganale," pp. 72, 77), a negligible impact on real wages implies a parallel increase in nominal wages, and therefore in domestic costs and prices, which does not seem consistent with the maintenance of external equilibrium.

described by Federico the assumption that "resources are given" is taken to an unusual extreme. The model allows no increase in the number of workers with particular skills, as if these skills could not be acquired; it allows no increase in the land devoted to specialized agriculture, as if when grain prices fell acre upon acre had not been converted to vineyard. The economy is, by assumption, in a straight-jacket: its capacity to react to changes in relative prices is curtailed *a priori*.

These same assumed rigidities presumably account for other peculiar results: that free trade would have revolutionized the structure of returns to different skills (with no connection to the cost of acquiring them); that free trade would not have increased the output of Italy's specialized agriculture, the sector where its international advantage was most obvious.[45]

If all this is so, Federico's result does not in fact mean what it is taken to mean. Rather than establish that the grain tariff had in fact a small impact on the real wages of unskilled workers, it ties that result to a counterfactual world in which Italy was not allowed to specialize in labor-intensive production; and if that is its burden the result is not surprising, not new, and above all no threat at all to the "optimistic" interpretation of the 1880s.

7. The tariff on grain and migration: ricardian trade and the standard approach

The economic analysis of migration is grafted onto the "comparative advantage" model of trade, it is not a natural offshoot. Ricardo's example was designed to illustrate the increase in the consumption of the English if they traded with the Portuguese, even if the latter are assumed to be more productive in every activity. The English would of course consume even more if instead of trading with the Portuguese they became themselves Portuguese, if they abandoned England for Portugal where everything, by assumption, is obtainable with less effort. As a weapon in the anti-protectionist controversy this last conclusion was of course worse than useless; Ricardo ruled it out by assuming that each country's resources are given, and not internationally mobile.

The traditional analysis of migration cleaves to Ricardo as much as it can: it considers labor not immobile, obviously, but "imperfectly mobile." Movement implies costs: one must pay for the voyage, one must give up

[45] Federico, "Protezione," pp. 469, 478.

one's income for the duration of the voyage and of the job search at destination, one must endure separation, one must face the unknown. These costs may be a profitable investment: they yield a future return, canonically identified with the attendant increase in the real wage for the rest of the migrant's life.

The precise object of the analysis is therefore *permanent* migration, not migration in general; but more about this later. The analysis is in any case rich: it immediately explains why migrants are typically young adults, at the beginning of their working lives and therefore with a maximum prospective gain; it explains why migration increases when the receiving countries prosper, and jobs are quickly found; it explains why one may be too poor to migrate, if the laws do not allow a contract of indenture that capitalizes one's earning at destination; it explains "chain migration," as earlier migrants help later ones fund the voyage, find jobs, and live in a community.[46]

This analysis is tacked onto the analysis of trade, sequentially so: "first" there is trade in goods, with is effects on relative prices and real wages, and "then" one sees whether and to what extent migration may remain advantageous.

In this logic transport improvements have an ambiguous effect on migration. On the one hand, they increase trade, reducing the interlocal differences in relative prices and (normally) in real wages. In the densely populated country land becomes less scarce, labor becomes less abundant, its low real wage rises; the opposite occurs in the thinly populated country, where the high real wage declines. Real returns to the factors of production converge: the benefit to migration falls because transport improvements reduce the difference in real wages.[47] On the other hand, transport improvements also reduce the cost of migration, because the voyage itself is faster and cheaper.

Tariffs are barriers to trade, just like high transport costs; but they are not barriers to migration. The grain tariff limited trade, limited the

[46] Below, Appendix 3, § 1. The model is applied to the Italian experience by R. Faini and A. Venturini, "Italian Emigration in the pre-War Period," in T. J. Hatton and J. G. Williamson, eds., *Migration and the International Labor Market, 1850–1939*, London 1994, pp. 72–90, and T. J. Hatton and J. G. Williamson, *The Age of Mass Migration: Causes and Economic Impact*, Oxford 1998, pp. 95–122.

[47] Imagine a country that imports grain and exports wine from and to "abroad." Measuring all prices in gold, for example, the price of grain in that country is its price "abroad" *plus* the transport cost, the price of wine its price "abroad" *less* its transport costs; the higher transport costs, the more domestic prices differ from those "abroad" (and so too, with a common technology, the real returns to the factors of production).

effect of transport improvements on relative real wages: it kept the return to migration high despite the improvement in transport costs. The grain tariff did not affect the cost of migration, which fell as transportation improved; in a labor-abundant country like Italy a policy that freezes relative prices by using tariffs to offset transport improvements seems designed to encourage emigration.

The protection obtained by Italy's grain rose from 1887 to 1895 both because the duty itself was progressively increased, and because the world price of grain progressively fell; that protection then declined because the duty remained unchanged, and the world price of grain steadily rose. The impetus to emigration created by the grain tariff thus followed a cycle that tended to offset the Kuznets cycle in the receiving countries, with a maximum around 1887, a minimum around 1895, and then a renewed upswing: the duty on grain increased overall migration but also reduced its cyclical fluctuations, as the push to leave Italy increased when the pull of the receiving countries fell, and vice versa.

8. The tariff on grain and migration: the trade model and relative mobility

The traditional analysis of migration is rich but not exhaustive: it considers only the permanent migrant, the *selfish* permanent migrant, concerned only with his personal consumption. His country of origin, which raised him, loses him with no countervailing benefit at all: had the plague taken him, the result would have been exactly the same.

Different objectives and effects characterize other migrants, the permanent migrant who leaves his family of origin but does not abandon it, who is concerned to assist it with his remittances, even more so the temporary migrant who works abroad to return home with his savings. These migrants have an effect on the balance of payments, on the equilibrium real exchange rate: the Southern migrants did not favor the industrialization of the North by loosening the balance of payments constraint with their remittances, as Luciano Cafagna claimed, rather, they strengthened the real exchange rate and limited Italy's industrial exports.[48] Such migrants do not look to their own consumption while living abroad, but to the purchasing power, back home, of what they set aside while working abroad: they are sensitive not only to relative real wages but

---

[48] Cafagna, "La formazione," pp. 398–399; also above, § 2 and note 16.

to relative *nominal* wages, to relative price levels, to the real exchange rate.

Ricardo's model of trade neglected commodity transport costs, that would have pointlessly complicated his exposition. Economists became used to thinking in terms of given, immobile resources, and of perfectly mobile goods; to considering resources at least relatively immobile, and goods uniformly mobile.

Trade is in fact determined as much by the relative mobility the "model of trade" neglects, as by the relative prices it considers; and that relative mobility depends on the one hand on the value of the delivered commodity unit, and on the other on the level of transport costs. Any transport cost is more easily overcome by high-value goods (per unit of weight) than by low-value goods; transport costs (per ton-mile) and distances that prohibit the movement of the latter do not prohibit the movement of the former. The higher the level of transport costs, the greater the mobility advantage of high-value goods: if the seas become infested by pirates the grain trade disappears, the spice and silk and silver trades continue. Only if transport costs disappear altogether are all goods equally (as well as perfectly) mobile.[49]

The higher transport costs, the further one is from the consuming center, the more relative mobility matters; and the mobility of labor lies between that of high-value goods and that of low-value goods. Not by chance, Africa exported high-value goods from the Gold and Ivory Coasts, and otherwise exported slaves, until steam navigation allowed the profitable export of Africa's low-value tropical goods. Not by chance, mountainous, land-locked Switzerland exported mercenaries until it developed its exports of high-value time-pieces: not by chance, the Swiss Guards are Swiss.[50]

The traditional models of trade and migration distinguish goods and resources, and consider the latter less mobile than the former. They are doubly misleading: labor is also a tradable good, and it is in fact more

---

[49] Below, Appendix 3, § 2.

[50] Below, Appendix 3, § 3–§ 4; also S. Fenoaltea, "Europe in the African Mirror: The Slave Trade and the Rise of Feudalism," *Rivista di storia economica* 15 (1999), pp. 123–165, and Id., "Economic Decline in Historical Perspective: Some Theoretical Considerations," *Rivista di storia economica* 22 (2006), pp. 3–39. The slave is a permanent migrant, but slaves are paid for, and thus equivalent not to the free (and selfish) permanent migrant but to the temporary migrant; humans are costly to transport per unit of weight because they require space and supplies, but they are nonethess of relatively high value, because moving a worker is a compact way of moving his future surplus over subsistence.

mobile than low-value goods. One area may find it convenient to export the services of its human resources by embodying them in goods, another to export them directly; the calculus is one and simultaneous, the temporary (or anyhow unselfish) migrant is from the perspective of trade a commodity like any other.

Temporary migration is thus better understood through the "model of trade," assimilating it to trade in goods, than through the "model of migration" itself. The model of migration teaches that the grain duty increased (permanent, selfish) emigration, because it reduced real wages; the model of trade (in goods and labor) adds that the grain duty *reduced* temporary emigration because protection raises nominal prices and wages and the real exchange rate. Protection limits imports and therefore exports, including the exports of labor services.

As recalled above, the movements of tariff rates and of commodity prices generated a cycle in actual protection. From 1887 to 1895, tariff rates rose and commodity prices fell; rising protection boosted permanent migration and curbed temporary migration. Subsequently, with stable tariffs and rising commodity prices, protection declined; there was ever less reason to leave Italy altogether, and ever more to support a family in Italy by working abroad. Italian intercontinental migration, at first overwhelmingly permanent, became from the 1890s increasingly temporary; one reason was of course the continuing progress in transportation technology, but another was the world-wide inflation that lowered Italy's barriers to trade.

9. The tariff on grain and migration: ricardian growth

The ricardian "model of trade" is, within its limits, a powerful instrument: it clarifies the logic of the reaction of the economy to the fall in the price of grain in the early 1880s, the logic of temporary migration. It shows that the grain tariff harmed industry and specialized agriculture; but the harm is limited to the transfer of resources from those sectors to cereal cultivation, the *net* damage to the economy is all but non-existent.

But to illuminate the grain tariff Ricardo crafted another instrument as well, which only appears to be aimed at different issues altogether. Ricardo is said to have pioneered abstract economic theory; his volume is in fact a tract against the Corn Laws, fully engaged in the great political battle of his day, and correspondingly not always objective or, one suspects, entirely candid. This is proved not so much by the "model of trade," which condemns protection in general, as by the "model of growth," which never mentions the Corn Laws but is aimed precisely at them.[51]

The growth model too is constructed with extraordinary intelligence. Where the trade model takes all resources as given, the growth model allows for the variation, over time, of labor and capital: these increase if they receive more than their "subsistence" return, and dwindle if they receive less. Only land is given, with two consequences. First, land differs from capital and labor: where these variable resources vanish if they are not adequately remunerated, land is that it is, the remuneration of land alone is not necessary for its maintenance. Second, as the variable resources accumulate land remains constant: the productivity and earnings of capital and labor accordingly decline because they are ever more abundant relative to the supply of land, land rents instead increase because land is ever more scarce relative to capital and labor.[52]

Growth therefore continues until the earnings of capital and labor decline to their subsistence levels, and all the surplus above that accrues to the land. At that point growth stops: not when and because the surplus falls to zero, but when and because the entire surplus accrues to the land-owning aristocracy that does not save and accumulate as the capitalists do. This characterization of England's aristocracy was of course a historical falsehood, for it was precisely the aristocracy that financed the massive investment in infrastructure that brought England to the threshold of the industrial revolution; but it is a falsehood that was absolutely necessary if the model was to achieve its polemical, political objective.[53]

In the early nineteenth century Britain's rising industrial classes challenged the hegemony of the landed aristocracy that imposed the Corn Laws. Ricardo's splendid model provided them with an entire arsenal. It tied the continuation of growth to the liberalization of the grain trade, which would allow Britain to maintain its workers with foreign corn and thus overcome the limits set by its own supply of land; it delegitimized land rent, and *a fortiori* its increases due to the Corn Laws, as socially unnecessary; and it delegitimized the political ascendancy of the landed aristocracy, the parasitic, consuming class whose private interest – unlike

---

[51] For example Backhouse, *A History*, p. 26; Fenoaltea, "Manchester," pp. 502–511; Id., "Politica doganale," pp. 70–73; Id., "Economic Decline," pp. 17–36, here partly summarized.

[52] Below, Appendix 4, § 1.

[53] Another falsehood assumed by Ricardo's model, and equally necessary to reach the desired conclusion, is that corn cannot simply be carried over from year to year; below, Appendix 4, § 1.

that of the productive classes who worked or saved – conflicted with the common good. The model portrayed the landowners as *ennemis du peuple*; covertly, and thus all the more effectively, it called for revolution.[54]

The model well portrays for all that the fundamental structure of traditional economies, the division of the total product of the land: part of it remunerates the labor and capital applied to the land itself, part is rent that maintains the urban-manufacturing sector that produces luxury goods and services for the landed aristocracy.

Ricardo's model is that of a closed economy, with its agricultural sector on the one hand and its complementary artisanal and commercial sector on the other; but it extends naturally to an open economy. Again, land is given. Again, capital and labor are variable, but they are variable because they are internationally mobile: their "subsistence" remuneration is that which just maintains *in situ* the extant stocks, a higher one induces immigration, a lower one emigration. Agricultural goods can naturally be exchanged for manufactures.

In every single nation the urban-manufacturing sector can be greater or smaller than that in Ricardo's autarkic equilibrium: a country can be without a manufacturing sector, if the landowners pay for imported luxuries by exporting their rents in kind; another can have an oversize manufacturing sector, maintained by the agricultural surplus of the foreign landowners to which it sells its goods. The "growth model" thus illustrates the distinction between a developed, industrial core and an underdeveloped, agricultural periphery, a distinction which the "trade model" misses completely and tends in fact to negate.[55]

The mobile-resource model of growth adds a great deal to the "model of trade."[56] In the traditional model of trade protection is harmful because resources are given, and given by chance: the (by chance) less densely populated country has a comparative advantage in (land-intensive) agricultural goods, the (by chance) more densely populated country a corresponding comparative advantage in (labor-intensive) industrial goods, and both can consume more if they trade freely with each other. The model of growth reverses cause and effect, and has the structure of trade determine relative demographic density: the "periphery" country is lightly

---

[54] Ricardo's "model of trade" emphasized that free markets are "good for everybody," his "model of growth" emphasized class conflict; the marxists would set aside the first and develop the second, mainstream ("bourgeois") economists set aside the second and develop the first.

[55] Below, Appendix 4, § 2.

[56] Below, Appendix 4, § 3.

populated because the industry that produces for its consumers, and is maintained by the surplus produce of its land, is located abroad.[57] It can develop by moving from the periphery-equilibrium to the autarky-equilibrium, by using industrial protection to attract to its soil those mobile resources it already maintains and whose product it already consumes. For the young American Republic, with its enormous agricultural surplus, its limitless land, the reduction of trade could indeed abet development.[58]

In a country with limited natural resources, like Italy (and, coal aside, England too), the autarky equilibrium is a poor one indeed. If it is to develop beyond that level it must clearly attract the world's mobile resources, nourish them with the surplus of others, manufacture for the rest of the world: it must become "core." In such countries the exclusion of foreign grain is a brake on development. That is the message of Ricardo's model of growth, the message England heeded: with the repeal of the Corn Laws it chose not only to devote more English capital and English labor to English industry, but to attract to England capital and labor then employed in foreign industry, to turn foreign industrial workers not into foreign farm workers but into English industrial workers. It chose in short not to displace foreign industry but to phagocytize it, to absorb it: in this not entirely innocent sense it chose to become "the workshop of the world."

At the same fork in the road Italy chose to protect its grain: it refused to progress far beyond autarky, it chose to repel, rather than to attract, the world's mobile resources. The grain duty forced those who would work in Italy to consume grain far more costly than that available on the world market. In an international context it was the equivalent of a punitive tax on production in Italy alone: it naturally diverted elsewhere those

---

[57] The "model of growth," protomarxist in its emphasis on class conflict, is such in the international context as well, in pointing to "the development of underdevelopment" through foreign trade. Imagine two autarkic economies, each with its artisans producing luxuries, and that the first has a more ancient and refined manufacturing sector than the second. When they come in contact the luxuries of the first will be preferred by the aristocracy even of the second; the second economy will therefore lose its manufacturing sector, and (at least in relative terms) lose population. Precolonial Africa, which paid for Indian cottons directly with its own people, is only the clearest, cruelest example of this mechanism (Fenoaltea, "Europe"; Id., "Economic Decline").

[58] Because it assumes given resources and excludes *a priori* that industrial protection could have attracted more to the United States, the "comparative advantage" model limits the possible national gain from industrial protection to the exploitation of America's near-monopoly as a supplier of raw cotton.

processing activities that are forever searching for low-cost locations, it diverted elsewhere investment and employment, capital and labor.

The traditional analysis of trade considers the grain tariff harmful because it led Italy to produce a mix of goods that was not the best among the production possibilities allowed by its given resources. The alternative analysis makes it clear that the grain tariff limited the accumulation of resources, that it reduced the entire range of production possibilities the "model of trade" takes as given. The duty on grain did not curb, as the "pessimists" claim, the peasants' flight from the land, as with the growth of earnings in alternative occupations they would abandon agriculture anyway; the grain tariff prevented them from finding such alternative occupations in Italy itself.[59] There is every reason to believe that the duty on grain was the greatest single cause of the Italian diaspora, of Italy's disappointing growth between Unification and the Great War.

10. The evolution of the literature

The evaluation of Italy's tariff policy is closely tied to the interpretation of the 1880s. Italy's economists of the time believed that the fall in transport costs and the expansion of trade had benefited the Italian economy, that the 1880s were prosperous, that the tariff of 1887 countered that prosperity. The historical literature of the last half-century is dominated by the opposite view: the expansion of trade damaged the Italian economy, the 1880s were depressed, the tariff of 1887 countered that depression. Both views are internally consistent; both cannot be right.

The battle has recently been rejoined; but even as it began Giovanni Federico fired off his estimates that deny the "crisis of the 1880s," and his arguments that protection had done no harm at all. It is not clear that these salvos were in fact coordinated; what is clear is that they came from the no-man's-land between the long-embattled trenches. Federico had taken up a dangerous position, exposed to attack on two sides.

But events have taken a curious turn. The arguments of the previous chapter have been found compelling, and the leading "pessimists" now agree that the 1880s were indeed prosperous. The arguments of the present chapter have instead failed utterly to impress the protectionists,

---

[59] Below, Appendix 4, § 4. On the effect on the real wage of the grain tariff on the one hand and emigration on the other see Fenoaltea, "Politica doganale," p. 72, and A. M. Taylor and J. G. Williamson, "Convergence in the Age of Mass Migration," *European Review of Economic History* 1 (1997), p. 40.

who dismiss them without so much as a reply: Federico himself ducks the issue, Gianni Toniolo and Vera Zamagni simply cite Federico's conclusions.[60] At the present time Federico is no longer alone: no-man's-land is the fashionable place to be.

The future course of the literature is not easy to predict. If the new majority view is indeed logically incoherent, it should not long survive; but the eventual outcome remains uncertain. The newly converted "optimists" may move past no-man's-land and jettison their protectionist views as well – or they may stick to their protectionism and revert to a logically consistent "pessimism," perhaps taking Federico with them. If, as it seems, "pessimism" and protectionism stand or fall together, neither can be considered dead until both have been buried.

But there is a further possibility, for the course of the literature may once again be shaped by deeper forces, by the story we wish to tell. Gerschenkron saw in Italy's commercial policy the *pièce de résistance* of public intervention in the economy; and he found it disastrous.[61] If one recognizes that it was exactly that – that the tariff was the main reason for Italy's stunted development, the main reason its dream of Great Power status dissolved in nightmare – one cannot tell a story that puts Italy's governing classes in a favorable light. If one is deeply *bien-pensant*, if one cannot write but approvingly of Italy's political leadership, there is no apparent harm in accepting that the 1880s were more prosperous than one had thought; but Italy's commercial policy must be defended, the damage done by the duties on steel and grain must be denied, and the refusal to engage the issue may be simple prudence.

The new majority view may lack logical coherence, and yet live on: it boasts hermeneutic coherence, and that foundation is immensely strong.

---

[60] G. Federico and V. Zamagni, both in P. Bolchini *et al.*, "A proposito di Stefano Fenoaltea, *L'economia italiana dall'Unità alla Grande Guerra*, Bari-Roma, 2006," *Rivista di storia economica* 22 (2006), pp. 347, 374; G. Toniolo, "Review of Stefano Fenoaltea (2006), *L'economia italiana dall'Unità alla Grande Guerra* (Rome and Bari: Laterza)," *Journal of Modern Italian Studies* 12 (2007), p. 131.

[61] Gerschenkron, "Notes," p. 80, and above, ch. 1, § 2.

5

Railways

1. The railway in history and in the literature

Transport costs determine the location of economic activity. Relatively immobile resources attract the relatively mobile, low-value goods high-value goods: man lives next to water, even in prehistory salt was traded over great distances.

Traditional technologies allowed relatively low transport costs only on water, on safe rivers or seas. On land, even on the sea if the cargo had to be defended, only the highest-value goods could bear the cost of long-distance transportation; low-value goods were limited to short distances, to local trade. An inland city not on a navigable waterway was nourished by the nearby countryside, and the short distances over which low-value goods could be moved set a limit to the city's size; over the centuries transportation technology barely changed, and Europe's cities did not grow beyond their medieval walls.

The resistance to movement is reduced if the road is improved. Investment in such improvement is particularly profitable where traffic is not only heavy but homogeneous, for with standard vehicles, of invariant gauge, the road itself can be reduced to two parallel strips: wooden tracks were laid down at the mines, to increase the hauling power of the draft animals.

In eighteenth-century England the iron industry rapidly improved its methods, much reducing the cost of castings, of wrought iron bars and plate. Iron tracks were laid down to serve general traffic, with horse-drawn cars and carriages: the common-carrier railway was born.

At the same time, England's fuel needs were being increasingly met by coal; and the coal mines needed to be drained. The first steam engines were used to pump them out: they were atmospheric-pressure engines, huge, terribly inefficient, but for that purpose at least economical. Out of them evolved by the end of the century the high-pressure steam-engine, relatively compact and sparing in its use of fuel, economical even far from the pit-head and therefore suitable for a multitude of purposes.

Early in the nineteenth century steam traction was successfully applied to the iron railway.[1] The steam railway proved a revolutionary invention: not only because it reached previously unimaginable speeds, but because for the first time in human history the cost of transportation over land fell to levels previously achieved only on water, with barges or cargo ships. For the first time in human history, land united instead of dividing: continental empires, previously ephemeral, became long-lasting; cities burst out of their historic walls (and equipped themselves with urban tramways), commuting appeared.[2] The steam railway would become the very symbol of the century, of Progress.

Economic historians too have been fascinated by the railway. For Rostow the railways were the "leading sector" in the industrial take-offs of the nineteenth century, in the United States and elsewhere; the earliest "cliometric" efforts questioned the inefficiency of slavery, and the importance of the railways. The first of these topics remained typically American, even though the analysis of New World slavery seemed contradicted by the prior experience of the Old; the second attracted young scholars from around the world, and the literature was soon enriched by numerous papers on the significance of the railway in different national contexts.[3]

The railway had been considered "important" both as a market for the metalmaking and engineering industries, and as a provider of transportation services. The pioneer cliometricians challenged both claims: in

---

[1] The cast-iron rails of the horse railways tended to shatter under the blows transmitted from the steam engines' pistons; they were therefore replaced by wrought-iron rails, which however rapidly wore down. Steel combines the resistance of cast iron to wear and compression and the resistance of wrought iron to tension and blows, but with traditional methods of production it was too expensive for anything but weapons. From the mid-nineteenth century technical progress dramatically cut the cost of steel as well, and the railways quickly switched to steel.

[2] To limit pollution, as defined in an age still inured to dung, urban tramways remained powered by horses, rather than by steam, until they were converted to electric traction at the end of the century.

[3] W. W. Rostow, *The Stages of Economic Growth: A Non-Communist Manifesto*, Cambridge 1960, pp. 54–55; R. W. Fogel and S. L. Engerman, eds., *The Reinterpretation of American Economic History*, New York 1971, pp. 187–203, 310–365; S. Fenoaltea, "Slavery and Supervision in Comparative Perspective: A Model," *Journal of Economic History* 44 (1984), pp. 635–668; P. K. O'Brien, ed., *Railways and the Economic Development of Western Europe*, London 1983.

the United States rails absorbed less iron than common nails, and railway transportation was not in fact cheaper than water transportation, on the canals that could have been built instead. The interpretation of this second point was much discussed, for the conclusion that the railway had not been "important" simply did not ring true. In strict logic, that America's railways may not have been *necessary* to open up the country does not mean that they had not in fact been *sufficient* to do so; the implausible, revisionist conclusion rested on a subtle redefinition of historical "importance," and the debate turned ultimately on semantic ambiguity.[4] All that aside, the substantive contribution of these early efforts was in the documentation of relative transport costs. The railway clearly cut transport costs to the extent that it displaced not water-borne modes but other overland modes, in essence horse-carts; with respect to canals, the railways' advantage was that they did not require water resources or mild temperatures, and especially that their less costly right-of-way allowed a more capillary development and thus required a smaller complement of expensive local horse-cart transportation.

In the Italian context the main theses on the importance of the railways predated these cliometric efforts. Railway transportation services were uppermost for Rosario Romeo, who believed that the "essential infrastructure" had to be in place before industry could take off, and also for Emilio Sereni, who believed that the railway had unified the domestic market; the railway market for industrial goods was uppermost for Alexander Gerschenkron, who considered the prior completion of the railway net one of the reasons Italy's "great spurt" was less vigorous than one might have expected.[5]

Both these contributions of Italy's railways have been examined by the present author; and in this case too the available evidence tends to subvert conventional views.[6]

---

[4] R. W. Fogel, *Railroads and American Economic Growth: Essays in Econometric History*, Baltimore 1964; S. Fenoaltea, "The Discipline and They: Notes on Counterfactual Methodology and the 'New' Economic History," *Journal of European Economic History* 2 (1973), pp. 729–746. The further controversy unleashed by R. W. Fogel and S. L. Engerman, *Time on the Cross: The Economics of American Negro Slavery*, Boston 1974, similarly turned largely on semantic ambiguity, in this case on the alternative meanings of "efficiency"; see S. Fenoaltea, "The Slavery Debate: A Note from the Sidelines," *Explorations in Economic History* 18 (1981), pp. 304–308.

[5] Above, ch. 1, § 2, § 4; E. Sereni, *Capitalismo e mercato nazionale in Italia*, 2[d] ed., Rome 1974 (1966).

[6] S. Fenoaltea, "Italy," in O'Brien, *Railways*, pp. 49–120, partly summarized in what follows. The tables in this chapter are transcribed, with certain simplifications, from that essay; some estimates of industrial production have since been amended (above, Tables 1.03, 2.01), but without affecting the conclusions they suggest. S. Fenoaltea, "Railroads

2. The development of the railways

The growth of railways was in no sense "manchesterian." The required investment was enormous, in public infrastructure, on land taken by eminent domain; it invited a public subsidy to construction, public control of operations and railway rates. Thus it was almost everywhere, thus it was in Italy; a happy consequence is that the historical, statistical documentation is here exceptionally rich.

The development of Italy's railways up to the Great War can be divided into four periods. From the opening of the first line (Naples–Portici) in 1839 to Unification, the first regional networks were built. By the end of the 1840s some 500 kilometers were in place: 50 around Naples, 200 in Tuscany (from Florence to Pisa and Leghorn and to Siena), 200 in (Austrian) Lombardy and Venetia (on the Milan–Venice line), and 50 in Piedmont (from Turin to Asti). Another 1,500 kilometers opened in the 1850s. The most significant growth was in Piedmont, which linked the major centers of the upper Po valley to each other and to the sea at Genoa; this net linked up at Novara with the line to Milan, Venice, and the Tarvisio mountain pass, at Alessandria with the line to Piacenza and Bologna. The separate Tuscan and Neapolitan nets also grew; in the Papal States, Rome was connected to Civitavecchia. In 1860 Italy's railway net was comparable to Spain's, the British, French, and German nets were many times greater (Table 5.01).

The second period, dear to Romeo, covers the next two decades: no fewer than 4,000 kilometers were built in the 1860s, another 2,500 in the 1870s. The railhead charged forth from Bologna to and along the Adriatic, reaching Ancona in 1861 and Lecce in 1866; at a less frantic pace it continued along the Ionic coast, reaching Reggio Calabria in 1875. The pre-existing networks were also rapidly linked up: Rome and Naples were connected in 1863, Florence and Bologna in 1864, Florence and Rome in 1866; the west-coast line was opened from Civitavecchia to

and Italian Industrial Growth, 1861–1913," *Explorations in Economic History* 9 (1972), pp. 325–351, was instead an unsuccessful attempt at methodological innovation. Where the standard "cliometric" approach measured the railways' impact on production by the extra output that could be obtained from given resources, that essay attempted to measure their contribution in an economy with elastic supplies of capital and labor. The analysis relied on a macroeconomic model, expanded to identify the relevant industrial sectors. It assumed perfect capital mobility, and suffered the familiar consequences of that assumption: (railway) investment had strong effects with the exchange at par, and none with a depreciated, floating exchange, even if the difference between the two exchange regimes could be mitigated by the hypothesis that railway investment was financed in part by money creation.

TABLE 5.01. *European railway networks (within the borders of 1913)*

	(1)	(2)	(3)	(4)	(5)
		1860		1913	
	area (thousand sq. km.)	population (millions)	railways (thousand km.)	population (millions)	railways (thousand km.)
Italy	287	25	2	35	18
Great Britain	228	23	15	42	33
France	536	35	9	39	41
Germany	541	37	12	68	64
Spain	504	16	2	20	15

Source: S. Fenoaltea, "Italy," in P. K. O'Brien, ed., *Railways and the Economic Development of Western Europe*, London 1983, p. 52.

Leghorn in 1867, from Leghorn through Genoa to the French border, across difficult terrain, in 1874. The main transpeninsular lines were also built, connecting Rome and Ancona in 1866, Naples and Bari in 1870, Salerno, Potenza, and Taranto in 1880; new lines also connected the major urban centers in Sicily, in Sardinia. In 1860 the major trunks were in place only in the North, and especially the Northwest; by 1880 they were in place in the peninsula and the major islands as well, the national trunks had essentially been completed (Figure 5.01).

The third period spans the next fifteen years. The Left gave a new impetus to railway construction, and between 1880 and 1895 another 6,500 kilometers were built. The last major trunk, from Salerno to Reggio Calabria along the difficult west coast of Southern Italy, was opened then; but most of the new lines built then were minor lines, of essentially local interest.

In the fourth period, from 1896 to 1913, new construction reverted to the slow pace of the earliest years; only some 2,500 kilometers were added in almost twenty years. On the eve of the Great War Italy's rail lines summed to 17,500 kilometers. Progress had been considerable compared to Italy itself at the time of Unification, but not compared to other European countries: Italy remained on a level with Spain, and far behind the Great Powers with which it compared itself (Table 5.01).

Administratively, the lines had originally been built and operated by a large number of private franchisees. Italy still has a number of small "franchise" railways, but the main network was thrice reorganized. In 1865 it was divided on a regional basis among the *Alta Italia* in the North, the *Romane* between Pisa and Florence and Naples, the *Meridionali* east of Bologna and Naples, the *Calabro-Sicule* (absorbed by the *Meridionali* in 1873), and the *Sarde*. In 1885, the main network, by then almost entirely repurchased by the State, was assigned to four operating companies: two minor ones in the main islands (the *Sicule* and the *Sarde*), and,

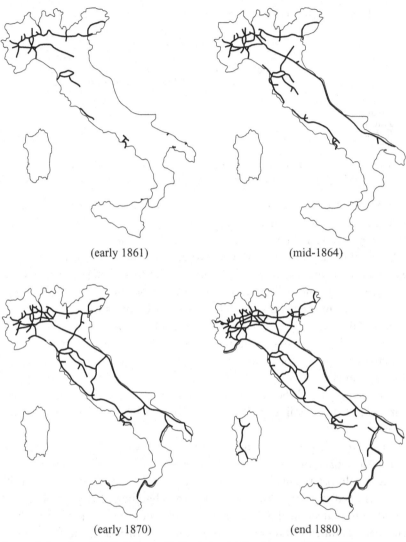

(early 1861)   (mid-1864)

(early 1870)   (end 1880)

Source: S. Fenoaltea, "Public Policy and Italian Industrial Development, 1861–1913"
(unpublished Ph.D. thesis, Harvard University, 1967), Fig. 17.

FIGURE 5.01. *The growth of the railways to 1880*

on the continent, two major longitudinal systems, the *Rete Mediterranea*
in the west and the *Rete Adriatica* in the east. The original contracts were
for twenty years, renewable; the fear that they might not be renewed led
the operating companies to limit investment and neglect maintenance,
and service deteriorated to the point that the termination of the contracts

TABLE 5.02. *Value added in rail- and tramway construction (million lire at 1911 prices; annual averages)*

	(1)	(2)	(3)	(4)	(5)
	rail- and tramway construction				total construc- tion
	new lines	improve- ments	main- tenance	total	
1861–1865	112	0	3	115	400
1866–1870	66	0	5	71	350
1871–1875	67	4	8	79	400
1876–1880	53	11	11	75	400
1881–1885	102	23	15	140	500
1886–1890	92	21	20	133	550
1891–1895	79	2	22	103	500
1896–1900	22	5	25	52	400
1901–1905	28	11	31	70	450
1906–1910	31	35	38	104	600
1911–1913	62	39	45	146	650

Source: S. Fenoaltea, "Italy," in P. K. O'Brien, ed., *Railways and the Economic Development of Western Europe*, London 1983, p. 61.

became inevitable. In 1905, the operation of the main network passed to the *Ferrovie della Stato*, and a large-scale program to rebuild the lines and renew the rolling stock was immediately launched.

After Unification, therefore, there were three main waves of railway investment. The first two waves, of new construction, were induced by political changes (Unification in 1861, the victory of the Left in 1876); the third wave, of reconstruction, was induced by the administrative shift from private to State operation.

3. Railways and the demand for industrial products

Alexander Gerschenkron emphasized the railways' demand for industrial products; its significance is gauged by Tables 5.02–5.04.

The railway-construction estimates (Table 5.02) document both the waves of new construction (to build new lines, and, increasingly, to improve extant lines) in the 1860s, the 1880s, and the pre-war years, and the steady growth of maintenance. Railway construction was a very significant component of total construction; it followed the typical Kuznets-cycle swing, like and even more than other construction, with a clearly destabilizing effect on the aggregate cycle.

The railway-rolling-stock estimates (Table 5.03) separate production and imports (measured, like production, not by value but by engineering-industry value added). Production and consumption (production plus net imports) display a cycle even sharper than that of construction, which

TABLE 5.03. *Engineering value added in rail- and tramway rolling stock (million lire at 1911 prices; annual averages)*

	(1)	(2)	(3)	(4)	(5)	(6)	(7)	(8)
						aggregate engineering[a]		
	rail- and tramway rolling stock				machinery only		total	
	produc-tion	imports	main-tenance	total	produc-tion	main-tenance	produc-tion	main-tenance
1861–1865	2.2	4.0	3.1	9.3	21	16	49	273
1866–1870	2.0	3.2	5.1	10.3	22	21	50	283
1871–1875	3.1	5.4	8.2	16.7	26	27	59	294
1876–1880	1.7	2.0	10.7	14.4	31	33	70	305
1881–1885	9.0	4.5	15.6	29.1	55	43	123	321
1886–1890	15.4	7.8	20.5	43.7	79	53	174	336
1891–1895	4.6	.1	22.7	27.4	52	62	113	351
1896–1900	11.8	2.3	27.1	41.2	65	74	139	369
1901–1905	19.8	6.2	34.6	60.6	83	93	176	394
1906–1910	45.8	21.0	44.4	111.2	166	114	347	422
1911–1913	53.5	3.1	54.6	111.2	200	135	412	446

[a] net of shipbuilding.

Source: S. Fenoaltea, "Italy," in P. K. O'Brien, ed., *Railways and the Economic Development of Western Europe*, London 1983, p. 62.

takes longer to complete.[7] Their trend was clearly upward, like that of construction for improvements, similarly tied to traffic growth; for the same reason value added in maintenance, by the railways' repair shops, steadily grew. One also notes the cyclical variation in the domestic share of the market: because over the short run world supply was more elastic than domestic supply, imports' share of the market briefly rose when consumption exploded, and fell to almost nothing when consumption contracted. The railways' needs were a conspicuous part of the market for "modern" engineering, the manufacture and maintenance of machines; it was naturally much smaller next to total engineering, especially at the beginning of the period at hand, when the industry's main activity was the maintenance of agricultural hand tools.

The metalmaking estimates (Table 5.04) also display the cycle and a rising trend. They document the importance of the railway market for Italy's ferrous-metals industry, and the import-substitution induced by the tariff. Interestingly, the railway market was dominated not by the direct demand for rails but increasingly, as metal replaced wood in the bodies of railway vehicles, by the engineering industry's derived demand for semi-finished metal. More generally, the railways' demand for metal

---

[7] Deliveries of rolling stock practically coincide with the opening of the lines, which typically required several years of construction; see S. Fenoaltea, "Railway Construction in Italy, 1861–1913," *Rivista di storia economica* 1 (1984), International Issue, pp. 27–54.

TABLE 5.04. *Metalmaking value added in rail- and tramway goods (million lire at 1911 prices; annual averages)*

	(1)	(2)	(3)	(4)	(5)	(6)
		rail- and tramway goods			total ferrous metal-making	
	rails					
	produc-tion	imports	other metal[a]	total		market share[b]
1861–1865	.0	1.2	.8	2.0	4.1	49
1866–1870	.0	1.0	1.0	2.0	3.6	42
1871–1875	.0	1.7	1.8	3.5	4.7	44
1876–1880	.0	2.4	1.4	3.8	7.0	54
1881–1885	.0	5.3	3.5	8.8	13.3	57
1886–1890	3.0	1.7	4.8	9.5	24.5	64
1891–1895	1.6	.4	2.2	4.2	18.5	75
1896–1900	.8	.7	3.6	5.1	24.5	81
1901–1905	1.4	.8	5.4	7.6	32.2	79
1906–1910	4.4	1.1	11.6	17.1	67.1	78
1911–1913	6.9	.1	11.3	18.3	90.9	83

[a] other metal produced or imported for rail- and tramway track and rolling stock.

[b] ratio of domestic production to domestic consumption, semi-finished ferrous metal (percent).

Source: S. Fenoaltea, "Italy," in P. K. O'Brien, ed., *Railways and the Economic Development of Western Europe*, London 1983, pp. 64–65.

was a very minor part of their demand for industrial goods: in value added terms their market for metalmaking never reached 20 million lire p. a., against peaks well over 100 million both for engineering and for construction. The visibly effective steel tariff had opposite effects on the metalmaking and engineering industries: had the mirage of the railways' demand for metal led to its adoption, the railways themselves would bear responsibility for Italy's stunted industrial development.[8]

The quantitative evidence does not support Gerschenkron's claim that Italy's "great spurt" (in manufacturing and mining) had been weakened by the prior completion of the railway net. Considered together, rather, the figures in Tables 5.02–5.04 document the change in the *composition* of the railways' demand, its shift over time from construction to manufacturing.

The initial construction of the railway lines, in the often difficult terrain of the Italian peninsula, required an enormous investment; but the larger part of the expense was for earth-moving, and comparatively little was for manufactured goods, for the the products of the metalmaking and engineering industries. As new construction dwindled and traffic increased railway demand became less visible but no less important. It shifted to the maintenance and improvement of the right-of-way, to the

[8] Fenoaltea, "Railroads," pp. 342–343.

maintenance and augmentation of the rolling stock; it shifted away from construction, and was increasingly directed at the engineering and metal-making industries.

Counting the cost of the raw materials, railway investment averaged some 180 million lire per year (at 1911 prices) both from 1861 to 1895, when most of Italy's railways were built, and from 1896 to 1913. In the first period about half that sum was absorbed by construction, another quarter by quarry products; the residual quarter was for metalmaking and engineering products, but over half of that was absorbed by coal and iron ore, and only 10 percent of the overall total was in fact manufacturing value added. In the second period the share of construction dropped to a third, that of quarry products to a tenth; the share of coal and iron ore rose to a quarter, that of metalmaking and engineering value added trebled to 30 percent, with the latter industry gaining relatively more. The point is strengthened by the steady growth of railway maintenance, initially of little weight but eventually comparable to investment, and about evenly divided between construction and engineering. The railway repair shops contributed a great deal to industrial value added, and to the formation of human capital.

In the 1880s the railways generated considerable demand, but mainly for pick-and-shovel work. Their consumption of manufactured goods was relatively minor: it does not seem to have had the potential to generate a "great spurt," even with a prohibitive tariff on engineering goods.

The railways' consumption of manufactured metal products was far greater in the early 1900s than in the 1880s, precisely because the railway net was already in place, and the railways' demand was dominated by the maintenance needs, and the investment in new rolling stock, typical of a mature system. The completion of the railway net in the nineteenth century did not reduce the railways' subsequent demand for manufactured goods, and lower the rate of industrial growth in the early twentieth: to the contrary, it increased the one, and raised the other.

4. The limits of railway transportation

The railway was the first modern, mechanical means of overland trans-portation. For Rosario Romeo this was its critical feature: without that "essential infrastructure," without the trunk lines built in the 1860s and '70s, Italy's industrial take-off could not have occurred at all. Emilio Sereni too focused on the transportation provided by the rail-ways: the peninsular trunks built by the Right unified the domestic market, and handed the consumers of the South to the industry of the North.[9]

In point of fact, Italy's railways do not appear to have had a revolutionary impact.

A crude initial calculation already suggests as much. In 1911, the railways loaded some 40 million tons of goods, including 11 million in the seaports (nearly half in Genoa, another quarter in Savona and Venice); letting domestic goods loaded in the seaports offset those imported directly by rail, the total tonnage of domestic goods loaded by the railways works out to some 29 million tons. In 1973, 1,168 million tons of goods were loaded by modern overland means (mostly not by railroads); deducting 217 million tons of imported goods, the tonnage of domestic goods transported by modern overland means works out to some 951 million tons, or 33 times the tonnage loaded by the railways in 1911.

The corresponding increase in production can be estimated from the increase in industrial and agricultural value added (plus the value of imports, reduced by half to allow for those consumed without further transformation), deflated by the increase in wholesale prices. The former increased some 2,900 times over, the second 430 times over; their ratio suggests that real, physical production increased some 6.7 times over. Transportation by modern overland means increased some 33 times over, or five times as much: in 1911 the railway provided only one fifth the transportation, per unit of physical output, provided in 1973 by all modern means together.[10]

Similar conclusions are suggested by Table 5.05, which lists the main groups of commodities transported by the *Ferrovie dello Stato* in 1911. Because these rankings depend in part on the underlying classification, and the disaggregation covers less than two thirds of the total actually shipped, important but highly disaggregated categories may be omitted altogether; but it is clear enough that over half the total tonnage moved by the railways consisted of fuels, construction materials, and the goods consumed and produced by agriculture.

Table 5.05 also compares railway transportation (by the *Ferrovie dello Stato*) with foreign trade and domestic production. Together, these figures

---

[9] Sereni, *Capitalismo e mercato nazionale*, pp. 71, 93; R. Romeo, *Risorgimento e capitalismo*, 3[d] ed., Rome-Bari 1998 (Bari 1959).

[10] This does not of course imply that total transportation per unit of output remained constant, and that the other four fifths were provided by traditional means: total transportation was surely much less, and it then paid to locate activity where it did not minimize production costs, but saved transportation costs.

TABLE 5.05. *Main commodities transported by the* Ferrovie dello Stato *in 1911 (million tons)*

	(1) ship-ments	(2) im-ports	(3) ex-ports	(4) domestic produc-tion	
1. lime and cement	1.7	.0	.0	2.6	
2. lumber	1.7	1.5	.0	1.1	
3. building stone	1.3	.0	.4	13.9	
4. bricks and tiles	1.2	.1	.1	7.8	
5. sand	.6	?	?	1.4	
6. asphalt	.1	.0	.0	.2	(rock only)
SUBTOTAL	6.8				
7. cereal and flour: wheat	1.8	1.5	.1	5.1	(cereal only)
8. cereal and flour: other	1.8	.6	.1	4.0	(cereal only)
9. wine	.9	.0	.1	4.8	
10. animal feed, straw, etc.	.5	?	?	23.4	(forage crops only)
11. sugar beet	.5	?	?	1.6	
12. animals	.4	.1	.0	.9	(slaughtered live weight)
13. grapes and must	.3	.0	.0	7.7	(grapes only)
14. citrus fruit	.3	.0	.4	1.0	
15. sugar, coffee, etc.	.3	.1	.0	.2	(crude sugar only)
SUBTOTAL	6.7				
16. coal, lignite, charcoal	6.0	9.8	.1	.7	(mine products only)
17. firewood	.3	.1	.0	2.5	
SUBTOTAL	6.3				
18. chemical fertilizer	.7	.0	.0	1.0	
19. phosphates, Thomas slag	.4	.6	.0	.0	
20. natural fertilizer	.4	.0	.0	?	
SUBTOTAL	1.5				
21. pig and scrap iron	.4	.6	.0	.7	
22. ingot and semi-f. metal	.3	.2	.0	1.1	(semi-finished metal only)
SUBTOTAL	.7				
23. yarn and cloth	.2	.0	.1	.3	(yarn only)
24. raw cotton	.2	.2	.0	.0	
25. other textile fibers	.1	.1	.1	.1	
SUBTOTAL	.5				
26. other chemicals	.4	.3	.1	.4	(final products only)
27. sulphur	.4	.0	.4	.4	(fused sulphur only)
28. mineral and vegetable oils	.3	.3	.1	.2	(petroleum and olive oil only)
29. paper	.2	.0	.0	.2	
TOTAL	23.8				

Source: S. Fenoaltea, "Italy," in P. K. O'Brien, ed., *Railways and the Economic Development of Western Europe*, London 1983, pp. 79–81.

suggest that the railways were heavily involved in the distribution of bulk imports: coal, in particular, and grain (with 1.3 million tons loaded at the seaports), artificial fertilizer (phosphates and Thomas slag), raw cotton, and probably lumber. The railways also seem to have collected bulk exports like sulphur, citrus fruit, perhaps marble (included with other building stone).

Wholly domestic transportation seems comparatively limited. Among bulk goods, only relatively valuable construction materials (lime and cement) and chemical fertilizer appear to have relied heavily on the railway; not by chance, they are commodities characterized by a relatively high unit value (by the standards of bulk goods), and by geographically diffused consumption (by construction and agriculture). Low-value construction materials, agricultural products, semi-finished industrial goods (metals) made limited use of the railways. The limited shipments of semi-finished industrial products surely reflect the territorial concentration of industry, perhaps even extensive vertical integration; but this feature of the industrial structure may itself be at least in part an adaptation to the high cost of transportation. The limited shipments of agricultural produce and other bulk goods point instead to a low level of interregional trade, to the persistence, on a large scale, of the traditional system of local trade between a city and the surrounding countryside.[11]

A *fortiori*, the peninsular trunks built in the 1860s and '70s do not appear to have unified the domestic market. This is confirmed by the fact that in the 1880s the railways still suffered from the competition of the traditional coasting trade, as will be seen in greater detail below. It is further, indirectly confirmed by the structure of Italy's foreign trade, and specifically the trade in grain.

Land-poor Italy was structurally an importer of grain; but as seen above its net imports were long the difference between conspicuous imports and smaller but far from insignificant exports.[12] In the early 1880s world grain prices collapsed, Italy's imports surged and exports fell to nothing; but in 1882 exports were still significant, near 100,000 tons, against an import volume approximately twice that. Italy's imports came primarily from Russia and Turkey. Forty percent of Italy's exports went to France, 30 percent to Iberia and Gibraltar, and another 30 percent to Switzerland and Austria; and only these last could have been transit trade serving the Cantons and Tyrol through Italian ports.

Had internal transport costs been relatively low and external transport costs relatively high, had the domestic market been more unified than the world market, Italy would have consumed all its own grain and imported only its further consumption. As it was, Italy's deficit regions did not absorb the exports of the regions with a surplus, rather, the ones bought abroad and the others sold abroad: despite the completion of

---

[11] Interregional trade was limited by migration, as well as by high transport costs, to the extent that remittances allowed the South to import manufactures without exporting a larger part of its agricultural output. But migration too is tied to transport costs: had the interior of the peninsula been less cut off from world markets, it would have tended to export more of its labor as value added to exported goods rather than directly as labor.

[12] Above, ch. 1, § 2.

TABLE 5.06. Comparative railway statistics, 1898[a]

	(1) R.M.	(2) R.A.	(3) Nord	(4) P.L.M.	(5) V.P.H.
A. Kilometers of line track	6,909	6,277	6,236	13,178	41,948
B. Traffic per km. of line track					
thousand passenger-kilometers	168	146	321	226	294
thousand ton-kilometers	178	173	496	406	531
thousand total traffic units	346	319	817	631	826
share of freight (percent)	51	54	61	64	64
C. Operating costs (lire per thousand traffic units)					
labor	27	25	14	14	15
fuel	6	5	2	3	3
other	9	10	7	7	8
TOTAL	42	40	22	24	26
total at Italian prices	42	40	28	29	32
D. Employment (per million traffic units)					
administration	.8	1.0	.3	.4	.5
track surveillance and maintenance	6.6	8.3	2.0	2.2	2.7
other	12.9	10.8	6.2	6.4	6.8
TOTAL	20.3	20.1	8.5	9.0	10.0

[a] Rete Mediterranea, Rete Adriatica, Chemins de Fer du Nord, Chemins de Fer de Paris à Lyon et à la Méditerranée, Vereinigte Prüssische und Hessische Staatseisenbahnen.

Source: S. Fenoaltea, "Italy," in P. K. O'Brien, ed., Railways and the Economic Development of Western Europe, London 1983, pp. 83–85.

the "essential infrastructure" Italy's different regions remained closer to foreign lands than to the other regions of Italy itself.

Italy's railways do not seem to have radically increased the internal mobility of commodities, to have transformed the economy, to have unified the domestic market: the evidence does not attribute to the railways, much less the trunks built in the 1860s and '70s, the crucial role they play in the interpretations of Sereni and Romeo.

5. The production cost of railway transportation

One might presume that the impact of Italy's railways was limited by the comparatively limited extent of the railway net itself (Table 5.01); but this hypothesis does not survive a deeper comparative analysis.

Table 5.06 transcribes some end-of-the-century data for the major Italian systems and a sample of foreign ones. It is immediately apparent that Italy's railways were not used at all intensively: total traffic per kilometer of line track was far below that carried elsewhere, freight traffic was particularly light.[13] Railway transportation was not limited by a

---

[13] Total traffic is conventionally measured in "traffic units," calculated as the simple sum of passenger-kilometers on the one hand and freight ton-kilometers on the other.

capacity constraint. Its supply was elastic; its use was limited by its user cost, itself determined on the one hand by the production cost of railway transportation, on the other by the margin between that cost and the price to the public.

In Italy the production cost of railway transportation – the operating cost, net of the fixed cost of the lines themselves – was relatively high, over two-thirds higher than the average of the present foreign sample. The conventional wisdom is that this was due to the high price of coal, which Italy had to import. In fact, fuel was everywhere a very minor cost item; that in Italy coal might cost two or three times as much as in France or Germany does not begin to explain the difference in operating costs. Other materials might also have been relatively expensive in Italy, but labor was cheaper, by about one fifth. If one calculates foreign costs at Italian prices the sample totals increase, but not very much; no more than a third of the actual difference in operating costs can be explained by the differences in local prices.[14]

The high operating costs of Italy's railways seem due primarily to the low productivity of labor, as employment per traffic unit was more than double that in the sample of foreign lines. Productivity was low across the board: in administration, in the maintenance and surveillance of the lines (where Italy appears particularly handicapped), and in the residual (sales and train crews, maintenance of the rolling stock).

Labor productivity was low even with the private operating companies, before public ownership could blunt the incentive to contain costs, before the State railways engaged in massive hiring; it seems due at least in part to an unfavorable natural and economic environment.

Railways operate at minimal costs if traffic is heavy and directionally balanced, if the tracks run straight and level. The topography of the Italian peninsula is far from ideal, even apart from the central mountain chain of the Apennines: today's high-speed lines are largely viaducts and tunnels, the original lines followed the snaking valleys. Grades and curves increase running times and maintenance costs, and limit cargo: they increase the consumption of labor and materials per unit of output. A greater initial investment, to improve the lines themselves, would have made for lower operating costs.

---

[14] This result is actually an overestimate, as the calculation alters the relative prices faced by foreign operators without allowing them to alter the input mix and minimize costs; by the same token, it establishes that the low labor productivity of Italian railway workers was only in part an adaptation to different relative prices.

Italy's railways were built on the cheap, not least because of the financial difficulties of the State that subsidized construction; but the lines' defects also reflect the imperfections of the concession contracts. Construction was subsidized per kilometer actually built, not per air-line kilometer between the end-points. Better tracks would have required added expenses for bridges and tunnels, and, by shortening the line, reduced subsidy income: the builders were encouraged to follow the meanders of the rivers, and today's commuters are still paying for that error.

The economic environment also made for high operating costs. Italy's railways were heavily involved in the distribution of bulk imports, in quantity far greater than the corresponding exports. They were in this sense the mirror-image of the colonial railways built to carry plantation or mine products to the sea: traffic was highly unbalanced, half the time the trains ran almost empty. The productivity of the crews, the ton-kilometers generated per employee were correspondingly reduced.[15] Limited domestic and total traffic in turn implied the underemployment of the railways' non-traveling workers, in operations and surveillance.

Railways had various categories of fixed costs, even apart from the system's original construction cost. For the firm, the minimal administrative staff represented a fixed cost; given the lines, the minimal operating and sales staff also represented a fixed cost. Such employment increased only if traffic grew beyond a certain level; only crew and maintenance costs were fully variable costs, tied to the transport service offered if not strictly to that actually generated (that is, to available ton-kilometers rather than actual ton-kilometers). Employment levels in Italy's railways, high per unit of output, were within the norm per kilometer of line: because the "fixed" component was tied in fact to the length of the lines themselves, while the "variable" component was not lower than where traffic was heavier because the unfavorable structure of demand and of the lines themselves reduced the output-productivity of the crews and maintenance staff.[16]

Railway transportation in Italy was expensive because the country's topography meant an abundance of curves and grades; because traffic was directionally unbalanced; because the fixed plant and large parts of the labor force were under-utilized. Railway transportation is a decreasing-cost activity, in Italy it was expensive because the railways were little used.

[15] L. Einaudi, *Cronache economiche e politiche di un trentennio*, 8 vols., Turin 1959–66, vol. 2, p. 286.

[16] All the systems in the sample employ 6 to 8 workers per kilometer of line track: the *Rete Mediterranea*, for example, had 20.3 workers per million traffic units and 0.346 million traffic units per kilometer of line track, or 7.0 workers per kilometer.

6. The user cost of railway transportation

The demand for transportation depends on its quality and price. In Italy, the quality of railway transportation seems never to have been particularly high: delivery schedules were so dilatory that even in the early 1900s horse-carts were faster for distances up to 200 kilometers. Service standards deteriorated further, generating widespread complaints, in particular circumstances: at the port of Genoa, where the railway infrastructure was simply inadequate to handle the growing traffic; on the entire system, over the transition from the private operators to the State railways, as the former finally neglected physical capital, and the latter initially diluted human capital.[17]

The price of railway transportation – its user cost – was instead relatively high, especially from a normative perspective. As economists have long known, prices provide correct information if they correspond to marginal costs, that is, if each price equals the additional cost incurred to produce an additional unit: consumers' decisions change production at the margin, and consumers are led to satisfy their needs at the lowest resource cost if the prices that determine their choices match marginal costs.

Railway transportation is a decreasing-cost activity. If average costs decline as production increases, marginal costs are necessarily less than average costs: a student's grade average declines if the additional, marginal grade is below the previous average. With "correct" prices, equal to marginal costs, decreasing-cost firms do not cover their average costs; efficient public intervention brings their prices into line with marginal costs, and covers the resulting operating loss with a subsidy. The subsidy must be per unit produced and sold, it must tie greater revenue to greater production: the point of the subsidy is to induce the firm to produce the quantity consumers are willing to purchase at the subsidized prices, equal to marginal costs.

In Italy the State set railway rates, and subsidized the railways: but it subsidized per kilometer of line rather than per traffic unit, and the rates it set were above even average costs. The State taxed traffic instead of subsidizing it, it discouraged use of the railway instead of encouraging it. Public policy did not aim at an efficient use of modern means of transportation: it seemed designed to build railways, not actually to use them.

---

[17] G. Baglioni, *Per la riforma ferroviaria*, Milan 1910; Einaudi, *Cronache*, vol. 2, pp. 291–296, 313–317, 578–619. In their first two years the *Ferrovie dello Stato* increased total employment by over 25 percent.

The main taxes on railway traffic took the form of public participation in the railways' *gross* revenues, at rates that declined over time from very high initial levels. The contracts with the early regional operators reserved to the State no less than 50 percent of gross revenue, the equivalent of a 100 percent excise tax: average railway rates had to be at least double average costs, minimal rates at least double marginal costs even if the railways charged different prices to different customers. After 1885 the State took 28 percent of the gross revenues of the main continental networks, the equivalent of a 39 percent excise tax; in 1898 the ratio of gross revenues to total (operating) costs equaled 1.38 for the *Rete Mediterranea*, and 1.47 for the *Rete Adriatica*.[18] After 1905 that ratio fell, to 1.20 on the State railways in 1911; but the reduction seems due to the explosion of unit costs with public operation rather than to a general reduction in railway rates, as these were raised across the board that very year.[19]

A system of prices equal to marginal costs is efficient, in the sense that it maximizes national income at market prices; but some components of national income are more easily monitored, and taxed, than others. The State has its own budget constraint, which naturally influences public intervention in the economy's markets; the State does not in fact aim at the optimization of the price system, and some taxes may understandably exceed, or subsidies fall short of, the theoretically optimal levels. But not even this can explain the particular policies adopted in Italy, the combination of heavy taxes that discouraged traffic and generous subsidies that encouraged construction.

The logic of that economic policy would appear to have been not economic but political. The typical investments in capital goods that are not used – that one hopes never to use – are the investments in military hardware: the Right that governed the newborn Kingdom of Italy and hurried to build the peninsular trunks may well have been sensitive to their military value, their capacity quickly to move troops to quell popular uprisings or, in the South where "bandit bands" long continued to disturb the official peace, a secessionist rebellion. To paraphrase Sereni, the bourgeois national government built the railways to unify not the domestic market, but the domestic theater of operations. Twenty years later, with the national State no longer in jeopardy, the political reasons

[18] The ratio of revenue to operating cost was even higher on the foreign railways considered in Table 5.06 (about 1.6 on the German system, almost 2.0 on the two French systems); but those railways were used altogether more intensively, and they were not visibly operating at decreasing costs.

[19] Law n. 310 of April 13, 1911 (arts. 14 e 15).

to subsidize railway construction were altogether pettier, a matter of electioneering, of strengthening a loyal MP by letting him bring to his district a lucrative contract to build a local railway. In both cases one can understand the emphasis on building the lines rather than on using them, the neglect of investments aimed at reducing future operating costs.

The records of the public authorities that determined railway rates document an episode that is at once revealing and incomprehensible. In 1886, twenty years after the completion of the all-rail route from the North to Apulia and Naples, the operating companies petitioned for reduced rates to meet the competition of the traditional sail-powered coasting trade; and their petition was turned down.[20]

The petition itself is revealing: it shows, against Sereni's thesis, that the peninsular trunks did not materially reduce transport costs between the North and the South, that they did not unify the domestic market. The relative costs of railway and maritime transportation were in fact such that the markets of the South were reached at lower costs from Northern Europe by sea, than from Northern Italy by rail. The South's high-cost industry, that had grown behind the high tariffs of the Kingdom of Naples, would appear to have felt the cold wind of competition when the much lower Piedmontese tariffs were extended nation-wide; the firms that survived do not appear to have suffered from the opening of the North-South railway route five or six years later.[21]

The State's refusal to allow a reduction in railway rates seems part of a permanent policy: Einaudi wrote in 1903 that "the State has always been the most convinced opponent of reductions in railway rates, out of fear that its share of total revenue might decline."[22]

Einaudi's account may well be true, but the argument and the policy remain incomprehensible. If the State wants to maximize the *gross* revenue of which it receives a given share, the rate it prefers must necessarily be *lower* than that preferred by the private operator who wants to maximize *net* revenue. If the State rationally maximized its revenues from the railways, *a fortiori* if it took the broader economy into account, it should

---

[20] R. Ispettorato generale delle strade ferrate, *Annali del consiglio delle tariffe delle strade ferrate 1886*, pp. 56–57. Further evidence of the continuing competitiveness of the coasting trade may be found for example in Commissione d'inchiesta sull'esercizio delle ferrovie italiane, *Atti*, Rome 1879–84, parte 1, vol. 2, pp. 83 and 99, vol. 3, p. 306.

[21] G. Luzzatto, *L'economia italiana dal 1861 al 1894*, Turin 1968 (Milan 1963), pp. 21–28, and below.

[22] Einaudi, *Cronache*, vol. 2, p. 90 (author's translation). Einaudi seems not to notice the logical problem hidden in his statement.

TABLE 5.07. *Returns on railway investment*

	(1) total investment (year end)^a	(2) operating revenue^a	(3) operating costs^a	(4) internal rate of return^b	(5) social rate of r. upper bound^b	(6) best estimate^b	(7) total network length^c
A. Total network							
in 1875	2,296	155.2	90.1	2.8	6.2	4.5	
in 1890	4,139	271.8	173.4	2.4	5.7	4.0	
in 1901	5,604	347.3	247.2	1.8	4.9	3.3	
in 1910	6,962	604.0	452.4	2.2	6.5	4.3	
B. Components of the network in 1910							
major Po valley lines	1,822	226.8	142.0	4.7	10.9	9.0	2,483
other major lines	2,107	191.2	164.3	1.3	5.8	3.1	4,114
minor lines	3,032	186.0	146.1	1.3	4.4	4.4	11,328
C. Minor lines earning per kilometer, in 1910							
less than 10.000 lire	833	32.3	30.2	.3	2.2	2.2	4,866
more than 10.000 lire	2,199	153.7	115.9	1.7	5.2	5.2	6,462

^{a} million lire.
^{b} percent per year.
^{c} kilometers.
Source: S. Fenoaltea, "Italy," in P. K. O'Brien, ed., *Railways and the Economic Development of Western Europe*, London 1983, p. 91.

have granted all petitions to reduce railway rates, and in fact imposed rates lower than those requested.[23]

7. The return on investment

A measure of the usefulness of Italy's railways is provided by the estimates of the return on investment in Table 5.07. Panel A reports the figures obtained, at various dates, for the entire system. The internal rate of return is calculated as the difference between operating revenue and operating costs, divided by total investment; it is always low, near 2 or 3 percent per year, and broadly declining over time (col. 4).[24]

The social rate of return adds to the numerator an estimate of consumers' surplus, the difference between the most users would have been willing to pay and what they actually paid. That surplus can be estimated only very roughly. An initial estimate assumes linear demand curves, and

[23] The railway company is constrained by the market demand curve, as in the textbook "monopoly" case. It accordingly maximizes net revenue (profits) by setting a price that yields a marginal revenue (which is less than the price, because the demand curve slopes downward) equal to marginal cost, which in turn is clearly positive. The price that maximizes gross revenue (and the share of that revenue accruing to the State) is necessarily lower, as it corresponds to a marginal revenue equal to zero.

[24] In 1875, for example, the internal rate of return equals $(155.2 - 90.1)/2{,}296 = 2.8$ percent.

that the State-imposed rates maximized operating revenue and therefore State income; these assumptions imply that consumers' surplus equaled half of total operating revenue (col. 5).[25]

As noted the rates that maximized gross operating revenue were lower than those that maximized net revenue, and accordingly generated a larger consumers' surplus. The State's income was a share of gross revenue until 1905, and then equal to net revenue; the rates that maximized public revenues were higher after the State took over operations, but the first general rate increase would appear to have been that of 1911. A State concerned with the economy at large as well as with its own revenue would have imposed lower rates, closer to marginal costs; but as also noted the Italian State appears to have imposed rates that were too high even to maximize its own revenues. The hypothesis that consumers' surplus equaled half of total revenue seems to that extent to overestimate that surplus.

This conclusion is strengthened by the likely non-linearity of the demand for railway transportation. The demand curve for transportation in general may be quasi-linear; but the demand curve for railway transportation surely becomes flatter as railway rates rise, for alternative modes become increasingly competitive.[26] In practice, therefore, the hypothesis that consumers' surplus equaled half of operating revenue is more than generous: the estimates it yields, near 6 percent per year, are clearly upper bounds.

The best estimates prudently reduce consumers' surplus to one quarter, rather than half, of operating revenue (col. 6). These figures are nearer 4 percent per year, or less than the internal rate of return to capital invested elsewhere at comparable risk.[27] The capital invested in Italy's railways did not yield enough to repay its cost, not even in the aggregate; at the

[25] If the demand curve is a straight line between a price P^* (for a zero quantity) and a quantity Q^* (for a zero price), gross revenue is maximized if the price equals $(P^*/2)$, which corresponds to a quantity $(Q^*/2)$. Gross income is then the rectangle $(P^*/2)(Q^*/2)$. Consumers' surplus corresponds to the triangle with base $(Q^*/2)$, and height $(P^* - (P^*/2)) = (P^*/2)$, equal to half of gross revenue. In 1875, for example, the social rate of return would equal $[155.2 + (155.2/2) - 90.1]/2,296 = 6.2$ percent.

[26] The demand for the product of a single firm at any price is the market demand at that price, less the total supplied at that price by all the other firms. If this supply is perfectly elastic at price P^* the residual demand is a broken line that is horizontal at price P^*, and identical to market demand at lower prices.

[27] That rate appears to have been close to 6 percent, and then, from the 1890s, 5 percent; see A. M. Biscaini Cotula and P. Ciocca, "Le strutture finanziarie: aspetti quantitativi di lungo periodo (1870–1970)," in F. Vicarelli, ed., *Capitale industriale e capitale finanziario: il caso italiano*, Bologna 1979, pp. 61–136. The social rate of return is to be compared to the internal rate in alternative investments if the capital invested in railways was imported or subtracted from marginal projects with negligible consumers' surplus.

margin, it surely yielded even less. This result is consistent with the conclusions suggested by the structure of taxes and subsidies: the investment
in Italy's railways was not justified on strictly economic grounds, there
must have been further benefits related for example to military or electoral
considerations.

The return to the successive waves of railway-net extensions cannot be
measured by the increases in invested capital (which includes improvements to pre-existing lines) and in operating income (which incorporates
trend and cyclical variations on the entire system); but a rough indication
can be obtained by considering the return to the different parts of the
network near the end of the period at hand.

The estimates in Table 5.07, Panel B divide the system into three parts:
the major North Italian lines in the Po valley, with their links to the sea
and the Alpine tunnels; the other major lines, in the peninsula and islands;
and the minor lines. These correspond very roughly to those built before
Unification, those built in the 1860s and '70s, and those built after 1880
(and, in the main, by 1895).

The internal rates of return point to a significant difference between
the major North Italian lines and the rest (col. 4): near 5 percent per year
for the former, a mere quarter of that figure for the latter. It bears notice
that the return to the minor lines was no lower than that on the peninsular
and island trunks, as their low revenues were apparently offset by their
low operating and especially construction costs. The traditional condemnation of the minor lines, based only on their low revenues, implicitly
assumes an investment (and operating cost) per kilometer as high as on
the major lines; the evidence does not warrant it.

The upper-bound estimates of the social rate of return are calculated
as above, with a consumers' surplus equal to half of operating revenue
(col. 5). The leaders are again the major Northern lines, with a return
near 11 percent per year, followed at a distance by the other major lines
(6 percent) and then the minor lines (4 percent).

The best estimates are here calculated with an eye to the plausible
variations in the difference between the initial estimate of consumers'
surplus and its actual amount (col. 6). That difference depends essentially
on the elasticity of demand for railway transportation, on the availabil-
ity of waterborne substitutes for the railway; and it was far from uniform. At one extreme there are the minor lines, typically land-locked,
with no substitute better than a horse-cart; the elasticity of demand was
below average, and the initial ("upper-bound") estimate can double as
the best estimate. The peninsular and island trunks were lines that followed or united the coasts; they were exposed to the competition of the

inexpensive coasting trade, and consumers' surplus was correspondingly limited.[28] For these lines, therefore, the best estimate sets that surplus equal to one fifth of operating revenue; the social rate of return appears low next to the cost of capital, and next to the return on the minor lines. For the major Northern lines the best estimate uses an intermediate figure, 35 percent of operating revenue, as internal navigation from the lakes to the Venetian lagoon continued to be used, and to provide an alternative to the railway, despite increasing neglect; the social rate of return remains conspicuous, near 9 percent per year.

The most wasteful part of the system seems accordingly to have been the peninsular and island trunks, and not, as commonly believed, the extensive network of minor lines. The latter included some 5,000 kilometers of lines earning less than 10,000 lire per year per kilometer, and the return on these was lower even than on the peninsular and island trunks (Panel C); but the corresponding investment was relatively small, and the other 6,500 kilometers of minor lines essentially covered the cost of the capital they absorbed.

The conclusion that the peninsular and island trunks were in fact the most wasteful part of the system is at odds with the traditional literature on the Italian railways; but it is perfectly in line with the "cliometric" analyses of other railways, which point to cost reductions that were substantial if the railway replaced horse carts in local transportation, and negligible if they replaced ships and barges on longer runs.

8. The impact of the railway: an evaluation

The new assessment of the peninsular trunks and of the minor lines entails a reappraisal of the railway-construction policies pursued in the early post-Unification decades.

The trunk lines built by the Right in the 1860s and '70s seem to have done little to reduce transport costs: to the extent that one can judge by their subsequent rate of return, their construction had to be driven by political and military considerations as well as by more narrowly economic motives. Those railways did not unify the domestic market, even less did they create the prerequisite for economic growth: the capital they absorbed would have yielded more in other uses, and the investment in railways retarded Italy's economic growth.

---

[28] The railway's superior speed and comfort no doubt gave it an edge in the movement of passengers and high-value goods; but for ordinary goods, as noted, the railways could not meet the user costs of the coasting trade without offering special discounts.

The Left built the last and perhaps the least useful of the major trunks, along the Southern coast from Salerno to Reggio Calabria; but the larger part of the minor lines built in the 1880s and '90s seem justified on purely economic grounds. Railway construction seems to have done more to reduce transport costs after 1880 than before; to the extent that the economic growth of the 1880s can be related to railway construction it is more plausibly related to the contemporaneous construction of the minor lines than to the prior construction of the peninsular trunks.

The Northern trunks, largely built before Unification (and subsequently much extended and improved), were indubitably the most useful part of the Italian railway net, even allowing for the alternative services obtainable from internal navigation. The actual extent and potential development of this alternative suggest that the railways were of particular significance for Piedmont, and the nearby Ligurian ports. In the upper Po valley, water resources may have been too limited to develop internal navigation without some cost to irrigated agriculture. All-water routes from Genoa and Savona to the Po were impeded perhaps by water-supply problems, certainly by the Ligurian Apennine; these were studied in the early nineteenth century, but they were never built, and those ports remained with a very limited hinterland until the railway provided an altogether more practical alternative.[29]

In the central and lower Po valley the railway's net benefit was altogether less, both because of the greater abundance of internal waterways, and because the railway itself diverted the upper valley's maritime traffic from the Adriatic coast to the Ligurian. Had infrastructure investment developed internal navigation rather than railways, Italy's industrial center would presumably have developed closer to the Adriatic, and been served through Venice rather than Genoa. The industrial progress of the upper Po valley, and its links to Liguria, are hard to imagine without the railway.

When all is said and done the most important Italian railways were those in the Northwest, built largely in the 1850s; and their major beneficiaries were Piedmont and Liguria. As he pursued the development of the railways, too, Camillo di Cavour well served the Kingdom of Sardinia.

---

[29] R. Commissione per lo studio di proposte intorno all'ordinamento delle strade ferrate, *Atti*, Rome 1903–06, vol. 5, parti 1–2, pp. 477, 482–489, 521.

6

North and South

1. The stages-of-growth models of Gerschenkron and Romeo

Italy's "Southern question" has been on the table for over a century. The failure of the South to industrialize and develop is at the heart of the question; the State's responsibility for that failure is at the heart of the historians' debate.[1]

The State's specifically regional policies are not at issue: in the half-century following Unification the special laws to further the development of specific areas were few, tardy, and in any case in favor of the South. Public investment in physical and human capital, too, reduced the initial disparities. The State spent heavily on roads and railroads, but disproportionately so in the South; the State imposed compulsory education, boosting literacy far more in the South than in the North.[2]

Tariff policy, much debated at the national level, had complex effects even within the North and the South. According to Italy's economists of the time the benefits obtained by the protected activities – some industries located primarily in the North, grain-growing widely diffused in the South – were outweighed by the damage suffered by the sectors that were

[1] R. Vaccaro, *Unità politica e dualismo economico in Italia (1861–1993)*, Padua 1995.
[2] Ibid., pp. 138–154; L. Cafagna, "Contro tre pregiudizi sulla storia dello sviluppo economico italiano," in P. Ciocca and G. Toniolo, eds., *Storia economica d'Italia. 1. Interpretazioni*, Rome-Bari 1998, p. 316; V. Zamagni, "Istruzione e sviluppo economico in Italia, 1861–1913," in G. Toniolo, ed., *Lo sviluppo economico italiano 1861–1940*, Bari 1973, pp. 190, 202, and V. Zamagni, "Istruzione e sviluppo economico: il caso italiano, 1861–1913," in G. Toniolo, ed., *L'economia italiana 1861–1940*, Bari 1978, pp. 140, 165.

naturally export-oriented: other industries again located primarily in the North, specialized agriculture important to the North but even more so to the South, where it was the only patently dynamic sector.[3] Those who believe protection promoted industrial growth, mainly in the North, and limited the "agrarian crisis," mainly in the South, see net benefits rather than net losses; but the effect on the North-South differential remains ambiguous, the difference between effects of the same sign.[4]

The stages-of-growth interpretations, which identify progress with industrial growth alone, radically simplify the problem. Alexander Gerschenkron evaluated public policy as an economist as well as a historian: he criticized not only the State's failure actively to promote industrial development in the 1880s, but also, and especially, the wrong-headed policies that slowed industrial growth during the "great spurt" of the Giolitti years. He did not consider the "Southern question," but the implications of his analysis are clear: the State slowed industrial growth in Italy, in Northern Italy; it limited, in the worst possible way, the widening of the North-South gap.[5]

Rosario Romeo's conclusions were the exact opposite of Gerschenkron's. In his interpretation public policy actively nourished the young nation's industrial progress. But the regional effects of those policy measures were highly differentiated. By avoiding agrarian reform (in the South), the State limited consumption by Southern peasants; by channeling the savings thus generated into the infrastructure, the State created the prerequisites for the industrialization of the North. Protection then subsidized Northern industry, at a cost to the South, which appeared in that market only as a consumer. The State's intervention benefited Italy overall, but it enriched the North and impoverished the South.[6]

Emilio Sereni held similar views. His focus too was on the creation of the infrastructure, of the railway lines that unified the domestic market

---

[3] For example L. Einaudi, *Cronache economiche e politiche di un trentennio*, 8 vols., Turin 1959–66, vol. I, pp. 135–136, 167–168; V. Pareto, *Lettres d'Italie. A cura di Gabriele De Rosa*, Rome 1973, pp. 48–50, 100–102; G. Sensini, *Le variazioni dello stato economico dell'Italia nell'ultimo trentennio del secolo XIX*, Rome 1904, pp. 70, 90. For a particularly impassioned denunciation of the harm wrought to Southern consumers and agricultural exporters see A. de Viti de Marco, *Un trentennio di lotte politiche*, Rome c.1930, pp. 25–30, 36, 42–52, 76, 135.

[4] For example V. Zamagni, *The Economic History of Italy, 1860–1990: Recovery after Decline*, Oxford 1993 (translation of Id., *Dalla periferia al centro: la seconda rinascita economica dell'Italia, 1861–1981*, Bologna 1990), pp. 116–117.

[5] Above, ch. 2, § 2.

[6] Above, ch. 2, § 4.

and allowed Northern industry to exploit Southern consumers: once again, the enrichment of the North impoverished the South.[7]

The analyses of Sereni and Romeo thus suggest that the South paid for the development of the North, of the Italian economy in general; they lend legitimacy to claims that the national State harmed the *Mezzogiorno*, that the South is entitled to reparations.

2. The stages-of-growth models of Bonelli and Cafagna

Luciano Cafagna finds such claims repugnant. He is himself a Southerner; but to his mind the North-South gap was not created by the national State, and the underdevelopment of the South harmed rather than helped the development of the national economy.

Already in the days of the Gerschenkron-Romeo debate Cafagna emphasized the initial North-South gap, inherited from the pre-Unification states and recently documented by Richard Eckaus; the North's environmental advantages, its more fertile land, its abundance of water for irrigation and motive power; the narrowness of the Southern market, that made it practically irrelevant to the industry of the North; the gradual nature of Italy's industrial development, which ill fit Romeo's chronology; the openness of the Italian economy, its ties, which Gerschenkron and Romeo neglected, to economic development abroad. At Unification, in fact, both the North and the South were "peripheries" exporting primary products to the industrial "core"; and Cafagna asked himself why these analogous starting points should have led to such different destinies.[8]

In a recent paper Cafagna returned to these problems, and answered that question – and dismantled, piece by piece, the foundations Romeo's interpretation gave to Southern claims for reparations. To do so he relied not on economic analysis, not on Gerschenkron's negative evaluation of public policy, but on the "Bonelli-Cafagna view" that had since been perfected. That interpretation retains the logical structure of Romeo's,

---

[7] E. Sereni, *Capitalismo e mercato nazionale in Italia*, 2^d ed., Rome 1974 (1966). The reduction of transport costs increased interregional trade, but this led to progress only where industrial production increased.

[8] L. Cafagna, "Intorno alle origini del dualismo economico in Italia," in A. Caracciolo, ed., *Problemi storici dell'industrializzazione e dello sviluppo*, Urbino 1965, pp. 103–150, reprinted with the addition of notes and subtitles in L. Cafagna, *Dualismo e sviluppo nella storia d'Italia*, Venice 1989, see pp. 187, 196, 200, 212, 216–217, 219–220. R. S. Eckaus, "The North-South Differential in Italian Economic Development," *Journal of Economic History* 20 (1961), pp. 285–317.

but much increases the relevant time frame. The "agrarian accumulation" that precedes industrial development lasted over a century: it took place primarily before Unification, it cannot have been the work of the national State. That accumulation, moreover, was essentially Northern, tied to the region's trade with the developed European economies, to the North's exports of silk: the Southern market was irrelevant, the forced saving of Southern peasants altogether secondary. Even the subsequent contribution of the State to the North's industrial progress was limited: the growth of the engineering industry, of the silk industry, of the cotton industry that was indeed protected but soon turned to exports was due to their competitive skills, it was not State-driven but "manchesterian."[9]

For Cafagna, clearly, the North-South gap cannot be attributed to political Unification; the North's greater wealth is the fruit of private enterprise, of its own efforts, not of a politically mediated transfer from the South. Rather, the North-South gap was ancient and deeply rooted; it grew after Unification, but simply because of "the obvious tendency to shift activity and investment to the areas that were already ahead and thus endowed with advantageous external economies and lower transaction costs."[10] This is Cafagna's conclusion: at Unification both North and South were underdeveloped peripheries, but the South was even more backward than the North; the North-South gap at the end is explained by the North-South gap at the beginning, exactly as Eckaus had argued long before.[11]

---

[9] Cafagna, "Contro tre pregiudizi," pp. 301–311. F. Bonelli, "Italian Capitalism: General Interpretative Guidelines," in G. Federico, ed., *The Economic Development of Italy since 1870*, Aldershot 1994, pp. 99–142 (translation of F. Bonelli, "Il capitalismo italiano. Linee generali di interpretazione, " in R. Romano, C. Vivanti, eds., *Storia d'Italia. Annali. 1. Dal feudalesimo al capitalismo*, Turin 1978, pp. 1193-1255) assigns a greater role to policy impulses (pp. 110–112), but the minimization of the role of the State is in the very logic of the interpretation, in the long "agrarian accumulation" that preceded Unification. That this slowed-down stages-of-growth interpretation thus disallows any Southern claims for reparations may be the ultimate reason Cafagna chose to identify his "waves" with a drawn-out rostowian take-off rather than with a proper economic cycle; see S. Fenoaltea, "Dualismo, ciclo e sviluppo nel pensiero di Luciano Cafagna," in E. Francia, ed., *Luciano Cafagna. Tra ricerca storica e impegno civile*, Venice 2007, pp. 167-174.

[10] Cafagna, "Contro tre pregiudizi," pp. 300–301, 317 (author's translation).

[11] Eckaus, "The North-South Differential," pp. 315–316 ("the economic level of the North was distinctly and significantly above that of the South at the time of unification . . . With different initial conditions it is not surprising that the disparities increased rather than diminished").

There are problems with this logic, however, even granting the assumption that such differentials tend naturally to widen rather than to narrow.[12] If it were so one could indeed conclude that the South failed to develop because it was already underdeveloped, but no more than that. The North may have been less backward than the South, but it was also backward next to the transalpine economies that were its trading partners; and among Europe's regions the backwardness of North Italy should have condemned it, exactly like the South, to perpetual underdevelopment.

In the logic of Cafagna's account the greater initial backwardness of the South would benefit development in the North only if these two regions exhausted the relevant universe, if they were the complementary halves of a closed world. That is not how Cafagna sees them, correctly so; and in any case that closed world would itself have to be a creature of the State, of a policy that interfered with the natural openness of the market. If one assumes in short that the State protected industry, anywhere in the country, the widening of the North-South gap may indeed be attributed, as Cafagna argues, to the natural advantages of the regions that were already ahead, without postulating policies deliberately harmful to the South.[13] But on that assumption one undercuts the thesis that the North's development was "manchesterian" rather than State-assisted; Southern claims for reparations would remain justified by the effects of public policy, if not by the policy-makers' intentions.

3. The "cyclical" interpretation and the weight of the past

When Cafagna and Eckaus assert that the regions which were initially ahead would "obviously" then grow faster than the rest they are in fact assuming that the real world is characterized by increasing, not decreasing, returns: intensification then reduces costs instead of increasing them, and that is why initial differences, even small, even random, tend not to disappear but to become ever larger. With increasing returns, too, there are multiple possible equilibria, and the eventual outcome is path-dependent, as when a marble is thrown into an egg-carton; in a world of decreasing returns there is instead only one possible equilibrium, and as when a marble is thrown into a hemispherical bowl the initial position matters only for the time it takes to reach that equilibrium.

[12] S. Fenoaltea, "Contro tre pregiudizi," *Rivista di storia economica* 20 (2004), pp. 95–96.
[13] Cafagna, "Contro tre pregiudizi," p. 317.

Eckaus was content to show that at Unification the North was already ahead of the South, but Cafagna's analysis is deeper than that: he describes the North's advantage as "radical," even "genetic."[14] That advantage is traced to a triad of resources, human, natural, and social. At Unification the North boasted far higher rates of literacy and primary schooling; far greater supplies of water, that allowed the intensification of agriculture and the development of manufacturing; and, most importantly, far better government, far greater security for people and property, far greater respect for the law. What Cafagna describes is the North's far greater *potential*: had it by chance been behind the South at Unification, it would surely have overtaken it.

Cafagna's analysis thus allows one to interpret the growing North-South gap either as the "natural" widening of an initial and possibly random disparity, or as the realization of potentials that were themselves different to begin with, as the reaching of an equilibrium that was foreordained and anything but random. The latter reading avoids the logical and political pitfalls of the former, and sits altogether more comfortably with his analysis of national economic growth, with his emphasis on the century-long "agrarian accumulation" that limited the very capacity of the national government to influence events and was itself limited essentially to the North. On either reading, however, Cafagna's analysis of the North-South differential is characterized by its long time frame, by the appeal to conditions at the time of Unification to explain events over the half-century that followed.

This manner of telling the story of the economy reflects a certain manner of seeing the economy itself. If resources are given and relatively immobile, if they must be patiently accumulated, economic equilibria are reached only with adequate time, and the choices of the past limit the options of the present. We are where we are because we hail whence we hail and are headed whither we are headed: the economy evolves in historic time.

If resources are highly mobile, and can quickly be acquired and as quickly lost, economic equilibria are quickly reached, and the past matters not: the real economy behaves much like financial markets, its time path represents not the slow convergence to a previously defined equilibrium but a random sequence of separate equilibria, each "immediately" achieved. We are where we are because this is where today we wish to be: history evolves in economic time, and the causes of events are to be sought not in the past but in the historical present.

---

[14] Ibid., pp. 301, 312.

Not all resources are equally or highly mobile; it is the relatively immobile, "local" resources that attract those that are relatively mobile. The attraction exerted by those local resources depends in turn on their nature and on the technology of the day, and changes, randomly, as the latter does. The Ruhr was transformed in a few years from a quiet agricultural valley into one of the world's great industrial centers not because of its prior "agrarian accumulation" but because its endowment of local resources then and only then attracted a complement of mobile resources.

In Italy, similarly, the greater development of the North after Unification is not to be explained by its greater initial potential, which it would have realized "immediately" and not over half a century. Rather, the greater growth of the North is to be traced to the greater growth of its very potential, which it always "immediately" realized: over time, that is to say, and thanks to the evolution of technology, the attractive power of the North's local resources progressively increased. The advantages of the Northern environment stressed by Cafagna retain their importance, but that importance is tied to the current moment, to the historical present, and not to past "initial conditions." That at the time of Unification the North and the South occupied similar positions in the international economy is simply irrelevant to their subsequent development: the problem that worried Cafagna, that lured him into an imprudent appeal to increasing returns, is not a problem at all.

4. The quantitative literature

The "Southern question" has been on the table for over a century, the literature discussing the regional disparities of Italy's industrial development fills libraries; but that endless debate has concerned mere conjectures, and the statistical reconstruction of industrial growth in Italy's regions (Figure 6.01) is only now getting under way.

The first point estimates of regional industrial production were compiled by Vera Zamagni, then a graduate student at Oxford, and published in 1978. They refer to 1911, and are derived primarily from Italy's first industrial census; they describe not the path of post-Unification development, but only its end result.[15]

Fourteen years later Alfredo Esposto presented regional estimates of industrial production in 1889–93; they are derived from the province-level

---

[15] V. Zamagni, *Industrializzazione e squilibri regionali in Italia. Bilancio dell'età giolittiana*, Bologna 1978; Ministero di agricoltura, industria e commercio, *Censimento degli opifici e delle imprese industriali al 10 giugno 1911*, 5 vols., Rome 1913–16.

FIGURE 6.01. *Italy's regions*

"industrial surveys" published between 1885 and 1903. Esposto compares his results to Zamagni's; his conclusions are reasonable but not robust, as they do not distinguish real changes from merely statistical differences generated by the differences in their sources and methods.[16]

Between Unification and the Great War the only statistical measures of the regional economies that were at least in principle comprehensive, repeated, and reasonably homogeneous over time were those provided by the demographic censuses. These were taken in 1861, 1871, 1881, 1901, and 1911; in 1891 the economy was in crisis, and to save money, alas, the census was skipped. From 1871 on these censuses contain detailed labor force statistics, by geographic unit, industry by industry.[17]

In the absence of more direct statistical evidence the diachronic analysis of regional industrial development has relied directly on these labor force figures. In 1970 Ornello Vitali published the first reconstruction of the evolution of the regions' industrial labor force; similar reconstructions

[16] A. G. Esposto, "Italian Industrialization and the Gerschenkronian 'Great Spurt': A Regional Analysis," *Journal of Economic History* 52 (1992), pp. 353–362; Dirstat (Direzione generale della statistica), *Annali di statistica*, serie IV, e.g., vols. 18–21, Rome 1887.

[17] Ministero di agricoltura, industria e commercio, *Statistica del Regno d'Italia. Censimento 31 dicembre 1871*, vol. 3, Rome 1876; Id., *Censimento della popolazione del Regno d'Italia al 31 dicembre 1881*, vol. 3, Rome 1884; Id., *Censimento della popolazione del Regno d'Italia al 10 febbraio 1901*, vol. 4, Rome 1904; Id., *Censimento della popolazione del Regno d'Italia al 10 giugno 1911*, vol. 5, Rome 1915.

brought forward to more recent times were subsequently presented by Vera Zamagni herself in 1987, and by Giorgio Fuà and Samuele Scuppa in 1988. But the evolution of the labor force is only an indirect indicator of the evolution of industrial production; curiously, too, all these analyses start with 1881, and make no use of the similarly detailed census figures for 1871.[18]

The new estimates of national industrial production have permitted a further step: the calculation of the first direct estimates of regional industrial production in the census years from 1871 to 1911, simply by allocating each industry's national value added to the different regions in proportion to their share of the corresponding labor force. The crude labor-force figures considered by the earlier literature are thus weighted by the (national average) value added per worker in the industry and calendar year at hand, automatically incorporating any intertemporal and intersectoral productivity differences. The neglected productivity differences are only those that are at once interregional, intratemporal, and intrasectoral; and these too decline as the industrial sectors are more narrowly specified.[19]

The initial estimates applied this method directly to the 15 industrial sectors identified in Table 1.02, and are correspondingly rough- and-ready. The roughest referred to the textile industries and to the utilities. The utilities estimates were weak because the industry was not separately identified by the census prior to 1911, and the earlier distributions reflected only the identifiable parts of the industry; the textile estimates were weak because the criteria used to distinguish female artisans from housewives clearly varied from region to region and census to census. The estimates for these two sectors have been entirely reconstructed on an annual basis, distinguishing individual products and stages of production,

[18] O. Vitali, *Aspetti dello sviluppo economico italiano alla luce della ricostruzione della popolazione attiva*, Rome 1970; V. Zamagni, "A Century of Change: Trends in the Composition of the Italian Labor Force, 1881–1981," *Historical Social Research* 44 (1987), no. 1, pp. 36–97; G. Fuà and S. Scuppa, "Industrializzazione e deindustrializzazione delle regioni italiane secondo i censimenti demografici 1881–1981," *Economia Marche* 7 (1988), pp. 307–327. The 1871 census does not contain regional labor-force figures, but these can readily be obtained by aggregating the appropriate provincial figures.

[19] S. Fenoaltea, "La crescita industriale delle regioni d'Italia dall'Unità alla Grande Guerra: una prima stima per gli anni censuari," Banca d'Italia, *Quaderni dell'Ufficio Ricerche Storiche*, n. 1, Rome 2001, and Id., "Peeking Backward: Regional Aspects of Industrial Growth in Post-Unification Italy," *Journal of Economic History* 63 (2003), pp. 1059–1102.

and using ancillary evidence as well as the distribution of the labor force; the corresponding census-year figures were extensively revised, but the hypotheses suggested by the initial estimates were not undermined.[20]

5. Aggregate industrial production: old and new estimates

The estimates considered here are an interim hybrid that combine the revised estimates for the textile industries and the utilities, and the preliminary census-based estimates for the other sectors.[21]

Summing over the 15 sectoral estimates specific to each region one obtains the estimates of aggregate regional production transcribed in Table 6.01, Panel A. Panel B presents these regional estimates as shares of the corresponding national total; both panels further present the corresponding absolute and relative variations between 1871 and 1911.

Panel C transcribes the regional shares of the national totals estimated by Zamagni and Esposto.[22] Esposto's estimates for 1889–93, obtained from independent data, with different methods, agree to a remarkable extent with the present figures for 1881 and 1901 transcribed in Panel B: the two sets of estimates tend to support each other.

Zamagni's estimates for 1911 differ systematically from the present estimates. They assign the industrial triangle (Piedmont, Liguria, and Lombardy) a share one third greater than that calculated here (some 55 percent, rather than 41); they appear to overstate regional disparities, in part systematically, in part by happenstance.

The systematic component is tied to the industrial census of 1911: it was Italy's first, and reflected the inexperience of the census bureau. As that industrial census was to coincide with the fifth population census, the household form was used to collect information on the industrial activity performed within the home, and by any (further) artisans who worked alone; a separate form was accordingly sent only to workshops

[20] On the peculiar weaknesses of the census data for the textile and utilities industries see Fenoaltea, "La crescita industriale," pp. 33–35, 39. The new regional textile series appeared in Id., "Textile Production in Italy's Regions, 1861–1913," *Rivista di storia economica* 20 (2004), pp. 145–174.

[21] These partial revisions account for the differences from the entirely census-based estimates in Fenoaltea, "Peeking Backward."

[22] Zamagni, *Industrializzazione*, p. 198; Esposto, "Italian Industrialization," p. 358. These estimates are examined in Fenoaltea, "Peeking Backward," pp. 1094–1100, partly summarized here.

TABLE 6.01. *Regional industrial production: aggregate estimates*

A. value added (million lire at 1911 prices)

	Pied.	Lig.	Lomb.	Ven.	Emilia	Tusc.	Mar.	Umbria
1911	643	263	1,093	422	361	411	107	74
1901	388	137	646	288	189	247	71	44
1881	256	82	375	196	134	162	54	27
1871	204	57	303	171	120	136	47	26
1911–1871	439	206	790	251	241	275	60	48
1911/1871	3.15	4.61	3.61	2.47	3.01	3.02	2.28	2.85

	Latium	Abr.	Camp.	Apulia	Bas.	Cal.	Sic.	Sard.
1911	175	90	417	203	33	106	385	84
1901	104	64	284	126	24	73	289	52
1881	73	53	220	93	24	61	213	40
1871	58	44	169	77	21	51	169	29
1911–1871	117	46	248	126	12	55	216	55
1911/1871	3.02	2.05	2.47	2.64	1.57	2.08	2.28	2.90

B. shares of the national total (percent)

	Pied.	Lig.	Lomb.	Ven.	Emilia	Tusc.	Mar.	Umbria
1911	13.21	5.41	22.45	8.66	7.41	8.45	2.21	1.53
1901	12.80	4.53	21.35	9.51	6.25	8.16	2.36	1.46
1881	12.48	3.97	18.17	9.51	6.47	7.84	2.62	1.29
1871	12.15	3.39	18.05	10.17	7.12	8.09	2.80	1.52
1911–1871	1.06	2.02	4.40	−1.51	.29	.36	−.59	.01
1911/1871	1.09	1.60	1.24	.85	1.04	1.04	.79	1.01

	Latium	Abr.	Camp.	Apulia	Bas.	Cal.	Sic.	Sard.
1911	3.59	1.84	8.56	4.18	.68	2.17	7.90	1.73
1901	3.44	2.11	9.39	4.16	.80	2.41	9.54	1.73
1881	3.55	2.57	10.66	4.51	1.18	2.97	10.30	1.94
1871	3.43	2.62	10.05	4.59	1.27	3.03	10.04	1.72
1911–1871	.16	−.78	−1.49	−.41	−.59	−.86	−2.14	.01
1911/1871	1.05	.70	.85	.91	.54	.72	.79	1.01

C. shares of the national total (percent): estimates by Zamagni (1911) and Esposto
  (1889–93)

	Pied.	Lig.	Lomb.	Ven.	Emilia	Tusc.	Mar.	Umbria
1911	17.5	7.9	29.1	8.9	6.1	8.1	1.5	1.3
1889–93	13.2	5.4	22.3	9.3	5.7	8.4	2.3	2.0

	Latium	Abr.	Camp.	Apulia	Bas.	Cal.	Sic.	Sard.
1911	3.4	1.0	6.3	2.7	.4	1.1	3.7	1.1
1889–93	3.3	2.1	9.1	4.0	.7	2.0	8.3	1.8

Sources: see text.

separate from the owner's residence and with at least two workers. As it turned out, the household form failed to do double duty, and did not in fact provide usable evidence of industrial activity. The "industrial census" accordingly tabulated only the partial figures derived from the other form; the demographic census counted 4.3 million industrial workers, the industrial census just 2.3 million. It missed more than the unemployed, more even than domestic workers and artisans that worked alone: it missed large factories too, if, like the Pirelli works in Milan, they were "not separate" – that is, at a different street address – from the owner's residence.

Bias creeps in because the coverage of the industrial census varied along the peninsula: it counted some two-thirds of the corresponding labor force in the Northwest (the industrial triangle), about half in the Center and Northeast, and just two-fifths in the South and major islands (the *Mezzogiorno*). That coverage varied, presumably, with the share of small-scale (domestic, artisanal) industry, perhaps with the share of factory-owners who had their shops and their home in a single compound, perhaps too with the share of factory-owners who were allowed by the local authorities not to respond at all; it would not appear to vary significantly with the incidence of unemployment, surely minimal everywhere in 1911 because of industry's rapid growth, and the enormous mobility, national and international, of labor.[23]

The industrial census counted employment, but in only part of industry; it is a partial, and geographically biased, sample of the underlying total. Zamagni never noticed the peculiar nature of her principal source: she estimated the regional distribution of industry directly from the census figures, and systematically overstated its concentration in the North.

A further series of errors worked by happenstance to reinforce this bias. The textile industry was the most heavily concentrated in the North, with almost three fourths of the national total in Piedmont and Lombardy

---

[23] Fenoaltea, "Peeking Backward," pp. 1086–1098. From 1901 to 1911 industrial growth generated an 18 percent increase in the industrial labor force, against a 6 percent increase in the population aged 15 to 65; measured external migration (undercounted, in fact, by the passport-based data) totaled 18 percent of the population at mid-decade; nominal and real wages rose smartly. Total unemployment was surely low, especially among industrial workers; nor does it appear to have been particularly low in the North. One reason is that overall regional growth does not appear to have been, in the North, above the national average; another is that the North held most of the textile industry, the only one with a total product, in 1911, sharply below its previous peak.

alone. Zamagni overestimated the size of this industry by almost half: she applied to the current value of production the share of value added indicated by the industrial census of the later 1930s, without correcting for the increase in that share that accompanied the reduction in materials costs with the fall in the relative price of raw cotton, and the substitution of cheap artificial silk for the expensive natural fiber.[24]

Against that, Zamagni underestimated, by half to three fourths, the value added of the industries least concentrated in the industrial triangle: those that processed leather, wood, and non-metallic minerals, and construction. In every case the distortion favored the North: Zamagni allowed these widely diffused industries a total weight similar to that of textiles alone, which the North utterly dominated, whereas they actually outweighed it by four to one.[25]

Esposto compared his estimates to Zamagni's, to illustrate the regional effects of the pre-war boom; the comparison actually illustrates the heterogeneity, and the different biases, of the estimates themselves.

6. The evolution of aggregate industrial production

The new estimates too are imprecise, but they do not seem to be systematically distorted; and because they are homogeneous they allow meaningful comparisons over time.[26]

The new aggregate estimates in Panel A of Table 6.01 point to industrial growth from 1871 to 1911 in every region. Output grows in every intercensal period, too (with the limited exception of Basilicata, which

---

[24] S. Fenoaltea, "The Growth of Italy's Silk Industry, 1861–1913: A Statistical Reconstruction," *Rivista di storia economica* 5 (1988), p. 308; Id., "The Growth of Italy's Cotton Industry, 1861–1913: A Statistical Reconstruction," *Rivista di storia economica* 17 (2001), p. 167.

[25] Zamagni, *Industrializzazione*, p. 198, allows 624 million lire to textiles and 747 million to the other four; the above estimates (Table 1.02) allow them 428 million and 1,643 million, respectively.

[26] The 1911 census data point to virtually identical horsepower in use per worker in the industrial triangle and in the rest of the country (Zamagni, *Industrializzazione*, p. 191); and these overstate the North's share of installed horsepower (and, presumably, of capital) because the census was taken in June, a period of abundant flow only in the glacier-fed rivers of the North. There is accordingly no reason to presume that value added per worker was systematically higher in the North. Nor would it matter much if the present estimates systematically underestimated the advantage of the more industrial regions: they would retain the usefulness of a thermometer, that allows comparisons of levels and changes even if the relative differences vary from Fahrenheit to Centigrade. The present results are described below as if they were exact, but only to avoid overburdening the text.

stagnates between 1881 and 1901): at this level of aggregation, with these benchmark dates, there are no cases or episodes of deindustrialization.[27]

Over the long run output growth rates differ widely, however, and the regional shares of the total correspondingly evolve (Panel B). The fastest growth was in the three regions of the Northwest triangle. The leader was Liguria, where production increased almost five-fold, raising the region's share by 60 percent; it was followed at a distance by Lombardy, with an almost four-fold increase in production and a one-quarter increase in the region's share, and at a further distance by Piedmont, with a more than three-fold increase in production and a one-tenth increase in the region's share. Piedmont was closely followed by Latium, Tuscany, and Emilia, where production just trebled, raising the regional share by 4 or 5 percent; in Sardinia and Umbria production almost trebled, and barely outstripped national growth. Elsewhere growth was less vigorous, and regional shares declined: by some 10 percent in Apulia, 15 in Venetia and Campania, 20 in the Marches and in Sicily, 30 in the Abruzzi and in Calabria, where output barely doubled. Basilicata fared worst: output grew by just 60 percent, and the region's share fell by almost half. Overall, the paths diverge: Lombardy's output, the greatest, was 14 times that of Basilicata, the least, in 1871, and no less than 33 times the latter in 1911.

The intermediate benchmarks suggest that the macro-regional divergence accelerated after 1881: the percentage share of the total attributed to the industrial triangle grows from 33.6 in 1871 to 34.6 in 1881, 38.7 in 1901, and 41.1 in 1911, that is, at average annual rates that rise from 0.3 percent in the first intercensal period to 0.6 in the second and third. A number of implications deserve to be noted, at least as working hypotheses.

The relative stasis of the regional shares from 1871 to 1881 is relevant to the long-running debate over the origins of Italy's dual economy. There is no evidence of a "Unification effect" harmful to the South, at least after 1871: either it had run its course, or it never existed at all. One is struck, rather, by the relative progress of Campania and Sicily in the initial sample decade, though it remains to be confirmed by sturdier figures.

The acceleration of the regional divergence in 1881, rather than in 1901, is instead relevant to the equally long-running debate over the

[27] Similarly, *mutatis mutandis*, Esposto, "Italian Industrialization," p. 362.

industrial growth of post-Unification Italy. Here too, the pre-war spurt seems no different from that of the 1880s: the regional estimates too agree poorly with Gerschenkron's view that the German-style mixed banks created in the 1890s led Italy's industrial take-off.

This same discontinuity in 1881 is relevant to the evaluation of major policy interventions, at the heart of both debates. On the one hand, indeed, it would seem tied to the shift to protection, that would have favored Northern industry; but this issue will be returned to below. On the other, it can be tied to growing territorial specialization induced by transport improvements; once again, the minor lines built largely between 1880 and 1895 appear to have had greater economic effects than the peninsular trunks built in the 1860s and '70s.[28]

7. Relative industrialization

The regions' shares of total product obviously reflect the regions' different size, as well as the different development of their industry. Table 6.02 reports, for each region, the male population over age 15 at the four census dates, as absolute numbers and as shares of the national total.[29] Table 6.03 in turn presents the regional indices of relative industrialization obtained as the ratio of the region's share of industrial production to its share of the male population over age 15. These tables too include measures of the absolute and relative changes over the entire forty-year span.[30]

The dynamics of that male population differ in various ways from those of industrial production. Relative changes are much smaller, and growth is no longer universal: the figures for Basilicata decline from 1871 on, those for the Abruzzi decline after 1901 and overall, those for

---

[28] Once again, obviously, the underlying assumptions are that the progressive extension of the railway net had correspondingly progressive effects on transport costs, without discontinuities tied to a hypothetical "completion" (perhaps of the "essential" part), and that the private sector responded without long delay.

[29] Only the male component of the population of working age is considered here, in part because of the uncertainties surrounding female participation rates, in part because the greater mobility of the male population guarantees a distribution closer to equilibrium.

[30] The calculated indices are pure numbers (like coefficients of variation). They are algebraically equivalent to the ratio of the industrial product per male over 15 in the region to the national average industrial product per male over 15; they can be considered approximations to ordinary coefficients of specialization, with the shares of the male population over 15 as proxies for the unknown shares of GDP.

TABLE 6.02. *Regional population: males over age 15*

A. absolute figures (million persons)

	Pied.	Lig.	Lomb.	Ven.	Emilia	Tusc.	Mar.	Umbria
1911	1.14	.42	1.53	1.02	.89	.90	.33	.23
1901	1.08	.37	1.40	.98	.82	.85	.33	.23
1881	1.02	.30	1.25	.93	.77	.77	.32	.21
1871	.97	.28	1.19	.89	.73	.74	.30	.19
1911–1871	.17	.14	.35	.13	.16	.16	.03	.04
1911/1871	1.17	1.49	1.29	1.15	1.21	1.21	1.10	1.19

	Latium	Abr.	Camp.	Apulia	Bas.	Cal.	Sic.	Sard.
1911	.45	.41	1.03	.67	.14	.39	1.21	.28
1901	.43	.44	.99	.63	.14	.39	1.14	.27
1881	.35	.43	.98	.52	.16	.40	.96	.24
1871	.32	.42	.93	.47	.17	.39	.84	.22
1911–1871	.13	−.01	.10	.20	−.03	.00	.36	.06
1911/1871	1.41	.98	1.10	1.44	.84	1.00	1.43	1.29

B. shares of the national total (percent)

	Pied.	Lig.	Lomb.	Ven.	Emilia	Tusc.	Marche	Umbria
1911	10.32	3.82	13.88	9.27	8.06	8.12	3.03	2.07
1901	10.32	3.53	13.32	9.37	7.79	8.14	3.19	2.18
1881	10.60	3.12	13.04	9.73	7.99	8.02	3.32	2.14
1871	10.73	3.11	13.12	9.83	8.10	8.18	3.34	2.14
1911–1871	−.41	.71	.76	−.56	−.04	−.06	−.21	−.07
1911/1871	.96	1.23	1.06	.94	1.00	.99	.91	.97

	Latium	Abr.	Camp.	Apulia	Bas.	Cal.	Sic.	Sard.
1911	4.06	3.71	9.33	6.06	1.26	3.54	10.92	2.55
1901	4.05	4.16	9.42	5.96	1.37	3.72	10.87	2.59
1881	3.63	4.43	10.19	5.46	1.70	4.18	9.98	2.48
1871	3.52	4.62	10.32	5.14	1.83	4.30	9.30	2.42
1911–1871	.54	−.91	−.99	.92	−.57	−.76	1.62	.13
1911/1871	1.15	.80	.90	1.18	.69	.82	1.17	1.05

Source: S. Fenoaltea, "Peeking Backward: Regional Aspects of Industrial Growth in Post-Unification Italy," *Journal of Economic History* 63 (2003), p. 1069.

Calabria simply stagnate. Over the long term the regions with the fastest growth, and a share that increases by over 5 percent, are (in descending order) Liguria, Apulia, Sicily, Latium, Lombardy and Sardinia. Emilia and Tuscany maintain an approximately constant share. The shares of the others decline: by some 3–4 percent in Piedmont and Umbria, 6 percent in Venetia, 9–10 percent in the Marches and Campania, some 20 percent in the Abruzzi and Calabria, and 30 percent in Basilicata. Again, the extremes diverge: the ratio of the highest regional population

TABLE 6.03. *Regional indices of relative industrialization*[a]

	Pied.	Lig.	Lomb.	Ven.	Emilia	Tusc.	Mar.	Umbria
1911	1.28	1.42	1.62	.93	.92	1.04	.73	.74
1901	1.24	1.28	1.60	1.01	.80	1.00	.74	.67
1881	1.18	1.27	1.39	.98	.81	.98	.79	.60
1871	1.13	1.09	1.38	1.03	.88	.99	.84	.71
1911–1871	.15	.33	.24	−.10	.04	.05	−.11	.03
1911/1871	1.13	1.30	1.17	.90	1.05	1.05	.87	1.04

	Latium	Abr.	Camp.	Apulia	Bas.	Cal.	Sic.	Sard.
1911	.89	.50	.92	.69	.54	.61	.72	.68
1901	.84	.51	1.00	.70	.58	.65	.88	.67
1881	.98	.58	1.05	.83	.70	.71	1.03	.78
1871	.97	.57	.97	.89	.69	.71	1.08	.71
1911–1871	−.08	−.07	−.05	−.20	−.15	−.10	−.36	−.03
1911/1871	.92	.88	.95	.78	.78	.86	.67	.96

[a] ratios of regional percentages of industrial value added to regional percentages of the male population over age 15.
Sources: see text.

(in Lombardy) to the lowest (in Basilicata) grows from 7 in 1871 to 11 in 1911.

In 1911, the industrial triangle clearly stands out: the three highest indices of relative industrialization are those for Lombardy (1.62), Liguria (1.42), and Piedmont (1.28). Elsewhere, only Tuscany has an index above one (1.04). It is followed by Venetia, Emilia, Campania, and Latium (.89–.93), Umbria, the Marches, and Sicily (.72–.74), Apulia and Sardinia (.68–.69), Calabria (.61), and finally Basilicata (.54) and the Abruzzi (.50). The three northwestern regions are also those with the most rapid growth in the index between 1871 and 1911: Liguria leads with a 30 percent increase, followed by Lombardy and Piedmont with increases of 17 and 13 percent, respectively. These are followed in turn by Tuscany, Emilia, and Umbria, with increases of 4–5 percent, and then, with increasing declines, Campania, and Sardinia (near −5 percent), Venetia, Latium, and the Abruzzi (near −10 percent), Calabria and the Marches (near −15 percent), Apulia and Basilicata (−22 percent), and Sicily (−33 percent). These changes in the index clearly pick up the broad features of Italy's industrial differentiation, with the Northwest in the lead, the South in relative decline, and the Center and Northeast in between.

The variations in the regional indices depend of course on the relative variation of the shares of industrial output on the one hand, and of the male population over 15 on the other. That population was highly mobile, and its redistribution presumably reflects the differential impact of stock-adjusting interregional and international migration; its relative growth accordingly measures the relative development of the regional economy as a whole, and the part played by industry emerges from a joint examination of the industrial share and the demographic share.

From this perspective one notices significant differences even within the industrial triangle. In Liguria and Lombardy – the regions with the highest index in 1911, and the fastest growth in the index from its level in 1871 – the growth in the region's share of national industrial production was accompanied by growth in its share of the male population, which in turn limits the growth of the index: these regions grew at above-average rates, and industry appears to have led their development. In Piedmont, in contrast, the growth of the region's share of total industry was much smaller, and much of the growth in the index comes from the *decline* in the share of the male population; the region appears to have been in overall relative decline, and to have fallen back on industry to compensate for the low vitality of the non-industrial sectors.

Elsewhere, over the long run the index grows only in Emilia, Tuscany, and Umbria. Here too, as in Piedmont, as the share of industry grew the share of the male population fell, but in Emilia and Tuscany the latter decline was minimal. The share of national industrial production grew slightly in Latium and Sardinia too; but their share of the male population grew even more rapidly, causing a fall in the index of relative industrialization, especially in Latium. Sardinia and especially Latium thus displayed relative progress overall, led by other sectors so vigorous that their industry declined as a share of the regional economy even as it grew as a share of national industry.

Almost all the other regions appear to be mirror-images of Lombardy and Liguria, with low industrial growth "leading," so to speak, low overall growth: the index declines, despite the fall in the share of the male population, because the share of industry fell even faster. In Venetia, the Marches, and Campania the former share fell 5 to 10 percent, the latter 15 to 20 percent; in Calabria and the Abruzzi, the shares fell some 20 percent, and 30 percent, respectively; in Basilicata, a failing region with a significant demographic decline even in absolute terms, the one fell some 30 percent, the other more than 45 percent.

The surprising exceptions are Apulia and Sicily. These appear as mirror-images of Piedmont: their shares of industry decline (by roughly a tenth and a fifth, respectively), but their indices decline even more (by roughly a fifth and a third, respectively), thanks to the spectacular growth in the share of the male population, comparable to that of Liguria (the overall leader, and winner of the industrial contest), and greater even than that of Latium (pulled along by the new national capital). Apulia and Sicily thus appear to be have enjoyed noteworthy relative progress, led by as yet unidentified sectors so vigorous as to offset the relative decline of their industry.[31]

Industrialization is considered the key to growth and modernization. The redistribution of the mobile labor force suggests that overall regional development was not tied in fact to industrial success. Figure 6.02 illustrates the relative growth of the regions' male population of working age, Figure 6.03 their relative industrialization: the contrast between the first (left panel) and the second (right panel) is as striking as it is unexpected.

8. The transformation of the map

The industrial triangle emerges clearly in 1911, but not at all in 1871 (Figure 6.02, left panel). At that date only Lombardy stands out, with an index near 1.40. Well behind, with indices near 1.10, come Piedmont, Liguria, and then Sicily. Venetia, Tuscany, Latium, and Campania cluster near the national norm; Emilia, the Marches, and Apulia are somewhat below it (near 0.90), Umbria, Basilicata, Calabria, and Sardinia lower still (near 0.70), and the Abruzzi lowest of all (under 0.60).

---

[31] The hypothesis that the Apulian and Sicilian economies were particularly vigorous stems as noted from the assumption that adult males were relatively mobile; the demographic growth of these regions would of course have very different implications, were it due to a high rate of natural reproduction and an inability to shed excess population. This alternative interpretation is ruled out by the data in Svimez (Associazione per lo sviluppo dell'industria nel Mezzogiorno), *Un secolo di statistiche italiane Nord e Sud, 1861–1961*, Rome 1961, p. 122. Between 1871 and 1911 in Apulia and Sicily demographic growth was well above the national average (respectively 40 and 35 percent of the geometric mean of the initial and final population, against 25 percent in the entire *Mezzogiorno* and 26 percent nation-wide); the rates of natural increase were barely above average (respectively 46 and 47 percent, against 41 percent in the entire *Mezzogiorno* and 40 percent nation-wide), and net migration rates were well below average (respectively 5 and 11 percent, against 16 percent in the entire *Mezzogiorno* and 14 percent nation-wide). At first blush neither Apulia nor Sicily appears to have developed a noticeable transit trade, nor of course national government services, so the leading sector was presumably specialized agriculture (respectively grapes and citrus fruit, possibly combined with sheep-raising).

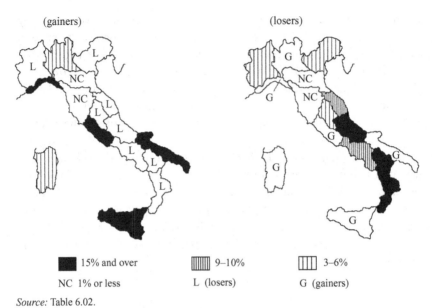

(gainers)   (losers)

■ 15% and over	▥ 9–10%	▯ 3–6%
NC 1% or less	L (losers)	G (gainers)

Source: Table 6.02.

FIGURE 6.02. *Percentage changes in regional shares of the male population
over age 15, 1871–1911*

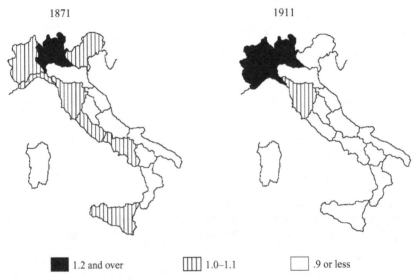

1871   1911

■ 1.2 and over	▥ 1.0–1.1	☐ .9 or less

Source: Table 6.03.

FIGURE 6.03. *Regional indices of relative industrialization, 1871 and 1911*

A basic feature of post-Unification Italy's industrial growth thus appears to be the broadening of industry's geographic base, from Lombardy alone to the three regions of the industrial triangle. As seen above, moreover, within that triangle industrialization seems altogether less vigorous in Piedmont than in Lombardy or (in particular) Liguria.

In 1871, the interregional differences are again less marked than in 1911: the ratio of the highest regional index to the lowest is just 2.4, against 3.2 forty years later. What is most striking, however, is so to speak the difference in the differences. As is evident from Figure 6.02 the industrial pattern of 1871 is not a muted version of that present forty years later, but a different one altogether. Apart from Lombardy which was then clearly exceptional, the industrial divide in 1871 ran essentially East-West rather than North-South. The gap between the industrial triangle and the *Mezzogiorno* evident in 1911 was clearly the result of changing current conditions, and not the path-dependent amplification of a disparity already present at Unification; the Eckaus-Cafagna hypothesis recalled above receives no support from the quantitative evidence.

The division by compass points is only a rough description, as Sardinia to the West was poorly endowed with industry, while Venetia to the East was near the national average; and in any case it gives no hint as to its logic. But the map suggests a more specific distinction, with rich implications. Lombardy again apart, the more industrialized regions appear to have been those that were most recently independent, or the home region of an independent state; the laggards were those long ruled from somewhere else (Sardinia, long attached to the Continent; Emilia, the Marches, and Umbria, long part of the Papal States; and the Abruzzi, Apulia, Basilicata, and Calabria, long subject to whomever was king in Naples).[32]

Lombardy apart, therefore, in 1871 Italy's industrial map seems to be that of a traditional *ancien régime* economy, the economy captured by Ricardo's "growth model": one in which "industry" is handicraft production for the ruling classes that spend tax revenues and land rents, export-oriented only if of world-beating quality, and naturally concentrated next to the court. The industrial, "*manu*facturing" regions are

---

[32] Sicily and the continental South had long been a single kingdom, but Sicily retained a significant if subsidiary capital.

those with the former capitals, of the preceding decades and centuries; the relatively non-industrial regions are those that had long been peripheral parts of broader political units.[33]

In such a context, the appropriate unit of analysis is not in fact the region, but (in Italy) the much smaller province. In a traditional economy, indeed, the surplus is drained from the entire subject territory and spent primarily in the capital; the outlying parts of the region with the capital are no different from the other regions. In the continental South that was once ruled from Naples, for example, the 1871 census counts almost 53,000 clothing and leather workers in the two provinces of Naples and Caserta (the Neapolitan Versailles), an average of 9,000 in the other provinces of Campania, and provincial averages of 7,000 to 11,000 in the Abruzzi, Apulia, Basilicata, and Calabria.[34] This is exactly what Ricardo's model leads one to expect.

The subsequent evolution of Italy's regional disparities seems tied to technical progress, to the diffusion of factory production and the concomitant decline of traditional, artisanal manufacturing. Factories are less sensitive than artisans to direct contact with their clients, not least because they produce inevitably for markets broader than the strictly local; their location is determined rather by the presence of local resources that minimize production costs and attract mobile capital and labor. The cheap energy and cheap transportation of the North exerted a stronger pull on factories than on artisans. By 1911 the former had largely displaced the latter; Italy's more industrial regions were then those of the upper Po valley, and their Ligurian outlet to the sea.[35]

The traditional system left its mark, in the survival elsewhere of luxury handicrafts, and for that matter continued in part to operate, as evidenced by the rapid growth of Latium, with the new national capital city of Rome. In 1871, symmetrically, Lombardy stands out as particularly and exceptionally modern, in a national economy still dominated by the traditional system. The decades from 1871 to 1911 thus seem to cover the central span of a drawn-out industrial revolution.

---

[33] Below, Appendix 4, § 2, and specifically case 4.

[34] Per hundred inhabitants these figures correspond respectively to 3.3 in the provinces of Caserta and Napoli, 2.3 in the other provinces of Campania, and 2.2 to 2.5 in the other regions of the continental South; but the absolute figures are the more meaningful, as the court attracts all industries, and even agriculture, which becomes more intensive next to the urban market.

[35] Below, Appendix 4, § 2, case 5.

9. The regions' industrial structure

Table 6.04 presents the regional estimates of 1911-price industrial value added, sector by sector, in the census years. Dividing each of these columns by its sum one obtains the estimates of each sector's share of regional production transcribed in Table 6.05.[36]

In general, at the present level of aggregation, the regional structures are very similar. In 1871, in particular, each region tends to reproduce, within itself, the structure of the entire country (Table 1.04); one sees there the inheritance of the political divisions, and the high internal transport costs, that limited trade and specialization. Political unification was immediate, economic unification came slowly with the improvement – itself limited – of internal transportation; the regions' industrial structure became progressively less similar, but not rapidly, and never dramatically.

The major differences appear in the mining sector, obviously dominated by natural endowments. The national average share, near 3 percent, reflects regional shares that are often near zero but much higher in the three regions with significant subsoil resources: Tuscany, where mining remained close to 5–6 percent of the regional total; Sicily, where mining's share grew from 13 percent in 1871 to 19 percent in 1901, and then collapsed, with the sulphur crisis, to some 12 percent in 1911; and above all Sardinia, where mining grew from 18 percent of the regional total in 1871 to 23–24 percent at the subsequent census dates.

The share of construction also varies, with a relatively high weight not so much in the regions with rapid population growth as in those with little other industry: for example in Basilicata and Calabria, as well as in Latium and Apulia, and not in Liguria or Lombardy. The influence of the Kuznets cycle is again apparent: almost everywhere the regional share of the construction industry is least in 1901, when it had yet to recover from the crisis of the 1890s.

The weight of the utilities also appears to vary systematically. In 1871 it was typically very small; the standout exception was Latium, with its peculiar inheritance of aqueducts. With the spread of power generation and the growth of municipal services this sector grew faster than any other, and by 1911 its weight was everywhere much greater. Latium retained its record, but comparably high shares were reached elsewhere, in the industrially backward regions where the utilities had nonetheless a

---

[36] The column sums from Table 6.04 are of course the regional totals presented in Table 6.01.

TABLE 6.04. *Regional industrial production: sector estimates (million lire of value added at 1911 prices)*

	Piedmont				Liguria			
	1871	1881	1901	1911	1871	1881	1901	1911
extractive ind.	2.0	.7	2.6	10.5	2.6	1.1	1.6	3.3
foodstuffs	55.5	55.2	76.2	96.1	13.7	17.3	23.7	39.3
tobacco	3.2	3.8	2.0	2.2	.6	.9	1.7	1.8
textiles	26.1	33.7	74.2	99.5	4.5	5.9	8.8	14.0
clothing	10.5	13.0	22.6	28.7	2.3	3.5	6.2	8.3
leather	14.4	18.9	27.8	26.3	4.1	5.8	9.5	9.2
wood	16.3	18.0	26.9	40.2	4.7	5.4	9.3	15.6
metalmaking	.8	2.5	6.4	13.0	.0	2.3	6.8	19.9
engineering	25.9	41.8	55.2	114.6	9.5	18.5	36.8	75.8
nonmet. min. prod.	5.5	8.4	12.6	35.9	1.7	1.9	3.7	10.1
chem., rubber	2.5	5.1	11.7	24.8	.7	1.5	3.5	10.8
paper, printing	5.0	8.5	19.3	36.9	2.8	3.3	5.8	11.0
sundry manuf.	1.4	.6	1.9	2.0	.6	1.5	.9	.6
manufacturing	166.9	209.5	336.7	520.1	45.3	67.4	116.7	216.3
construction	33.2	44.9	36.8	78.6	8.1	12.0	14.0	31.7
utilities	1.9	2.7	11.5	34.2	1.0	1.5	5.0	12.2

	Lombardy				Venetia			
	1871	1881	1901	1911	1871	1881	1901	1911
extractive ind.	2.4	2.9	3.5	8.8	1.5	2.3	2.6	4.8
foodstuffs	84.4	89.8	131.2	159.2	45.6	44.7	61.8	73.7
tobacco	1.8	2.4	2.0	3.7	2.3	2.5	2.0	1.5
textiles	50.2	63.3	156.9	211.7	13.5	18.3	35.8	50.2
clothing	17.3	21.4	31.4	39.5	8.6	8.9	13.9	17.5
leather	19.4	23.6	38.7	40.3	11.3	14.2	18.7	19.6
wood	23.6	26.0	47.8	77.0	16.0	16.2	26.2	43.4
metalmaking	1.3	3.2	8.7	26.1	.6	.9	1.6	2.8
engineering	37.4	52.7	84.9	195.8	25.3	32.4	41.2	75.1
nonmet. min. prod.	7.5	10.8	16.0	51.1	8.8	12.6	22.7	28.3
chem., rubber	2.6	5.0	24.0	32.4	1.2	2.8	5.6	10.7
paper, printing	8.4	13.0	32.7	67.0	4.2	4.8	10.0	18.6
sundry manuf.	1.6	1.5	3.9	11.7	1.0	.5	.6	1.7
manufacturing	255.3	312.7	577.0	915.4	138.3	158.9	240.0	343.1
construction	43.8	57.4	51.4	122.7	29.7	33.8	40.7	60.1
utilities	1.6	2.4	14.5	46.6	1.2	1.5	4.7	14.0

certain presence: for example in Umbria, which developed its hydroelectric potential, and in Basilicata, seat of the initial conduit of the Apulian aqueduct.[37] The major producers in 1911 were Piedmont and Lombardy,

---

[37] These shares reflect the conventions of the industrial classifications, which assign the production of electric energy to the electric utilities only if it is sold to third parties; the in-house production of power is assigned instead to the consuming industry, with the result for example that the production of electric energy to supply the electrochemicals industry is part of the utilities in Umbria, but of chemicals in the Abruzzi. This practice is followed

TABLE 6.04 *(continued)*

	Emilia				Tuscany			
	1871	1881	1901	1911	1871	1881	1901	1911
extractive ind.	1.1	1.9	1.6	3.0	6.3	9.8	14.5	25.7
foodstuffs	32.0	31.2	48.1	78.9	33.6	34.0	46.8	53.8
tobacco	3.2	2.2	2.3	2.5	1.7	3.4	5.2	5.4
textiles	6.9	7.6	3.9	5.3	6.8	8.5	16.8	18.4
clothing	8.3	11.0	19.2	23.3	13.0	15.0	19.3	42.0
leather	11.7	14.0	20.9	22.8	10.7	13.5	20.9	21.6
wood	10.4	11.7	17.5	29.6	11.3	12.1	21.0	31.7
metalmaking	.3	.6	.8	2.0	.6	1.8	5.5	14.4
engineering	15.7	20.7	27.2	59.5	17.7	22.9	31.0	57.7
nonmet. min. prod.	2.4	2.8	4.1	21.6	7.4	9.6	16.0	35.9
chem., rubber	1.5	2.0	4.9	13.1	2.0	2.6	5.7	16.5
paper, printing	2.4	3.1	6.7	13.7	4.1	4.9	11.4	26.2
sundry manuf.	.5	.3	.8	2.4	1.2	2.0	1.9	1.4
manufacturing	95.2	107.1	156.5	274.6	110.0	130.3	201.5	324.8
construction	22.7	23.7	28.4	72.6	18.1	20.0	27.1	51.6
utilities	.6	1.0	2.8	10.9	1.4	1.9	4.1	9.3

	Marches				Umbria			
	1871	1881	1901	1911	1871	1881	1901	1911
extractive ind.	.8	1.2	.9	1.7	.1	.0	.6	1.6
foodstuffs	10.7	9.7	12.5	15.1	6.8	6.4	7.5	9.5
tobacco	1.6	1.4	1.6	1.6	.0	.0	.0	.1
textiles	3.5	3.9	3.8	4.0	1.4	1.4	2.1	4.7
clothing	3.7	4.2	6.5	8.2	1.3	1.2	2.0	2.8
leather	5.3	6.5	10.4	10.3	2.8	3.5	5.8	5.8
wood	3.7	4.1	6.0	8.8	2.2	2.3	3.9	4.7
metalmaking	.2	.2	.4	.5	.1	.3	3.4	7.7
engineering	7.9	9.9	11.9	15.8	4.4	5.3	8.1	9.0
nonmet. min. prod.	1.2	1.7	2.2	8.3	.9	1.1	1.3	3.7
chem., rubber	.5	.6	1.2	3.6	.1	.2	1.2	5.0
paper, printing	.9	2.2	4.5	7.5	.4	.6	1.3	3.0
sundry manuf.	.3	.2	.3	.5	.1	.0	.0	.0
manufacturing	39.3	44.5	61.2	84.2	20.5	22.4	36.7	56.0
construction	6.9	8.3	7.5	15.9	4.8	4.2	5.8	10.1
utilities	.1	.2	1.8	5.7	.2	.2	1.2	6.7

but the sector's share was limited there by the extensive development of manufacturing; the lowest shares appear in Sardinia, in Apulia, in Calabria, where there were few active plants and the provision of municipal services was correspondingly limited.

here because the logically consistent alternative would require assigning to the power-producing industry all power production, electric and non-electric; failing that, again for example, the textile industry would contract if it inserted electric generators between its steam engines and its textile machinery.

TABLE 6.04 (*continued*)

	Latium				Abruzzi			
	1871	1881	1901	1911	1871	1881	1901	1911
extractive ind.	.6	.8	.7	2.6	.0	.1	.3	1.4
foodstuffs	16.3	18.2	26.1	25.8	12.8	13.9	14.7	16.8
tobacco	1.0	1.0	1.0	1.0	.0	.0	.0	.0
textiles	1.2	1.3	.5	.6	.8	1.3	.9	1.4
clothing	2.1	3.1	6.1	9.8	3.5	5.0	5.7	6.6
leather	5.1	6.3	10.4	10.7	5.6	7.2	11.6	11.2
wood	4.8	5.0	8.6	11.0	3.3	3.5	5.6	8.7
metalmaking	.3	.6	.7	1.5	.2	.1	.1	.7
engineering	8.2	11.1	15.6	28.6	8.2	10.6	12.0	14.2
nonmet. min. prod.	2.0	3.0	3.4	8.5	1.2	1.6	2.0	6.7
chem., rubber	.7	.8	1.7	3.7	.4	.4	1.1	3.2
paper, printing	1.9	4.7	10.3	21.0	.3	.4	1.1	2.2
sundry manuf.	.2	.3	.3	1.2	.1	.1	.1	.3
manufacturing	43.6	55.3	84.6	123.3	36.4	44.1	54.8	72.0
construction	10.7	13.4	12.1	32.9	7.2	8.4	7.5	13.6
utilities	2.8	3.9	6.8	16.4	.3	.3	1.2	2.6

	Campania				Apulia			
	1871	1881	1901	1911	1871	1881	1901	1911
extractive ind.	1.3	2.8	1.5	4.2	3.0	4.5	4.3	6.3
foodstuffs	45.5	59.3	65.7	82.1	24.4	23.8	28.2	46.6
tobacco	1.2	1.7	2.2	3.1	.1	.1	.2	2.2
textiles	17.3	13.1	13.6	12.5	1.4	1.3	1.5	2.1
clothing	9.5	11.9	16.9	22.8	3.7	5.4	6.8	10.8
leather	16.1	22.2	35.7	37.9	7.8	10.8	17.8	18.8
wood	14.8	17.5	25.7	37.7	5.4	7.1	12.0	20.6
metalmaking	1.4	1.9	3.2	11.3	.2	.2	.3	1.1
engineering	21.9	34.3	50.3	77.1	10.0	12.6	23.8	30.5
nonmet. min. prod.	4.6	5.8	7.8	13.7	1.8	2.3	4.8	10.1
chem., rubber	2.6	4.5	7.9	15.8	1.4	1.6	3.0	6.8
paper, printing	4.6	7.3	11.6	21.0	.4	.8	2.1	4.8
sundry manuf.	1.5	3.8	5.0	3.9	.1	.1	.1	.5
manufacturing	141.0	183.3	245.5	338.8	56.5	66.0	100.5	154.9
construction	25.3	32.5	29.4	58.7	17.5	22.4	20.4	39.7
utilities	1.2	1.7	8.1	15.3	.1	.2	.8	2.5

The other and largest major group is the manufacturing sector; and within it too regional patterns appear very similar, especially in 1871. The foodstuffs industry was then everywhere the largest of the sectors identified here, followed at a distance by engineering (in fact blacksmithing, engaged in the maintenance of agricultural tools), and then by the processing of (non-food) vegetable and animal products; the textile industry was larger than the engineering industry only in Lombardy, and comparable to it in Piedmont and Campania.

TABLE 6.04 *(continued)*

	Basilicata				Calabria			
	1871	1881	1901	1911	1871	1881	1901	1911
extractive ind.	.0	.1	.2	.8	.9	.8	1.0	1.3
foodstuffs	6.4	6.1	6.3	6.8	15.7	17.5	19.6	24.2
tobacco	.0	.0	.0	.0	.0	.0	.0	.0
textiles	.2	.4	.2	.2	1.4	2.0	2.6	2.2
clothing	1.2	1.3	1.4	1.7	3.5	3.6	5.1	6.6
leather	2.7	3.7	4.7	4.7	6.2	8.5	12.3	13.8
wood	1.8	1.7	2.2	3.5	4.3	5.5	8.3	12.7
metalmaking	.0	.0	.0	.0	.0	.1	.0	.0
engineering	3.9	4.5	4.4	5.1	8.1	9.4	9.5	12.7
nonmet. min. prod.	.5	.6	.7	1.3	1.0	1.3	1.6	5.3
chem., rubber	.1	.4	.3	.5	.3	.8	1.3	4.3
paper, printing	.1	.1	.3	.3	.3	.3	.9	1.5
sundry manuf.	.0	.0	.0	.0	.1	.1	.0	.2
manufacturing	16.9	18.9	20.4	24.1	40.8	49.1	61.2	83.5
construction	4.3	5.3	3.2	6.0	8.9	11.3	9.8	19.4
utilities	.1	.1	.3	2.4	.3	.3	.9	1.7

	Sicily				Sardinia			
	1871	1881	1901	1911	1871	1881	1901	1911
extractive ind.	21.3	32.4	54.4	46.0	5.2	9.8	11.9	20.0
foodstuffs	45.4	55.3	66.2	82.0	6.5	8.5	9.6	17.2
tobacco	4.4	1.3	1.1	1.9	.0	.2	.8	.9
textiles	4.6	3.9	2.2	1.5	.1	.1	.2	.2
clothing	5.0	10.7	8.6	12.3	.6	.9	1.3	2.2
leather	17.5	23.9	39.3	41.2	2.5	3.5	5.6	5.7
wood	11.4	12.7	23.4	33.1	2.1	2.3	3.6	7.8
metalmaking	1.0	.5	1.0	1.5	.0	.0	.2	.4
engineering	22.4	24.2	33.3	45.1	4.7	6.1	7.9	11.5
nonmet. min. prod.	4.1	6.7	9.3	16.7	.4	.6	.9	2.9
chem., rubber	2.4	2.6	4.6	16.4	.1	.1	.4	.5
paper, printing	1.2	1.7	4.2	6.5	.2	.3	.6	1.1
sundry manuf.	.5	.3	.3	.5	.1	.0	.0	.2
manufacturing	119.8	143.9	193.4	258.7	17.1	22.7	30.9	50.5
construction	26.4	35.0	36.2	70.9	6.4	7.3	8.9	12.5
utilities	1.1	1.7	4.9	9.3	.2	.3	.7	1.0

Sources: see text.

This interregional similarity was reduced over time as transportation improved and the industrial triangle developed. In 1911 an industrial structure similar to that of 1871, with the foodstuffs industry perceptibly the largest, survived in Emilia and in much of the South (Apulia, Basilicata, Calabria, Sicily, and Sardinia). Elsewhere the engineering industry, then at a cyclical peak, had reached parity or near-parity with the foodstuffs industry; it had become perceptibly the largest in Piedmont and

TABLE 6.05. *Sector shares of aggregate industrial production,*
by region (percent)

	Piedmont				Liguria			
	1871	1881	1901	1911	1871	1881	1901	1911
extractive ind.	1.0	.3	.7	1.6	4.6	1.4	1.1	1.3
foodstuffs	27.2	21.4	19.6	14.9	24.0	21.1	17.3	14.9
tobacco	1.5	1.5	.5	.3	1.1	1.1	1.3	.7
textiles	12.8	13.1	19.1	15.5	7.9	7.2	6.4	5.3
clothing	5.2	5.0	5.8	4.5	4.1	4.2	4.5	3.2
leather	7.1	7.3	7.2	4.1	7.2	7.1	6.9	3.5
wood	8.0	7.0	6.9	6.2	8.3	6.5	6.8	5.9
metalmaking	.4	1.0	1.7	2.0	.0	2.6	4.9	7.5
engineering	12.7	16.2	14.2	17.8	16.7	22.5	26.8	28.8
nonmet. min. prod.	2.7	3.3	3.3	5.6	3.0	2.3	2.7	3.8
chem., rubber	1.2	2.0	3.0	3.9	1.3	1.8	2.6	4.1
paper, printing	2.5	3.3	5.0	5.7	4.8	4.0	4.2	4.2
sundry manuf.	.7	.2	.5	.3	1.1	1.8	.7	.2
manufacturing	81.8	81.3	86.9	80.8	79.5	82.3	85.0	82.1
construction	16.3	17.4	9.5	12.2	14.2	14.6	10.2	12.0
utilities	.9	1.1	3.0	5.3	1.7	1.8	3.6	4.6

	Lombardy				Venetia			
	1871	1881	1901	1911	1871	1881	1901	1911
extractive ind.	.8	.8	.5	.8	.9	1.1	.9	1.1
foodstuffs	27.8	23.9	20.3	14.6	26.7	22.8	21.5	17.5
tobacco	.6	.6	.3	.3	1.3	1.3	.7	.4
textiles	16.6	16.9	24.3	19.4	7.9	9.3	12.4	11.9
clothing	5.7	5.7	4.9	3.6	5.0	4.5	4.8	4.2
leather	6.4	6.3	6.0	3.7	6.6	7.2	6.5	4.6
wood	7.8	6.9	7.2	7.0	9.3	8.3	9.1	10.3
metalmaking	.4	.8	1.3	2.4	.4	.5	.5	.7
engineering	12.3	14.0	13.1	17.9	14.8	16.5	14.3	17.8
nonmet. min. prod.	2.5	2.9	2.5	4.7	5.2	6.4	7.9	6.7
chem., rubber	.9	1.3	3.7	3.0	.7	1.4	2.0	2.5
paper, printing	2.8	3.5	5.1	6.1	2.5	2.5	3.5	4.4
sundry manuf.	.5	.4	.6	1.1	.6	.2	.2	.4
manufacturing	84.3	83.3	89.3	83.7	81.0	80.9	83.4	81.3
construction	14.4	15.3	8.0	11.2	17.4	17.2	14.1	14.2
utilities	.5	.6	2.2	4.3	.7	.8	1.6	3.3

in Lombardy, and especially in Liguria, where it overtook foodstuffs by 1881 and was by 1911 almost twice as large.

The textile industry displays a different pattern. In Piedmont, in Lombardy, in Venetia, in a minor key in Tuscany too, its share grew to a peak in 1901, thanks also to the turn-of-the-century crisis of the cyclical industries; its share then declined as the latter recovered, but in 1911 it remained the largest industry in Lombardy and the second-largest, after

TABLE 6.05 *(continued)*

	Emilia				Tuscany			
	1871	1881	1901	1911	1871	1881	1901	1911
extractive ind.	.9	1.4	.8	.8	4.6	6.0	5.9	6.2
foodstuffs	26.7	23.4	25.4	21.9	24.7	21.0	18.9	13.1
tobacco	2.6	1.6	1.2	.7	1.2	2.1	2.1	1.3
textiles	5.8	5.7	2.0	1.5	5.0	5.2	6.8	4.5
clothing	7.0	8.2	10.2	6.5	9.6	9.2	7.8	10.2
leather	9.7	10.5	11.0	6.3	7.8	8.3	8.5	5.2
wood	8.7	8.8	9.3	8.2	8.3	7.5	8.5	7.7
metalmaking	.3	.5	.4	.6	.4	1.1	2.2	3.5
engineering	13.1	15.5	14.4	16.5	13.0	14.1	12.6	14.0
nonmet. min. prod.	2.0	2.1	2.2	6.0	5.5	6.0	6.5	8.7
chem., rubber	1.3	1.5	2.6	3.6	1.5	1.6	2.3	4.0
paper, printing	2.0	2.3	3.6	3.8	3.0	3.0	4.6	6.4
sundry manuf.	.4	.2	.4	.7	.9	1.2	.8	.3
manufacturing	79.6	80.2	82.7	76.0	81.0	80.4	81.5	78.9
construction	19.0	17.7	15.0	20.1	13.3	12.4	11.0	12.5
utilities	.5	.7	1.5	3.0	1.0	1.1	1.7	2.3

	Marches				Umbria			
	1871	1881	1901	1911	1871	1881	1901	1911
extractive ind.	1.6	2.3	1.3	1.6	.3	.1	1.4	2.2
foodstuffs	22.6	17.9	17.5	14.1	26.5	24.0	16.9	12.8
tobacco	3.4	2.6	2.2	1.5	.0	.0	.0	.1
textiles	7.4	7.2	5.3	3.7	5.6	5.2	4.7	6.3
clothing	7.9	7.7	9.1	7.7	4.9	4.6	4.6	3.8
leather	11.2	11.9	14.6	9.6	11.1	13.0	13.1	7.8
wood	7.8	7.5	8.4	8.2	8.6	8.7	8.7	6.3
metalmaking	.4	.4	.6	.5	.4	1.2	7.7	10.3
engineering	16.7	18.3	16.7	14.7	17.4	19.9	18.3	12.1
nonmet. min. prod.	2.5	3.2	3.0	7.7	3.6	3.9	3.0	5.0
chem., rubber	1.0	1.0	1.6	3.4	.5	.9	2.8	6.8
paper, printing	2.0	4.1	6.4	7.0	1.6	2.3	2.9	4.0
sundry manuf.	.6	.3	.4	.5	.3	.1	.1	.1
manufacturing	83.4	82.0	85.7	78.3	80.4	83.7	82.9	75.2
construction	14.7	15.3	10.5	14.8	18.7	15.6	13.0	13.6
utilities	.3	.4	2.5	5.3	.6	.6	2.7	9.0

engineering, in Piedmont. Elsewhere its share continuously declined; the decline was especially great in Campania, where the industry was tied to the processing of the traditional fibers displaced by cotton, and especially sudden in Emilia, where the initial processing of hemp fell rapidly in the 1890s.[38]

[38] Fenoaltea, "Textile Production in Italy's Regions," pp. 167, 170.

TABLE 6.05 *(continued)*

	Latium				Abruzzi			
	1871	1881	1901	1911	1871	1881	1901	1911
extractive ind.	1.0	1.1	.6	1.5	.1	.2	.4	1.5
foodstuffs	28.3	24.8	25.1	14.7	29.1	26.1	23.1	18.7
tobacco	1.7	1.4	.9	.6	.0	.0	.0	.0
textiles	2.1	1.8	.5	.3	1.8	2.5	1.4	1.6
clothing	3.6	4.2	5.8	5.6	8.0	9.4	8.9	7.3
leather	8.8	8.6	10.0	6.1	12.8	13.6	18.1	12.5
wood	8.3	6.9	8.3	6.3	7.6	6.6	8.8	9.7
metalmaking	.5	.8	.6	.8	.5	.1	.2	.8
engineering	14.2	15.1	15.0	16.3	18.7	20.0	18.7	15.9
nonmet. min. prod.	3.4	4.1	3.3	4.8	2.7	3.1	3.2	7.5
chem., rubber	1.2	1.1	1.7	2.1	.8	.8	1.6	3.6
paper, printing	3.3	6.3	9.9	12.0	.6	.8	1.7	2.4
sundry manuf.	.3	.3	.3	.7	.1	.1	.1	.3
manufacturing	75.7	75.3	81.2	70.4	82.8	83.2	85.9	80.4
construction	18.5	18.3	11.6	18.8	16.4	15.9	11.8	15.2
utilities	4.8	5.3	6.6	9.3	.6	.6	1.9	2.9

	Campania				Apulia			
	1871	1881	1901	1911	1871	1881	1901	1911
extractive ind.	.8	1.3	.5	1.0	3.9	4.8	3.4	3.1
foodstuffs	26.9	26.9	23.1	19.7	31.6	25.6	22.3	22.9
tobacco	.7	.8	.8	.7	.1	.1	.2	1.1
textiles	10.3	6.0	4.8	3.0	1.8	1.4	1.2	1.1
clothing	5.6	5.4	6.0	5.5	4.8	5.8	5.4	5.3
leather	9.5	10.1	12.5	9.1	10.1	11.6	14.1	9.2
wood	8.8	7.9	9.0	9.0	7.0	7.6	9.5	10.1
metalmaking	.8	.8	1.1	2.7	.2	.2	.2	.5
engineering	13.0	15.6	17.7	18.5	12.9	13.5	18.9	15.0
nonmet. min. prod.	2.7	2.6	2.7	3.3	2.4	2.5	3.8	5.0
chem., rubber	1.5	2.1	2.8	3.8	1.8	1.7	2.4	3.4
paper, printing	2.7	3.3	4.1	5.0	.5	.8	1.7	2.4
sundry manuf.	.9	1.7	1.7	.9	.1	.1	.1	.2
manufacturing	83.5	83.2	86.3	81.2	73.3	70.9	79.8	76.1
construction	15.0	14.7	10.3	14.1	22.6	24.1	16.2	19.5
utilities	.7	.8	2.9	3.7	.1	.2	.7	1.2

Metalmaking was, in 1871, negligible everywhere. In 1911 it was still tiny at the national level (Table 1.04), but it had become no less than the third industry in Liguria, and even in Umbria, where the Terni works rivaled foodstuffs and engineering.

In many regions of the Center and South leather-working increased its share until 1901; at the turn of the century it was a strong third in the Marches, in Umbria, in Latium, in the entire *Mezzogiorno*.

TABLE 6.05 *(continued)*

	Basilicata				Calabria			
	1871	1881	1901	1911	1871	1881	1901	1911
extractive ind.	.0	.4	.6	2.5	1.8	1.3	1.4	1.2
foodstuffs	30.1	24.9	25.9	20.5	30.8	28.5	26.9	22.9
tobacco	.0	.0	.0	.0	.0	.0	.0	.0
textiles	1.1	1.7	1.0	.7	2.7	3.3	3.5	2.1
clothing	5.5	5.4	5.8	4.9	6.8	5.9	7.0	6.2
leather	12.8	15.0	19.6	14.1	12.2	13.9	16.9	13.1
wood	8.3	7.0	8.9	10.6	8.4	8.9	11.4	12.0
metalmaking	.1	.1	.0	.0	.1	.1	.0	.0
engineering	18.2	18.5	18.1	15.2	15.9	15.2	13.0	12.0
nonmet. min. prod.	2.2	2.6	2.9	3.9	1.9	2.1	2.2	5.0
chem., rubber	.5	1.5	1.4	1.4	.7	1.2	1.7	4.0
paper, printing	.3	.5	1.1	.8	.5	.5	1.2	1.4
sundry manuf.	.0	.1	.1	.1	.2	.1	.0	.2
manufacturing	79.1	77.2	84.7	72.2	80.2	79.9	84.0	78.9
construction	20.3	21.9	13.5	18.1	17.5	18.3	13.5	18.3
utilities	.5	.5	1.2	7.3	.5	.5	1.2	1.6

	Sicily				Sardinia			
	1871	1881	1901	1911	1871	1881	1901	1911
extractive ind.	12.7	15.2	18.8	11.9	17.9	24.4	22.7	23.8
foodstuffs	26.9	26.0	22.9	21.3	22.4	21.2	18.3	20.4
tobacco	2.6	.6	.4	.5	.0	.5	1.4	1.1
textiles	2.7	1.8	.7	.4	.3	.2	.3	.3
clothing	2.9	5.0	3.0	3.2	1.9	2.3	2.4	2.6
leather	10.4	11.2	13.6	10.7	8.6	8.7	10.6	6.8
wood	6.8	5.9	8.1	8.6	7.3	5.8	6.9	9.2
metalmaking	.6	.2	.4	.4	.1	.1	.3	.5
engineering	13.3	11.4	11.5	11.7	16.2	15.3	15.1	13.7
nonmet. min. prod.	2.5	3.2	3.2	4.3	1.4	1.6	1.7	3.5
chem., rubber	1.4	1.2	1.6	4.3	.3	.3	.8	.6
paper, printing	.7	.8	1.5	1.7	.6	.6	1.2	1.2
sundry manuf.	.3	.1	.1	.1	.2	.0	.0	.2
manufacturing	71.0	67.6	66.9	67.2	59.2	56.7	59.0	60.1
construction	15.7	16.5	12.5	18.4	22.1	18.2	17.0	14.9
utilities	.6	.8	1.7	2.4	.8	.7	1.3	1.2

Sources: see text.

10. The regions' comparative advantages

Dividing the sector-specific regional estimates of 1911-price industrial value added in Table 6.04 by their year-specific row sums one obtains the estimates of each region's share of each sector's national production transcribed in Table 6.06. Dividing these last by the regional shares of

TABLE 6.06. *Regional shares of aggregate industrial production,
by sector (percent)*

	Piedmont				Liguria			
	1871	1881	1901	1911	1871	1881	1901	1911
extractive ind.	4.0	.9	2.5	7.4	5.3	1.6	1.5	2.3
foodstuffs	12.2	11.2	11.8	11.6	3.0	3.5	3.7	4.8
tobacco	15.0	18.1	9.0	7.9	3.0	4.5	7.9	6.3
textiles	18.6	20.3	22.9	23.2	3.2	3.6	2.7	3.3
clothing	11.2	10.8	13.1	11.8	2.5	2.9	3.6	3.4
leather	10.1	10.2	9.6	8.8	2.9	3.1	3.3	3.1
wood	12.0	11.9	10.9	10.4	3.5	3.5	3.8	4.0
metalmaking	11.2	16.6	16.5	14.5	.1	14.3	17.4	18.9
engineering	11.2	13.2	12.2	13.8	4.1	5.8	8.1	9.2
nonmet. min. prod.	10.8	11.9	11.6	13.8	3.3	2.7	3.4	3.9
chem., rubber	13.2	16.3	15.0	14.8	3.8	4.7	4.5	6.4
paper, printing	13.6	15.2	15.7	15.3	7.4	5.8	4.7	4.6
sundry manuf.	15.0	5.1	12.1	7.3	6.8	13.1	5.8	2.3
manufacturing	12.4	12.8	13.4	13.5	3.4	4.1	4.6	5.6
construction	12.1	13.2	10.8	11.3	3.0	3.5	4.1	4.5
utilities	13.5	13.9	16.6	17.9	7.0	7.5	7.2	6.4

	Lombardy				Venetia			
	1871	1881	1901	1911	1871	1881	1901	1911
extractive ind.	4.9	4.0	3.4	6.2	3.0	3.2	2.5	3.3
foodstuffs	18.5	18.3	20.4	19.3	10.0	9.1	9.6	8.9
tobacco	8.6	11.4	9.2	13.3	10.9	12.0	9.1	5.4
textiles	35.9	38.1	48.4	49.4	9.6	11.0	11.1	11.7
clothing	18.4	17.8	18.2	16.2	9.2	7.4	8.0	7.2
leather	13.5	12.7	13.3	13.4	7.9	7.6	6.4	6.5
wood	17.3	17.2	18.9	19.9	11.7	10.7	10.6	11.2
metalmaking	18.2	21.3	22.3	24.9	8.6	6.0	4.0	2.7
engineering	16.2	16.6	18.7	23.6	10.9	10.2	9.1	9.1
nonmet. min. prod.	14.7	15.2	14.6	19.6	17.3	17.8	20.8	10.9
chem., rubber	13.7	16.3	30.7	19.3	6.3	9.0	7.2	6.4
paper, printing	22.6	23.2	26.6	27.7	11.4	8.6	8.1	7.7
sundry manuf.	17.5	14.0	24.0	43.2	11.0	4.5	3.5	6.2
manufacturing	19.0	19.1	22.9	23.8	10.3	9.7	9.5	8.9
construction	16.0	16.9	15.2	17.6	10.9	9.9	12.0	8.6
utilities	11.2	12.3	20.9	24.4	8.7	7.6	6.8	7.3

the male population of working age (Table 6.02) one obtains the
sector-specific indices of relative industrialization transcribed in Table 6.07; these are of course analogous to those already calculated for
industry as a whole (Table 6.03).

These indices reveal some further patterns. In 1871, in particular, the
regional indices for the food sector are strikingly close to those for total
manufacturing: food processing seems to follow other manufacturing in
the residential centers of the upper classes, confirming the *ancien régime*

TABLE 6.06 *(continued)*

	Emilia				Tuscany			
	1871	1881	1901	1911	1871	1881	1901	1911
extractive ind.	2.2	2.6	1.6	2.1	12.8	13.8	14.2	18.1
foodstuffs	7.0	6.4	7.5	9.5	7.4	6.9	7.3	6.5
tobacco	15.0	10.3	10.4	9.0	8.0	16.3	23.7	19.2
textiles	5.0	4.6	1.2	1.2	4.9	5.1	5.2	4.3
clothing	8.9	9.2	11.1	9.6	13.9	12.5	11.2	17.3
leather	8.1	7.5	7.2	7.6	7.5	7.2	7.2	7.2
wood	7.7	7.8	7.1	7.7	8.3	8.0	8.5	8.2
metalmaking	4.8	4.0	2.1	1.9	8.5	12.3	14.1	13.7
engineering	6.8	6.5	6.0	7.2	7.7	7.2	6.9	7.0
nonmet. min. prod.	4.6	3.9	3.7	8.3	14.6	13.6	14.7	13.8
chem., rubber	8.1	6.3	6.3	7.8	10.4	8.5	7.3	9.8
paper, printing	6.4	5.5	5.5	5.7	11.1	8.7	9.3	10.8
sundry manuf.	5.4	2.9	5.0	8.7	13.3	17.9	11.8	5.2
manufacturing	7.1	6.5	6.2	7.1	8.2	8.0	8.0	8.5
construction	8.3	7.0	8.4	10.4	6.6	5.9	8.0	7.4
utilities	4.4	5.0	4.1	5.7	10.2	9.4	6.0	4.9

	Marches				Umbria			
	1871	1881	1901	1911	1871	1881	1901	1911
extractive ind.	1.5	1.7	.9	1.2	.2	.0	.6	1.1
foodstuffs	2.3	2.0	1.9	1.8	1.5	1.3	1.2	1.1
tobacco	7.6	6.8	7.2	5.7	.0	.0	.0	.3
textiles	2.5	2.3	1.2	.9	1.0	.8	.6	1.1
clothing	4.0	3.5	3.8	3.4	1.3	1.0	1.2	1.2
leather	3.7	3.5	3.6	3.4	2.0	1.9	2.0	1.9
wood	2.7	2.7	2.4	2.3	1.6	1.5	1.6	1.2
metalmaking	2.5	1.6	1.0	.5	1.5	2.1	8.8	7.3
engineering	3.4	3.1	2.6	1.9	1.9	1.7	1.8	1.1
nonmet. min. prod.	2.3	2.4	2.0	3.2	1.8	1.5	1.2	1.4
chem., rubber	2.4	1.8	1.5	2.2	.6	.8	1.6	3.0
paper, printing	2.5	3.9	3.7	3.1	1.1	1.1	1.1	1.2
sundry manuf.	3.3	1.5	1.6	1.9	.8	.4	.2	.1
manufacturing	2.9	2.7	2.4	2.2	1.5	1.4	1.5	1.5
construction	2.5	2.4	2.2	2.3	1.7	1.2	1.7	1.5
utilities	1.0	1.0	2.5	3.0	1.1	.8	1.7	3.5

nature of the economy of the time.[39] In the case of the leather-working industries, in turn, the variations over time and space in their shares of regional industry turn out to correspond to relatively constant production per capita: as if consumption per capita were everywhere similar, and

---

[39] Since the censuses captured the urban foodstuffs industry better than its rural counterpart (a part-time activity of the agricultural population), the actual relation may have been less rigid than the present estimates suggest; but it is unlikely to have been very different.

TABLE 6.06 *(continued)*

	Latium				Abruzzi			
	1871	1881	1901	1911	1871	1881	1901	1911
extractive ind.	1.1	1.1	.7	1.8	.1	.2	.3	1.0
foodstuffs	3.6	3.7	4.1	3.1	2.8	2.8	2.3	2.0
tobacco	4.7	4.7	4.3	3.6	.0	.0	.0	.0
textiles	.9	.8	.2	.1	.6	.8	.3	.3
clothing ,	2.2	2.6	3.5	4.0	3.8	4.2	3.3	2.7
leather	3.6	3.4	3.6	3.6	3.9	3.9	4.0	3.7
wood	3.5	3.3	3.5	2.9	2.5	2.3	2.3	2.3
metalmaking	3.9	3.7	1.7	1.4	3.3	.5	.3	.7
engineering	3.5	3.5	3.4	3.5	3.6	3.3	2.6	1.7
nonmet. min. prod.	3.9	4.2	3.1	3.3	2.3	2.3	1.9	2.6
chem., rubber	3.7	2.6	2.2	2.2	1.9	1.4	1.3	1.9
paper, printing	5.1	8.3	8.4	8.7	.8	.8	.9	.9
sundry manuf.	1.9	2.2	1.7	4.6	.6	.5	.5	.9
manufacturing	3.2	3.4	3.4	3.2	2.7	2.7	2.2	1.9
construction	3.9	3.9	3.6	4.7	2.6	2.5	2.2	2.0
utilities	20.0	19.9	9.9	8.6	2.0	1.7	1.7	1.4

	Campania				Apulia			
	1871	1881	1901	1911	1871	1881	1901	1911
extractive ind.	2.6	3.9	1.5	3.0	6.2	6.4	4.2	4.5
foodstuffs	10.0	12.1	10.2	9.9	5.4	4.8	4.4	5.6
tobacco	5.7	8.3	9.8	11.2	.5	.3	.9	7.9
textiles	12.4	7.9	4.2	2.9	1.0	.8	.5	.5
clothing	10.1	9.9	9.8	9.4	3.9	4.5	3.9	4.4
leather	11.2	11.9	12.3	12.6	5.4	5.8	6.1	6.3
wood	10.9	11.6	10.4	9.8	4.0	4.7	4.8	5.3
metalmaking	20.1	12.3	8.1	10.8	2.4	1.5	.7	1.0
engineering	9.5	10.8	11.1	9.3	4.3	4.0	5.3	3.7
nonmet. min. prod.	9.1	8.1	7.1	5.3	3.6	3.3	4.4	3.9
chem., rubber	13.7	14.6	10.1	9.4	7.2	5.1	3.8	4.1
paper, printing	12.5	13.0	9.5	8.7	1.1	1.4	1.7	2.0
sundry manuf.	16.1	34.5	31.1	14.5	.5	.4	.6	1.9
manufacturing	10.5	11.2	9.7	8.8	4.2	4.0	4.0	4.0
construction	9.2	9.5	8.7	8.4	6.4	6.6	6.0	5.7
utilities	8.3	8.4	11.7	8.0	.8	.7	1.2	1.3

the leather industry (unlike the foodstuffs industry) produced for rural consumers as well as urban ones.

The sector-specific indices too point to heterogeneity within the industrial triangle: from this perspective Piedmont and Lombardy appear similar, Liguria different. Liguria specialized quickly and strongly in metalmaking and (heavy) engineering: coal landed at the sea-ports, and to avoid the costs of further transshipments and transportation these

TABLE 6.06 *(continued)*

	Basilicata				Calabria			
	1871	1881	1901	1911	1871	1881	1901	1911
extractive ind.	.0	.1	.1	.6	1.9	1.1	1.0	.9
foodstuffs	1.4	1.2	1.0	.8	3.4	3.6	3.0	2.9
tobacco	.0	.0	.0	.0	.0	.0	.0	.0
textiles	.2	.2	.1	.1	1.0	1.2	.8	.5
clothing	1.3	1.1	.8	.7	3.7	3.0	3.0	2.7
leather	1.9	2.0	1.6	1.6	4.4	4.6	4.2	4.6
wood	1.3	1.1	.9	.9	3.1	3.6	3.4	3.3
metalmaking	.3	.2	.0	.0	.5	.5	.1	.0
engineering	1.7	1.4	1.0	.6	3.5	3.0	2.1	1.5
nonmet. min. prod.	.9	.9	.6	.5	1.9	1.9	1.5	2.0
chem., rubber	.6	1.2	.4	.3	1.8	2.5	1.6	2.5
paper, printing	.2	.2	.2	.1	.7	.6	.7	.6
sundry manuf.	.0	.1	.1	.1	1.3	.5	.2	.6
manufacturing	1.3	1.2	.8	.6	3.0	3.0	2.4	2.2
construction	1.6	1.6	1.0	.9	3.3	3.3	2.9	2.8
utilities	.8	.6	.4	1.3	1.8	1.4	1.3	.9

	Sicily				Sardinia			
	1871	1881	1901	1911	1871	1881	1901	1911
extractive ind.	43.5	45.6	53.3	32.4	10.5	13.7	11.6	14.1
foodstuffs	10.0	11.3	10.3	9.9	1.4	1.7	1.5	2.1
tobacco	21.1	6.4	5.1	6.9	.0	1.0	3.4	3.3
textiles	3.3	2.3	.7	.3	.1	.0	.0	.1
clothing	5.3	8.9	5.0	5.1	.6	.8	.7	.9
leather	12.2	12.8	13.5	13.7	1.7	1.9	1.9	1.9
wood	8.4	8.4	9.5	8.6	1.5	1.5	1.5	2.0
metalmaking	13.8	3.0	2.7	1.5	.3	.2	.4	.4
engineering	9.7	7.6	7.3	5.5	2.0	1.9	1.7	1.4
nonmet. min. prod.	8.1	9.5	8.5	6.4	.8	.9	.8	1.1
chem., rubber	12.4	8.5	5.9	9.7	.4	.4	.5	.3
paper, printing	3.1	3.1	3.4	2.7	.5	.5	.5	.4
sundry manuf.	6.0	2.3	1.6	1.8	.5	.1	.1	.7
manufacturing	8.9	8.8	7.7	6.7	1.3	1.4	1.2	1.3
construction	9.7	10.3	10.7	10.2	2.3	2.1	2.6	1.8
utilities	7.8	8.4	7.1	4.9	1.6	1.4	1.0	.5

Sources: see text.

fuel-intensive industries located directly on the coast. Piedmont and to an even greater extent Lombardy appear characterized instead by the breadth of their industrial comparative advantage (at least at the present level of aggregation, which does not preclude different results with a finer grid): in 1911 of the twelve manufacturing indices those below unity are just three in Piedmont and not even one in Lombardy, while the high indices (1.3 or more) are six in Piedmont and no fewer than nine in Lombardy.

TABLE 6.07. *Regional indices of relative industrialization, by sector*[a]

	Piedmont				Liguria			
	1871	1881	1901	1911	1871	1881	1901	1911
extractive ind.	.4	.1	.2	.7	1.7	.5	.4	.6
foodstuffs	1.1	1.1	1.1	1.1	1.0	1.1	1.0	1.2
tobacco	1.4	1.7	.9	.8	1.0	1.4	2.2	1.6
textiles	1.7	1.9	2.2	2.3	1.0	1.1	.8	.9
clothing	1.0	1.0	1.3	1.1	.8	.9	1.0	.9
leather	.9	1.0	.9	.8	.9	1.0	.9	.8
wood	1.1	1.1	1.1	1.0	1.1	1.1	1.1	1.1
metalmaking	1.1	1.6	1.6	1.4	.0	4.6	4.9	5.0
engineering	1.0	1.2	1.2	1.3	1.3	1.9	2.3	2.4
nonmet. min. prod.	1.0	1.1	1.1	1.3	1.1	.9	1.0	1.0
chem., rubber	1.2	1.5	1.5	1.4	1.2	1.5	1.3	1.7
paper, printing	1.3	1.4	1.5	1.5	2.4	1.9	1.3	1.2
sundry manuf.	1.4	.5	1.2	.7	2.2	4.2	1.7	.6
manufacturing	1.2	1.2	1.3	1.3	1.1	1.3	1.3	1.5
construction	1.1	1.2	1.1	1.1	1.0	1.1	1.2	1.2
utilities	1.3	1.3	1.6	1.7	2.3	2.4	2.0	1.7

	Lombardy				Venetia			
	1871	1881	1901	1911	1871	1881	1901	1911
extractive ind.	.4	.3	.3	.4	.3	.3	.3	.4
foodstuffs	1.4	1.4	1.5	1.4	1.0	.9	1.0	1.0
tobacco	.7	.9	.7	1.0	1.1	1.2	1.0	.6
textiles	2.7	2.9	3.6	3.6	1.0	1.1	1.2	1.3
clothing	1.4	1.4	1.4	1.2	.9	.8	.9	.8
leather	1.0	1.0	1.0	1.0	.8	.8	.7	.7
wood	1.3	1.3	1.4	1.4	1.2	1.1	1.1	1.2
metalmaking	1.4	1.6	1.7	1.8	.9	.6	.4	.3
engineering	1.2	1.3	1.4	1.7	1.1	1.0	1.0	1.0
nonmet. min. prod.	1.1	1.2	1.1	1.4	1.8	1.8	2.2	1.2
chem., rubber	1.0	1.2	2.3	1.4	.6	.9	.8	.7
paper, printing	1.7	1.8	2.0	2.0	1.1	.9	.9	.8
sundry manuf.	1.3	1.1	1.8	3.1	1.1	.5	.4	.7
manufacturing	1.4	1.5	1.7	1.7	1.0	1.0	1.0	1.0
construction	1.2	1.3	1.1	1.3	1.1	1.0	1.3	.9
utilities	.9	.9	1.6	1.8	.9	.8	.7	.8

The industrial triangle was then followed by Tuscany and Campania, with indices for all manufacturing near the national average, and about as many sector-specific indices above 1.3 as below 1.0. Next, with ever lower indices for all manufacturing and typically no more than a single sector-specific index above 1.3, came Venetia and Emilia, then the Marches, Umbria, Latium, and Apulia; last, with indices for all manufacturing around 0.5–0.6 and no fewer than eleven out of twelve sector-specific indices below 1.0, came the Abruzzi, Basilicata, Calabria, Sicily, and Sardinia.

TABLE 6.07 *(continued)*

	Emilia				Tuscany			
	1871	1881	1901	1911	1871	1881	1901	1911
extractive ind.	.3	.3	.2	.3	1.6	1.7	1.7	2.2
foodstuffs	.9	.8	1.0	1.2	.9	.9	.9	.8
tobacco	1.9	1.3	1.3	1.1	1.0	2.0	2.9	2.4
textiles	.6	.6	.2	.2	.6	.6	.6	.5
clothing	1.1	1.1	1.4	1.2	1.7	1.6	1.4	2.1
leather	1.0	.9	.9	.9	.9	.9	.9	.9
wood	.9	1.0	.9	.9	1.0	1.0	1.0	1.0
metalmaking	.6	.5	.3	.2	1.0	1.5	1.7	1.7
engineering	.8	.8	.8	.9	.9	.9	.8	.9
nonmet. min. prod.	.6	.5	.5	1.0	1.8	1.7	1.8	1.7
chem., rubber	1.0	.8	.8	1.0	1.3	1.1	.9	1.2
paper, printing	.8	.7	.7	.7	1.4	1.1	1.1	1.3
sundry manuf.	.7	.4	.6	1.1	1.6	2.2	1.5	.6
manufacturing	.9	.8	.8	.9	1.0	1.0	1.0	1.0
construction	1.0	.9	1.1	1.3	.8	.7	1.0	.9
utilities	.5	.6	.5	.7	1.2	1.2	.7	.6

	Marches				Umbria			
	1871	1881	1901	1911	1871	1881	1901	1911
extractive ind.	.5	.5	.3	.4	.1	.0	.3	.6
foodstuffs	.7	.6	.6	.6	.7	.6	.5	.6
tobacco	2.3	2.0	2.2	1.9	.0	.0	.0	.1
textiles	.7	.7	.4	.3	.5	.4	.3	.5
clothing	1.2	1.0	1.2	1.1	.6	.5	.5	.6
leather	1.1	1.0	1.1	1.1	.9	.9	.9	.9
wood	.8	.8	.8	.7	.8	.7	.7	.6
metalmaking	.7	.5	.3	.2	.7	1.0	4.0	3.5
engineering	1.0	.9	.8	.6	.9	.8	.8	.5
nonmet. min. prod.	.7	.7	.6	1.1	.8	.7	.6	.7
chem., rubber	.7	.5	.5	.7	.3	.4	.7	1.4
paper, printing	.8	1.2	1.2	1.0	.5	.5	.5	.6
sundry manuf.	1.0	.5	.5	.6	.4	.2	.1	.1
manufacturing	.9	.8	.8	.7	.7	.6	.7	.7
construction	.8	.7	.7	.8	.8	.6	.8	.7
utilities	.3	.3	.8	1.0	.5	.4	.8	1.7

The evolution of the sector-specific indices suggests that the success of the industrial triangle was tied to growing shares of growing sectors; in the South the sector-specific shares generally declined, and the few that rose refer as often as not to sectors that were themselves declining.[40] But this is mere accounting, and not yet economics. In a closed economy, to be sure, sector-specific growth rates depend essentially on income elasticities

---

[40] So too, once again, Esposto, "Italian Industrialization," p. 362.

TABLE 6.07 *(continued)*

	Latium				Abruzzi			
	1871	1881	1901	1911	1871	1881	1901	1911
extractive ind.	.3	.3	.2	.4	.0	.0	.1	.3
foodstuffs	1.0	1.0	1.0	.8	.6	.6	.6	.5
tobacco	1.3	1.3	1.1	.9	.0	.0	.0	.0
textiles	.2	.2	.0	.0	.1	.2	.1	.1
clothing	.6	.7	.9	1.0	.8	.9	.8	.7
leather	1.0	.9	.9	.9	.9	.9	1.0	1.0
wood	1.0	.9	.9	.7	.5	.5	.5	.6
metalmaking	1.1	1.0	.4	.3	.7	.1	.1	.2
engineering	1.0	1.0	.8	.8	.8	.8	.6	.5
nonmet. min. prod.	1.1	1.2	.8	.8	.5	.5	.4	.7
chem., rubber	1.1	.7	.5	.5	.4	.3	.3	.5
paper, printing	1.4	2.3	2.1	2.1	.2	.2	.2	.2
sundry manuf.	.6	.6	.4	1.1	.1	.1	.1	.2
manufacturing	.9	.9	.8	.8	.6	.6	.5	.5
construction	1.1	1.1	.9	1.2	.6	.6	.5	.5
utilities	5.7	5.5	2.4	2.1	.4	.4	.4	.4

	Campania				Apulia			
	1871	1881	1901	1911	1871	1881	1901	1911
extractive ind.	.3	.4	.2	.3	1.2	1.2	.7	.7
foodstuffs	1.0	1.2	1.1	1.1	1.0	.9	.7	.9
tobacco	.6	.8	1.0	1.2	.1	.1	.2	1.3
textiles	1.2	.8	.4	.3	.2	.1	.1	.1
clothing	1.0	1.0	1.0	1.0	.8	.8	.7	.7
leather	1.1	1.2	1.3	1.4	1.1	1.1	1.0	1.0
wood	1.1	1.1	1.1	1.0	.8	.9	.8	.9
metalmaking	2.0	1.2	.9	1.2	.5	.3	.1	.2
engineering	.9	1.1	1.2	1.0	.8	.7	.9	.6
nonmet. min. prod.	.9	.8	.8	.6	.7	.6	.7	.6
chem., rubber	1.3	1.4	1.1	1.0	1.4	.9	.6	.7
paper, printing	1.2	1.3	1.0	.9	.2	.3	.3	.3
sundry manuf.	1.6	3.4	3.3	1.5	.1	.1	.1	.3
manufacturing	1.0	1.1	1.0	.9	.8	.7	.7	.7
construction	.9	.9	.9	.9	1.2	1.2	1.0	.9
utilities	.8	.8	1.2	.9	.1	.1	.2	.2

(and of course on substitution effects, if relative costs change), and the more dynamic regions will be those with an advantage in the faster-growing sectors. In a small open economy, on the other hand, production is not constrained by domestic, or even world, consumption, and the more dynamic sectors may be such simply because they are located in the regions that are relatively more capable of development.

To take a specific example, consider the textile industry, largely concentrated in the North. Had Italy been a closed economy, a prohibition

TABLE 6.07 *(continued)*

	Basilicata				Calabria			
	1871	1881	1901	1911	1871	1881	1901	1911
extractive ind.	.0	.1	.1	.5	.4	.3	.3	.3
foodstuffs	.8	.7	.7	.7	.8	.9	.8	.8
tobacco	.0	.0	.0	.0	.0	.0	.0	.0
textiles	.1	.1	.1	.0	.2	.3	.2	.1
clothing	.7	.6	.6	.5	.9	.7	.8	.8
leather	1.0	1.2	1.2	1.2	1.0	1.1	1.1	1.3
wood	.7	.7	.6	.7	.7	.9	.9	.9
metalmaking	.2	.1	.0	.0	.1	.1	.0	.0
engineering	.9	.8	.7	.5	.8	.7	.6	.4
nonmet. min. prod.	.5	.5	.5	.4	.4	.4	.4	.6
chem., rubber	.3	.7	.3	.2	.4	.6	.4	.7
paper, printing	.1	.1	.2	.1	.2	.1	.2	.2
sundry manuf.	.0	.1	.1	.1	.3	.1	.1	.2
manufacturing	.7	.7	.6	.5	.7	.7	.7	.6
construction	.9	.9	.7	.7	.8	.8	.8	.8
utilities	.4	.4	.3	1.0	.4	.3	.3	.3

	Sicily				Sardinia			
	1871	1881	1901	1911	1871	1881	1901	1911
extractive ind.	4.7	4.6	4.9	3.0	4.3	5.5	4.5	5.5
foodstuffs	1.1	1.1	.9	.9	.6	.7	.6	.8
tobacco	2.3	.6	.5	.6	.0	.4	1.3	1.3
textiles	.4	.2	.1	.0	.0	.0	.0	.0
clothing	.6	.9	.5	.5	.2	.3	.3	.4
leather	1.3	1.3	1.2	1.3	.7	.8	.7	.7
wood	.9	.8	.9	.8	.6	.6	.6	.8
metalmaking	1.5	.3	.2	.1	.1	.1	.1	.1
engineering	1.0	.8	.7	.5	.8	.8	.7	.5
nonmet. min. prod.	.9	1.0	.8	.6	.3	.4	.3	.4
chem., rubber	1.3	.9	.5	.9	.2	.2	.2	.1
paper, printing	.3	.3	.3	.2	.2	.2	.2	.2
sundry manuf.	.6	.2	.1	.2	.2	.0	.0	.3
manufacturing	1.0	.9	.7	.6	.5	.6	.5	.5
construction	1.0	1.0	1.0	.9	1.0	.9	1.0	.7
utilities	.8	.8	.7	.4	.7	.6	.4	.2

[a] ratios of regional percentages of sector value added to regional percentages of the male population over age 15.
Sources: see text.

on Northern textile manufacturing would have shifted the industry to the South (with secondary adjustments, but almost certainly a net improvement in the South's industrial performance). But Italy was an open economy. At the national level the relative growth of the textile industry was tied to the evolution of external trade, as substantial net imports of textiles gave way to equally substantial net exports; and this may have happened because textile manufacturing could grow in the North. Had some prohibition prevented the development of the Northern textile industry, the counterfactual alternative need not be the development of the textile industry in the South (let alone one successfully producing for world markets); rather, industrial growth might still have occurred largely in the North, and simply shifted to some other export-oriented branch of manufacturing, with a continued national import balance in textiles.

The more plausible hypothesis is the latter. The regions of the industrial triangle appear to have enjoyed a comparative advantage not in a few specific sectors, but practically throughout manufacturing: their industrial advantage appears to have been general, and not sector-specific.[41] The further implication is that the tariff cannot be said to have favored the North by protecting the industries in which it was particularly strong; rather, the North would have become strong in any protected industry, and absent tariff protection it would have become strong in any industry favored by free trade.[42]

The North's general advantages in factory production may have reflected, as Cafagna suggested, not only its natural resources, its water, its topography, but its social resources as well: one can easily imagine that the "amoral familism" of the South did not hinder traditional, small-scale artisanal manufacturing (or agriculture), but did increase the costs of larger-scale, factory industry.[43] Social resources are obviously inherited from the past, as natural resources are; and like the latter their power to attract mobile resources depends on the technology of the moment. The different social environment does not alter the essential conclusion suggested above: Italy's dualism developed after Unification because the evolution of the technology of production, and of organization, increasingly favored location in the North.

---

[41] For a statistical analysis see ch. 6A below.

[42] Above, ch. 4, § 9.

[43] "Amoral familism" is the absence of ethical constraints on behavior outside the family circle, and as such an obstacle to economic development, as argued in E. C. Banfield, *The Moral Basis of a Backward Society*, Glencoe IL 1958. Recent studies exploring these themes include B. A'Hearn, "Institutions, Externalities, and Economic Growth in Southern Italy: Evidence from the Cotton Textile Industry, 1861–1914," *Economic History Review* 51 (1998), pp. 734–762, and Id., "Could Southern Italians Cooperate? *Banche Popolari* in the *Mezzogiorno*," *Journal of Economic History* 60 (2000), pp. 67–93.

11. The relocation of the textile industry

This picture is enriched by the new regional series for the textile industry, which distinguish individual fibers and stages of production.[44] Overall the textile industries of Lombardy and Piedmont were the leaders in 1861, and again, even more sharply, in 1913: their shares increased from one third to one half, and from one sixth to one quarter, respectively, of the national total. Venetia too increased its share, from one twelfth in 1861 to one ninth in 1913; the other regions lost ground, or held on to a share that was ever very small.

For all that the time series do not seem to illustrate the path-dependent strengthening of initial disparities. Textile production in Campania was in 1861 close to that of Piedmont, and almost twice that of Venetia; in 1913 it was but an eighth of the former and a quarter of the latter. The disaggregation by fiber also ties the relative growth of the textile industries in Lombardy and Piedmont not to the progress of their traditional and initially dominant components, but to the great success of their relatively new cotton industry; and in Venetia too regional growth was tied to initially secondary fibers (wool and cotton).[45]

The roots of the success of the Northern regions seem once again environmental rather than historical. The traditional hand-processing of textile fibers was as ancient and ubiquitous as traditional agriculture, which it naturally complemented as an off-season activity. Machine processing relied on expensive equipment, which was not to be left idle. That apparently gave a strong advantage to the locations with a year-round supply of water (for power, and also, in the specific case of textiles, for the repeated washing of the material); and in Italy such locations abound only on the northern edge of the Po valley, where the Alpine run-off offsets the lack of summer rain. In the North, moreover, and in part because of its extensive irrigated agriculture, ambient humidity was high throughout the year; textile fibers were there less brittle, and more resistant to the strains of machine processing, than in the dry summer air of the

---

[44] Fenoaltea, "Textile Production in Italy's Regions." The new series for the utilities are here less useful, as the industry was obviously tied to local markets (or waterfalls).

[45] The shares of the Lombard and Piedmontese industries increased mainly between 1880 and 1900 (the years of the cotton boom induced by tariff protection: above, chapter 4, § 3); the increase in the share of Venetia's industry was instead concentrated in the decade and a half after 1866, as if it had been a one-time gain tied to its transfer to the Kingdom (ibid., pp. 148, 163).

South. Over the half-century at hand the fastest-growing textile industries were those that first and best lent themselves to the adoption of machinery; and for that very reason they located increasingly at the feet of the Alps.

The processing of hemp and linen proved difficult to mechanize. The industry declined over time even in absolute terms, dragging down the shares of the regions that owed to it their initial strength: Emilia, Sicily, and above all Campania. The industry began to grow again just before the War, when its technical problems were finally solved; but the new factories located in the North, and not in the industry's traditional basins.

It is also apparent that in 1871 the textile industries in Piedmont and Venetia were far more mechanized, on average, than those in Lombardy; and this suggests that "protoindustrial" production was much less significant, when factory production got under way, in the former regions than in the latter. Piedmont and Venetia would thus appear to have been endowed with "initial advantages" only because the time series begin when they do; if the numbers could be extended back another few decades those regions too would appear as upstarts.

The specific case of the textile industry would thus confirm that the post-Unification growth of the North's industry was due to what was happening then, and not to what had happened earlier. The North developed industry not because it had accumulated a wealth of silkworms, but (like the Ruhr) because the evolution of technology made it *at that time* a low-cost location; and this could remain true even if the initial distribution of industry among Italy's regions turned out to be more similar to the later one than the now available estimates suggest.

All this argues against the path dependencies, or slow approaches to equilibrium, envisioned by Cafagna. But it would appear to support his central argument that the reasons for the relative progress of the North were deep, "genetic," and independent of the policies of the national State.

Moreover, the textile industry's relocation to the North seems tied to only one of Cafagna's triad of resources, the natural, in effect water: the water that flowed in the rivers, the water suspended in the air. Human resources, the literacy rates that were in any case evolving in favor of the South, seem entirely irrelevant. So too, in the case at hand, social resources, the rule of law that may be necessary but is certainly not sufficient: Emilia too lacked mountain glaciers, the textile industry declined there as in Siciliy and Campania.

12. Regional imbalances and the "failure" of liberal Italy

One can hardly ask the State to increase natural resources, to make snow fall where it does not; it can at most, and certainly should, protect the country's natural endowment, and contain its destructive exploitation. One can and should ask the State to guarantee security, to enforce the law; but one must also recognize that a country's State, like its Church, is an expression of its society, and its nature cannot be quickly changed without a Terror.

Once again the emphasis on resource mobility seems to lead back to one of Cafagna's claims, in this case that the national State not only did not but *could not have* exerted a major influence on Italy's dual economy. The reason is not in the slow metabolism of the economy, in the century-long "agrarian accumulation," in the predetermination of post-Unification paths by the regions' initial conditions; it is in the role of natural resources, that attracted industry ever more to the North instead of to the South. The reason is different, but the conclusion seems much the same.

But resource mobility has further implications, for the more mobile resources are attracted by the less mobile. Natural resources are relatively immobile, but their power to attract depends on the available technology: the analysis ties industry's preference for the North to a certain technology, to the technology, specifically, of the first industrial revolution.

That technology was characterized by its intensive use of natural resources. Progress then saved labor, substituting machines; it did not save raw materials, it enormously increased (in part because of the low efficiency of those early prime movers) the consumption of energy. That is why the "natural" industries of the day were those that consumed local raw materials, that burned local coal or exploited local waterfalls; the textile industry may be an extreme case, but not for all that unrepresentative. These were the forces that shaped Europe's early industrialization, not by countries but everywhere by regions, the regions with the resources that mattered.[46]

That mattered then, with that technology. But it was not always so. With traditional technologies labor was relatively unproductive, and heavily influenced costs; more importantly, technology was itself

[46] N. J. G. Pounds, *An Historical Geography of Europe 1800–1914*, Cambridge 1985; S. Pollard, *Peaceful Conquest: The Industrialization of Europe 1760–1970*, Oxford 1981.

embodied in the workers, and not, as it would later be, to the extreme of the production line of Henry Ford (and Charlie Chaplin), in the machines.

With traditional technologies the least mobile resource was in fact human capital, technical skill, the secrets of the trade. The industrial leadership pre-modern Italy had conquered and maintained for centuries was based not on its natural resources – Italy then exported cloths of English wool, finished with Levantine mordants and dyes – but on a monopoly of the best technology; and when it lost that monopoly it lost its industry.[47]

The first industrial revolution obscured that model, it seemed superseded even to Luigi Einaudi, an economist steeped as few have been in economic history; that it was still current was proved just across the Alps, by the watch-making industry developed by the Swiss as a substitute for migration from a resource-poor environment.[48]

That model returned to the fore with the second industrial revolution, the science-based revolution of electrical equipment and organic chemistry. Its new products consumed few raw materials and little energy, and were, like Swiss watches, of high value per unit weight; and like watch-making it would succeed where the best technical skills were diffused among the masters and the men.[49] It is to the diffusion of technical skills, to the *de facto* imitation of contemporary Switzerland and pre-modern Italy, that Germany would owe its economic success, so admirable in itself, so tragic in its consequences.

Italy too had its technical schools, Milan's *Politecnico*, its Pirelli works; but these remained exceptions. Italy did not imitate the Swiss model of high craftsmanship, a model perhaps too deeply rooted in the

[47] R. T. Rapp, "The Unmaking of the Mediterranean Trade Hegemony: International Trade Rivalry and the Commercial Revolution," *Journal of Economic History* 35 (1975), pp. 499–525 (and S. Fenoaltea, "Lo sviluppo economico dell'Italia nel lungo periodo: riflessioni su tre fallimenti," in Ciocca and Toniolo, *Storia economica d'Italia.* 1, pp. 15–29). The "natural advantage" then enjoyed by Italy was rather that of its geographic position, that made it "the crossroads of different economic civilizations" (P. Malanima, *L'economia italiana. Dalla crescita medievale alla crescita contemporanea*, Bologna 2002, p. 188; author's translation).

[48] S. Fenoaltea, "Einaudi commentatore e protagonista della politica economica: aspetti dell'età giolittiana," *Rivista di storia economica* 20 (2004), p. 277; D. S. Landes, *Revolution in Time: Clocks and the Making of the Modern World*, Cambridge MA 1983.

[49] This was noted just after 1900 by de Viti de Marco, *Un trentennio*, p. 25.

institutions and "social capital" of that free people; nor did it imitate the German model of nurturing the advanced industries by promoting technical education.

Rather, Italy repeated, as a late imitator, the first industrial revolution; and that is why industry concentrated in the North.

6A

North and South: A Sectoral Analysis

1. Sectoral imbalances

The upper panel of Table 6A.01 presents the sums of the absolute deviations from 1.0 of the sector-specific regional indices of relative industrialization reported in Table 6.07 in the four census years. These sums are themselves indices of regional disparities: if for a given sector each region has a share of production exactly in line with its share of the male population of working age all the local indices equal 1.0, and the sum of the deviations is zero. With perfect concentration fifteen regional indices equal zero, so the sum of their deviations equals 15; the other index is equal to 100 percent divided by its region's percentage share of the male population, and therefore varies with the identity of that region. In 1911, for example, the limit values of the sum of the deviations equal 21.2, if the sector is entirely in Lombardy (the most populous region, with 13.9 percent of the males considered and a maximum local index of 7.2), and 90.9 if it is entirely in Basilicata (the least populous, with 1.3 percent of the males considered and a maximum local index of 76.9). The sum of the absolute deviations from 1.0 is thus an index of geographic concentration on the implicit assumption of uniform dispersion within each region.[1]

---

[1] The fact that the upper limit of the index is not pre-defined may be perplexing, but it must be recognized as entirely logical: it means that with perfect concentration in a single geographic unit the index continues to grow as the geographic disaggregation is increased and the relevant unit becomes smaller. The index would instead stop growing as one narrowed the geographic specification if the industry were, say, entirely Lombard, but uniformly dispersed within Lombardy itself; and this is as it should be.

TABLE 6A.01. *Regional indices of relative industrialization, by sector: sums of the absolute deviations from 1.0*

A. simple sums

	1871	1881	1901	1911
extractive ind.	16.5	17.9	17.5	14.8
foodstuffs	2.6	3.3	3.4	3.6
tobacco	10.9	10.1	10.7	8.8
textiles	10.0	10.8	13.7	14.2
clothing	4.5	4.0	4.7	4.8
leather	1.6	1.8	2.1	2.7
wood	3.1	2.9	3.2	3.1
metalmaking	7.5	11.9	17.1	17.0
engineering	2.0	3.5	4.9	6.7
nonmet. mineral products	5.6	6.0	6.8	5.3
chemicals, rubber	5.9	5.8	7.7	6.1
paper, printing	9.3	9.7	8.7	8.9
sundry manufacturing	9.2	15.6	13.0	10.2
manufacturing	3.0	3.8	4.5	5.1
construction	2.1	2.9	2.5	3.4
utilities	11.8	12.0	9.3	8.5

B. sums weighted by the sector shares of national value added

	1871	1881	1901	1911
extractive ind.	48	63	60	43
foodstuffs	70	79	72	61
tobacco	14	10	7	5
textiles	83	87	147	125
clothing	25	23	27	24
leather	14	16	20	17
wood	25	21	26	24
metalmaking	3	8	22	37
engineering	27	54	74	114
nonmet. mineral products	17	21	24	28
chemicals, rubber	6	9	20	21
paper, printing	20	26	36	45
sundry manufacturing	5	8	7	5
manufacturing	240	301	374	402
construction	34	48	28	49
utilities	9	11	20	33

Sources: see text.

Despite this limitation, the behavior of the sums of the absolute deviations is not without interest. Considering first the four major groups one notes that the lowest values are always referred to construction, producer of immobile consumer durables and therefore closely tied to population itself, followed by manufacturing, tied then more than now to a direct contact between producers and consumers. The sum for the utilities is noticeably higher, especially in the early years when municipal services begin to appear in the more progressive cities, and highest of all for mining, obviously because subsoil resources were relatively concentrated.

The sum related to manufacturing grows continually over time, presumably as transport improvements made for increasing specialization. The sums for the other major groups follow different paths. For the utilities, the decline in the sum in question between 1881 and 1911 seems due to the diffusion of municipal services. For construction, the sum seems to follow the Kuznets cycle, presumably because new construction was more concentrated, as well as more volatile, than maintenance.[2] For mining, finally, the noticeable drop in the sum from 1901 to 1911 seems tied in part to the sulphur crisis that cut Sicily's share from over one half to under one third, and in part once again to the construction cycle, on the obvious assumption that low-grade construction materials were more widely distributed than ores.

Within the manufacturing group almost every sector-specific sum increases over time. The leather-goods industry is always the least concentrated, followed by foodstuffs and woodworking. In 1871 the engineering industry, dominated by blacksmithing, is barely more concentrated than leather; but with the growth of modern machinery-production this sector concentrates faster than any other, and by 1911 its sum is relatively high.

In 1871 the most concentrated sector is the tobacco-products industry, which appears at once anomalous, and characteristic of the traditional surplus-collecting economy. It is absent or nearly so in the peripheral regions of the former multi-regional states, as from the peripheral parts of the other regions: not of course for lack of consumers, but almost certainly because it generated conspicuous rents, and was tied to the administrative centers to improve monitoring. In 1871 the paper, sundry, metalmaking, and textile industries are also relatively concentrated; in 1911 the most concentrated are precisely these last two (with the former the leading sector in Liguria and Umbria, the latter the leading sector in Lombardy and Piedmont), followed by sundry manufacturing, paper, and tobacco (and, at a distance, engineering).

---

[2] Total 1911-price value added in construction appears to have been 18 percent below the previous peak (1863) in 1871, at a new high just one percent above the previous peak (1874) in 1881, 24 percent below the previous peak (1886) in 1901, and at a new high (5 percent above the previous year's new high, and 57 percent above the 1886 peak) in 1911: above, Table 1.03.

2. Sectoral contributions to regional imbalances

In the lower panel of Table 6A.01 the sums presented as such in the upper panel are weighted by each sector's share of total national production (from Table 1.04), to bring out each sector's contribution to overall industrial concentration. The weighted sums obtained for such highly concentrated but relatively tiny sectors as tobacco, metalmaking, and sundry manufacturing are of course relatively small; in 1871, indeed, the largest weighted sum is that for the foodstuffs industry, which was not highly concentrated but overwhelmingly large. Here too, however, economic causality involves more than mere accounting; if as suggested above food-processing simply followed other manufacturing one must look elsewhere for the lead.

The textile sector here appears particularly significant. Over time, indeed, the weighted sum for food-processing declines as that sector lags behind the others; the weighted sum for textiles grows, most markedly between 1881 and 1901, when thanks in part to the cyclical contraction of durables production it is far above that for any other sector. From 1901 to 1911 the cyclical upswing brings the weighted sum for engineering above that for textiles, which instead falls slightly; the other sectors are all far behind.

A final indicator can be obtained by comparing the weighted sum for manufacturing as a whole to the sum of the weighted sums for its component sectors.[3] If all the regions had identical structures, indeed, the regional indices would be identical across sectors and equal to that for total manufacturing; the weighted sum for all manufacturing would therefore coincide with the sum of the weighted sums for its various elements.[4] Different regions need not be equally involved in manufacturing; but their relative advantages would clearly apply to all manufacturing, and not to specific sectors.

Imagine instead a situation in which all regions are equally advantaged in total manufacturing, but with offsetting specializations in the different sectors. In this case, with only specific relative advantages but no general ones, the weighted sum for manufacturing as a whole is by hypothesis

---

[3] The comparison is within Panel B: for example, in 1911 the weighted sum for manufacturing as a whole is 402 (as reported), the sum of the weighted sums for its component sectors is $(61 + 5 + 125 \cdots + 45 + 5)$.

[4] Because the weights are the sectors' shares of total national production, the weight attached to manufacturing as a whole is of course the sum of the weights attached to its components.

zero, while positive values are obtained for the sector-specific weighted sums, and so therefore for the sum of these sums.

The ratio of the sum of the sector-specific weighted sums to the weighted sum for all manufacturing thus equals one if comparative advantages in manufacturing are entirely general and not at all sector-specific, and grows without limit as one approaches the symmetric polar case in which such advantages are strictly sector-specific but not at all general. In the case at hand, the sum of the sector-specific weighted sums equals 309 in 1871, 362 in 1881, 482 in 1901, and 506 in 1911; its ratio to the weighted sum for manufacturing as a whole equals 1.29 in 1871, 1.20 in 1881, 1.29 in 1901, and 1.26 in 1911. Over its possible range from one to infinity this ratio is very close to one, and practically constant over time. Once again, therefore, the figures suggest that the more industrial regions enjoyed essentially general advantages.[5]

---

[5] This result too is preliminary, of course, but it is relatively robust. If the sector-specific product per worker which the present figures assume constant were in fact systematically higher in the more industrial regions, it would obviously continue to hold; in fact, it would only be subverted if that product per worker were systematically *lower* in those regions, in all sectors (so the more industrial regions disappear) or at least in some (so their advantages are no longer general). For very recent evidence that among Italy's regions strong industrial growth was associated with a relative *lack* of specialization even in subsequent decades see G. Cainelli, R. Leoncini, and A. Montini, "Struttura produttiva e sviluppo regionale di lungo periodo in Italia," *Moneta e Credito* 44 (2001), pp. 461–485.

7

The State of Play

1. Italy and the world economy: cyclical movements

The economic development of post-Unification Italy cannot be understood by examining Italy alone. Italy was already then part of a wider world characterized by the ready movement of goods, ideas, men and money; it developed as and to the extent that the mobile resources of that transnational economy chose to locate on Italian soil.

From 1861 to 1913 Italy's total product grew, even in per-capita terms, relatively steadily. It did not always grow from year to year: agriculture was the dominant sector, especially in the early years, and total product fell if bad weather or outbreaks of disease caused poor harvests. But these downturns were short-lived, and over the medium term agricultural production grew without significant interruption.

The longer cycle was in the industrial sector; it grew stronger over time, and became much the major source of aggregate production movements. Within that sector, the cycle was specific to the industries that produced durable goods – construction, engineering – and those that supplied their raw materials. The dominant economic cycle in post-Unification Italy was an investment cycle.

The upswings of that investment cycle were the quinquennia from Unification to 1865 and again from 1869 to 1874, under the Right; the decade from 1879 to 1887, dominated politically by Depretis; and the even longer period, from 1896 to the War, dominated by Giolitti. The sustained growth of investment in the Depretis and Giolitti years told throughout the economy: in the 1880s and again in the *belle époque* cyclically high growth rates were registered by the industries producing non-durables, by the services, by real wages, by aggregate consumption. The production of durables fell from 1865 to 1869, stagnated from 1874 to 1879, fell especially in the long crisis from 1887 to 1896; this last too was transmitted to the other sectors, and over that decade there was little net growth in real wages and per-capita product.

The real cycle in investment, and in total product, seems to have had its immediate causes in international finance, in the changing supply of foreign capital: investment in Italy grew when foreign capital was abundant and poured in, and fell when it became scarce and flowed back out. The initial wave of foreign investment, in the early 1860s, seems tied to the high expectations generated by Unification; it did not survive the military defeats, and budget crisis, of 1866. In those years Italy's own successes and failures first encouraged, and then discouraged, foreign investors: the cycle in capital imports and domestic investment can be traced to domestic developments.

Over the next forty-odd years Italy appears instead as a passive participant in a world-wide cycle. The confidence with which savers in the British center viewed investment abroad waxed and waned: in the London market developing countries' bonds were in favor in the early 1870s, in the 1880s and in the *belle époque*, out of favor in the late 1870s and in the 1890s. Italy was then just another foreign country: the tide of foreign investment ebbed and flowed in Italy as in the entire financial periphery, without visible connection to policy decisions in Italy itself.

Italy seems to have distinguished itself from the rest of the periphery, as it had done before 1866, only on the very eve of the European war. By 1913 it was again relatively favored by foreign investors – perhaps thanks to the victorious war against Turkey, mirror-image of the earlier defeat at the hands of Austria.

2. Italy and the world economy: long-term growth

To a first approximation, therefore, after about 1870 the cyclical movements of the Italian economy do not seem to have been induced by changes in national policies. The effects of those policies are to be sought elsewhere, in the long-term rate of growth, in the significant but disappointingly limited development of the economy.

In 1913 Italy's population was larger and more prosperous than in 1861. It was healthier and better educated: the benefits of the public investments in the nation's schools and aqueducts are clear enough.

The gains from extending the railway net throughout the peninsula and the islands are not so clear. The new lines were too often justified by more than their economic benefits: first by their strategic value, to ensure military control of the regions newly annexed by the Piedmontese crown, and then by sordidly political returns. Worse, the enormous investment in the system was largely wasted, as the high railway rates imposed by the State discouraged traffic: Italy's railways were little used, and did little to unify the domestic market.

Clear harm was wrought by Italy's import duties. Italy is densely populated, resource-poor, unsuited to autarkic development: it can provide Italians with work at incomes comparable to those obtainable abroad only if it attracts processing activities, if it imports raw materials and exports finished products. In the later nineteenth century the reduction in world transport costs and import prices hurt Italy's disadvantaged sectors, that were in any case to be scaled down; it clearly benefited the economy at large, and most especially Italy's abundant labor.

Italy's tariffs rejected those benefits. The duty on steel made the engineering industry uncompetitive in the export market, and prevented it from continuing to grow even as the domestic market contracted; the duty on wheat limited the development of all industry, and of labor-intensive specialized agriculture as well. Protection increased the real costs of producing in Italy. It diverted production, and mobile resources, from Italy's soil; the number of Italians abroad rose into the millions.

The industries that in post-Unification Italy grew to serve world markets were those that had pioneered the first industrial revolution, industries that made heavy use of energy and imported materials. They were attracted to the Ligurian coast and the year-round rivers of the foothills of the Alps: it is in this period that Italy's industry concentrated in the "northwest triangle."

Italy did not develop industries at the cutting edge of technology: it came to export cheap cotton textiles rather than chemicals or electrical equipment, the new products of the day. New industries are attracted by specialized human resources, by research and technical skills, far more than by natural resources. They could have been attracted to Italy, and not only to the Northwest; but this more modern, more rapid, less regionally unbalanced growth would have required a stimulus the State failed signally to provide.

That stimulus was not the subsidization of particular industries with tariffs and government contracts: one cannot identify *ex ante* the industries (or the stocks) that will prove to be, twenty or thirty years hence, those in which it would have been clever to invest, and in any case the result of such assistance is rarely more than a greenhouse plant. The more fruitful stimulus is rather the creation of an environment in which high-technology industry develops spontaneously, in whatever form the market and the path of human invention may determine: an environment rich in technical skills, nourished by a nationwide system of secondary and post-secondary technical schools – and by a panoply of scholarships to allow the training of the bright children even of the working classes. Milan did much, on its own initiative; the State did all too little.

Half a century after Unification Italians in Italy would have been more numerous and more prosperous had the State not limited international trade, had it developed technical education and opened it to merit: had Italy's ruling classes been willing to promote the nation's progress even at the cost of renewing themselves.

3. The breeze of battle

This is the interpretation suggested by the evidence, and analytical tools, available at the present time. How much or how long it may convince before it is consigned to the rubbish-tip of scholarship, one cannot now tell: the issue will be determined by the scholars of tomorrow.

First refusal belongs of course to the scholars of today, in fact to the author's close colleagues who reviewed the Italian edition of this work. Within this group initial reactions vary, by individual and by topic; but in general they manifest little interest in the railroads – perhaps because we have at last outgrown our childhood toys – and, surprisingly, in the regional aspects of Italy's growth. Even the discovery that employment apparently grew altogether faster in Apulia and in Sicily than in the industrial triangle – so momentous in its implications (and, so far along a working life, at once so tantalizing and so bitter) – passes unnoticed.[1]

The age-old issue of Italy's tariff policy receives attention, but the debate remains mired where it was: those who defended protection do not respond to the criticism of their arguments and evidence, and obdurately reiterate their views. The further controversy over the crisis of the 1880s appears instead to be drawing to a close, at least on the surface: the

---

[1] Their silence may be unrepresentative: other quantitative historians (and the author himself) are actively improving the regional estimates, and this strand of the literature may rapidly evolve in the very near future.

long hegemonic "pessimistic" view of that decade is given up for dead, its opposite embraced. But on a deeper level this issue is linked to the preceding, for if the increase in trade – the "grain invasion" – of the early 1880s generated prosperity rather than depression, the subsequent tariff hikes must have had the opposite effect. A protectionist is in fact a closet "pessimist," and neither issue can be considered resolved until the two are resolved coherently.

The thesis that the major production movements in pre-War Italy were a simple investment cycle spawned by the shifts in Britain's willingness to supply capital to the periphery earns mostly negative reviews. Only a few declare themselves satisfied that Italy, as a small country, danced to an imported tune; rather more seem concerned to recover a proper story that traces the vigor of the pre-war upswing to domestic innovations and national heroes. These early shots are ranging fire, and not surprisingly many go badly astray; but one in particular may have scored a useful hit.

It has been suggested that in the Giolitti years, and thanks to Giolitti's policies, the Italian economy grew unusually fast because it was then, by its own lamentable standards, unusually competitive. The suggestion is intriguing, not least because the same has been said of the years of the "economic miracle" in the aftermath of the Second World War.

4. The tasks of economic history

Economic policy is not always subservient to vested interests. But the more it is motivated by higher ideals – the more it seeks actively to further the nation's progress – the more it is hostage to the perception of the economy's past, of the inherited problems to be solved and the solutions they imply.

In the decades that followed the Second World War Italy made a massive, fruitless effort to reduce regional disparities. The *Cassa per il Mezzogiorno* aimed to speed development and increase employment in the South by building infrastructure and subsidizing industrial *capital*; the subsidies attracted capital- and subsidy-intensive petrochemicals that ruined the coastal environment and prevented the growth of labor-intensive tourist services.

These spectacularly wrong-headed policies are explained in part by the development economics of the day, by its neglect of traditional microeconomics in favor of keynesian macro-planning, and, worse, of Leontief-style micro-planning that simply ignored the principle of substitution.[2] But their tap-root was in the then current understanding of economic history, in the presumption that growth proceeds in stages, that development is necessarily industrial, that Italy's own industrial progress had been held back by a lack of infrastructure and a lack of local capital.

Italy's regional policies were consistent with the Italian interpretation of Italy's past, the interpretation of Rosario Romeo. It matters not whether the politicians distilled their frenzy from the pen of an economic historian, or whether Romeo himself borrowed his interpretation from the madmen in authority. The point here is that the economic history of the day endorsed economic policy: it did not provide, as it should have, evidence that would have given the politicians pause.

Would the policies of the *Cassa* not have been different, had Italy's economic historians drawn from the past the lesson that local development is not limited by local capital, because capital is mobile, but by the profitability of producing, and employing labor, there rather than elsewhere? the lesson that in post-Unification Italy employment grew faster in Apulia and Sicily, where industry lagged, than in Lombardy or Piedmont? Would Italy suffer today the consequences of half a century of errors, had its economic history not been interpreted as it had been?

Economic history is not mere antiquarianism. It is culture, it is our sense of who we are, of the road we are traveling, of the next step we are to take: it is politics.

---

[2] R. S. Eckaus, "The Factor Proportions Problem in Underdeveloped Areas," *American Economic Review* 45 (1955), pp. 539–565. See also S. Fenoaltea, "I due fallimenti della storia economica: il periodo post-unitario," *Rivista di politica economica* 97 (2007), nn. 3–4, pp. 341–358, here partly summarized.

APPENDICES

TARIFFS, TRADE, MIGRATION, AND GROWTH

Appendix 1

Tariffs and Market Prices

1. The possible cases

The possible effect of a tariff on the market price of the protected good is illustrated in Figure A1.01. From one graph to the other domestic demand, the world price, and the tariff are kept constant, and the assumption of a competitive domestic market is maintained; domestic supply varies. At the world price foreign producers can provide, and foreign consumers absorb, "unlimited" quantities of the good in question: the home country is assumed small, in the sense that its own sales and purchases cannot materially affect world-market equilibrium.

In the first case domestic supply and demand intersect at a price above the world price augmented by the entire tariff: the tariff limits imports, but does not eliminate them. In this case the domestic market price exceeds the world price by the full amount of the tariff: foreign supply allows domestic consumers to purchase goods without paying more than the world price plus the tariff, and at that (tariff-inclusive) price domestic demand exceeds domestic supply.

In the second case domestic supply and demand intersect at a price that exceeds the world price, but by less than the tariff. The domestic price is generated directly by that intersection: the tariff eliminates the imports that would otherwise take place, but precisely because it is thus prohibitive the domestic market price exceeds the world price by only *part* of the tariff itself.

In the third case domestic supply and demand intersect at a price lower even than the world price. The world price will then prevail on the domestic market as well: domestic producers can sell at that price

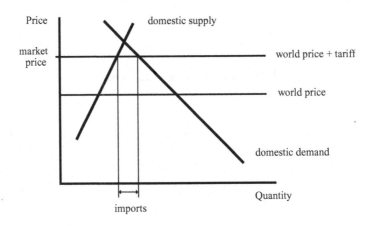

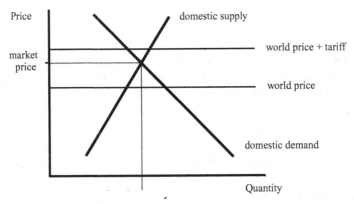

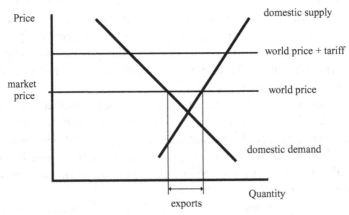

FIGURE A1.01. *The effect of a tariff on market price*

to foreign consumers, and will not sell to domestic consumers at a price lower than that. At the world price domestic supply exceeds domestic demand: the home country exports the good instead of importing it, and the tariff has no effect at all.

2. The case of cotton

In the case of a homogeneous good the above three cases are mutually exclusive; if it is exported, the only relevant case is the third.

But cotton goods were not homogeneous, and one can imagine three separate markets, respectively for high-, medium-, and low-quality goods. At the beginning of the half-century at hand all three markets corresponded to the first case, with equilibrium imports. By its end Italy exported cotton goods, but only of low quality. At that point all three cases held simultaneously: the third case prevailed in the market for low-quality goods, but in that market alone, while the first and second prevailed for high- and medium-quality goods. The tariffs on these goods remained effective, raising prices and domestic output.

The cotton tariff was thus effective, increasing domestic production and its average quality, despite Italy's exports of (low-quality) cotton goods.

Appendix 2

The Ricardian Model of Trade

1. The gains from trade

The ricardian model of trade can be illustrated by Figure A2.01. The axes measure the physical quantities of grain and of wine; in the sense to be explained forthwith, these represent land-intensive goods (cereals), and labor-intensive goods (the products of specialized agriculture, and industry), respectively.

Curve $W4$–$G4$ is our production possibilities curve (with our given resources, and our technology); under autarky it also represents our consumption possibilities. The autarky equilibrium is, by assumption, point *(1)*, that is, $(W1, G3)$. At point *(1)*, the production possibilities curve is tangent to the "price line" (not illustrated on the graph): the slope of the former, which corresponds to the goods' relative costs, equals the slope of the latter, which corresponds to their relative prices.

In the world market, by assumption, relative prices differ: grain is relatively cheaper, the price line is correspondingly flatter. If our country opens itself to free trade, domestic relative prices align themselves to world relative prices. The production equilibrium therefore shifts from *(1)* to *(2)*, that is, to the point where the slope of our production possibilities curve equals the slope of free-trade price line: "grain" production falls from $G3$ to $G2$, "wine" production grows from $W1$ to $W2$. The free-trade consumption-possibilities curve is the price line tangent, in *(2)*, to the production possibilities curve; we can consume more "wine," and more "grain," than under autarky, and the new consumption equilibrium will be a point on the segment *(2)*–$G5$ above, and to the right of, point *(1)*.

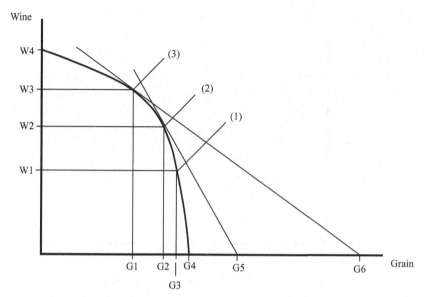

FIGURE A2.01. *The gains from trade*

These are the gains from trade: they stem solely from the differences between relative costs (relative prices) in the home market under autarky, and in the foreign market. Absolute costs, which appear nowhere on the graph, are irrelevant; "comparative advantages" suffice.

With an increase in the difference between domestic autarky relative prices and world relative prices – with a fall in the relative price of imported grain – the free-trade production equilibrium moves further away from the autarky equilibrium, and *the gains from trade increase.* In Figure A2.01 the new world price line is even flatter, and the production point moves from (2) to (3); "grain" production falls further, to G_1, "wine" production grows further, to W_3. One sector suffers a crisis, the other enjoys a boom; but consumption increases across the board, as the consumption equilibrium moves from a point on the line (2)–G_5 to a point on the line (3)–G_6, ever further above, and to the right of, point (1).

The move from point (2) to point (3) has effects that are entirely analogous to those of the move from point (1) to point (2): those who consider harmful the fall in the price of grain in the early 1880s must be prepared to deny that trade itself is beneficial, to assert a preference for autarky.

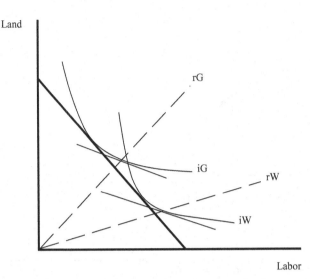

FIGURE A2.02. *The factor-intensity of production*

2. The factor-intensity of production

As the production equilibrium changes, so do the relative earnings of the factors of production.

It is assumed that the different branches of production use the same factors of production, but with different intensities, that is, in different proportions. In Figure A2.02, the axes measure the factors of production, land and labor. The curves in the graph illustrate two "isoquants," *iG* for "grain" and *iW* for "wine": these indicate the various combinations of land and labor that yield a given quantity of "grain" on the one hand, and "wine" on the other. The parallel lines are "isocosts," that is, the locus of combinations of land and labor with a constant total cost; their (common) slope corresponds to the relative prices of the factors of production.

A given output is obtained at minimum cost where the isoquant meets the lowest possible isocost, that is, at the illustrated tangencies; the rays *rG* and *rW* that pass through those tangencies indicate the cost-minimizing land–labor ratio in the production of "grain," and of "wine." If the production functions are very simple (homothetic, with constant returns to scale), a single isoquant represents the entire function: given relative factor prices one can produce more or less of any good, but changes in the level of production appear simply as proportionate movements along the given ray, and the factor proportions that minimize costs remain unchanged.

Figure A2.02 assumes that "grain" is land-intensive, and "wine" labor-intensive, in the specific sense that with any given relative factor price the cost-minimizing land–labor ratio is higher in "grain" than in "wine." If the relative price of labor increases, the isocosts become steeper, and the tangency points climb up the isoquants: the rays rG and rW rotate counterclockwise, but (on these assumptions) rG remains steeper than rW.

In the initial case illustrated by Figure A2.02, the quantity of "wine" corresponding to iW costs less than the quantity of "grain" corresponding to iG: iW is tangent to an isocost lower than that tangent to iG. But if the relative price of labor increases until the isocost becomes as steep as the illustrated bold line, and tangent at once to iG and to iW, those two quantities will have an identical cost: as the relative price of labor increases, so does the relative price of the labor-intensive good.

Where land abounds and labor is scarce, land is cheap and so is "grain," labor is dear and so is "wine"; and vice versa. Italy was far more densely populated than the world's great plains: its comparative advantage was correspondingly in labor-intensive goods, that of the great plains in land-intensive goods. Italy therefore imported grain, and exported wine (and other labor-intensive products, including silk).

3. Production and factor prices

Figure A2.03 illustrates the links between the production equilibrium and factor prices (the incomes of laborers and landowners). The graph is the same as that of Figure A2.02; the isoquants have been omitted (but must not be forgotten), the available supplies of land and labor have been added: T^* land and L^* labor are the "given resources" that (with the given isoquants) generate the production possibilities illustrated in Figure A2.01.

The bold-face lines represent the initial equilibrium. Given the relative factor prices that generate the cost-minimizing land–labor ratios indicated respectively by $rG1$ and $rW1$, and given the output levels that correspond to the isoquants that pass respectively through $(Tg1, Lg1)$ and through $(Tw1, Lw1)$, $Tg1$ land and $Lg1$ labor are employed in the production of "grain," and $Tw1$ land and $Lw1$ labor in the production of "wine"; the parallelogram constructed on those rays and points has its apex at (T^*, L^*), and both factor markets are in (full-employment) equilibrium.

Imagine now a reduction in the relative price of grain. In Figure A2.01 the production equilibrium moves up the production possibilities curve, away from $G4$ and toward $W4$. With the prevailing factor

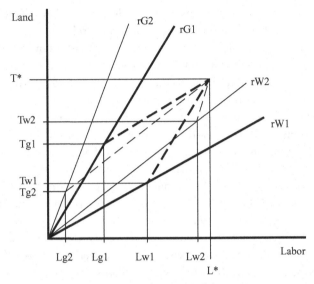

FIGURE A2.03. *Production and factor prices*

prices, in Figure A2.03 production moves along the currently prevailing rays, up and to the right along *rW1*, down and to the left along *rG1*. But the reduction in "grain" production releases land and labor in proportions that differ from those in which the increase in "wine" production absorbs them: too much land, not enough labor, are put on the market. The apex of the parallelogram moves down and to the right: the total demand for land falls short of the available supply, the total demand for labor exceeds it.

This disequilibrium in the factor markets leads to an adjustment in their relative prices, upward for labor, downward for land: the wage–rental ratio rises.

This change in relative factor prices induces movement along the isoquants, and a change in factor proportions, in all branches of production (Figure A2.02): the rays *rG* and *rW* rotate counterclockwise and become steeper. In all production, less labor is used per acre: *all agriculture becomes less (labor) intensive.* In all production, a given output is obtained with more land, and less labor, than before: *yields per acre fall across the board.*

A new equilibrium may be reached for example with the rays *rG2* and *rW2*: there is again full employment of both factors of production, but with fewer resources devoted to the now lower production of "grain" – (*Tg2, Lg2*) instead of (*Tg1, Lg1*) – and more to the now higher production of "wine," which employs (Tw_2, Lw_2) instead of (Tw_1, Lw_1). The parallelogram changes shape, but its apex remains locked on the equilibrium point (T^*, L^*). As the relative price of "grain" falls, so does the relative price of land, the factor of production used intensively by "grain"; the reduction in the labor-intensity of every cultivation exactly offsets the change in the product mix in favor of the more labor-intensive good.

Appendix 3

Migration and Relative Mobility

1. The model of migration

The standard model of migration considers it an investment, to be undertaken if the present value of the benefits exceeds that of its costs.

The costs of migration include two main elements: the direct cost of travel (the ticket plus ancillary expenses), and the opportunity cost of the time spent in travel and searching for work at destination (the income the migrant would otherwise have earned during that time). These costs are calculated in real terms, deflating the nominal figures by the price of the basket of goods the migrant consumes.

The corresponding benefit is the present value of the increase in the real wage over the rest of the migrant's working life. Assuming a constant flow over time, the migrant's calculus can be reduced to a comparison between the real cost c and the real benefit $b = k(w_d - w_o)$, where w_d and w_o are the real wages respectively at destination and at the origin, and k is the corresponding capitalization factor (which varies inversely with the discount rate, and positively with the length of the expected working life). Labor thus moves from where real wages are low to where real wages are high; migration increases the migrant's real marginal product, and correspondingly increases world output.

This approach highlights various aspects of migration itself, and of its relation to trade. Migration may be blocked by a liquidity constraint, so that only those with adequate capital can actually move; this constraint is loosened by friends and relatives already abroad, who can advance the ticket price, and help the migrant find work. The benefits of migration are greater, the longer the remaining working life; the young gain by migration more than the old. The cost of migration is lower if and when the host economy prospers, and work is quickly found; the point matters, because one migrates only once, and will accordingly chose the moment that yields the greatest net benefit.[1]

The cost of migration obviously falls if transport costs fall. But a reduction in transport costs normally increases trade, induces specialization as the various countries exploit their comparative advantages, and reduces the interlocal differences in the relative prices of the factors of production as well as of goods. In relative terms real wages fall where labor is scarce, and rise where labor is abundant: the fall in transport costs reduces the benefits, as well as the costs, of migration. Transport improvements thus have an ambiguous effect on migration, favoring it to the extent that the fall in costs precedes the real adjustments that reduce the benefits. In labor-abundant countries protection unambiguously favors migration, as it limits trade and the reduction in the benefits of migration that would otherwise accompany the reduction in its costs.

2. Relative mobility and trade

The ricardian model of trade demonstrates, as it was designed to demonstrate, the gains from trade based on comparative advantages. To this end transport costs are an unnecessary complication, which Ricardo rightly ignores. In fact, however, trade is *jointly* determined by differences in autarky relative prices (the comparative advantages the model incorporates) and in the relative mobility of different commodities (the transport costs the model ignores): the "comparative advantage" model of trade is polemically perfect, but empirically defective, and especially so for historical purposes, as transport costs weighed far more heavily in the past than they do now.

Define the coefficient of mobility m for any given good as the ratio between its unit value in the destination market P_d net, and gross, of the transport cost T: $m = (P_d - T)/P_d$. Transport costs depend on weight and distance, and not, or to be precise much less, on the value of the good transported; keeping distance constant, m increases with P_d, and is correspondingly greater for goods of high value per unit weight.

---

[1] If alternative investments are not mutually exclusive, all those with a positive net present value are worth undertaking; if they are, only the one with the highest such value is to be pursued.

If transport costs are negligible, T vanishes, and $m = 1$ for all goods, which are equally (and "perfectly") mobile; the higher transport costs, the greater the relative mobility of high-value goods. Consider for example two goods, A and B, with destination prices (P_{da} and P_{db}) equal to 100 and 60, respectively, per unit of weight. If for that unit of weight $T = 30$, $m_a = .70$, $m_b = .50$, and $m_a = 1.40m_b$. If $T = 45$, $m_a = .55$, $m_b = .25$, and $m_a = 2.20m_b$; with $T = 60$, $m_a = 0.40$, $m_b = 0$: their ratio becomes infinite, and transporting B is unprofitable even if the good itself is, at the point of origin, absolutely free.

The merchant invests a sum S, and seeks the maximum gain when the goods are sold at destination. At the goods' point of origin S buys either $A = S/P_{oa}$ or $B = S/P_{ob}$; the merchant's receipts at destination are $AP_{da}m_a$ in the one case and $BP_{db}m_b$ in the other. The more advantageous export is A if $AP_{da}m_a > BP_{db}m_b$; but $AP_{oa} = BP_{ob} = S$, so A will be exported in preference to B if $(P_{ob}/P_{oa})m_a > (P_{db}/P_{da})m_b$. If $m_a > m_b$ the traded good will be A rather than B even if, to a lesser extent, $(P_{ob}/P_{oa}) < (P_{db}/P_{da})$, that is, even if the relative price of A at the point of origin is relatively *high*.

With negligible transport costs $m_a = m_b = 1$, and the traded goods are necessarily those with a low relative price at the point of origin: if transport costs are negligible, the "comparative advantage" model that neglects them adequately describes the logic of trade. The higher transport costs – the more one moves back in time, the more one considers widely separated markets – the greater the mobility advantage of high-value goods, and the greater the likelihood that relative mobility will overwhelm comparative advantage.[2]

3. Relative mobility and permanent migration

The standard model of migration should apply to the slave trade as well as to free migration (and in fact better to the former, as the economic calculus that determines migration is not complicated by the migrant's emotional ties); and before the great nineteenth-century migrations from Europe much the largest flow of migrants was represented by the trade in slaves from sub-Saharan Africa primarily to the New World, but also to the old-settled lands on the shores of the Mediterranean and the Indian Ocean.

---

[2] One notes that to explain comparative advantages one need consider only two goods; to take relative mobility into account one must add a third good, for the contrary flow, or assume that exports cover a tribute rather than imports.

This forced migration was paradoxical, however, as Africa itself was relatively underpopulated; the real marginal product of labor was there relatively high, and the cost of moving the slaves clearly exhausted any increase in that product associated with the slaves' relocation. Africanist historians, familiar with African conditions, attempt to resolve that paradox by appealing to various forms of market failure, but their hypotheses are strained; the paradox is instead easily resolved if one recalls that the slave trade was indeed a trade, and that trade is shaped by relative mobility as well as by relative prices.

The slave is a commodity. The slave's value P_s is the capitalization of the surplus (the slave's marginal product less the slave's subsistence) obtained over the slave's expected life: $P_s = k(W - P_b B_s)$, where k is the capitalization coefficient (analogous to that above), W is the slave's implicit wage (confiscated by the owner), P_b the price of subsistence goods, and B_s the slave's subsistence. In real terms, $(P_s/P_b) = k((W/P_b) - B_s)$: the slave is worth k times the periodic surplus, and therefore worth more where the real wage and the surplus are higher.

If a territory produces only subsistence goods, it can export these, or the slaves that would produce them; but subsistence goods are low-value goods, much less mobile than the slave (who contains a lifetime of future surplus). If transport costs are high it is more economical to transport slaves even if the real wage is lower at destination. Repeating the logic of the previous section (with slaves S replacing good A), slaves will be exported in preference to goods if $(P_{ob}/P_{os})m_s > (P_{db}/P_{ds})m_b$; with $m_s > m_b$ this condition is met even if, to a lesser extent, $(P_{ob}/P_{os}) < (P_{db}/P_{ds})$, that is, even if the real wage (and therefore the relative price of slaves) is higher at the point of origin than at destination.

The standard model of migration – permanent but voluntary – fails to explain the slave trade, a permanent but involuntary migration; and it fails because it recognizes the cost of moving the migrants but neglects the alternative cost of moving goods, because it recognizes $m_s < 1$ but not $m_b < 1$. If all goods were perfectly mobile, indeed, transport costs would limit the slave trade alone, and with $m_s < 1 = m_b$ slaves would be exported only if $(P_{ob}/P_{os}) > (P_{db}/P_{ds})$, that is, under the same conditions that would generate (permanent) voluntary migration.

Assume for simplicity that all prices are measured in gold, which is (almost) perfectly mobile. If all goods are perfectly mobile $P_{db} = P_{ob}$, and the difference between P_{ds} and P_{os} that sustains the slave trade requires as above that labor be more productive at destination: permanent migration, voluntary or not, would always climb a productivity gradient. With imperfectly mobile goods, the "law of one price" reduces to the condition that differences in local prices cannot exceed the cost of transporting the goods (plus tariffs, if any). In the case of the African slave trade the involuntary migrants climbed not a productivity gradient but a price gradient: international equilibrium required that African price *levels* be relatively low, low enough to generate *nominal* wages and therefore slave prices themselves low enough to sustain the slave trade. The slave trade was driven not by relative productivity, but by the real exchange rate.[3]

Migration that reduces the worker's marginal product seems to reduce world product, but that is not so. If transport costs are significant otherwise identical goods in different places are different goods, and their aggregate is meaningless.[4] The African slave trade was a market equilibrium because it was economically efficient, in the precise sense that it maximized consumption at the migrants' destination given consumption at the origin; and it did so by minimizing not the costs of production alone, but the total costs of production and transportation.

4. Relative mobility and temporary migration

The voluntary equivalent of the slave trade is not the free permanent migration of the standard model, but free *temporary* migration.

The permanent migrant of the standard model is entirely selfish. The decision to migrate considers only the migrant's own consumption; the migrant simply abandons the old country, which receives nothing in return. The slave is sold, at an f.o.b. price that capitalizes the surplus to be earned at destination (net of course of transport costs): the slave sold abroad is an export, and sustains the real exchange rate. The temporary migrant who works abroad to save, and remits or repatriates those savings, affects the real exchange rate as the slave does; and to maximize those savings the migrant may live abroad at a subsistence minimum, like a slave, and like a slave contribute to the home country's balance of payments the entire surplus earned abroad (net again of transport costs).

---

3 The "law of one price" in all markets of the world, tariffs apart, and the related "purchasing power parity" hypothesis both stem from the neglect of commodity transport costs. With significant transport costs, and significant differences in the relative mobility of different countries' exports, price levels tend systematically to diverge. See below, Appendix 4, § 3.

4 Transport costs are analogous to the costs of industrial transformation. If one neglected these and failed to perceive that processed wool differs from raw wool, for example, weight losses in industrial processing would similarly seem to reduce "the total supply of wool."

The not-entirely-selfish permanent voluntary migrant, who also remits savings, is an intermediate form; the exact equivalent of the slave is the permanent voluntary migrant so unselfish as to remain abroad, living at mere subsistence, and remitting the entire surplus earned above that minimum.

The selfish permanent migrant is motivated only by the difference in real wages, and is not influenced by the exchange rate. Slave exports depend on the real exchange rate; and so does temporary, or at least unselfish, voluntary migration. Let all prices be measured once again in gold, and imagine that subsistence costs less in the country of origin: $P_{ob} < P_{db}$. The real wage of the selfish migrant is simply W_d/P_{db}; the real wage abroad of the temporary (or unselfish – the point will not be repeated) migrant is instead $w_{et} = (1 - q)(W_d/P_{db}) + q(W_d/P_{ob})$, where q is the share of the local wage that is saved and repatriated.

If temporary migration exists it must be advantageous, that is, $w_{et} > W_o/P_{ob}$; but clearly, if $P_{ob} < P_{db}$, $w_{et} > W_d/P_{db}$. Like the slave trade and unlike permanent voluntary migration, temporary migration is not ruled out if $W_d/P_{db} < W_o/P_{ob}$: like the slave, the temporary migrant may move *down* a real wage gradient, so long as the move is *up* a price (and nominal savings) gradient. The same considerations that explain the paradox of the slave trade explain the paradox for example of the Irish in Britain, who apparently (judging from anthropometric measures) moved toward *lower* real wages.[5]

Like the slave trade, temporary migration can of course also climb a productivity gradient. But the real wage abroad of the temporary migrant who saves and remits remains tied to the real exchange rate, for it will be higher, for a given real wage abroad, the lower the home country's real exchange rate P_{ob}/P_{db}: the same conditions that encourage the slave trade encourage temporary migration.[6]

[5] Similar considerations explain urban movements that reduce measured real wages without recourse to the putative appeal of the "bright city lights": see S. Fenoaltea, "Economic Decline in Historical Perspective: Some Theoretical Considerations," *Rivista di storia economica* 22 (2006), pp. 3–39.

[6] Temporary migration and the slave trade differ ultimately in two ways. The minor point concerns the relative timing of the foreign earnings from the export of labor services on the one hand and the performance of those services on the other: in the slave trade the first anticipate the second, with voluntary migration the second precedes the first. The major point concerns the trade-off between transport costs and coercion costs. Per year of work abroad temporary migration consumes more than twice as much transportation, but avoids coercion; the slave trade has been eroded not by prohibition (in the face of continued profitability) but by the fall in transport costs, and the attendant increase in the mobility of goods and of labor itself, that rendered it unprofitable.

Like the slave, therefore, the temporary migrant is analytically a commodity, better understood through the model of trade rather than through the standard model of migration. Commodity exports are determined by relative prices (comparative advantages) and relative mobility, and the higher transport costs the greater the role of the latter. The mobility of the human commodity, slave or temporary migrant, lies between that of high-value goods on the one hand and that of low-value goods on the other; slaves and temporary migrants will come from lands burdened by high transport costs and not blessed by exportable supplies of gold, spices, or manufactures.

Protection limits trade and factor-price convergence: where labor is abundant protection reduces the real wage and encourages permanent migration. But protection limits imports, boosts the real exchange rate, and limits exports: all exports, including those of the human commodity, the services of temporary migrants.

Appendix 4

The Ricardian Model of Growth

1. The model of growth

The ricardian model of growth can be illustrated by Figure A4.01. Grain is measured on the vertical axis, labor on the horizontal. The curve illustrates the quantity of grain produced by a given number of agricultural workers. It is a standard production function, characterized by diminishing returns to labor because land is given. As the agricultural labor force increases, therefore, grain output increases but less than proportionately: labor's marginal product (the slope of the curve) decreases, and so does its average product (the slope of the ray from the origin to the relevant point on the curve). The illustrated ray out of the origin is in a sense the inverse of the curve. It illustrates the number of workers "produced" by a given quantity of grain; its slope corresponds to the "subsistence" wage, that is, the wage that keeps the labor force constant. The labor force would increase with a higher wage, and decrease with a lower one; in long-run equilibrium, wages must be at "subsistence," so defined.

The intersection of the illustrated curves (G_3, L_3) identifies the equilibrium of a communist society (which distributes the total product equally among the people, and if necessary forces them to work), and also of a society with private property, so long as it is equally distributed (so that the per-capita return to land tops up the less-than-subsistence per-capita return to labor, and everybody again winds up consuming the average product).

Ricardo models a capitalist economy, with landed property in the hands of an aristocracy so limited in numbers that its own consumption of grain is negligible; and in that economy growth is limited on the one

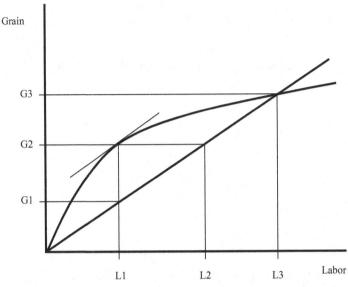

FIGURE A4.01. *The model of growth*

hand because land cannot grow in step with capital and labor, and on the other because the aristocracy does not save and accumulate.

Land is in fixed supply; as capital and labor increase land becomes ever more scarce, and its rental value increases.[1] Land is given, rent is not necessary to maintain it as profits and wages are necessary to maintain capital and labor: the rent of land is entirely surplus, it is "rent" in the technical sense of our textbooks.[2]

The aristocracy does not save and accumulate. In Ricardo's model grain is the capital that maintains the workers from harvest to harvest; but the only *productive* capital, which reproduces itself, is that which maintains the agricultural labor force. The part of the harvest that accrues as rent to the aristocracy is *unproductive* capital, dissipated as luxury-good consumption: it maintains workers, but workers who are themselves

---

[1] Ricardo thought of differential rent rather than of the pure scarcity rent generated even with homogeneous land, but the point is here immaterial.
[2] "Surplus" is income that can be expropriated without losing the services of the factor of production. Most star athletes would continue to play even if paid much less, as their earnings in any alternative profession would typically be much lower; when teams "owned" players, their salaries were much lower, and the surplus accrued to the team owners. Economists call surplus "rent" precisely because the first surplus to be identified as such was the return to land, so characterized by Ricardo.

"unproductive" in the sense that they produce luxuries rather than grain, that is, new capital.

In Ricardo's model land rent increases as population grows, and growth ends when the entire surplus over the subsistence of the agricultural labor force accrues as rent to the aristocracy: at that point profits (the difference between the harvest obtained by the capitalist farmer and the sum of the rent to the land and the wages of the laborers) are zero, capital stops growing, and so does the labor force that capital maintains.

Marginal analysis allows greater precision. With wages equal to the workers' marginal product, growth ends when that product falls to "subsistence." In the graph the equilibrium corresponds to output G_2: G_1 is the "productive" capital, the agricultural wages-fund that maintains L_1 "productive" workers, and $(G_2 - G_1)$ is the rent dissipated in the maintenance of $(L_2 - L_1)$ "unproductive" workers.

This is in fact the capitalist equilibrium, determined by the market (given concentrated property in land): no capitalist farmer will hire workers once their marginal product falls below the wage, and with equilibrium ("subsistence") wages the agricultural labor force cannot exceed L_1. To blame the aristocracy for the economy's failure to grow right up to (G_3, L_3) Ricardo must assume both that landowners consume their entire income and that grain cannot simply be stored from year to year. Ricardo explicitly assumed the first condition (which in the English context was more nearly false than true); he did not mention the second, and may well have failed altogether to notice it.

But that second condition is essential, for without it the first has no bite. If grain cannot be kept simply by being stored, the capitalist can maintain it from year to year only by passing it back through the land; capital that is not reinvested in grain production is simply lost. The alternative to the laborer's marginal product is no longer the capital itself but, by the next harvest, nothing at all; labor is profitably hired even if the marginal product is less than the wage, so long as it is positive. If landowners too behave like weberian capitalists, the entire harvest becomes productive capital; with non-storable grain the product G_2 supports L_2 "productive" (agricultural) laborers, who reproduce a larger capital, and so on right up to the equilibrium (G_3, L_3). If grain is allowed to be stored in the model as it is in fact, growth ends instead at G_2 (with L_2 workers, of whom L_1 "productive") because of capitalism, because land is privately held and property is concentrated, and not, as Ricardo seems determined to prove by fair means or foul, because of the profligacy of the aristocracy.

The implications of Ricardo's analysis are obvious. If England is to continue to grow it must overcome the constraint imposed by its own endowment of land: it must eliminate the Corn Laws and maintain its workers with cheap imported grain. The reduction in the price of grain reduces land rents, absorbed by the parasitic class, to the advantage of the productive classes, the capitalists who save and the laborers who work. The *fictio* that free trade is "good for everybody" is here abandoned: the abolition of the Corn Laws would harm the landowning aristocracy which then ruled England, but that class deserves punishment because it is the enemy of the people.

2. The model of growth and trade

Ricardo's model misrepresents England, with its aristocracy that in fact invested and promoted economic growth; it represents altogether better the traditional *ancien régime* societies, with their landowning aristocracies of *gattopardi* and *boyarin* who consume land rents and taxes and maintain the artisans that produce luxury goods.

Ricardo's model is of a closed economy, but it extends very naturally to an open economy, with mobile resources. It is enough to substitute space for time: the equilibrium wage remains, as defined, that which keeps the labor force constant, but the adjustment in the latter is attributed to migration rather than to the balance of births and deaths.

The equilibrium remains in part that of Figure A4.01: the agricultural labor force remains L_1, the agricultural wages-fund G_1, the rent accruing to the landowners $(G_2 - G_1)$; but the overall equilibrium depends on the structure of trade. If the country exports in kind part of the return to land, the total wages-fund will be less than G_2, and the total labor force less than L_2 – and vice versa, obviously, in the opposite case.

Figure A4.02 twice reproduces Figure A4.01. It imagines two countries (or regions) with identical agricultural sectors and "subsistence" wages; it is constructed by rotating one of the copies of Figure A4.01 through 180°, and superimposing the two autarky equilibria (G_2, L_2). For one of them, R_1, the axes are the conventional ones; for the other, R_2, they are inverted, and are read respectively downward and from right to left. The agricultural labor force of R_2 is accordingly $(L_4 - L_3)$, equal to L_1; and so on. Total grain output is G_4, and it maintains a total labor force L_4.

Figure A4.02 can illustrate a variety of typical cases. The first is autarky equilibrium, without trade: the two countries have identical agricultural

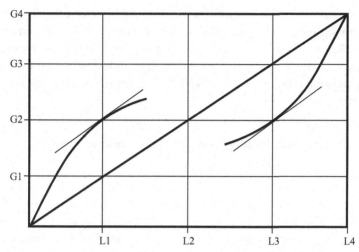

FIGURE A4.02. *The model of growth and trade*

sectors, and equivalent manufacturing sectors, employing $(L2 - L1) = (L3 - L2)$. The second is equilibrium with "equal trade," an exchange of manufactures for manufactures (the woolens of the one against the linens of the other); the geometry of the equilibrium is unchanged.

The third is equilibrium with "unequal trade," of the agricultural surplus of one country against the manufactures of the other. Imagine that $R2$ exports its agricultural rent in kind: its labor force is then only the agricultural labor force $(L4 - L3)$, consuming $(G4 - G3)$, the labor force of $R1$ is instead $L3$, maintained by the domestic grain product $G2$ plus the imported foreign rent $(G3 - G2)$. The artisans who produce for the aristocracy of $R2$, and are maintained by its rental income, are overseas, in $R1$.

In the fourth case $R1$ and $R2$ are considered two regions of a single state. Imagine that the capital, the court, the residence of the entire aristocracy are in $R1$, and that the artisans locate near their clients: the geometry remains that of the preceding case, and the only difference is that the flow of rents from $R2$ has no counter-flow, it is a payment not for imports but of a rent (and tax) obligation.

This fourth case is pertinent to this day, to the extent that the taxes drained from the entire country maintain the political and administrative structures of the capital city. Figure A4.02 illustrates interregional trade in a modern economy in yet another way, without the class distinctions so dear to Ricardo. In this fifth case region $R2$ exports its agricultural surplus and imports the manufactures produced by region R_1; the geometry remains that of the preceding two cases, but the interpretation again differs. Region R_1 is again industrial, but not because it is the region of residence of the artisans' clients; rather, it is industrial because it possesses immobile resources ("waterfalls") that attract industry and mobile resources.

3. The model of growth and the model of trade

The "model of growth" enriches and in part overturns the ("comparative advantage") "model of trade." The latter would show that free trade "benefits all," at least all countries if not all individuals within those countries. The former turns on much more than an increase in total consumption (which in practice is in any case very small): it brings into focus the distinction between core and periphery that the "model of trade" misses altogether, and ties the growth of industry to the growth of the entire economy.

In the "model of trade" resources are given. The country that is (by chance) thinly populated enjoys a comparative advantage in (land-intensive) agriculture; it exports its agricultural surplus, and imports the manufactures of the country that is (by chance) densely populated and thus enjoys a comparative advantage in (labor-intensive) industry. In the "model of growth" demographic density is endogenous. The densely populated country will be that which wins the race to become the workshop of the world; the thinly populated country will be that which loses that race and remains agricultural. The "model of growth" subverts the anti-mercantilist message of the "model of trade": it fully justifies the policies aimed at developing non-agricultural exports, the luxury-good industries and the carrying trade.[3]

---

[3] The implications of these arguments are numerous. Hume's specie-flow mechanism was and is interpreted as proof of the futility of mercantilist policies aimed at increasing the domestic supply of circulating gold. Hume himself knew that protection would increase equilibrium prices and attract gold, and argued on separate grounds that smuggling rendered it ineffective. But there is much more to be said. Mercantilist policies aimed at developing non-agricultural exports (of manufactured luxuries and transport services), at transforming a country from "periphery" to "core"; and such a transformation clearly attracted gold, through two mechanisms. First, at given prices, the transformation meant growth in the economy's resource base and in the volume of transactions. Second, and more importantly, in the presence of significant transport costs the transformation implied a rise in the equilibrium price level as well. The reason is that the costs of a ship's outbound and inbound leg are joint costs; equilibrium requires that these joint costs be covered by

The "model of growth" thus illustrates the possible benefits of protection as of free trade. By embracing free trade England, the industrial leader, abandoned autarky to become core: in the above taxonomy it moves as R_1 from the first case to the third (at the cost of the rest of the world, that symmetrically abandons autarky to become periphery). North America was instead an affluent periphery, that exported an enormous agricultural surplus and imported manufactures; it was region R_2 of that third case. Industrial protection moved it towards the autarky equilibrium, from the third case above to the first: it thus attracted to its soil the industrial workers overseas that it already maintained and whose products it already consumed.

4. The model of growth and the tariff on grain

Far better than the model of trade, the model of growth brings out the harm the grain tariff inflicted on the Italian economy, and its effects on migration. Imagine an economy with two sectors, producing respectively grain G and manufactures M with labor L subject to diminishing returns: $G = g(L_G)$ with $g' > 0$, $g'' < 0$, and $M = m(L_M)$ with $m' > 0$, $m'' < 0$. Grain is the subsistence good, so the real wage is simply g'. The total labor force is by definition the sum of its two components: $L_T = L_G + L_M$. Labor-market equilibrium requires equal (real and nominal) wages in the two sectors; given the prices (P) of the goods produced, $g' = (P_M/P_G)m'$.

The introduction of a grain tariff reduces (P_M/P_G), and therefore the marginal productivity, measured in grain, of manufacturing labor. In the "model of trade" the total labor force L_T is given; labor-market equilibrium is restored by moving labor from M to G, reducing g' and

---

the joint return, but within this constraint the relative earnings on the two trips are determined by relative demand. Trade balances in value, not in volume; manufactured goods are far more valuable per ton than primary products, and many tons of grain pay for one ton of cloth. The transport capacity actually generated is that needed to transport, and thus will be borne (almost) entirely by, the low-value good; the high-value good does not use the available capacity, and is transported (almost) free of charge. The "law of one price" thus (almost) holds for manufactures, but not for agricultural goods, which have a much lower price in the country that exports them; the price level is thus systematically higher in the manufacturing country than in the agricultural country, and mercantilist policies were anything but ineffective. By the same token "purchasing power parity" is not to be expected: it reflects the assumption that transport costs are negligible, innocent enough in Ricardo's "comparative advantage" demonstration of the gains from trade, but critical, and unwarranted, in Hume's context, because the specie-flow argument that price levels tend to equilibrium implies a common price level, independent of national development policy, only in the absence of transport costs.

increasing m' until the change in the relative price of the goods is offset by the change in relative physical productivities. In the "model of growth" the equilibrium wage g' is given (and equal to that obtainable abroad, net of transfer costs). Labor-market equilibrium is therefore restored without changing L_G: the change in the relative price of the goods is offset entirely by increasing m', that is, by reducing L_M. But L_G is unchanged: the decline in manufacturing labor is not a transfer to the other sector but a net loss, a decline in L_T. In the "model of trade" total employment is given, and the grain tariff cuts the real wage; in the "model of growth" the real wage is given, and the grain tariff cuts total employment.

In Figure A2.01, as noted, the "model of trade" has the economy respond to the grain tariff by moving along a given production possibilities curve: the production of wine (or manufactures) falls but that of grain increases, the net loss is minimal. In the "model of growth" as the production of wine (or manufactures) declines that of grain does *not* increase: in Figure A2.01 the grain tariff implies a movement directly toward the grain axis, a shift for example from (W_3, G_1) not to (W_2, G_2) but to (W_2, G_1). Capital and labor abandon the country: the economy's resource base declines, and its production possibilities shrink, in this example from the curve that passed through (W_3, G_1) and (W_2, G_2) to one passing through (W_2, G_1).

By emphasizing the mobility of resources the "model of growth" associates development not just with a better use of the economy's resources, but with their accumulation, the capacity to attract them and retain them. The grain tariff denied Italy the cheap grain of the world's great plains, and obliged those who would produce in Italy to maintain their labor with the expensive grain of Italy's arid hills. It handicapped production in Italy alone: it diverted production, and employment, overseas.

References

Abramowitz, M., "The Nature and Significance of Kuznets Cycles," *Economic Development and Cultural Change* 9 (1961), pp. 225–248.

Abramowitz, M., "The Passing of the Kuznets Cycle," *Economica* 140 (1968), pp. 349–367.

[R.] Accademia dei Lincei, *Cinquanta anni di storia italiana*, 3 vols., Milan 1911.

A'Hearn, B., "Institutions, Externalities, and Economic Growth in Southern Italy: Evidence from the Cotton Textile Industry, 1861–1914," *Economic History Review* 51 (1998), pp. 734–762.

A'Hearn, B., "Could Southern Italians Cooperate? *Banche Popolari* in the Mezzogiorno," *Journal of Economic History* 60 (2000), pp. 67–93.

Amatori, F., D. Bigazzi, R. Giannetti, L. Segreto, eds., *Storia d'Italia. Annali. 15. L'industria*, Turin 1999.

Assante, F., ed., *Il movimento migratorio italiano dall'Unità nazionale ai giorni nostri*, 2 vols., Geneva 1978.

Backhouse, R., *A History of Modern Economic Analysis*, Oxford 1985.

Baglioni, G., *Per la riforma ferroviaria*, Milan 1910.

Baia Curioni, S., *Modernizzazione e mercato. La borsa di Milano nella "nuova economia" dell'età giolittiana (1888–1914)*, Milan 2000.

Balletta, F., "Emigrazione italiana, cicli economici e rimesse (1876–1976)," in G. Rosoli, ed., *Un secolo di emigrazione italiana 1876–1976*, Rome 1978, pp. 65–96.

Banfield, E. C., *The Moral Basis of a Backward Society*, Glencoe IL 1958.

Barberi, B., *I consumi nel primo secolo dell'Unità d'Italia*, Milan 1961.

Bardini, C., A. Carreras, P. Lains, "The National Accounts for Italy, Spain and Portugal," *Scandinavian Economic History Review* 43 (1995), pp. 115–147.

Battilossi, S., *Annali*, P. Ciocca, G. Toniolo, eds., *Storia economica d'Italia. 2*, Rome-Bari 1999.

Baxter, M., R. G. King, "Measuring Business Cycles: Approximate Band-Pass Filters for Economic Time Series," *Review of Economics and Statistics* 81 (1999), pp. 575–593.

Bianchi, B., "Appendice statistica: il rendimento del consolidato dal 1862 al 1946," in F. Vicarelli, ed., *Capitale industriale e capitale finanziario: il caso italiano*, Bologna 1979, pp. 139–167.

Biscaini Cotula, A. M., P. Ciocca, "Le strutture finanziarie: aspetti quantitativi di lungo periodo (1870–1970)," in F. Vicarelli, ed., *Capitale industriale e capitale finanziario: il caso italiano*, Bologna 1979, pp. 61–136.

Bloomfield, A. I., *Patterns of International Investment Before 1914* (Princeton Studies in International Finance No. 21), Princeton 1968.

Bolchini, P., et al., "A proposito di Stefano Fenoaltea, *L'economia italiana dall'Unità alla Grande Guerra*, Bari-Roma, 2006," *Rivista di storia economica* 22 (2006), pp. 331–375.

Bonelli, F., "Il capitalismo italiano. Linee generali di interpretazione," in R. Romano, C. Vivanti, eds., *Storia d'Italia. Annali. 1. Dal feudalesimo al capitalismo*, Turin 1978, pp. 1193–1255.

Bonelli, F., "Italian Capitalism: General Interpretative Guidelines," in G. Federico, ed., *The Economic Development of Italy since 1870*, Aldershot 1994, pp. 99–142 (translation of F. Bonelli, "Il capitalismo italiano. Linee generali di interpretazione, "in R. Romano, C. Vivanti, eds., *Storia d'Italia. Annali. 1. Dal feudalesimo al capitalismo*, Turin 1978, pp. 1193–1255).

Cafagna, L., "L'industrializzazione italiana. La formazione di una 'base industriale' in Italia fra il 1896 e il 1914," *Studi storici* 2 (1961), pp. 690–724, reprinted in Id., *Dualismo e sviluppo nella storia d'Italia*, Venice 1989, pp. 323–357.

Cafagna, L., "Intorno alle origini del dualismo economico in Italia," in A. Caracciolo, ed., *Problemi storici dell'industrializzazione e dello sviluppo*, Urbino 1965, pp. 103–150, reprinted with the addition of notes and subtitles in L. Cafagna, *Dualismo e sviluppo nella storia d'Italia*, Venice 1989, pp. 187–220.

Cafagna, L., "The Industrial Revolution in Italy, 1830–1914," in C. M. Cipolla, ed., *The Fontana Economic History of Europe*, vol. 4, Glasgow 1972, pp. 279–328.

Cafagna, L., "La politica economica e lo sviluppo industriale," in *Stato e società dal 1876 al 1882: atti del XLIX Congresso di storia del Risorgimento italiano (Viterbo, 30 settembre – 5 ottobre 1978)*, Rome 1980, pp. 141–157, reprinted in Id., *Dualismo e sviluppo nella storia d'Italia*, Venice 1989, pp. 261–278.

Cafagna, L., "Protoindustria o transizione in bilico? (A proposito della prima onda dell'industrializzazione italiana)," *Quaderni storici* 54 (1983), pp. 971–984, reprinted in Id., *Dualismo e sviluppo nella storia d'Italia*, Venice 1989, pp. 359–372.

Cafagna, L., "La formazione del sistema industriale: ricerche empiriche e modelli di crescita," *Quaderni della Fondazione G. G. Feltrinelli* 25 (1983), pp. 27–38, reprinted in Id., *Dualismo e sviluppo nella storia d'Italia*, Venice 1989, pp. 385–399.

Cafagna, L., *Dualismo e sviluppo nella storia d'Italia*, Venice 1989.

Cafagna, L., "Discussion of the Origins of Italian Economic Dualism," in G. Federico, ed., *The Economic Development of Italy Since 1870*, Aldershot 1994, pp. 634–653 (translation of L. Cafagna, *Dualismo e sviluppo nella storia d'Italia*, Venice 1989, pp. 187–220).

Cafagna, L., "Contro tre pregiudizi sulla storia dello sviluppo economico italiano," in P. Ciocca, G. Toniolo, eds., *Storia economica d'Italia. 1. Interpretazioni*, Rome-Bari 1998, pp. 297–325.

Cafagna, L., N. Crepax, eds., *Atti di intelligenza e sviluppo economico. Saggi per il bicentenario della nascita di Carlo Cattaneo*, Bologna 2001.

Cainelli, G., R. Leoncini, A. Montini, "Struttura produttiva e sviluppo regionale di lungo periodo in Italia," *Moneta e Credito* 44 (2001), pp. 461–485.

Cairncross, A., *Home and Foreign Investment, 1870–1913: Studies in Capital Accumulation*, Cambridge 1953.

Cairncross, A., "Economic Growth and Stagnation in the United Kingdom before the First World War," in M. Gersovitz, C. F. Diaz Alejandro, G. Ranis, M. R. Rosenzweig, eds., *The Theory and Experience of Economic Development: Essays in Honor of Sir W. Arthur Lewis*, London 1982, pp. 287–299.

Caracciolo, A., ed., *Problemi storici dell'industrializzazione e dello sviluppo*, Urbino 1965.

Caracciolo, A., ed., *La formazione dell'Italia industriale*, Bari 1969.

Cardarelli, S., et al., *Ricerche per la storia della Banca d'Italia. Volume I*, Collana storica della Banca d'Italia, serie "contributi," vol. I, Bari 1990.

Carocci, G., *Giolitti e l'età giolittiana*, Turin 1961.

Carreras, A., "La producció industrial espanyola i italiana des de mitjan segle XIX fins a l'actualitat" (unpublished Ph.D. thesis, Universitat Autònoma de Barcelona, 1983).

Carreras, A., "La producción industrial en el muy largo plazo: una comparación entre España e Italia de 1861 a 1980," in L. Prados, V. Zamagni, eds., *El desarrollo económico en la Europa del Sur: España e Italia en perspectiva histórica*, Madrid 1992, pp. 173–210.

Carreras, A., "Un ritratto quantitativo dell'industria italiana," in F. Amatori, D. Bigazzi, R. Giannetti, L. Segreto, eds., *Storia d'Italia. Annali. 15. L'industria*, Turin 1999, pp. 179–272.

Castronovo, V., *Storia economica d'Italia*, Turin 1995.

Cerrito, E., "Depressioni. Caratteri e genesi della depressione di fine XIX secolo, più altre tre (e un'altra ancora)," *Studi storici* 44 (2003), pp. 927–1005.

Ciccarelli, C., S. Fenoaltea, "Business Fluctuations in Italy, 1861–1913: The New Evidence," *Explorations in Economic History* 44 (2007), pp. 432–451.

Ciocca, P., "Einaudi e le turbolenze economiche fra le due guerre," *Rivista di storia economica* 20 (2004), pp. 279–308.

Ciocca, P., *Ricchi per sempre? Una storia economica d'Italia (1796–2005)*, Turin 2007.

Ciocca, P., "Interpreting the Italian Economy in the Long Run," *Rivista di storia economica* 24 (2008), pp. 241–246.

Ciocca, P., G. Toniolo, eds., *Storia economica d'Italia. 1. Interpretazioni*, Rome-Bari 1998.

Ciocca, P., G. Toniolo, eds., *Storia economica d'Italia. 2. Annali* (by S. Battilossi), Rome-Bari 1999.

Ciocca, P., G. Toniolo, eds., *Storia economica d'Italia. 3.1. Le strutture dell'economia*, Rome-Bari 2002.

Ciocca, P., G. Toniolo, eds., *Storia economica d'Italia. 3.2. I vincoli e le opportunità*, Rome-Bari 2003.

Ciocca, P., A. Ulizzi, "I tassi di cambio nominali e 'reali' dell'Italia dall'Unità nazionale al Sistema Monetario Europeo (1861–1979)," in S. Cardarelli *et al.*, *Ricerche per la storia della Banca d'Italia. Volume I*, Collana storica della Banca d'Italia, serie "contributi," vol. I, Bari 1990, pp. 341–368.

Cipolla, C. M., ed., *The Fontana Economic History of Europe*, vol. 4, Glasgow 1972.

Cipolla, C. M., *Before the Industrial Revolution: European Society and Economy, 1000–1700*, New York 1980.

Clough, S. B., *The Economic History of Modern Italy*, New York 1964.

Cohen, J. S., "Financing Industrialization in Italy, 1894–1914: The Partial Transformation of a Late-Comer," *Journal of Economic History* 27 (1967), pp. 363–382.

Cohen, J. S., G. Federico, *The Growth of the Italian Economy, 1820–1960*, Cambridge 2001.

Coletti, F., "Dell'emigrazione italiana," in R. Accademia dei Lincei, *Cinquanta anni di storia italiana*, vol. 3, Milan 1911, pp. 1–284.

Commissione d'inchiesta sull'esercizio delle ferrovie italiane, *Atti*, 3 parts in 7 vols., Rome 1879–84.

[R.] Commissione per lo studio di proposte intorno all'ordinamento delle strade ferrate, *Atti*, 10 vols., Rome 1903–06.

Confalonieri, A., *Banca e industria in Italia, 1894–1906*, 3 vols., Milan 1974–76.

Confalonieri, A., *Banca e industria in Italia dalla crisi del 1907 all'agosto 1914*, 2 vols., Milan 1982.

Cottrau, A., *Le industrie meccaniche e il regime doganale*, Rome 1891.

Croce, B., *Storia d'Italia dal 1871 al 1915*, 9th ed., Bari 1967 (1927).

Da Pozzo, M., G. Felloni, *La borsa valori di Genova nel secolo XIX*, Turin 1964.

De Bernardi, A., ed., *Questione agraria e protezionismo nella crisi economica di fine secolo*, Milan 1977.

de Cecco, M., "L'Italia grande potenza: la realtà del mito," in P. Ciocca, G. Toniolo, eds., *Storia economica d'Italia. 3.2. I vincoli e le opportunità*, Rome-Bari 2003, pp. 3–36.

de Viti de Marco, A., "Finanze e politica doganale," *Giornale degli economisti* ser. 2, 2-I (1891), pp. 30–47, partially reprinted in A. De Bernardi, ed., *Questione agraria e protezionismo nella crisi economica di fine secolo*, Milan 1977, pp. 179–184.

de Viti de Marco, A., *Un trentennio di lotte politiche*, Rome c. 1930.

Direzione generale delle dogane e imposte indirette, *Movimento commerciale del Regno d'Italia nell'anno . . .* , annual.

Dirstat (Direzione generale della statistica), *Annali di statistica*, serie IV, Rome 1884–1910.

Dirstat (Direzione generale della statistica), *Annuario statistico italiano*, 1878ff.

Easterlin, R. A., *Population, Labor Force, and Long Swings in Economic Growth: The American Experience*, New York 1968.

Eckaus, R. S., "The Factor Proportions Problem in Underdeveloped Areas," *American Economic Review* 45 (1955), pp. 539–565.

Eckaus, R. S., "The North-South Differential in Italian Economic Development," *Journal of Economic History* 20 (1961), pp. 285–317.

Edelstein, M., *Overseas Investment in the Age of High Imperialism: The United Kingdom, 1850–1914*, New York 1982.

Einaudi, L., *Cronache economiche e politiche di un trentennio*, 8 vols., Turin 1959–66.

Ercolani, P., "Documentazione statistica di base," in G. Fuà, ed., *Lo sviluppo economico in Italia*, vol. 3, Milan 1969, pp. 380–460.

Esposto, A. G., "Italian Industrialization and the Gerschenkronian 'Great Spurt': A Regional Analysis," *Journal of Economic History* 52 (1992), pp. 353–362.

Faini, R., A. Venturini. "Italian Emigration in the pre-War Period," in T. J. Hatton, J. G. Williamson, eds., *Migration and the International Labor Market, 1850–1939*, London 1994, pp. 72–90.

Falchero, A. M., A. Giuntini, G. Nigro, L. Segreto, eds., *La storia e l'economia. Miscellanea di studi in onore di Giorgio Mori*, 2 vols., Varese 2003.

Federico, G., "Per una analisi del ruolo dell'agricoltura nello sviluppo economico italiano: note sull'esportazione di prodotti primari (1863–1913)," *Società e storia* 5 (1979), pp. 379–441.

Federico, G., "Per una valutazione critica delle statistiche della produzione agricola italiana dopo l'Unità (1860–1913)," *Società e storia* 15 (1982), pp. 87–130.

Federico, G., "Commercio dei cereali e dazio sul grano in Italia (1863–1913). Una analisi quantitativa," *Nuova rivista storica* 68 (1984), pp. 46–108.

Federico, G., "Il valore aggiunto dell'agricoltura," in G. M. Rey, ed., *I conti economici dell'Italia. 2. Una stima del valore aggiunto per il 1911*, Collana storica della Banca d'Italia, serie "statistiche storiche," vol. I.II, Bari 1992, pp. 3–103.

Federico, G., ed., *The Economic Development of Italy Since 1870*, Aldershot 1994.

Federico, G., "Introduction," in Id., ed., *The Economic Development of Italy Since 1870*, Aldershot 1994, pp. xi–xliii.

Federico, G., *Il filo d'oro. L'industria mondiale della seta dalla restaurazione alla grande crisi*, Venice 1994.

Federico, G., "Una stima del valore aggiunto dell'agricoltura italiana," in G. M. Rey, ed., *I conti economici dell'Italia. 3°°. Il valore aggiunto per gli anni 1891, 1938, 1951*, Collana storica della Banca d'Italia, serie "statistiche storiche," vol. I.III.2, Rome-Bari 2000, pp. 3–112.

Federico, G., "Protezione e sviluppo economico italiano: molto rumore per nulla?" in L. Cafagna, N. Crepax, eds., *Atti di intelligenza e sviluppo economico. Saggi per il bicentenario della nascita di Carlo Cattaneo*, Bologna 2001, pp. 451–489.

Federico, G., "L'agricoltura italiana: successo o fallimento?" in P. Ciocca, G. Toniolo, eds., *Storia economica d'Italia. 3.1. Le strutture dell'economia*, Rome-Bari 2002, pp. 99–136.

Federico, G., "Le nuove stime della produzione agricola italiana, 1860–1910: primi risultati e implicazioni," *Rivista di storia economica* 19 (2003), pp. 357–381.

Federico, G., "Heights, Calories and Welfare: A New Perspective on Italian Industrialization, 1854–1913," *Economics and Human Biology* 1 (2003), pp. 289–308.

Federico, G., K. O'Rourke, "Much Ado About Nothing? Italian Trade Policy in the 19th Century," in S. Pamuk, J. G. Williamson, eds., *The Mediterranean Response to Globalisation before 1950*, London 2000, pp. 269–296.

Federico, G., A. Tena, "Was Italy a Protectionist Country?" *European Review of Economic History* 2 (1998), pp. 73–97.

Federico, G., A. Tena, "Did Trade Policy Foster Italian Industrialization? Evidence from Effective Protection Rates, 1870–1930," *Research in Economic History* 19 (1999), pp. 111–130.

Federico, G., G. Toniolo, "Italy," in R. Sylla, G. Toniolo, eds., *Patterns of European Industrialization: The Nineteenth Century*, London 1991.

Feinstein, C. H., *National Income, Expenditure and Output of the United Kingdom, 1855–1965*, Studies in the National Income and Expenditure of the United Kingdom, vol. 6, Cambridge 1972.

Fenoaltea, S. "Public Policy and Italian Industrial Development, 1861–1913" (unpublished Ph.D. thesis, Harvard University, 1967).

Fenoaltea, S., "Decollo, ciclo, e intervento dello Stato," in A. Caracciolo, ed., *La formazione dell'Italia industriale*, Bari 1969, pp. 95–114.

Fenoaltea, S., "Railroads and Italian Industrial Growth, 1861–1913," *Explorations in Economic History* 9 (1972), pp. 325–351.

Fenoaltea, S., "The Discipline and They: Notes on Counterfactual Methodology and the 'New' Economic History," *Journal of European Economic History* 2 (1973), pp. 729–746.

Fenoaltea, S. "Le ferrovie e lo sviluppo industriale italiano, 1861–1913," in G. Toniolo, ed., *Lo sviluppo economico italiano 1861–1940*, Bari 1973, pp. 157–186, and again in G. Toniolo, ed., *L'economia italiana 1861–1940*, Bari 1978, pp. 105–135 (translation of S. Fenoaltea, "Railroads and Italian Industrial Growth, 1861–1913," *Explorations in Economic History* 9 [1972], pp. 325–351).

Fenoaltea, S., "Riflessioni sull'esperienza industriale italiana dal Risorgimento alla prima guerra mondiale," in G. Toniolo, ed., *Lo sviluppo economico italiano 1861–1940*, Bari 1973, pp. 121–156, and again in G. Toniolo, ed., *L'economia italiana 1861–1940*, Bari 1978, pp. 69–104.

Fenoaltea, S., "Real Value Added and the Measurement of Industrial Production," *Annals of Economic and Social Measurement* 5 (1976), pp. 113–139.

Fenoaltea, S., "The Slavery Debate: A Note from the Sidelines," *Explorations in Economic History* 18 (1981), pp. 304–308.

Fenoaltea, S., "The Growth of the Utilities Industries in Italy, 1861–1913," *Journal of Economic History* 42 (1982), pp. 601–627.

Fenoaltea, S., "Italy," in P. K. O'Brien, ed., *Railways and the Economic Development of Western Europe*, London 1983, pp. 49–120.

Fenoaltea, S., "Railway Construction in Italy, 1861–1913," *Rivista di storia economica* 1 (1984), International Issue, pp. 27–54.

Fenoaltea, S., "Slavery and Supervision in Comparative Perspective: A Model," *Journal of Economic History* 44 (1984), pp. 635–668.

Fenoaltea, S., "Public Works Construction in Italy, 1861–1913," *Rivista di storia economica* 3 (1986), International Issue, pp. 1–33.

Fenoaltea, S., "Construction in Italy, 1861–1913," *Rivista di storia economica* 4 (1987), International Issue, pp. 21–54.

Fenoaltea, S., "The Extractive Industries in Italy, 1861–1913: General Methods and Specific Estimates," *Journal of European Economic History* 17 (1988), pp. 117–125.

Fenoaltea, S., "The Growth of Italy's Silk Industry, 1861–1913: A Statistical Reconstruction," *Rivista di storia economica* 5 (1988), pp. 275–318.

Fenoaltea, S., "International Resource Flows and Construction Movements in the Atlantic Economy: The Kuznets Cycle in Italy, 1861–1913," *Journal of Economic History* 48 (1988), pp. 605–637.

Fenoaltea, S., "Il valore aggiunto dell'industria italiana nel 1911," in G. M. Rey, ed., *I conti economici dell'Italia. 2. Una stima del valore aggiunto per il 1911*, Collana storica della Banca d'Italia, serie "statistiche storiche," vol. I.II, Bari 1992, pp. 105–190.

Fenoaltea, S., "Politica doganale, sviluppo industriale, emigrazione: verso una riconsiderazione del dazio sul grano," *Rivista di storia economica* 10 (1993), pp. 65–77.

Fenoaltea, S., "Lo sviluppo economico dell'Italia nel lungo periodo: riflessioni su tre fallimenti," in P. Ciocca, G. Toniolo, eds., *Storia economica d'Italia. 1. Interpretazioni*, Rome-Bari 1998, pp. 3–41.

Fenoaltea, S., "Europe in the African Mirror: The Slave Trade and the Rise of Feudalism," *Rivista di storia economica* 15 (1999), pp. 123–165.

Fenoaltea, S., "The Growth of Italy's Wool Industry, 1861–1913: A Statistical Reconstruction," *Rivista di storia economica* 16 (2000), pp. 119–145.

Fenoaltea, S., "The Growth of Italy's Cotton Industry, 1861–1913: A Statistical Reconstruction," *Rivista di storia economica* 17 (2001), pp. 139–171.

Fenoaltea, S., "La crescita industriale delle regioni d'Italia dall'Unità alla Grande Guerra: una prima stima per gli anni censuari," Banca d'Italia, *Quaderni dell'Ufficio Ricerche Storiche*, n. 1, Rome 2001.

Fenoaltea, S., "Manchester, manchesteriano... *dekwakoncoz*?" in L. Cafagna, N. Crepax, eds., *Atti di intelligenza e sviluppo economico. Saggi per il bicentenario della nascita di Carlo Cattaneo*, Bologna 2001, pp. 491–511.

Fenoaltea, S., "Textile Production in Italy, 1861–1913," *Rivista di storia economica* 18 (2002), pp. 3–40.

Fenoaltea, S., "Production and Consumption in Post-Unification Italy: New Evidence, New Conjectures," *Rivista di storia economica* 18 (2002), pp. 251–298.

Fenoaltea, S., "Lo sviluppo dell'industria dall'Unità alla Grande Guerra: una sintesi provvisoria," in P. Ciocca, G. Toniolo, eds., *Storia economica d'Italia. 3.1. Le strutture dell'economia*, Rome-Bari 2002, pp. 137–193.

Fenoaltea, S., "Notes on the Rate of Industrial Growth in Italy, 1861–1913," *Journal of Economic History* 63 (2003), pp. 695–735.

Fenoaltea, S., "Peeking Backward: Regional Aspects of Industrial Growth in Post-Unification Italy," *Journal of Economic History* 63 (2003), pp. 1059–1102.

Fenoaltea, S., "Product Heterogeneity, Trade and Protection: The Cotton Industry in Post-Unification Italy," in A. M. Falchero, A. Giuntini, G. Nigro, L. Segreto, eds., *La storia e l'economia. Miscellanea di studi in onore di Giorgio Mori*, vol. 1, Varese 2003, pp. 275–287.

Fenoaltea, S., "Contro tre pregiudizi," *Rivista di storia economica* 20 (2004), pp. 87–106.

Fenoaltea, S., "Textile Production in Italy's Regions, 1861–1913," *Rivista di storia economica* 20 (2004), pp. 145–174.

Fenoaltea, S., "Einaudi commentatore e protagonista della politica economica: aspetti dell'età giolittiana," *Rivista di storia economica* 20 (2004), pp. 271–278.

Fenoaltea, S., "The Growth of the Italian Economy, 1861–1913: Preliminary Second-Generation Estimates," *European Review of Economic History* 9 (2005), pp. 273–312.

Fenoaltea, S., "Economic Decline in Historical Perspective: Some Theoretical Considerations," *Rivista di storia economica* 22 (2006), pp. 3–39.

Fenoaltea, S., *L'economia italiana dall'Unità alla Grande Guerra*, Rome-Bari, 2006.

Fenoaltea, S., "The Reconstruction of Historical National Accounts: The Case of Italy," presented at the International Economic History Congress, Helsinki, 2006, session 103.

Fenoaltea, S. "Dualismo, ciclo e sviluppo nel pensiero di Luciano Cafagna," in E. Francia, ed., *Luciano Cafagna. Tra ricerca storica e impegno civile*, Venice 2007, pp. 167–174.

Fenoaltea, S., "I due fallimenti della storia economica: il periodo post-unitario," *Rivista di politica economica* 97 (2007), nn. 3–4, pp. 341–358.

Fenoaltea, S., *Italian Industrial Production, 1861–1913: A Statistical Reconstruction* (in progress).

Fenoaltea, S., C. Bardini, "Il valore aggiunto dell'industria," in G. M. Rey, ed., *I conti economici dell'Italia. 3°°. Il valore aggiunto per gli anni 1891, 1938, 1951*, Collana storica della Banca d'Italia, serie "statistiche storiche," vol. I.III.2, Rome-Bari 2000, pp. 113–238.

Fishlow, A., "Lessons from the Past: Capital Markets during the 19th Century and the Interwar Period," *International Organization* 39 (1985), pp. 383–439.

Fogel, R. W., *Railroads and American Economic Growth: Essays in Econometric History*, Baltimore 1964.

Fogel, R. W., S. L. Engerman, eds., *The Reinterpretation of American Economic History*, New York 1971.

Fogel, R. W., S. L. Engerman, *Time on the Cross: The Economics of American Negro Slavery*, Boston 1974.

Francia, E., ed., *Luciano Cafagna. Tra ricerca storica e impegno civile*, Venice 2007.

Fratianni M., F. Spinelli, "Currency Competition, Fiscal Policy and the Money Supply Process in Italy from Unification to World War I," *Journal of European Economic History* 14 (1985), pp. 473–499.

Fuà, G., *Notes on Italian Economic Growth 1861–1964*, Milan 1966.

Fuà, G., ed., *Lo sviluppo economico in Italia*, vols. 2–3, Milan 1969.

Fuà, G., *Crescita economica. Le insidie delle cifre*, Bologna 1993.

Fuà, G., S. Scuppa, "Industrializzazione e deindustrializzazione delle regioni italiane secondo i censimenti demografici 1881–1981," *Economia Marche* 7 (1988), pp. 307–327.

Gerschenkron, A., "Economic Backwardness in Historical Perspective," in B. F. Hoselitz, ed., *The Progress of Underdeveloped Areas*, Chicago 1952, pp. 3–29, reprinted in A. Gerschenkron, *Economic Backwardness in Historical Perspective*, Cambridge MA 1962, pp. 3–30.

Gerschenkron, A., "Notes on the Rate of Industrial Growth in Italy, 1881–1913," *Journal of Economic History* 15 (1955), pp. 360–375, reprinted in Id., *Economic Backwardness in Historical Perspective*, Cambridge MA 1962, pp. 72–89.

Gerschenkron, A., "Rosario Romeo e l'accumulazione primitiva del capitale," *Rivista storica italiana* 71 (1959), pp. 557–586.

Gerschenkron, A., *Economic Backwardness in Historical Perspective*, Cambridge MA 1962.

Gerschenkron, A., "Rosario Romeo and the Original Accumulation of Capital," in Id., *Economic Backwardness in Historical Perspective*, Cambridge MA 1962, pp. 90–118 (translation of Id., "Rosario Romeo e l'accumulazione primitiva del capitale," *Rivista storica italiana* 71 [1959], pp. 557–586).

Gerschenkron, A., "The Approach to European Industrialization: A Post-Script," in Id., *Economic Backwardness in Historical Perspective*, Cambridge MA 1962, pp. 355–364.

Gerschenkron, A., "Description of an Index of Italian Industrial Development, 1881–1913," in Id., *Economic Backwardness in Historical Perspective*, Cambridge MA 1962, pp. 367–421.

Gerschenkron, A., *Continuity in History and Other Essays*, Cambridge MA 1968.

Gerschenkron, A., "The Industrial Development of Italy: A Debate with Rosario Romeo (with a Postscript)," in Id., *Continuity in History and Other Essays*, Cambridge, MA 1968, pp. 98–127 (translation of A. Gerschenkron, R. Romeo, "Lo sviluppo industriale italiano [testo del dibattito tenuto a Roma, presso la Svimez, il 13 luglio 1960]," *Nord e Sud* 23 [1961], pp. 30–56).

Gerschenkron, A., R. Romeo, "Lo sviluppo industriale italiano (testo del dibattito tenuto a Roma, presso la Svimez, il 13 luglio 1960)," *Nord e Sud* 23 (1961), pp. 30–56.

Gersovitz, M., C. F. Diaz Alejandro, G. Ranis, M. R. Rosenzweig, eds., *The Theory and Experience of Economic Development: Essays in Honor of Sir W. Arthur Lewis*, London 1982.

Giannetti, R., "Sviluppo globale e sviluppo nazionale: riflessioni a partire da Stefano Fenoaltea, *L'economia italiana dall'Unità alla Grande Guerra*, Bari, Laterza, 2006," *Rivista di politica economica* 97 (2007), nn. 3–4, pp. 407–419.

Giusti, F., "Bilanci demografici della popolazione italiana dal 1861 al 1961," in Istat (Istituto centrale di statistica), *Sviluppo della popolazione italiana dal 1861 al 1961, Annali di statistica*, serie VIII, vol. 17, Rome 1965, pp. 87–122.

Gould, J. D., "European Inter-Continental Emigration. The Road Home: Return Migration from the USA," *Journal of European Economic History* 9 (1980), pp. 41–112.

Gramsci, A., *Il Risorgimento*, Turin 1949.

Habakkuk, H. J., "Fluctuations in House-Building in Britain and the United States in the Nineteenth Century," *Journal of Economic History* 22 (1962), pp. 198–230.

Harley, C. K., "The Interest Rate and Prices in Britain, 1873–1913: A Study of the Gibson Paradox," *Explorations in Economic History* 14 (1977), pp. 69–89.

Harvey, A. C., A. Jaeger, "Detrending, Stylized Facts and the Business Cycle," *Journal of Applied Econometrics* 8 (1993), pp. 231–247.

Hatton, T. J., J. G. Williamson, eds., *Migration and the International Labor Market, 1850–1939*, London 1994.

Hatton, T. J., J. G. Williamson, *The Age of Mass Migration: Causes and Economic Impact*, Oxford 1998.

Homer, S., *A History of Interest Rates*, New Brunswick 1963.

Hoselitz, B. F., ed., *The Progress of Underdeveloped Areas*, Chicago 1952.

[R.] Ispettorato generale delle strade ferrate, *Annali del consiglio delle tariffe delle strade ferrate*, annual.

Istat (Istituto centrale di statistica), *Indagine statistica sullo sviluppo del reddito nazionale dell'Italia dal 1861 al 1956*, *Annali di statistica*, serie VIII, vol. 9, Rome 1957.

Istat (Istituto centrale di statistica), *Le rilevazioni statistiche in Italia dal 1861 al 1956*, 4 vols., *Annali di statistica*, serie VIII, vols. 5–8, Rome 1957–59.

Istat (Istituto centrale di statistica), *Sommario di statistiche storiche italiane, 1861–1955*, Rome 1958.

Istat (Istituto centrale di statistica), *Sviluppo della popolazione italiana dal 1861 al 1961*, *Annali di statistica*, serie VIII, vol. 17, Rome 1965.

Kelley, A. C., "Demographic Change and Economic Growth: Australia, 1861–1911," *Explorations in Entrepreneurial History* 5 (1968), pp. 207–277.

Kuznets, S. S., "Economic Growth and Income Inequality," *American Economic Review* 45 (1955), pp. 1–28.

Kuznets, S. S., *Capital in the American Economy: Its Formation and Financing*, Princeton 1961.

Landes, D. S., *Revolution in Time: Clocks and the Making of the Modern World*, Cambridge MA 1983.

Lauricella, F., "Emigrazione italiana di massa in Argentina e in Brasile e ciclo agricolo (1876–1896)," in F. Assante, ed., *Il movimento migratorio italiano dall'Unità nazionale ai giorni nostri*, vol. 2, Geneva 1978, pp. 349–385.

Lewis, W. A., *Growth and Fluctuations, 1870–1913*, London 1978.

Livi Bacci, M., "I fattori demografici dello sviluppo economico," in G. Fuà, ed., *Lo sviluppo economico in Italia*, vol. 2, Milan 1969, pp. 17–95.

Luzzatto, G., *L'economia italiana dal 1861 al 1894*, Turin 1968 (Milan 1963).

Maddison, A., "A Revised Estimate of Italian Economic Growth, 1861–1989," *BNL Quarterly Review* 177 (1991), pp. 225–241.

Maddison, A., *Monitoring the World Economy, 1820–1992*, Paris 1995.

Maddison, A., *The World Economy: A Millennial Perspective*, Paris 2001.

Malanima, P., *La fine del primato. Crisi e riconversione nell'Italia del Seicento*, Milan 1998.

Malanima, P., *L'economia italiana. Dalla crescita medievale alla crescita contemporanea*, Bologna 2002.

Marcuzzo M. C., L. H. Officer, A. Rosselli, eds., *Monetary Standards and Exchange Rates*, London 1997.

Marolla, M., M. Roccas, "La ricostruzione della bilancia internazionale dei servizi e trasferimenti unilaterali dell'anno 1911," in G. M. Rey, ed., *I conti economici dell'Italia. 2. Una stima del valore aggiunto per il 1911*, Collana storica della Banca d'Italia, serie "statistiche storiche," vol. I.II, Bari 1992, pp. 241–282.

Mazzola, U., "L'aumento del dazio sul grano," *Giornale degli economisti*, ser. 2, 2-I (1891), pp. 190–198, partially reprinted in A. De Bernardi, ed., *Questione agraria e protezionismo nella crisi economica di fine secolo*, Milan 1977, pp. 185–190.

Ministero di agricoltura, industria e commercio, *Statistica del Regno d'Italia. Censimento 31 dicembre 1871*, vol. 3, Rome 1876.

Ministero di agricoltura, industria e commercio, *Censimento della popolazione del Regno d'Italia al 31 dicembre 1881*, vol. 3, Rome 1884.

Ministero di agricoltura, industria e commercio, *Censimento della popolazione del Regno d'Italia al 10 febbraio 1901*, vol. 4, Rome 1904.

Ministero di agricoltura, industria e commercio, *Censimento degli opifici e delle imprese industriali al 10 giugno 1911*, 5 vols., Rome 1913–16.

Ministero di agricoltura, industria e commercio, *Censimento della popolazione del Regno d'Italia al 10 giugno 1911*, vol. 5, Rome 1915.

Ministero per la Costituente. *Rapporto della commissione economica presentato all'Assemblea costituente. II. Industria. I. Relazione*, 2 vols., Rome 1947.

Mitchell, B. R., *European Historical Statistics*, London 1975.

Mokyr, J., "Demand vs. Supply in the Industrial Revolution," *Journal of Economic History* 37 (1977), pp. 981–1008.

Nardozzi, G., "The Italian 'Economic Miracle'," *Rivista di storia economica* 19 (2003), pp. 139–180.

O'Brien, P. K., ed., *Railways and the Economic Development of Western Europe*, London 1983.

O'Leary, P. J., W. A. Lewis, "Secular Swings in Production and Trade, 1870–1913," *The Manchester School of Economic and Social Studies* 23 (1955), pp. 113–152.

Pamuk, S., J. G. Williamson, eds., *The Mediterranean Response to Globalisation before 1950*, London 2000.

Pareto, V., *Lettres d'Italie. A cura di Gabriele De Rosa*, Rome 1973.

Pedone, A., "Il bilancio dello Stato e lo sviluppo economico italiano: 1861–1963," *Rassegna economica* 31 (1967), pp. 285–341.

Pescosolido, G., *Agricoltura e industria nell'Italia unita*, Rome-Bari 1994.

Pescosolido, G., *Unità nazionale e sviluppo economico*, Rome-Bari 1998.

Pollard, S., *Peaceful Conquest: The Industrialization of Europe 1760–1970*, Oxford 1981.

Pounds, N. J. G., *An Historical Geography of Europe 1800–1914*, Cambridge 1985.

Prados, L., V. Zamagni, eds., *El desarrollo económico en la Europa del Sur: España e Italia en perspectiva histórica*, Madrid 1992.

Rapp, R. T., "The Unmaking of the Mediterranean Trade Hegemony: International Trade Rivalry and the Commercial Revolution," *Journal of Economic History* 35 (1975), pp. 499–525.

Rey, G. M., ed., *I conti economici dell'Italia. 2. Una stima del valore aggiunto per il 1911*, Collana storica della Banca d'Italia, serie "statistiche storiche," vol. I.II, Bari 1992.

Rey, G. M., "Introduzione," in Id., ed., *I conti economici dell'Italia. 2. Una stima del valore aggiunto per il 1911*, Collana storica della Banca d'Italia, serie "statistiche storiche," vol. I.II, Bari 1992, pp. vii–xxii.

Rey, G. M., ed., *I conti economici dell'Italia. 3°°. Il valore aggiunto per gli anni 1891, 1938, 1951*, Collana storica della Banca d'Italia, serie "statistiche storiche," vol. I.III.2, Rome-Bari 2000.

Rey, G. M., "Nuove stime di contabilità nazionale (1891–1911): primi risultati," *Rivista di storia economica* 19 (2003), pp. 315–339.

Ricardo, D., *On the Principles of Political Economy and Taxation*, London 1817.

Romano, R., C. Vivanti, eds., *Storia d'Italia. Annali. 1. Dal feudalesimo al capitalismo*, Turin 1978.

Romeo, R., "La storiografia politica marxista," *Nord e Sud* 21 (1956), pp. 5–37, 22 (1956), pp. 16–44.

Romeo, R., "Problemi dello sviluppo capitalistico in Italia dal 1861 al 1887," *Nord e Sud* 44 (1958), pp. 7–60, 45 (1958), pp. 23–57.

Romeo, R., *Risorgimento e capitalismo*, 3^d ed., Rome-Bari 1998 (Bari 1959).

Romeo, R., *Breve storia della grande industria in Italia*, Rocca San Casciano 1961.

Rosoli G., ed., *Un secolo di emigrazione italiana 1876–1976*, Rome 1978.

Rossi, N., A. Sorgato, G. Toniolo, "I conti economici italiani: una ricostruzione statistica, 1890–1990," *Rivista di storia economica* 10 (1993), pp. 1–47.

Rossi, N., G. Toniolo, G. Vecchi, "Is the Kuznets Curve Still Alive? Evidence from Italian Household Budgets, 1881–1961," *Journal of Economic History* 61 (2001), pp. 904–925.

Rostow, W. W., *The Stages of Economic Growth: A Non-Communist Manifesto*, Cambridge 1960.

Saul, S. B., "House Building in England, 1890–1914," *Economic History Review* 15 (1962), pp. 119–137.

Sensini, G., *Le variazioni dello stato economico dell'Italia nell'ultimo trentennio del secolo XIX*, Rome 1904.

Sereni, E., *Il capitalismo nelle campagne (1860–1900)*, Turin 1947.

Sereni, E., *Capitalismo e mercato nazionale in Italia*, 2^d ed., Rome 1974 (1966).

Solomou, S., *Phases of Economic Growth: Kondratieff Waves and Kuznets Swings*, Cambridge 1987.

Somogyi, S., "Nuzialità," in Istat (Istituto centrale di statistica), *Sviluppo della popolazione italiana dal 1861 al 1961*, Annali di statistica, serie VIII, vol. 17, Rome 1965, pp. 321–397.

Sori, E., *L'emigrazione italiana dall'Unità alla seconda guerra mondiale*, Bologna 1979.

Stringher, B., "La Gran Bretagna e le concorrenze mondiali," *Nuova Antologia di Scienze, Lettere ed Arti*, serie III, 3 (1886), pp. 710–738.

Stringher, B., "Il commercio con l'estero e il corso dei cambi," *Nuova Antologia di Scienze, Lettere ed Arti*, serie III, 54 (1894), pp. 15–43.

Stringher, B., "Gli scambi con l'estero e la politica commerciale," in R. Accademia dei Lincei, *Cinquanta anni di storia italiana*, vol. 3, Milan 1911, pp. 1–186.

Svimez (Associazione per lo sviluppo dell'industria nel Mezzogiorno), *Un secolo di statistiche italiane Nord e Sud, 1861–1961*, Rome 1961.
Sylla, R., G. Toniolo, eds., *Patterns of European Industrialization: The Nineteenth Century*, London 1991.
Sylos Labini, P., *Problemi dello sviluppo economico*, Bari 1970.
Tagliacarne, G., "Lo sviluppo dell'industria italiana e il commercio estero," in Ministero per la Costituente, *Rapporto della commissione economica presentato all'Assemblea costituente. II. Industria.I. Relazione*, vol. 2, Rome 1947, pp. 33–92.
Tattara, G., "Paper Money but a Gold Debt: Italy on the Gold Standard," *Explorations in Economic History* 40 (2003), pp. 122–142.
Tattara, G., M. Volpe, "Italy, the Fiscal Dominance Model, and the Gold-Standard Age," in M. C. Marcuzzo, L. H. Officer, A. Rosselli, eds., *Monetary Standards and Exchange Rates*, London 1997, pp. 229–263.
Taylor, A. M., J. G. Williamson, "Convergence in the Age of Mass Migration," *European Review of Economic History* 1 (1997), pp. 27–63.
Thomas, B., *Migration and Economic Growth: A Study of Great Britain and the Atlantic Economy*, Cambridge 1954.
Thomas, B., *Migration and Urban Development: A Reappraisal of British and American Long Cycles*, London 1972.
Toniolo, G., ed., *Lo sviluppo economico italiano 1861–1940*, Bari 1973.
Toniolo, G., "Effective Protection and Industrial Growth: The Case of Italian Engineering," *Journal of European Economic History* 6 (1977), pp. 659–673.
Toniolo, G., ed., *L'economia italiana 1861–1940*, Bari 1978.
Toniolo, G., *Storia economica dell'Italia liberale 1850–1918*, Bologna 1988.
Toniolo, G., *An Economic History of Liberal Italy, 1850–1918*, London 1990 (translation of Id., *Storia economica dell'Italia liberale 1850–1918*, Bologna 1988).
Toniolo, G., "La storia economica dell'Italia liberale: una rivoluzione in atto," *Rivista di storia economica* 19 (2003), pp. 247–263.
Toniolo, G., "Sviluppo nonostante lo Stato," *Il Sole-24 Ore* 142, n. 172 (June 25, 2006), p. 41.
Toniolo, G., "Review of Stefano Fenoaltea (2006), *L'economia italiana dall'Unità alla Grande Guerra* (Rome and Bari: Laterza)," *Journal of Modern Italian Studies* 12 (2007), pp. 130–132.
Vaccaro, R., *Unità politica e dualismo economico in Italia (1861–1993)*, Padua 1995.
Vecchi, G., "I bilanci familiari in Italia: 1860–1960," *Rivista di storia economica* 11 (1994), pp. 9–95.
Vicarelli, F., ed., *Capitale industriale e capitale finanziario: il caso italiano*, Bologna 1979.
Vitali, O., "La stima del valore aggiunto a prezzi costanti per rami di attività," in G. Fuà, ed., *Lo sviluppo economico in Italia*, vol. 3, Milan 1969, pp. 463–477.
Vitali, O., *Aspetti dello sviluppo economico italiano alla luce della ricostruzione della popolazione attiva*, Rome 1970.
Vitali, O., "Gli impieghi del reddito nell'anno 1911," in G. M. Rey, ed., *I conti economici dell'Italia. 2. Una stima del valore aggiunto per il 1911*, Collana

storica della Banca d'Italia, serie "statistiche storiche," vol. I.II, Bari 1992, pp. 283–337.

Williamson, J. G., *American Growth and the Balance of Payments, 1820–1913: A Study of the Long Swing*, Chapel Hill 1964.

Williamson, J. G., "The Impact of the Corn Laws Just Prior to Repeal," *Explorations in Economic History* 27 (1990), pp. 123–156.

Zamagni, V., "Istruzione e sviluppo economico in Italia, 1861–1913," in G. Toniolo, ed., *Lo sviluppo economico italiano 1861–1940*, Bari 1973, pp. 187–240.

Zamagni, V., "Istruzione e sviluppo economico: il caso italiano, 1861–1913," in G. Toniolo, ed., *L'economia italiana 1861–1940*, Bari 1978, pp. 137–178.

Zamagni, V., *Industrializzazione e squilibri regionali in Italia. Bilancio dell'età giolittiana*, Bologna 1978.

Zamagni, V., "A Century of Change: Trends in the Composition of the Italian Labor Force, 1881–1981," *Historical Social Research* 44 (1987), no. 1, pp. 36–97.

Zamagni, V., *Dalla periferia al centro: la seconda rinascita economica dell'Italia, 1861–1981*, Bologna 1990.

Zamagni, V., "Il valore aggiunto del settore terziario italiano nel 1911," in G. M. Rey, ed., *I conti economici dell'Italia. 2. Una stima del valore aggiunto per il 1911*, Collana storica della Banca d'Italia, serie "statistiche storiche," vol. I.II, Bari 1992, pp. 191–239.

Zamagni, V., *The Economic History of Italy, 1860–1990: Recovery after Decline*, Oxford 1993 (translation of Id., *Dalla periferia al centro: la seconda rinascita economica dell'Italia, 1861–1981*, Bologna 1990).

Zamagni, V., P. Battilani, "Stima del valore aggiunto dei servizi," in G. M. Rey, ed., *I conti economici dell'Italia. 3°°. Il valore aggiunto per gli anni 1891, 1938, 1951*, Collana storica della Banca d'Italia, serie "statistiche storiche," vol. I.III.2, Rome-Bari 2000, pp. 239–371.

Index

The take-off of the Giolitti years

Léon Délagrange at the controls of the Voisin N. 3 with which, in June 1908, he performed the first-ever heavier-than-air flights in Italy. (Photo © Musée de l'Air et de l'Espace/Paris-Le Bourget. Reproduced by permission.)

Printed in the United States
by Baker & Taylor Publisher Services

Printed in the United States
by Baker & Taylor Publisher Services